Book of Rhymes

A Laxative for Creative Constipation®

Book of Rhymes

A Laxative for Creative Constipation®

Romane Armand

Kombít Media

Published by Kombít Media

Developmental Editor: Otis Kopp
Managing Editor: Sidney Baptista
Associate Editor: Michael McAlexander
Cover Design: Weapon Agency and Josh Williams
Layout Design: Lani Dame

Printed in the U.S.A

To Pops

Table of Contents

Preface

This book was compiled over the course of 14 years to expand your rhyming options. It has rescued me from writer's block on countless songwriting occasions. It has even helped me to become a Guinness World Record holder. Reading the book from cover to cover prepared me to achieve the world's Longest Freestyle Rap record, in which I improvised rap lyrics for 24 hours straight with no more than a 3-second break. I know that this powerful tool will stretch your imagination and spark your creativity.

Like many creative works, this book is the product of a collective effort. To my editor and friend Otis, thank you for being a part of this project from the very beginning and for helping to water this seed. Much love to my mentors Laura Mayo and John Hoffmire, who believed in me before I believed in myself. Salute to my fellow rhymers Sid, Schylar and Michael for your help with editing. A shout-out to my talented designer friends Lani, Ash and Josh for making this book look so dope, inside and out.

My enormous gratitude to the Kickstarter supporters whose contributions helped to get this book over the finish line. Thank you to Laura & Gary Mayo, Ashley Day, the Meaders family, the McCoy family, Lisa Johnston, Joel Armand, Jang Lee, Tristan Loughlin, Mareo & Emilie McCracken, Jason Mighdoll, Amber Cabral, Schumann Robert, Greg and Janna Smith, Tim Clark & family, Dr. Darron Smith, Bible Belt Brewing Company, Marisa Dobson, the Peden and Blackerby families, Quint Randle, Michael McAlexander, the Ellsworth family, the Saint-Louis family, the Peck family, Justin Lewis, Derrick Duplessy, Scott W. Jones, Wendy Blowtree, Quin Allen, Nathalie Armand-Bradley, the Hoffmire family and Ben Jack's Music.

Enjoy!

Romane Armand

Introduction

Book of Rhymes: A Laxative for Creative Constipation is a collection of words assembled into groups based on the way they rhyme. It is designed to significantly increase your number of rhyming word options. What makes this book unique is that it takes a holistic approach to rhyming by including three forms of rhyme: Exact Rhyme, Family Rhyme, and Slant Rhyme.

Exact Rhymes are words that share an identical rhyme sound, in which the stressed vowel sound and succeeding consonant sounds are the same. *Candy* and *handy* form an exact rhyme because they both share the *andy* rhyme sound. Decades ago, exact rhyme was the prominent rhyme type in English verse and song lyrics, as illustrated here in the Frank Sinatra song *My Way*.

> And now, the end is <u>near</u>
> And so I face the final <u>curtain</u>
> My friend, I'll say it <u>clear</u>
> I'll state my case, of which I'm <u>certain</u>

Since the days of *My Way*, writers have branched out considerably when it comes to rhyming. They no longer feel restricted to only using exact rhyme. They have realized that two words do not have to share an identical rhyme sound in order to rhyme. That is why this generation embraces the use of broader forms of rhyme such as Family Rhyme and Slant Rhyme.

Family Rhymes are words that share phonetically related rhyme sounds, in which the stressed vowel sound is identical and succeeding consonant sounds are part of the same phonetic family. *Happy, chatty, tacky, flabby, baggy,* and *daddy* form a family rhyme because they all share the same stressed vowel sound (the short A sound) and their succeeding consonant sounds belong to the same phonetic family (Plosives). Below are the different phonetic families and their accompanying constant sounds.

Plosives:	p, t, k, b, g, d
Fricatives:	f, th, s, sh, ch, v, TH, z, zh
Nasals:	m, n, ng

If you have ever heard a singer use the words *baby* and *lady* together in a rhyme, then you have heard a family rhyme before. Family rhymes are regularly used in the lyrics of popular music and in contemporary verse, as illustrated here in the Beyoncé song *Irreplaceable*.

> In the closet that's my <u>stuff</u>
> Yes, if I bought it, please don't <u>touch</u>
> And keep talking that mess that's <u>fine</u>
> But could you walk and talk at the same <u>time</u>
> And it's my name that is on that <u>tag</u>
> So remove your bags let me call you a <u>cab</u>

Introduction

In terms of sound, the difference between family rhyme and exact rhyme is hardly noticeable. This gives you the benefit of gaining more rhyming word options without losing much of a sonic connection. A limitation of family rhyme is that there still exist words that do not have rhymes. In order to find rhymes for these 'hard to rhyme words' we use an even broader form of rhyme called, Slant Rhyme.

Slant Rhymes are words that share similar rhyme sounds, in which the stressed vowel sound is identical and succeeding consonant sounds are different as well as unrelated. *Orange, foreign, Warren,* and *Florence* form a slant rhyme. Hip-hop is one of the genres where slant rhymes are commonplace as illustrated here in the Eminem song *Infinite.*

> My coiled hands around this microphone are *lethal*
> One thought in my *cerebral* is deeper than a jeep full of *people*

To the ear, *lethal, cerebral,* and *people* rhyme well because they share a strong sonic connection. However, not all slant rhymes are created equal. The requirements for what can be defined as a slant rhyme are very broad. Technically, the words *people* and *sneaky* form a slant rhyme. This book targets quality slant rhymes that share a strong sonic connection, therefore, *people* and *sneaky* are not listed in the same group. Instead, *sneaky* is listed with words like *peachy, easy, sweetie, weekly, sleepy,* and *kiwi.*

Words Included in this book go above and beyond just words that can be found in a standard dictionary. It features popular slang like *foodie* and *selfie*, phrases like *drama queen* and *camera shy,* as well as the names of famous people, things, and places like *Oprah, GoPro,* and *Disneyland.*

Words Not Included in this book are highly offensive, vile, and vulgar words. Specifically, any word that is not permitted on American daytime network television has been left out. This is an adult reference book that does contain words that may not be suitable for children but omits words that will likely offend many groups of people. Additionally, many highly technical and obscure words have been left out of this book in order to provide space for more frequently used, popular, or relevant terms to many poets, advertisers, and songwriters.

How To Use This Book

1. Identify Syllables within a Word

Think of a word that you want to find rhymes for. Now identify the syllables within that word. Below is an example using the word 'lady.'

Word-	lady
Syllables-	la·dy

2. Locate the 'Rhyme Sound' of the Word

Every word contains a part that is utilized to make rhyme connections. This is called the **rhyme sound**. Locate the rhyme sound by saying the word out loud and listening for which syllable contains the **stressed vowel sound** (it has the highest pitch). The rhyme sound begins at the point of the stressed vowel sound and continues through to the end of the word.

Vowel Sounds-	la·dy
Stressed Vowel Sound-	a
Rhyme Sound-	ady

3. Search Alphabetically

Now search alphabetically for the rhyme sound. This will lead you to the rhyme sound group. The rhyme sound group represents a unifying label for words that share sonically similar rhyme sounds (sound-alikes). Its spelling **always starts with a vowel** (A, E, I, O, U or Y). Beneath the rhyme sound group will be a list of rhyming words organized by their number of syllables.

ADY

baby
lady
shady

bag lady
cry baby

4. Cross-references

Sometimes, you will find a **cross-reference** instead of a list of rhyming words. Don't worry, this means that either this particular rhyme sound can be spelled more than one way; or that it has been combined with similar rhyme sounds to form a larger rhyme sound group. **Simply search for the cross-reference** and it will lead you to a list of rhyming words. For example, if you are seeking words that rhyme with 'baby', below is what you will find when searching for the rhyme sound ABY.

ABY (see ADY)

How To Use This Book

Numbered Rhyme Sounds

Some words end in the same spelling but have completely different sounds. When the same spelling can represent more than one sound, an identification number is added to the rhyme sound for each pronunciation of the sound. For example, you will find two separate listings for the rhyme sound OW.

OW 1	OW 2
beau	bough
blow	bow
bow	brow
bro	chow
crow	ciao
doe	cow
dough	how
faux	now
floe	ow
flow	plow

Example Words and Rhyme Sounds

Identifying the rhyme sound of a word takes a little bit of practice. After a few tries, it becomes easy. Below are some example words and their rhyme sounds in order to help you to get familiar with identifying the rhyme sound.

WORD	RHYME SOUND
back	ACK
market	ARKET
native	ATIVE
Roosevelt	ELT
member	EMBER
dental	ENTAL
enlighten	IGHTEN
dignify	IGNIFY
locally	OCALLY
aerobic	OBIC
pressure cooker	OOKER
rural	URAL
numerous	UMEROUS
spy	Y

A

Rhyme Sounds

A 1

aah
baa
bah
blah
bra
fa
ha
hah
la
ma
pa
rah
schwa
shah
spa
trois
ya
yah

ah hah
bourgeois
cha-cha
foie gras
ga-ga
grandpa
ha-ha
health spa
hoopla
hurrah
moola
oompah
patois
Pooh-Bah
tah-dah
Utah
wah-wah

baklava
blah, blah, blah
Bogota
brouhaha
la de da
last hurrah
ma-and-pa
Mardi Gras
nursing bra
Omaha
ooh and aah

oompah-pah
padded bra
Panama
que sera
tra la la
training bra
Wichita

comsi comsa
Lady Gaga

que sera, sera

A 2 (see AY)
AA (see A 1)
AB 1 (see AD 1)
AB 2 (see OD)
ABA (see ADA 1)
ABACI (see ASSIFY)
ABACUS (see ALYSIS)
ABAN (see ATION 1)
ABBA (see ASMA)
ABBAGE (see ATIC 1)
ABBATH (see ATIC 1)
ABBER 1 (see ACKER)
ABBER 2 (see OLLAR)
ABBERED (see ATTERED)
ABBERING (see ATTERING)
ABBESS (see ASHES)
ABBEY (see ALLEY)
ABBIE (see ALLEY)

ABBIER

ashier
baggier
battier
blabbier
brassier
brattier
chattier
classier
crabbier
crappier
dallier
drabbier
fattier
flabbier
flappier
flashier

gabbier
gassier
grabbier
grassier
happier
jazzier
nappier
nastier
nattier
rallier
rattier
saggier
sappier
sassier
savvier
scabbier
shabbier
shaggier
snappier
tabbier
tackier
tallier
tattier
trashier
wackier

slaphappier
unhappier

dilly-dallier

ABBIEST (see AGGIEST)
ABBILY (see ALITY)

ABBINESS

ashiness
bagginess
battiness
blabbiness
brassiness
brattiness
cattiness
chattiness
classiness
crabbiness
craftiness
cragginess
crappiness

daffiness
draftiness
fattiness
flabbiness
flagginess
flashiness
gabbiness
gassiness
glassiness
grassiness
happiness
jazziness
massiness
nappiness
nastiness
nattiness
patchiness
rattiness
sackiness
sagginess
sappiness
sassiness
scabbiness
scrappiness
scratchiness
shabbiness
shagginess
slabbiness
snappiness
splashiness
swagginess
tackiness
trashiness
wackiness
waxiness

unhappiness

ABBING 1 (see ACKING)
ABBING 2 (see OCKING)
ABBIT (see ATIC 1)
ABBITRY (see ALITY)
ABBLE 1 (see ACKLE)
ABBLE 2 (see OTTLE)
ABBLED (see ADDLED)
ABBLER 1 (see ACKLER)
ABBLER 2 (see OBBLER)
ABBLING 1 (see ACKLING)
ABBLING 2 (see OBBLING)
ABBLY (see OCKEY)
ABBOT (see ATIC 1)

ABBOTT (see ATIC 1)
ABBY 1 (see ALLEY)
ABBY 2 (see OCKEY)
ABBYING (see ALLYING)
ABDOMEN (see AFRICAN)
ABE (see ADE 1)
ABEL (see ABLE)
ABELED (see ABLED)
ABER (see ATOR)
ABI (see OCKEY)
ABIA (see ANIA)
ABIAL (see ADIAL)
ABIAN (see ANIUM)
ABIAS (see ANEOUS)
ABID (see ATIC 1)
ABIES (see ADIES)
ABIN (see ATTEN)
ABINET (see ASSIONATE)
ABINETRY (see ALITY)
ABIT (see ATIC 1)
ABITANT (see ASSIONATE)
ABITING (see ABLISHING)
ABITUS (see ALYSIS)

ABLE

Abel
able
acheful
anal
angel
anile
Babel
bagel
baneful
basal
basil
blameful
cable
cradle
fable
faceful
facial
faithful
fatal
fateful
gainful
gazeful
glacial
graceful

grateful
hateful
hazel
label
ladle
Mabel
maple
nasal
natal
naval
navel
painful
papal
plateful
playful
Rachel
racial
sable
shameful
spatial
stable
staple
strayful
swayful
table
tasteful
waistful
wakeful
wasteful

appraisal
betrayal
biracial
card table
crap table
defrayal
disable
disdainful
disgraceful
dismayful
distasteful
enable
end table
finagle
horse stable
inveigle
mislabel
palatial
pool table
portrayal

postnasal
postnatal
prenatal
round table
St. Basil
times table
timetable
turntable
unable
unfaithful
ungraceful
ungrateful
unstable
Witch Hazel

billiard table
Cain and Abel
coffee table
dressing table
farm to table
interracial
jumper cable
on the table
Ping-Pong table
reappraisal
rock the cradle
TV cable
warning label

conference table
designer label
head of the table
telephone cable
Tower of Babel
under the table
willing and able

ABLED

cabled
cradled
fabled
labeled
ladled
mapled
stapled
tabled

disabled

enabled
finagled
inveigled
mislabeled

ABLESS (see OLISH)
ABLET (see ATIC 1)

ABLING

abling
cabling
cradling
ladling
mapling
stabling
stapling
tabling

disabling
enabling
encradling
finagling

ABLISH (see ATIC 1)

ABLISHING

barracking
barreling
battening
blackening
caroling
carrying
fashioning
fastening
fattening
flattening
gaveling
gladdening
habiting
lavishing
maddening
marrying
parenting
parroting
quarreling
rationing
ravishing

saddening
slackening
tarrying
tasseling
traveling
varying

card-carrying
cohabiting
disparaging
embarrassing
establishing
inhabiting
miscarrying
refashioning
refastening
remarrying
unfastening
unraveling
unvarying

Christmas caroling
disestablishing
intermarrying
preestablishing
reestablishing

ABLISHMENT (see ASSIONATE)
ABLO (see OTTO 1)
ABNER (see ACKER)
ABO (see OTTO 1)
ABOON (see ALUE)
ABOR (see ATOR)
ABORATE (see ACERATE)
ABORED (see AVORED)
ABORING (see AVORING)
ABRA (see ADA 1)
ABRAM (see ATION 1)
ABRE (see OLLAR)
ABRIC (see ATIC 1)
ABSENCE (see ALLON)
ABSENT (see ACHMENT)
ABULOUS (see ALYSIS)
ABY (see ADY)
AC 1 (see ACK)
AC 2 (see OT)
AC 3 (see AW)
ACA (see ADA 1)
ACANCY (see ACIOUSLY)
ACANT (see ATION 1)
ACARD (see ATTERED)

ACAS 1 (see AWLESS)
ACAS 2 (see ACES)

ACATE

alate
clavate
gradate
hamate
malate
pacate
placate
playmate
vacate

ACCA (see ADA 1)
ACCATO (see OTTO 1)
ACCENT (see ATTEN)
ACCESS (see ASHES)
ACCHUS (see AWLESS)
ACCID (see ATIC 1)
ACCIDENT (see ASSIONATE)
ACCINATE (see ACERATE)
ACCLIMATE (see ACERATE)

ACCO

afro
basso
Caddo
Castro
Hasbro
lasso
macco
macro
tasco
whacko
zacco

chebacco
El Paso
fiasco
goracco
sargasso
Tabasco
tobacco

Donnie Brasco
Fidel Castro

Abraham Maslow
Lupe Fiasco

ACCRA (see ADA 1)
ACCURATE (see ASSIONATE)

ACE 1

ace
ache
ape
bake
base
bass
baste
Blake
brace
brake
break
cake
cape
case
chafe
chase
chaste
crepe
dace
Drake
drape
eighth
face
faith
fake
flake
gape
grace
grape
H
haste
jake
lace
lake
mace
make
nape
pace
paste
place
quake

race
rake
rape
safe
sake
scape
scrape
shake
shape
snake
space
spake
stake
steak
take
tape
taste
trace
vape
vase
waif
waist
wake
waste

abase
agape
air base
air brake
apace
arms race
at stake
awake
backache
backspace
bad taste
beefcake
big break
Bill Gates
birthplace
boldface
bookcase
briefcase
car race
cardcase
cheesecake
cupcake
daybreak
debase
deface

disgrace
displace
distaste
dog race
dogface
dollface
drag race
earache
earthquake
efface
egg-shape
embrace
encase
enlace
erase
escape
fair shake
fast break
fast pace
fireplace
first base
footrace
forsake
freebase
fruitcake
glass case
go ape
good taste
grubstake
handshake
headache
headspace
heart-shape
heartache
heartbreak
home base
horserace
hot cake
housebreak
in case
intake
jailbreak
keep pace
keepsake
landscape
last place
lay waste
lose face
lunch break
make haste

milkshake
misplace
misshape
mistake
muckrake
Myspace
namesake
neckbrace
newsbreak
no place
off-base
opaque
outbreak
outpace
paleface
pancake
Park Place
partake
pear-shape
play safe
posthaste
rat race
red tape
remake
replace
reshape
retake
retrace
sackrace
save face
Scotch tape
seascape
shipshape
shoelace
shortcake
showcase
showplace
snail's pace
snowflake
someplace
sour grape
staircase
straight face
suitcase
sweepstake
tax break
test case
third base
toothache
toothpaste

touch base
tough break
two-face
typeface
unchaste
undrape
unlace
unsafe
uptake
workplace
workspace

about-face
aerospace
aftertaste
angel face
anyplace
babyface
basket case
bellyache
birthday cake
bouillabaisse
bow and scrape
breathing space
change of pace
coffee break
coffee cake
commonplace
cut-and-paste
Daphne Blake
database
demo tape
doublespace
doubletake
every place
face-to-face
fall from grace
fire escape
flying ace
freckleface
funny face
get a break
give and take
go to waste
Goober Grape
Great Grape Ape
Harlem Shake
haste makes waste
hatchet face
hiding place

human race
in a scrape
in good shape
innerspace
interface
interlace
interspace
just in case
know your place
knowledge base
Leatherface
Lost in Space
make or break
makeup case
marketplace
meeting place
MPH
Norman Bates
not a trace
out of place
out of shape
outerspace
overtake
paper chase
Pearly Gates
pennant race
pepper steak
piece of cake
pillow case
pokerface
polling place
power base
pure and chaste
rattlesnake
relay race
resting place
saving grace
seedless grape
self-efface
service break
set the pace
Shake 'n' Bake
show your face
Smiley Face
Steak 'n' Shake
steeplechase
stock-car race
stomachache
storage space
sugarbake

take a break
take the cake
tickertape
undertake
upper case
way off base
wedding cake
wide-awake
wild-goose chase

acquired taste
bent out of shape
blue in the face
chariot race
cigarette case
commercial break
egg on your face
federal case
for goodness sake
get to first base
gimme a break
hazardous waste
in any case
jewelry case
magnetic tape
nuclear waste
satin and lace
slap in the face
United States
upside-down cake
vanity case
videotape
watering place
whip into shape
wide-open space

icing on the cake
Justin Timberlake
open and shut case
political race
slow on the uptake

America's Cup Race

ACE 2 (see OCKEY)
ACEABLE (see ATIONAL 1)
ACEAN (see ATION 1)
ACEFUL (see ABLE)
ACEFULLY (see ACIOUSLY)
ACELET (see ATIVE)
ACEMENT (see ATION 1)

ACENT (see ATION 1)
ACENTLY (see ACIOUSLY)
ACEO (see ATIO 1)
ACEOUS (see ACES)
ACER (see ATOR)

ACERATE

acclimate
acerate
acetate
activate
adulate
caffeinate
calibrate
califate
capitate
captivate
cavitate
fascinate
gravitate
lacerate
magistrate
masticate
masturbate
maturate
salivate
saturate
vaccinate

assassinate
collaborate
deactivate
decaffeinate
decapitate
elaborate
extrapolate
inactivate
procrastinate
reacclimate
reactivate
remasticate
revaccinate
unmagistrate
unsaturate

oversaturate
supersaturate

overelaborate

ACES

aces
acreage
aimless
Amos
anus
Avis
baitless
bases
basest
basics
basis
bassist
blameless
braces
brainless
bravest
Cambridge
cases
chainless
chases
chasteness
claimless
dameless
Danish
dateless
Davis
dazes
drainage
faces
faintest
faintness
faithless
fakeness
fameless
famous
fateless
flameless
fracas
frameless
freightless
gainage
gainless
gameless
gamest
gateless
gazes
graces
gracious

graveness
gravest
grazes
greatest
greatness
hazes
heinous
laces
lamest
lateness
latest
lazes
mateless
matrix
mavis
mazes
nameless
painless
phases
places
plainness
plateless
quaintest
races
racist
rainless
Ramist
rapist
rateless
sadist
safest
sageness
sagest
sameness
shameless
skateless
spaces
spacious
squamous
stainless
stateless
statist
straightest
straightness
strainless
strangeness
strangest
tamest
tasteless
tazes

traces
traitless
traitress
vagueness
vaguest
vases
veinless
wainage
waitress
waveless
weightless

amazes
audacious
aviatrix
biramous
bodacious
boldfaces
bookcases
briefcases
capacious
car races
cardcases
contagious
courageous
curvaceous
defaces
dog races
dogfaces
drag races
embraces
erases
escapist
fallacious
fireplaces
flirtatious
footraces
glass cases
good gracious
hiatus
horseraces
in cases
innateness
irateness
iratest
landscapist
Las Vegas
loquacious
mendacious
Miles Davis

neckbraces
oasis
off-bases
ornateness
outpaces
outrageous
palefaces
playmateless
predacious
pugnacious
rampageous
rapacious
replaces
retraces
sackraces
sagacious
salacious
sedateness
sedatest
sequacious
shoelaces
showcases
showplaces
staircases
straight faces
suitcases
tenacious
test cases
two-faces
ungracious
Uranus
veracious
vexatious
vivacious
voracious
workplaces
world-famous

advantageous
Albert Camus
basket cases
Bette Davis
breathing spaces
change of paces
commonplaces
data bases
dominatrix
efficacious
flying aces
frecklefaces

funny faces
goodness gracious
hatchet faces
hiding places
ignoramus
interlaces
interspaces
Jody Davis
makeup cases
marketplaces
meditatist
meeting places
ostentatious
pennant races
pillow cases
pokerfaces
polling places
relay races
resting places
self-effaces
stock-car races
storage spaces
wild-goose chases

chariot races
cigarette cases
disadvantageous
federal cases
get to first bases
jewelry cases
Rosie The Waitress
vanity cases
wide-open spaces

open-and-shut-cases
political races

ACET (see ATIC 1)
ACETATE (see ACERATE)
ACH 1 (see ASS 1)
ACH 2 (see OT)
ACH 3 (see ACE 1)
ACHA (see ADA 1)
ACHABLE (see ACTABLE)
ACHARY (see ALITY)
ACHE 1 (see ACE 1)
ACHE 2 (see ASS 1)
ACHE 3 (see ALLEY)
ACHEFUL (see ABLE)
ACHEL (see ABLE)
ACHELOR (see ALENDAR)

ACHES 1 (see ASHES)
ACHES 2 (see ASHES)
ACHI (see OCKEY)
ACHIEST (see ANEOUS)
ACHINESS (see AKINESS)
ACHING 1 (see ATING)
ACHING 2 (see ACKING)
ACHINGLY (see AKINGLY)

ACHIO

daddio
patio

mustachio
pistachio

Leonardo Dicaprio

ACHMED (see AULTED)

ACHMENT

absent
advent
fragment
hatchment
stagnant

attachment
coagment
detachment
dispatchment

reattachment

ACHO (see OTTO 1)
ACHT (see OT)
ACHTING (see OCKING)
ACHTZE (see OCKEY)
ACHY (see ADY)
ACIA (see ASIA)
ACIAL (see ABLE)
ACIALLY (see ACIOUSLY)
ACIATE (see ATIATE)
ACID (see ATIC 1)
ACIDNESS (see ALYSIS)
ACIDY (see ALITY)
ACIE (see ADY)

ACIENT (see ATION 1)
ACIER 1 (see AKIER)
ACIER 2 (see ATOR)
ACIEST (see ANEOUS)
ACIFIST (see ALYSIS)
ACIFY (see ASSIFY)
ACILE (see ACKLE)
ACILY (see AVERY)
ACING (see ATING)
ACIOUS (see ACES)

ACIOUSLY

agency
aimlessly
blatantly
faithfully
famously
fatally
gracefully
graciously
gratefully
latency
masonry
painfully
papacy
patiently
racially
shamelessly
spaciously
tastefully
vacancy
vagrancy

audaciously
capaciously
complacently
contagiously
courageously
disgracefully
fallaciously
freemasonry
loquaciously
mendaciously
mistakenly
outrageously
pugnaciously
rapaciously
sagaciously
salaciously

tenaciously
ungraciously
veraciously
vivaciously
voraciously

advantageously
efficaciously
unashamedly

disadvantageously
inefficaciously
nonadvantageously

ACIST (see ACES)
ACIT (see ATIC 1)
ACITLY (see ALITY)
ACITY (see ALITY)

ACK

act
app
apt
at
back
bat
black
brat
cap
cat
chap
chat
clack
clap
claque
crack
crap
dap
drat
fact
fat
flack
flap
flat
frat
Gap
gat
gnat
hack

hap
hat
jack
knack
Knapp
lac
lack
lap
Mac
map
mat
nap
pack
pact
pat
phat
plaque
prat
quack
rack
rap
rapt
rat
sac
sack
sap
sat
scrap
shack
slack
slap
slat
smack
snack
snap
spat
splat
stack
stat
strap
tack
tact
tap
tat
that
thwack
track
tract
trap
vat

wack	detract	jet black
whack	dingbat	jockstrap
wrack	distract	kayak
wrap	dognap	keep track
yak	doormat	kersplat
yap	drawback	kickback
zap	dunce cap	kidnap
	enact	knapsack
abstract	entrap	kneecap
adapt	enwrap	known fact
aflap	exact	Kodak
agap	extract	laid-back
Amtrak	fall back	last act
ASCAP	fall flat	laugh at
at bat	fast track	laugh track
attack	fat cat	look back
attract	feedback	lose track
backpack	fight back	love pat
backslap	fire hat	love sac
backtrack	firetrap	Love Shack
bad rap	first act	low-fat
bareback	flapjack	lunch sack
bark at	flashback	mishap
begat	floormat	mousetrap
blackjack	format	mudflap
bobcat	fullback	mudpack
bootstrap	gas cap	muskrat
bounce back	giftwrap	nightcap
bra strap	give back	nonfat
brass hat	greenback	offtrack
brickbat	halfback	oh snap
burlap	hardhat	old bat
bushwhack	hatchback	old chap
buyback	hatrack	old hat
call back	haystack	on tap
catnap	heel tap	on track
chinstrap	high hat	one-track
chitchat	hijack	outback
class act	hold back	packrat
clothes rack	horseback	pay back
cognac	hubcap	peek at
cold pack	humpback	pitch-black
combat	hunchback	placemat
comeback	icecap	playact
compact	icepack	playback
contact	impact	protract
contract	in fact	prozac
cravat	infract	racetrack
cutback	intact	ransack
deathtrap	Iraq	Rat Pack

rat trap
react
recap
redcap
refract
repack
retrack
retract
right track
roadmap
rollback
sandtrap
setback
sex act
shellac
shoerack
short stack
sidetrack
six-pack
skullcap
skyjack
slapjack
slow track
smokestack
sneeze at
snowcap
soft pack
soundtrack
speed trap
steel trap
stop gap
straw hat
stray cat
subtract
sun hat
swayback
switchback
take back
talk back
that's that
throwback
thumbtack
Tic Tac
tie rack
tie tack
tomcat
Top Cat
top hat
transact
unpack

unsnap
unstrap
unwrap
way back
white rat
whitecap
wildcat
wingback
wink at
wiretap
wisecrack
wolf pack
wombat
wrong track
yell at

acrobat
alley cat
almanac
applejack
Arafat
army brat
artifact
autocrat
baby fat
baby-sat
baccarat
back to back
bacon fat
baseball cap
beat the rap
booby trap
bottlecap
bureaucrat
caddie shack
Cadillac
camelback
cardiac
cataract
chew the fat
chicken fat
chili mac
copycat
counteract
cowboy hat
crackerjack
cul-de-sac
democrat
desert rat
diamondback

diplomat
dirty rat
Fanny Pack
final act
fraidy cat
gender gap
gingersnap
habitat
Hacky Sack
handicap
heart attack
hit the sack
hobie cat
I get that
inexact
inside track
interact
interlap
jumping jack
kitty cat
laundromat
lumberjack
maniac
Men in Black
missile gap
money back
nurse's cap
off the rack
off the track
out of whack
overact
overlap
paper sack
paperback
Parent Trap
pass the hat
Photostat
piggyback
pitapat
pitterpat
plutocrat
Pontiac
pussycat
quarterback
railroad track
razorback
reenact
retroact
rheostat
riot act

sailor hat
Saran Wrap
scaredy cat
shoulder strap
shut your trap
single-track
smell a rat
take a nap
take the rap
technocrat
thermostat
thinking cap
this and that
Thundercat
thunderclap
tit for tat
tourist trap
turtleback
union jack
vampire bat
warning track
weather map
welcome mat
where it's at
whippersnap
zodiac

after the fact
aristocrat
before the fact
behind your back
blind as a bat
calico cat
Cat In The Hat
cigarette pack
clean up your act
clickety-clack
counterattack
Felix The Cat
flat on your back
go to the mat
hard nut to crack
insomniac
Jehoshaphat
knife in the back
Linda Ronstadt
matter of fact
on the attack
overreact
panic attack

pat on the back
pick up the slack
right off the bat
sharp as a tack
shirt off your back
spaghetti strap
stab in the back
ten-gallon hat
tough nut to crack
yakkity-yak

aphrodisiac
career diplomat
Farmer's Almanac
generation gap
hemophiliac
hypochondriac
mind like a steel
trap
pedophiliac

at the drop of a hat
jumpin' Jehoshaphat
physical handicap

Monday morning quarterback

Ain't Nobody Got Time For That

ACKABLE (see ACTABLE)
ACKAGE (see ATIC 1)
ACKAL (see ACKLE)
ACKARD (see ATTERED)
ACKEN (see ATTEN)
ACKENED (see ASTENED)
ACKENER (see ALENDAR)
ACKENING (see ABLISHING)

ACKER

Abner
actor
adder
after
asker
backer
backward
badder
badger
baffler

bagger
basher
batter
baxter
blabber
blacker
bladder
blaster
blather
bragger
brasher
cadger
Calor
capper
captor
capture
Casper
caster
castor
catcher
chapper
chapter
chatter
clacker
clapper
clasher
clasper
clatter
cracker
crafter
crapper
crasher
crasser
dafter
dagger
dapper
dasher
drafter
dragger
factor
faster
fatter
flagger
flapper
flasher
flatter
fracture
gabber
gaffer
gagger

gapper
gasher
gasper
gasser
gather
gladder
gnasher
grabber
grafter
grappler
hacker
hatcher
hatter
jabber
Jasper
jazzer
lacquer
ladder
lagger
lasher
latcher
lather
latter
laugher
laughter
laxer
madder
mapper
masher
masker
master
matcher
matter
nabber
nagger
napper
Nasser
packer
pallor
passer
pastor
pasture
patcher
patter
plaster
platter
quacker
racker
raffler
rafter

rapper
raptor
rapture
rasher
rasper
rather
razzer
sacker
sadder
sagger
sasser
scatter
scrapper
scratcher
shafter
shatter
slacker
slapper
slasher
slather
smacker
smasher
snacker
snagger
snatcher
splasher
splatter
stabber
stacker
staffer
stagger
stasher
stature
strapper
swagger
tacker
tagger
tapper
tasker
tatter
taxer
thrasher
thwacker
tracker
tractor
trapper
valor
vaster
wagger
waxer

whacker
wrapper
yakker
yapper
yatter
zapper

abstractor
adapter
amasser
attacker
attractor
back scratcher
backpacker
backslapper
backstabber
backtracker
bandmaster
broadcaster
brown bagger
bushwhacker
bypasser
cadaver
catnapper
come after
compactor
contactor
contractor
contraster
dance master
Day After
detractor
disaster
dispatcher
distracter
dogcatcher
egg hatcher
enactor
enrapture
entrapper
exacter
extractor
eye-catcher
firecracker
flycatcher
foot dragger
forecaster
gallbladder
gate-crasher
giftwrapper

gray matter
gum wrapper
harasser
headmaster
hereafter
hijacker
kidnapper
linebacker
lipsmacker
madcapper
Mick Jagger
mismatcher
Mixmaster
newscaster
no matter
nutcracker
palaver
postmaster
price slasher
protractor
purse snatcher
ransacker
reactor
recapture
red snapper
refractor
regather
relaxer
repacker
retractor
ringmaster
Ritz Cracker
rope ladder
run after
safecracker
sandbagger
sandblaster
scoutmaster
sidetracker
skyjacker
steadfaster
stepladder
subtractor
surpasser
tail wagger
take after
taskmaster
thereafter
toe tapper
trespasser

typecaster
uncapper
unpacker
unstrapper
unwrapper
View-Master
wiretapper
wisecracker
woolgather
zigzagger

antimatter
benefactor
body snatcher
chiropractor
choirmaster
cloak-and-dagger
Cootie Catcher
counteractor
ever after
final chapter
flabbergaster
ghetto blaster
handicapper
handicrafter
hereinafter
interactor
jibber-jabber
lath and plaster
lollygagger
lord and master
manufacture
mix-and-matcher
money grabber
morning after
overactor
overlapper
party crasher
pick up after
pitter-patter
RH factor
simulcaster
subject matter
thereinafter
trash compactor
up the ladder
whippersnapper
William Shatner
windchill factor

animal cracker
character actor
corporate ladder
counterattacker
family matter
forever after
gist of the matter
overreactor
weather forecaster

ACKEREL (see ACTABLE)
ACKERY (see ALITY)
ACKET (see ATIC 1)
ACKETLESS (see ALYSIS)
ACKETY (see ALITY)
ACKEY (see ALLEY)
ACKIE (see ALLEY)
ACKIER (see ABBIER)
ACKIEST (see AGGIEST)
ACKILY (see ALITY)
ACKINESS (see ABBINESS)

ACKING

acting
adding
asking
axing
backing
bagging
bashing
basking
batching
batting
blabbing
blacking
blasting
bragging
capping
cashing
casting
castling
catching
chapping
chatting
clacking
clapping
clashing
clasping
crabbing

cracking
crafting
crapping
crashing
dabbing
dashing
dazzling
drafting
dragging
fasting
faxing
flagging
flapping
flashing
frazzling
gabbing
gadding
gaffing
gagging
gapping
gasping
gassing
gnashing
grabbing
grafting
grappling
grasping
hacking
hashing
hassling
hatching
having
jabbing
jacking
jagging
jazzing
lacking
lagging
lapping
lapsing
lashing
lasting
latching
laughing
madding
mapping
mashing
masking
massing
matching

matting
nabbing
nagging
napping
packing
padding
passing
patching
patting
quacking
racking
rafting
rapping
rasping
ratting
sacking
sagging
sapling
sapping
sassing
scrapping
scratching
shacking
slacking
slapping
slashing
slatting
smacking
smashing
snacking
snagging
snapping
snatching
spazzing
splashing
splatting
stabbing
stacking
staffing
stashing
strapping
swagging
tacking
tagging
tapping
tatting
taxing
thatching
thrashing
thwacking

tracking
trapping
trashing
wagging
waxing
whacking
wracking
wrapping
yakking
yapping
zagging
zapping

abstracting
amassing
attaching
attacking
attracting
back scratching
backpacking
backslapping
backstabbing
backtracking
bedazzling
bombasting
broadcasting
bushwacking
bypassing
catnapping
chitchatting
class acting
collapsing
combatting
compacting
contacting
contracting
contrasting
detaching
detracting
didacting
dispatching
distracting
dognapping
elapsing
enacting
entrapping
enwrapping
exacting
extracting
eye-catching

floor matting
flycasting
footpadding
forecasting
gay-bashing
giftwrapping
gut-grabbing
harassing
hijacking
impacting
infracting
kidnapping
lambasting
leg waxing
lipsmacking
longlasting
miscasting
mismatching
nonmatching
outclassing
outlasting
protracting
ransacking
reacting
recapping
refracting
rehashing
relapsing
relaxing
rematching
repacking
retracking
retracting
sandbagging
sandblasting
sidetracking
skin grafting
skyjacking
subtracting
surpassing
thumbtacking
toe-tapping
tomcatting
tonguelashing
tooth-capping
transacting
trespassing
typecasting
unclasping
unlashing

unlatching
unpacking
unsnagging
unsnapping
unstrapping
unwrapping
wiretapping
wisecracking
zigzagging

autographing
boobytrapping
counteracting
cradle-snatching
everlasting
flabbergasting
handicapping
interacting
interlapping
lollygagging
lumberjacking
mix-and-matching
overacting
overdrafting
overlapping
overmatching
overstaffing
overtaxing
paragraphing
photographing
photostatting
piggybacking
pistolpacking
pitterpatting
playacting
quarterbacking
razzledazzling
reattaching
reattacking
reenacting
retroacting
simulcasting
telecasting
telegraphing

counterattacking
overreacting
whitewater rafting
yakkity-yakking

ACKLE

addle
agile
apple
astral
axle
babble
baffle
bashful
battle
brashful
cackle
castle
cattle
cavil
chapel
crackle
dabble
dazzle
drabble
facile
fragile
frazzle
gabble
gaffle
gaggle
gavel
grapple
gravel
haggle
hassle
jackal
paddle
pascal
passel
prattle
rabble
raffle
rascal
rattle
ravel
razzle
saddle
scrabble
shackle
snaggle
Snapple
straddle
straggle

tackle
tassel
tattle
travel
vassal
waggle

astraddle
bad apple
bedazzle
bedraggle
Big Apple
dog-paddle
New Castle
pineapple
ramshackle
rehaggle
sandcastle
Seattle
sidesaddle
skedaddle
unravel
unsaddle
unshackle
White Castle

Adam's apple
baby rattle
block and tackle
Eddie Haskell
fiddle-faddle
fishing tackle
flying tackle
ice cream paddle
losing battle
razzle-dazzle
tabernacle
tittle-tattle
wedding chapel

ACKLER

addler
babbler
battler
dabbler
gaggler
haggler
paddler

rattler
saddler
shackler
straddler
tackler
tattler

cage rattler
skedaddler
unsaddler

baby rattler

ACKLESS (see ASHES)

ACKLING

babbling
baffling
battling
cackling
crackling
dabbling
haggling
paddling
prattling
raffling
rattling
saddling
shackling
snaggling
spackling
straddling
straggling
tackling
tattling
waggling

skedaddling
unsaddling

ACKLY (see ALLEY)
ACKMENT (see ASSMENT)
ACKNESS (see ASHES)
ACKNEY (see ALLEY)
ACKO (see ACCO)
ACKROOM (see ALUE)
ACKSON (see ACTION)
ACKWARD (see ACKER)
ACKY (see ALLEY)

ACLE 1 (see OTTLE)
ACLE 2 (see ACKLE)
ACME (see ALLEY)
ACMES (see ADDIES)
ACNE (see ALLEY)
ACO 1 (see OTTO 1)
ACO 2 (see ADO 2)
ACON (see ATION 1)
ACQUER (see ACKER)
ACQUES (see OT)
ACQUET (see ATIC 1)
ACRA (see ADA 1)
ACRE (see ATOR)
ACREAGE (see ACES)
ACRED (see ADED)
ACRO (see ACCO)
ACRON (see ACTION)
ACRUM (see ASM)
ACT (see ACK)

ACTABLE

actable
actual
addable
admiral
affable
baggable
cackerel
capital
capitol
cappable
casual
catchable
classical
factional
factual
fallible
faxable
flappable
fractional
gradual
hatchable
latchable
lateral
laughable
mackerel
magical
mappable
matchable

national
natural
packable
pactional
paddable
paginal
palpable
patchable
practical
radical
rational
scratchable
smashable
snatchable
tactical
taxable
trackable
tractional
vaginal
waxable

abstractional
attachable
attackable
attractable
bilateral
climaxable
collateral
combatable
compactible
compatible
contactable
contractable
contractual
detachable
detractable
diagonal
dispatchable
distractable
enactable
erratical
exactable
extractable
fanatical
grammatical
hexagonal
impactable
impalpable
impractical
infallible

irrational
mathematical
nonrational
octagonal
pentagonal
reactable
reactional
recappable
redactional
relaxable
sabbatical
sporadical
subfractional
subtractable
syntactical
transactable
transactional
transactual
transnational
trilateral
unfallible
unflappable
unlatchable
unmatchable

ambilateral
antinational
antirational
biographical
Cape Canaveral
counterfactual
demographical
equilateral
geographical
holy mackerel
interactional
international
longilateral
multilateral
multinational
pornographical
problematical
quadrilateral
reattachable
satisfactual
septilateral
supernational
supernatural
supranational
typographical

unattachable
unattackable
ungrammatical
unilateral

bibliographical
inequilateral

autobiographical

ACTED (see ATIC 1)
ACTER (see ACKER)
ACTERY (see ALITY)
ACTIBLE (see ACTABLE)
ACTIC (see ATIC 1)
ACTICAL (see ACTABLE)
ACTICALIZE (see ATURALIZE)
ACTICALLY (see ATICALLY)
ACTICE (see ASHES)
ACTING (see ACKING)

ACTION

Acron
action
ashen
caption
dragon
faction
fashion
flagon
fraction
Jackson
passion
ration
Saxon
traction
wagon
waxen

abstraction
adaption
attraction
bandwagon
class action
closed caption
compaction
compassion
contraction
contraption

court action

detraction

dispassion

distraction

extraction

grand passion

high fashion

impaction

inaction

infraction

live action

protraction

reaction

refraction

retraction

see action

snapdragon

subtraction

take action

transaction

Volkswagen

Anglo-Saxon

battlewagon

chain reaction

counteraction

covered wagon

covert action

direct action

gut reaction

interaction

Janet Jackson

malefaction

Michael Jackson

out of fashion

paddy wagon

police action

prolonged-action

reflex action

Reggie Jackson

retroaction

satisfaction

star attraction

station wagon

dissatisfaction

drug interaction

piece of the action

affirmative action

Puff, the Magic Dragon

Samuel L. Jackson

ACTIONAL (see ACTABLE)

ACTIONALIZE (see ATURALIZE)

ACTIONATE (see ASSIONATE)

ACTIVATE (see ACERATE)

ACTIVE (see ATIC 1)

ACTIVELY (see ALITY)

ACTIVIST (see ALYSIS)

ACTLESS (see ASHES)

ACTLY (see ALLEY)

ACTMENT (see ASSMENT)

ACTNESS (see ASHES)

ACTOR (see ACKER)

ACTORED (see ATTERED)

ACTORING (see ATTERING)

ACTORY (see ALITY)

ACTRESS (see ASHES)

ACTUAL (see ACTABLE)

ACTUALIZE (see ATURALIZE)

ACTUALLY (see ATICALLY)

ACTURE (see ACKER)

ACTURED (see ATTERED)

ACTURER (see ALENDAR)

ACTURING (see ATTERING)

ACTUS (see ASHES)

ACULA (see AFRICA)

ACULAR (see ALENDAR)

ACULOUS (see ALYSIS)

ACULTY (see ALITY)

ACURA (see AFRICA)

ACUUM (see ALUE)

ACY (see ADY)

AD 1

ad

add

bad

badge

bag

blab

brad

brag

cab

cad

cadge

Chad

clad

crab

dab

dad

dag

drab

dradge

drag

fab

fad

fadge

flab

flag

gab

gad

gag

glad

grab

grad

had

hag

jab

jag

lab

lad

lag

mad

madge

nab

nag

pad

padge

plaid

rag

sad

sag

scab

scad

shad

shag

slab

snag

stab

stag

swag

tab

tad

tag

wag

zag

Ahab
airbag
backstab
Baghdad
barf bag
beanbag
bedpad
Carlsbad
check pad
comrade
confab
cornpad
crash pad
crawdad
desk pad
dishrag
dogtag
doodad
egad
feedbag
fleabag
flight bag
footpad
forbade
gone mad
grab bag
granddad
handbag
hexad
ice bag
ink pad
jet lag
keypad
launch pad
like mad
man-made
Maytag
my bad
nametag
nomad
not bad
note pad
post-grad
prefab
price tag
ragbag
ragtag
red tag
rehab
sand crab

sandbag
scratch pad
scumbag
scuzzbag
Sinbad
Skypad
sleazebag
smack-dab
teabag
too bad
tote bag
trashbag
unclad
want ad
washrag
white flag
zigzag

airsick bag
boiling mad
bowling bag
checkered flag
chew the rag
crying jag
doggie bag
duffel bag
Galahad
gift of gab
have it bad
heating pad
Hubble brag
humble brag
in the bag
ironclad
ivy-clad
landing pad
launching pad
laundry bag
litterbag
lollygag
luggage tag
mom and dad
money bag
not so bad
photo lab
punching bag
running gag
saddlebag
scalawag
scallywag

shopping bag
shoulder pad
sleeping bag
steno pad
Stridex Pad
taxicab
Trinidad
undergrad

classified ad
Olympiad
scantily clad

American flag
helicopter pad

AD 2 (see OD)

ADA 1

Accra
aga
Allah
aqua
Baja
basta
brava
challah
Dakka
Dascha
Gaza
gotcha
gotta
grata
guava
hasta
Hoffa
java
kasha
kata
kava
lava
lotsa
maasha
Malta
matzah
Mazda
Opera
oughta

papa

pasha

pasta

Paula

Plaza

poppa

Prada

sacra

saga

salsa

Sasha

Shaka

tapa

vodka

Acosta

armada

Bahamas

casaba

Chapala

Chautauqua

Chewbacca

Chihuahua

cicada

de nada

Granada

Hakuna Matata

horchata

impala

koala

La Costa

Maraca

Marsala

Misawa

Nevada

pajamas

pentacra

piazza

piñata

reata

ricotta

schemata

soap opera

sonata

squamata

Sriracha

stemmata

stigmata

Sumatra

toccata

tostada

Zapata

Ali Baba

ambulacra

chupacabra

enchilada

Ensenada

Frank Sinatra

Guatemala

lavalava

oblongata

polyacra

simulacra

carne asada

Chevy Impala

Erik Estrada

pina colada

aficionada

Afrika Bambaataa

interambulacra

Phantom of the Opera

Sierra Nevada

the whole enchilada

ADA 2 (see ASIA)

ADABLE

aidable

baitable

braidable

capable

drapable

failable

flayable

gradable

grazeable

layable

mailable

nailable

payable

playable

raidable

rapable

sailable

savable

sayable

scalable

scrapable

shadable

shapable

skateable

sprayable

swayable

tailable

tapable

tradable

trailable

wadable

weighable

assailable

available

awaitable

betrayable

blockadable

conveyable

curtailable

defrayable

degradable

delayable

derailable

dissuadable

escapable

evadable

impalable

incapable

inhalable

invadable

obeyable

okayable

persuadable

placadable

portrayable

regalable

relayable

repayable

replayable

reshapeable

retailable

surveyable

undrapable

unshapable

upbraidable

upgradable

barricadable
inescapable
marinadable
promenadable
serenadable
unassailable
unavailable

biodegradable

ADAGE (see ATIC 1)
ADAM (see ASM)
ADAMANT (see ASSIONATE)
ADATE (see ACATE)
ADD (see AD 1)
ADDABLE (see ACTABLE)
ADDED 1 (see ATIC 1)
ADDED 2 (see OLID)
ADDEN (see ATTEN)
ADDENING (see ABLISHING)
ADDER 1 (see ACKER)
ADDER 2 (see OLLAR)
ADDEST (see ATIC 1)
ADDICT (see ATIC 1)
ADDIE (see ALLEY)

ADDIES

acmes
baddies
caddies
daddies
fatties
laddies
mashies
nasties
paddies
patsies
patties
taffies

Laffy-Taffies

angioplasties

ADDILY (see ALITY)
ADDIN (see ATTEN)
ADDING 1 (see ACKING)
ADDING 2 (see ALLING)
ADDIO (see ACHIO)

ADDITIVE (see ALYSIS)
ADDLE 1 (see ACKLE)
ADDLE 2 (see OTTLE)

ADDLED

addled
appled
axled
babbled
battled
castled
dabbled
dazzled
grappled
haggled
hassled
paddled
prattled
rattled
raveled
saddled
scaffold
straddled
tasseled
tattled
traveled

dog-paddled
embattled
skedaddled
unraveled
unsaddled

razzle-dazzled

ADDLER 1 (see ACKLER)
ADDLER 2 (see OBBLER)
ADDLING 1 (see ACKLING)
ADDLING 2 (see OBBLING)
ADDO (see ACCO)
ADDUX (see ATIC 1)
ADDY (see ALLEY)
ADDYING (see ALLYING)

ADE 1

Abe
age

aid
aide
babe
bade
blade
braid
cage
dade
fade
Gabe
gauge
Glade
grade
jade
lade
laid
made
maid
page
paid
plague
rage
raid
sage
shade
spade
stage
staid
suede
they'd
trade
vague
wade
wage

abrade
afraid
arcade
assuage
backstage
Band-Aid
barmaid
Belgrade
birdcage
black plague
blockade
bridesmaid
brigade
cascade
charade

crusade
Dark Age
degrade
dissuade
downgrade
downstage
engage
enrage
evade
fair trade
first aid
front page
gas gauge
grenade
handmade
high grade
homemade
housemaid
Ice Age
inlaid
invade
Kincaid
Kool-Aid
lampshade
limeade
mermaid
milkmaid
nightshade
nursemaid
of age
offstage
old age
old maid
onstage
outrage
parade
persuade
pervade
pomade
postpaid
prepaid
pureed
rampage
relaid
remade
repaid
ribcage
school age
self-made
sound stage

space age
steep grade
stockade
Stone Age
sunshade
switchblade
teenage
tirade
top grade
unpaid
upbraid
upgrade
upstage
well-made

accolade
act your age
all the rage
awkward age
barricade
Broadway stage
cattle plague
center stage
chambermaid
come of age
custom-made
dairymaid
disengage
escalade
escapade
even trade
everglade
final grade
fire brigade
foreign aid
foreign trade
Gatorade
golden age
hand grenade
hearing aid
hit parade
Honest Abe
Iron Age
legal age
legal aid
lemonade
lion cage
make the grade
marinade
marmalade

masquerade
Medicaid
metermaid
middle age
Minute Maid
newborn babe
over age
overlaid
overpaid
panty raid
razor blade
ready-made
reengage
renegade
retrograde
Rose Parade
Rubbermaid
serenade
shoulder blade
stock-in-trade
tailormade
teacher's aid
title page
ultrasuede
unafraid
under age
underlaid
underpaid
weather gauge
welfare aid

balance of trade
bubonic plague
Easter parade
government aid
Little Mermaid
minimum wage
penny arcade
pneumonic plague
temperature gauge
Thomas Kincaid
visual aid

ADE 2 (see OD)
ADE 3 (see AD 1)

ADED

aided
aphid
basted
braided
David
faded
graded
hatred
jaded
laded
naked
pasted
raided
sacred
shaded
spaded
tasted
traded
waded
wasted

abraded
blockaded
cascaded
crusaded
degraded
dissuaded
downgraded
evaded
invaded
paraded
persuaded
pervaded
upgraded

barricaded
masqueraded
serenaded

ADEMY (see ALITY)
ADEN (see ATION 1)
ADENCE (see ATEMENTS)
ADEQUATE (see ALYSIS)
ADER (see ATOR)
ADERIE (see OMETRY)
ADES (see ADIES)
ADGE (see AD 1)
ADGELESS (see ASHES)
ADGER (see ACKER)

ADGERED (see ATTERED)
ADGERING (see ATTERING)
ADGET (see ATIC 1)
ADGETRY (see ALITY)
ADGILY (see ALITY)
ADIA 1 (see ANIA)
ADIA 2 (see AFIA)

ADIAL

cranial
gavial
gradial
labial
radial

acranial
adagial
bilabial
corradial
domanial
gonadial
perradial
sporadial
subcranial

dentilabial
epicranial
infralabial
interradial
intracranial
multiradial
octocranial
pericranial
semiradial
supracranial

ADIAN (see ANIUM)
ADIANT (see ANEOUS)
ADIATE (see ATIATE)
ADIC (see ATIC 1)
ADICAL (see ACTABLE)
ADICALIZE (see ATURALIZE)
ADICALLY (see ATICALLY)
ADIE (see ADY)
ADIENT (see ANEOUS)
ADIER (see AKIER)

ADIES

crazies
Hades
ladies
navies
rabies
scabies

bag ladies
landladies
Mercedes

ADIEST (see ANEOUS)
ADINESS (see AKINESS)
ADING (see ATING)
ADINGLY (see AKINGLY)
ADIO (see ATIO 1)
ADISH (see ATIC 1)
ADISON (see AFRICAN)
ADIST (see ACES)
ADIUM (see ANIUM)
ADIUS (see ANEOUS)
ADJ (see OD)
ADJECTIVE (see ALYSIS)
ADLE (see ABLE)
ADLED (see ABLED)
ADLEY (see ALLEY)
ADLING (see ABLING)
ADLOW (see OTTO 1)
ADLY (see ALLEY)
ADMIRAL (see ACTABLE)
ADNESS (see ASHES)
ADO 1 (see OTTO 1)

ADO 2

bueno
Cato
dado
Drano
halo
Kato
KO
MAACO
NATO
Plato
rainbow
sago
Waco
yayo

Laredo
potato
tomato
tornado
Vallejo
volcano

couch potato
green tomato
hot potato
Reading Rainbow
San Diego
small potato
Taco Bueno
Winnebago

Carmen Sandiego

fettuccine Alfredo

ADOLFF (see AYOFF)
ADON (see AYON)
ADONAI (see ASSIFY)
ADOW (see ALLOW 1)
ADRIAN (see ANIUM)
ADT (see ACK)
ADUAL (see ACTABLE)
ADUALLY (see ATICALLY)
ADUATE (see ALYSIS)
ADULATE (see ACERATE)
ADVENT (see ACHMENT)

ADY

achy
Amy
baby
Bailey
basely
braidy
brainy
caky
Casey
chastely
crazy
daily
daisy
eighty
flaky
gaily

Gracie
Grady
grainy
gravely
gravy
greatly
Haiti
hasty
hazy
Jamie
Janey
Jay-Z
Katie
lacy
lady
lately
lazy
mainly
mangy
matey
maybe
namely
navy
paisley
pastry
pasty
plainly
quaky
racy
rainy
rangy
Sadie
safely
safety
sanely
scaly
shady
shaky
shapely
snaky
spacy
staidly
stately
tasty
Tracy
vainly
veiny
wavy
weighty
zany

arcanely
bag lady
church lady
Count Basie
crybaby
Dick Tracy
First Lady
fugazey
germanely
grandbaby
Greg Brady
humanely
inanely
innately
insanely
irately
Israeli
Jan Brady
landlady
Mike Brady
milady
mundanely
old lady
ornately
profanely
sedately
shillelagh
Slim Shady
stir-crazy
Tom Brady
ungainly
unwavy
urbanely

cockamamie
inhumanely
miscellany
Peter Brady
scatterbrainly
ukulele
upsy-daisy

Barnum and Bailey
fresh as a daisy
Johnny-come-lately

AE (see AY)
AELI (see ADY)
AESAR (see EATER 1)
AF (see ASS 1)
AFE (see ACE 1)

AFEL (see OTTLE)
AFELY (see ADY)
AFER (see ATOR)
AFERED (see AVORED)
AFERY (see AVERY)
AFEST (see ACES)
AFETY (see ADY)
AFF 1 (see ASS 1)
AFF 2 (see OFF)
AFFABLE (see ACTABLE)
AFFE (see ASS 1)
AFFEINATE (see ACERATE)
AFFER 1 (see ACKER)
AFFER 2 (see OLLAR)
AFFIC (see ATIC 1)
AFFIES (see ADDIES)
AFFIEST (see AGGIEST)
AFFILY (see ALITY)
AFFINESS (see ABBINESS)
AFFING (see ACKING)
AFFLE 1 (see ACKLE)
AFFLE 2 (see OTTLE)
AFFLER (see ACKER)
AFFLING (see ACKLING)
AFFLY (see OCKEY)
AFFMENT (see ASSMENT)
AFFOLD (see ADDLED)
AFFY (see ALLEY)
AFFYING (see ALLYING)

AFIA

Austria
Bosnia
Claudia
mafia
Nadia
nausea

insomnia

AFING (see ATING)

AFRICA

Acura
Africa
Agitha
algebra
Attica

Avila
Dracula
maxima
scapula
spatula

diaspora
Metallica
sciatica
South Africa

Nissan Maxima

AFRICAN

abdomen
African
javelin
Madison
masculine
Vatican

Kim Kardashian

AFRO (see ACCO)
AFT 1 (see ASS 1)
AFT 2 (see ASH 2)
AFTED (see ATIC 1)
AFTER (see ACKER)
AFTIEST (see AGGIEST)
AFTINESS (see ABBINESS)
AFTING 1 (see ACKING)
AFTING 2 (see ALLING)
AFTMENT (see ASSMENT)
AFTY (see ALLEY)
AG (see AD 1)
AGA 1 (see ADA 1)
AGA 2 (see ASIA)
AGAN (see ATION 1)
AGANS (see ATEMENTS)
AGATE (see ATIC 1)
AGE 1 (see ADE 1)
AGE 2 (see OD)
AGE 3 (see OFF)
AGEANT (see ATTEN)
AGEDY (see ALITY)
AGEL (see ABLE)
AGEMENT (see ATION 1)
AGEN 1 (see ATION 1)
AGEN 2 (see ACTION)
AGENCY (see ACIOUSLY)

AGENESS (see ACES)
AGENT (see ATION 1)
AGENTS (see ATEMENTS)
AGEOUS (see ACES)
AGEOUSLY (see ACIOUSLY)
AGER 1 (see ATOR)
AGER 2 (see OLLAR)
AGERED (see AVORED)
AGERING (see AVORING)
AGEST (see ACES)
AGGA (see ASMA)
AGGABLE (see ACTABLE)
AGGAGE (see ATIC 1)
AGGARD (see ATTERED)
AGGEDLY (see ALITY)
AGGEDY (see ALITY)
AGGER (see ACKER)
AGGERING (see ATTERING)
AGGIE (see ALLEY)
AGGIER (see ABBIER)

AGGIEST

ashiest
baggiest
battiest
braggiest
brashiest
brassiest
brattiest
catchiest
cattiest
chattiest
classiest
crabbiest
craftiest
craggiest
crappiest
daffiest
draftiest
draggiest
fattiest
flabbiest
flaggiest
flappiest
flashiest
gabbiest
gassiest
glassiest
grabbiest

grassiest
happiest
jaggiest
jazziest
massiest
nastiest
nattiest
patchiest
plashiest
quackiest
quaggiest
raspiest
rattiest
saggiest
sappiest
sassiest
scabbiest
scattiest
scrappiest
scratchiest
shabbiest
shaggiest
snaggiest
snappiest
snatchiest
snazziest
splashiest
tackiest
tattiest
trashiest
vastiest
wackiest
whackiest
wrathiest

slaphappiest
unhappiest

AGGILY (see ALITY)
AGGINESS (see ABBINESS)
AGGING (see ACKING)
AGGIO (see ARIO 2)
AGGLE (see ACKLE)
AGGLED (see ADDLED)
AGGLER (see ACKLER)
AGGLING (see ACKLING)
AGGLY (see ALLEY)
AGGOT (see ATIC 1)
AGGOTY (see ALITY)
AGGREGATE (see ALYSIS)
AGGY (see ALLEY)

AGIA (see ASIA)
AGIAL (see ADIAL)
AGIC (see ATIC 1)
AGICAL (see ACTABLE)
AGICALIZE (see ATURALIZE)
AGICALLY (see ATICALLY)
AGILE (see ACKLE)
AGINAL (see ACTABLE)
AGINATE (see ASSIONATE)
AGINE (see ATTEN)
AGINER (see ALENDAR)
AGINESS (see AKINESS)
AGING 1 (see ATING)
AGING 2 (see OCKING)
AGINGLY (see AKINGLY)
AGION (see ATION 1)
AGIOUS (see ACES)
AGIOUSLY (see ACIOUSLY)
AGISTRATE (see ACERATE)
AGITHA (see AFRICA)
AGLE (see ABLE)
AGLED (see ABLED)
AGLESS (see ASHES)
AGLING (see ABLING)
AGM (see AN 1)
AGMENT (see ACHMENT)
AGNANT (see ACHMENT)
AGNE 1 (see AIN 1)
AGNE 2 (see ONNA)
AGNET (see ATIC 1)
AGNEY (see ALLEY)
AGNIFY (see ASSIFY)
AGNUM (see ASM)
AGO 1 (see OTTO 1)
AGO 2 (see ADO 2)
AGON (see ACTION)
AGONAL (see ACTABLE)
AGONFLY (see ASSIFY)
AGONIST (see ALYSIS)
AGONY (see ALITY)
AGRANCE (see ATEMENTS)
AGRANCY (see ACIOUSLY)
AGRANT (see ATION 1)
AGUCHI (see UTY)
AGUE 1 (see ADE 1)
AGUE 2 (see OD)
AGUENESS (see ACES)
AGUEST (see ACES)
AGULAR (see ANGULAR)
AH (see A 1)
AHED (see OD)
AHING (see AWING)
AHLER (see OLLAR)

AHMA (see ONNA)
AHMAN (see OTTEN)
AHN (see ON 1)
AHOE (see OTTO 1)
AHT (see OT)
AHUA (see ADA 1)
AI (see Y)
AIAH (see ASIA)
AIC (see ATIVE)
AICA (see ASIA)
AICAN (see ATION 1)
AID 1 (see ADE 1)
AID 2 (see EAD 1)
AID 3 (see AD 1)
AIDA (see IA)
AIDABLE (see ADABLE)
AIDE (see ADE 1)
AIDED (see ADED)
AIDEN (see ATION 1)
AIDER (see ATOR)
AIDING (see ATING)
AIDLY (see ADY)
AIDY (see ADY)
AIF (see ACE 1)
AIG (see EAD 1)
AIGHT (see ATE 1)
AIGHTEN (see ATION 1)
AIGHTER (see ATOR)
AIGHTEST (see ACES)
AIGHTNESS (see ACES)
AIGN (see AIN 1)
AIGNABLE (see AINABLE)
AIGNER (see AINER)
AIGNING (see AINING)
AIGNMENT (see ATION 1)
AIGON (see YLON)

AIL

ail
ale
bail
bale
Braille
Dale
fail
frail
gale
grail
hail
hale

jail
mail
male
nail
pail
pale
quail
rail
sail
sale
scale
snail
stale
tail
tale
they'll
trail
veil
wail
whale
Yale

airmail
assail
avail
blackmail
bulk mail
Clydesdale
coattail
cocktail
curtail
derail
detail
doornail
ducktail
email
entail
exhale
fan mail
female
fire sale
fish scale
fishtail
for sale
full-scale
grand scale
guardrail
handrail
hangnail
hate mail

hightail
impale
inhale
jump bail
junk mail
large-scale
make bail
make sail
on sale
outsail
pass-fail
payscale
pigtail
prevail
rattail
regale
resale
retail
set sail
shirttail
small scale
telltale
thumbnail
toenail
travail
unveil
upscale
voicemail
white sale
wholesale

Abigail
bill of sale
Chip 'n' Dale
Chippendale
clearance sale
cottontail
countervail
epic fail
estate sale
express mail
fairy tale
fingernail
garage sale
ginger ale
Holy Grail
in detail
killer whale
lonesome trail
monorail

nature trail
never fail
nightingale
out on bail
overscale
press-on nail
rummage sale
sliding scale
tattletale
tip the scale
tooth and nail
water pail
without fail
year-end sale
yellowtail

Milburn Drysdale
registered mail
thin as a rail
to no avail

AILABLE (see ADABLE)
AILAND (see IGHTEN)
AILANT (see ATION 1)

AILER

bailer
Bayer
Baylor
failer
failure
flailer
flayer
frailer
gayer
grayer
hailer
haler
jailer
layer
mailer
Mayer
mayor
nailer
paler
player
prayer
railer
sailor

scaler
slayer
sprayer
staler
stayer
tailer
tailor
Taylor
trailer
wailer
weigher
whaler

airmailer
assailer
betrayer
bewailer
blackmailer
bricklayer
conveyor
curtailer
defrayer
derailer
detailer
displayer
entailer
essayer
exhaler
hightailer
impaler
inhaler
Lord's Prayer
naysayer
obeyer
portrayer
prevailer
purveyor
regaler
retailer
surveyor
taxpayer
team player
top layer
unveiler
waylayer
wholesaler

cassette player
ozone layer
record player

say a prayer
tattletailer

Elizabeth Taylor

AILERING (see AVORING)
AILEY (see ADY)
AILIFF (see ATIVE)

AILING

ailing
bailing
baling
failing
galing
hailing
jailing
mailing
nailing
paling
railing
sailing
scaling
tailing
trailing
wailing

airmailing
assailing
bewailing
blackmailing
curtailing
derailing
detailing
entailing
exhaling
handrailing
hightailing
impaling
inhaling
prevailing
regaling
retailing
unfailing
unveiling

AILINGLY (see AKINGLY)
AILLE (see AIL)
AILLES (see Y)

AILMENT

ailment
bailment
wailment

assailment
availment
bewailment
curtailment
derailment
empalement
engrailment
entailment
exhalement
impalement
prevailment
regalement

disentailment

AILOR (see AILER)
AILORED (see AVORED)
AILORING (see AVORING)
AILURE (see AILER)
AILY (see ADY)
AIM (see AIN 1)
AIMANT (see ATION 1)
AIMENT (see ATION 1)
AIMER (see AINER)
AIMING (see AINING)
AIMLESS (see ACES)
AIMLESSLY (see ACIOUSLY)

AIN 1

aim
bane
blame
brain
Cain
came
cane
chain
change
claim
crane
dame
Dane
deign

drain
fame
feign
flame
frame
gain
game
grain
Jane
lame
lane
maim
main
Maine
name
pain
pane
plain
plane
rain
range
reign
rein
same
sane
shame
slain
Spain
sprain
stain
strain
strange
swain
tame
train
twain
vain
vein
wane

abstain
acclaim
aflame
airplane
arcane
arraign
arrange
attain
ball game
became

big game
birdbrain
bloodstain
brain drain
brand name
butane
campaign
card game
champagne
chess game
choke chain
chow mein
close range
cocaine
complain
con game
constrain
contain
defame
derange
detain
disclaim
disdain
dog chain
domain
door frame
downrange
Elaine
engrain
estrange
exchange
exclaim
explain
eye strain
fair game
fast lane
first name
food chain
free rein
free-range
freight train
gold chain
Great Dane
hairbrain
humane
in vain
inane
inflame
insane
John Wayne

left brain
long-range
loose change
Lorraine
mainframe
maintain
Mark Twain
membrane
migraine
misname
mundane
nickname
obtain
octane
oil change
old flame
ordain
pen name
pertain
pet name
Plain Jane
proclaim
profane
propane
raise Cain
reclaim
refrain
regain
remain
rename
restrain
retain
retrain
right brain
romaine
seaplane
sex change
shortchange
slow lane
small change
Soul Train
surname
sustain
take aim
terrain
timeframe
tire chain
Ukraine
unchain
untame

urbane
war game

acid rain
aeroplane
all the same
appertain
ascertain
ball and chain
candy cane
cellophane
change of name
Charlemagne
claim to fame
Cootie Game
counterclaim
daisy chain
Dating Game
diaper change
Dick and Jane
disarrange
down the drain
driving range
entertain
exact change
fast-food chain
featherbrain
feel no pain
firing range
for a change
foreordain
freezing rain
give free rein
given name
gravy train
growing pain
guessing game
Hall of Fame
hurricane
hydroplane
inhumane
interchange
John Coltrane
just the same
Kurt Cobain
lovers lane
maiden name
married name
Mary Jane
Michael Cane

middle name
monoplane
never change
Notre Dame
Novocain
off the chain
out of range
overcame
overstrain
parlor game
passing lane
picture frame
pink champagne
play the game
post exchange
potty-train
prearrange
preordain
put to shame
rattlebrain
rearrange
rifle range
rock cocaine
scatterbrain
smear campaign
stake a claim
stock exchange
sugar cane
toilet-train
wagon train
waiting game
weathervane
windowframe
windowpane

against the grain
all in the same
bicycle lane
Big Daddy Kane
capital gain
Erica Kane
eternal flame
foreign exchange
memory lane
name of the game
Newlywed Game
no pain, no gain
Olympic flame
Olympic game
public domain

Shania Twain
skin in the game
sympathy pain
varicose vein
video game
wordly acclaim

ahead of the game
eminent domain
low-down dirty shame
money down the drain
polyurethane

political campaign

AIN 2 (see EN)

AINABLE

chainable
changeable
cranable
drainable
feignable
gainable
sprainable
stainable
strainable
trainable

abstainable
arraignable
arrangeable
attainable
bloodstainable
campaignable
complainable
constrainable
containable
detainable
disdainable
engrainable
estrangeable
exchangeable
explainable
maintainable
obtainable
ordainable
pertainable

profanable
refrainable
regainable
restrainable
retainable
retrainable
sustainable
unchainable
unchangeable

appertainable
ascertainable
entertainable
foreordainable
hydroplanable
interchangeable
overstrainable
prearrangeable
preordainable
rearrangeable

AINAGE (see ACES)
AINBOW (see ADO 2)
AINDER (see AINER)
AINE (see AIN 1)

AINER

aimer
blamer
chamber
changer
claimer
danger
drainer
fainter
feigner
feinter
flamer
framer
gainer
gamer
Kramer
lamer
maimer
manger
namer
painter
planer
quainter

ranger
reigner
reiner
saner
shamer
sprainer
stainer
strainer
stranger
tainter
tamer
trainer
vainer

abstainer
acclaimer
arraigner
arranger
attainer
campaigner
complainer
constrainer
container
defamer
deranger
detainer
disclaimer
endanger
exchanger
exclaimer
explainer
inaner
inflamer
Lone Ranger
maintainer
mundaner
obtainer
ordainer
profaner
reclaimer
refrainer
regainer
remainder
remainer
restrainer
retainer
shortchanger
sustainer
urbaner
weight gainer

ascertainer
diaper changer
disarranger
entertainer
fingerpainter
forest ranger
inhumaner
interchanger
money changer
out of danger
overstrainer
perfect stranger
rearranger

Mighty Morphin' Power Ranger

AINFUL (see ABLE)
AINFULLY (see ACIOUSLY)
AINIER (see AKIER)

AINING

aiming
blaming
braining
caning
chaining
changing
claiming
craning
deigning
draining
feigning
flaming
framing
gaining
gaming
laming
maiming
naming
paining
raining
ranging
reigning
reining
shaming
spraining
staining
straining

taming
training

abstaining
acclaiming
arraigning
arranging
attaining
campaigning
complaining
containing
defaming
detaining
disclaiming
exchanging
exclaiming
explaining
free-ranging
inflaming
maintaining
nicknaming
obtaining
ordaining
pertaining
reclaiming
refraining
regaining
remaining
renaming
restraining
retaining
retraining
spring training
sustaining
unchaining

appertaining
ascertaining
diaper-changing
disarranging
entertaining
everchanging
foreordaining
interchanging
overstraining
prearranging
preordaining
rearranging

on the job training

sensitivity training

AININGLY (see AKINGLY)
AINLESS (see ACES)
AINLY (see ADY)
AINMENT (see ATION 1)
AINNESS (see ACES)
AINST (see ENT)

AINT

ain't
faint
feint
paint
quaint
saint
taint

acquaint
complaint
constraint
repaint
restraint
war paint

fingerpaint
reacquaint
self-restraint

Latter-day Saint

AINTANCE (see ATEMENTS)

AINTED

fainted
feinted
painted
tainted

acquainted
repainted

fingerpainted
get acquainted
reacquainted

AINTENANCE (see ATEMENTS)
AINTER (see AINER)
AINTEST (see ACES)

AINTINESS (see AKINESS)
AINTING (see ATING)
AINTNESS (see ACES)
AINY (see ADY)
AIQUIRI (see ALITY)
AIR (see ARE 1)
AIRABLE (see ARABLE)
AIRE 1 (see ARE 1)
AIRE 2 (see EAR 1)
AIRED (see ARED 1)
AIRIE (see ARY)
AIRIER (see ARRIER)
AIRILY (see ERITY1)
AIRING (see ARING)
AIRLESS (see ARENESS)
AIRLY (see ARY)
AIRNESS (see ARENESS)
AIRY (see ARY)
AISAL (see ABLE)
AISANT (see ATION 1)
AISE (see AVE 1)
AISER (see ATOR)
AISIN (see ATION 1)
AISING (see ATING)
AISLEY (see ADY)
AISON (see AYON)
AISSE (see ACE 1)
AIST (see ACE 1)
AISTFUL (see ABLE)
AISY (see ADY)
AIT 1 (see ATE 1)
AIT 2 (see AY)
AITABLE (see ADABLE)
AITED (see ATED)
AITEN (see ATION 1)
AITER (see ATOR)
AITERING (see AVORING)
AITH (see ACE 1)
AITHFUL (see ABLE)
AITHFULLY (see ACIOUSLY)
AITHLESS (see ACES)
AITI (see ADY)
AITIAN (see ATION 1)
AITING (see ATING)
AITINGLY (see ATINGLY)
AITLESS (see ACES)
AITOR (see ATOR)
AITRESS (see ACES)
AIVE (see AVE 1)
AIVER (see ATOR)
AIVING (see ATING)
AJA (see ADA 1)
AJESTY (see ALITY)

AJOR (see ATOR)
AJORED (see AVORED)
AJORING (see AVORING)
AJUN (see ATION 1)
AK (see ACK)
AKA (see ADA 1)
AKABLY (see AVERY)
AKE (see ACE 1)
AKED (see ADED)
AKEFUL (see ABLE)
AKEN (see ATION 1)
AKENESS (see ACES)
AKENLY (see ACIOUSLY)
AKER (see ATOR)
AKERY (see AVERY)
AKI 1 (see OCKEY)
AKI 2 (see ALLEY)

AKIER

brainier
brakier
cakier
clavier
crazier
flakier
flamier
gamier
glazier
grainier
grapier
grazier
hazier
lacier
lakier
lazier
mazier
pavier
quakier
racier
rainier
shadier
shakier
snakier
wavier

AKIEST (see ANEOUS)

AKINESS

achiness
caginess
daintiness
flakiness
hastiness
laziness
manginess
pastiness
quakiness
ranginess
scaliness
shadiness
shakiness
snakiness
tastiness
waviness
zaniness

AKING (see ATING)

AKINGLY

achingly
bakingly
bravingly
cravingly
failingly
grazingly
quakingly
ragingly
railingly
ravingly
savingly
scathingly
takingly
wailingly

amazingly
breathtakingly
debasingly
degradingly
depravingly
engagingly
mistakingly
painstakingly
prevailingly
unavailingly
unfailingly

entertainingly
retrogradingly

AKKA (see ADA 1)
AKKER (see ACKER)
AKKING (see ACKING)
AKY (see ADY)

AL 1

Al
Cal
gal
Hal
pal
Sal
shall
Val

canal
chorale
corral
decal
locale
low-cal
morale
pen pal

chaparral
ear canal
femme fatale
musicale
rationale
root canal

Erie Canal
Guadalcanal

AL 2 (see ALL 1)
ALA 1 (see ADA 1)
ALA 2 (see ASIA)
ALABLE (see ADABLE)
ALACE (see ATIC 1)
ALACHI (see ASSIFY)
ALAD (see ATIC 1)
ALADY (see ALITY)
ALAN (see ALLON)
ALANCE (see ALLON)
ALANT (see ATION 1)
ALARY (see ALITY)

ALATE 1 (see ACATE)
ALATE 2 (see ATIC 1)
ALAXY (see ALITY)
ALBUM (see ALLION)
ALC (see ALP)
ALCHEMIST (see ALYSIS)
ALCIUM (see ALIUM)
ALCO (see OTTO 1)
ALCOLM (see ALLION)
ALCON (see ALLION)
ALCONY (see ALITY)
ALCULUS (see ALYSIS)
ALCUM (see ALLION)
ALD (see AULT)
ALDER (see ALTER)
ALDI (see OCKEY)
ALDIE (see OCKEY)
ALDING (see ALLING)
ALDO (see OTTO 1)
ALDY (see OCKEY)
ALE 1 (see AIL)
ALE 2 (see AL 1)
ALE 3 (see OLLY 1)
ALEA (see ASIA)
ALEC (see ATIC 1)
ALECK (see ETIC)
ALEIGH (see OLLY 1)
ALEM (see ATION 1)
ALEMENT (see AILMENT)
ALENCE (see ATEMENTS)

ALENDAR

aperture
bachelor
barrister
battener
blackener
calendar
caliber
challenger
character
chavender
fastener
fattener
flattener
kalendar
lavender
mariner
massacre
passenger

Salinger
scavenger

ambassador
encalendar
imaginer
McAlister
spectacular
vernacular

manufacturer

Kevin McCallister

ALENT (see ATTEN)
ALER (see AILER)
ALERIE (see ALITY)
ALESS (see AWLESS)
ALEX (see ATIC 1)
ALF 1 (see ASS 1)
ALF 2 (see ALP)
ALGEBRA (see AFRICA)
ALGIC (see OTIC)
ALGO (see OTTO 1)
ALGUM (see ALLION)
ALI 1 (see OLLY 1)
ALI 2 (see ALLEY)
ALIA (see ASIA)
ALIAN 1 (see ANIUM)
ALIAN 2 (see ALLION)
ALIAS (see ARIOUS)
ALIBER (see ALENDAR)
ALIBRATE (see ACERATE)
ALIC (see ATIC 1)
ALICE (see ATIC 1)
ALID 1 (see ATIC 1)
ALID 2 (see OLID)
ALIEN (see ANIUM)
ALIFATE (see ACERATE)
ALIFY (see OLLIFY)
ALIGNANCE (see IVALENCE)
ALILEE (see ALITY)
ALIN (see OTTEN)
ALINESS (see AKINESS)
ALING (see AILING)
ALINGER (see ALENDAR)
ALION (see ALLION)
ALISTER (see ALENDAR)

ALITY

acidy
actively
agony
allergy
alogy
apathy
avidly
baggily
balcony
basketry
battery
blasphemy
cabinetry
cadgily
calorie
Calvary
Cassidy
cavalry
cavity
chastity
chattery
classically
classily
clattery
crappily
daffily
daiquiri
dastardly
dragony
factory
faculty
faddily
fallacy
fattily
flabbily
flashily
flattery
gadgetry
galaxy
Galilee
gallantry
gallery
gravity
happily
hatchery
jazzily
lactory
lavishly

maggoty
majesty
malady
mastery
mattery
Napoli
nastily
passively
patchery
quackery
rabbitry
rackety
raggedly
raggedy
rapidly
rhapsody
salary
sappily
scrappily
snappily
strategy
tacitly
tattery
thatchery
tractory
tragedy
travesty
Valerie
wackily
wagony
Zachary

academy
analogy
anatomy
art gallery
audacity
brutality
capacity
catastrophe
causality
centrality
crustalogy
depravity
detractory
Dick Dastardly
fatality
formality
frugality
legality

locality
mammalogy
mendacity
mentality
morality
mortality
neutrality
normality
olfactory
oralogy
paralogy
petralogy
phylactery
plurality
pugnacity
reality
refractory
sagacity
slaphappily
tenacity
tetralogy
tonality
totality
unhappily
veracity
vitality
vivacity
vocality
voracity

abnormality
actuality
bestiality
calefactory
commonality
cordiality
criminality
David Cassidy
genealogy
generality
geniality
hospitality
idealogy
illegality
immorality
immortality
incapacity
informality
joviality
law of gravity

liberality
manufactory
mineralogy
mutuality
nationality
partiality
Peanut Gallery
personality
perspicacity
practicality
principality
punctuality
rationality
satisfactory
sensuality
sexuality
solar battery
speciality
technicality
triviality
visuality
whimsicality

asexuality
assault and battery
center of gravity
congeniality
conviviality
dissatisfactory
eventuality
excalifactory
genethlialogy
impartiality
instrumentality
irrationality
municipality
originality
sentimentality
spirituality
universality
unsatisfactory

artificiality
confidentiality
constitutionality
individuality
superficiality

ALIUM

calcium
kalium
Valium

dentalium
gnaphalium
potassium
rhophalium

argentalium

ALIVATE (see ACERATE)
ALK (see OT)
ALKABLE (see OGICAL)
ALKATIVE (see OSITIVE)
ALKEN (see OTTEN)
ALKER 1 (see OLLAR)
ALKER 2 (see OLLAR)
ALKIE (see OCKEY)
ALKINESS (see OCKINESS)
ALKING 1 (see OCKING)
ALKING 2 (see ALLING)
ALKY (see OCKEY)

ALL 1

all
awl
ball
bawl
brawl
call
crawl
doll
drawl
fall
gall
hall
haul
loll
mall
maul
moll
pall
Paul
Saul
scrawl
shawl

small
sprawl
squall
stall
tall
trawl
wall
y'all
yawl

air ball
appall
at all
atoll
banal
baseball
beanball
bird call
blackball
cabal
catcall
catchall
close call
cornball
crank call
cue ball
cure-all
curveball
dance hall
downfall
eightball
end-all
enthrall
eyeball
fire wall
fireball
fly ball
Foosball
football
footfall
forestall
foul ball
free-fall
fuzzball
golf ball
goofball
Great Wall
gumball
hairball
handball

hard ball
highball
house call
install
jump ball
Ken doll
kickball
landfall
last call
long haul
meatball
mess hall
miscall
name-call
Nepal
Nerf Ball
nightfall
oddball
on call
pall-mall
phone call
pinball
pitfall
play ball
pool hall
pratfall
rag doll
rainfall
recall
roll call
screwball
scuzzball
seawall
short haul
sick call
snowball
snowfall
softball
speedball
spitball
St. Paul
stonewall
tell all
toll call
town hall
U-Haul
Warhol
whitewall
will-call
windfall

withdrawal
wolf call
you-all

above all
after all
all in all
baby doll
Barbie doll
basketball
beck and call
Berlin Wall
billiard ball
bowling ball
butterball
cannonball
carryall
caterwaul
cattle call
city hall
climb the wall
collect call
come to call
cotton ball
coverall
crystal ball
curtain call
disenthrall
distress call
down the hall
end it all
fancy ball
free-for-all
have a ball
judgment call
know it all
knuckleball
Leventhal
living doll
local call
Lucille Ball
matzo ball
Montreal
music hall
nature's call
obscene call
off-the-wall
on the ball
one and all
overall

overcall
overhaul
paper doll
popcorn ball
pro football
return call
Seconal
Senegal
shopping mall
Southern drawl
still and all
study hall
Taj Mahal
ten feet tall
tennis ball
tether ball
touch football
volleyball
wake-up call
wall-to-wall
waterfall
Western Wall
wherewithal

Australian crawl
Carnegie Hall
carry the ball
clarion call
courtesy call
debutante ball
drive up the wall
go to the wall
hole in the wall
justice for all
long-distance call
Magic 8-Ball
make your skin crawl
Neanderthal
once and for all
push to the wall
table football
Tammany Hall

Arsenio Hall
be-all and end-all
behind the eight ball
community hall
go over the wall
over the long haul
up against the wall

writing on the wall

ALL 2 (see AL 1)
ALLABEES (see OLOGIES)
ALLABLE (see OGICAL)
ALLACE (see AWLESS)
ALLACY (see ALITY)
ALLAD (see ATIC 1)
ALLAH (see ADA 1)
ALLANT (see ATTEN)
ALLANTRY (see ALITY)
ALLAS (see ATIC 1)
ALLEN 1 (see OTTEN)
ALLEN 2 (see ALLON)
ALLENGE (see ALLON)
ALLENGED (see ASTENED)
ALLENGER (see ALENDAR)
ALLEON (see AMPION)
ALLER (see OLLAR)
ALLERGY (see ALITY)
ALLERY (see ALITY)
ALLET (see ATIC 1)

ALLEY

abbey
Abby
acme
acne
Aggie
aggy
alley
aptly
Ashley
ashy
Asti
baddie
badly
baggy
batty
blabby
blackly
Bradley
brashly
brassy
bratty
cabbie
caddie
Cagney
Cali

catchy
Cathy
catty
chassis
chatty
clacky
clashy
classy
crabby
crafty
crappy
crassly
daddy
daffy
dally
Daphne
drafty
draggy
faddy
fasty
fatty
flabby
flappy
flashy
flatly
flaxy
gabby
galley
gappy
gassy
ghastly
gladly
glassy
grabby
graspy
grassy
hackney
happy
Jackie
jazzy
khaki
lackey
Lassie
lastly
laxly
madly
Maggie
mashie
matty
maxi

Maxie
naggy
nappy
nasty
natty
paddy
pappy
patchy
patsy
patty
plashy
quacky
rally
rashly
raspy
ratty
sacky
sadly
saggy
Sally
sappy
sassy
savvy
scabby
scraggly
scrappy
scratchy
shabby
shaggy
snaggy
snappy
snazzy
splashy
swaggy
tabby
tacky
taffy
tally
tatty
taxi
trappy
trashy
valley
vastly
wacky
waggy
waxy

abstractly
Apache

back alley
big daddy
blind alley
compactly
Death Valley
exactly
golf caddie
granddaddy
grandpappy
Iraqi
Kate Bradley
pep rally
Pine Valley
rice paddy
ship's galley
slaphappy
steadfastly
tea caddy
unhappy
unsavvy
zigzaggy

Abernathy
baby daddy
bowling alley
Chatty Cathy
Cincinnati
dilly dally
football rally
laffy-taffy
make it snappy
Mexicali
Milton Bradley
not exactly
Short N' Sassy
sugar daddy
Tallahassee
The Great Gatsby
Tin Pan Alley
trigger-happy
up your alley

angioplasty
Peppermint Patty
Silicon Valley

ALLIBLE (see ACTABLE)
ALLIC (see ATIC 1)
ALLICA (see AFRICA)
ALLID (see ATIC 1)
ALLIER (see ABBIER)

ALLING

balding
balking
balling
balming
bawling
bogging
bombing
brawling
calling
calming
caulking
causing
clogging
crawling
dogging
drawling
falling
flogging
fogging
frauding
galling
hauling
hogging
jogging
lauding
lofting
logging
lolling
mauling
nodding
palling
palming
pausing
plodding
podding
prodding
scalding
scrawling
shodding
sodding
solving
sprawling
squalling
stalling
tomming
trawling
trodding
wadding

wafting
waltzing

A-bombing
absolving
alofting
appalling
applauding
becalming
befalling
befogging
birdcalling
blackballing
bulldogging
catcalling
convolving
defogging
defrauding
devolving
dissolving
embalming
enthralling
evolving
eyeballing
fire bombing
forestalling
free-falling
hot-rodding
hotdogging
installing
involving
marauding
napalming
pratfalling
ramrodding
recalling
resolving
revolving
snowballing
spit-wadding
stonewalling
time bombing
unclogging
unshodding
unwadding

Avon calling
cataloging
caterwauling
cattle prodding

circumvolving
disenthralling
intervolving
overhauling
preresolving
problem solving
redissolving
reinvolving
waterbombing
waterlogging

atomic bombing
nuclear bombing

ALLION

album
algum
falcon
Malcolm
scallion
stallion
talcum
vallum

battalion
black stallion
corallum
Italian
medallion
rapscallion

intervallum

Millennium Falcon

ALLIS (see AWLESS)
ALLISTER (see ALENDAR)

ALLON

absence
Alan
Allen
balance
challenge
gallon
talon

off balance

counterbalance
Jimmy Fallon
Woody Allen

ALLOP (see ATIC 1)
ALLOR (see ACKER)
ALLOT (see ATIC 1)
ALLOUS (see ATIC 1)

ALLOW 1

aloe
alto
arrow
ballow
callow
fallow
gallow
hallow
mallow
marrow
narrow
pharaoh
sallow
salvo
shadow
shallow
sparrow
tallow
tarot

allhallow
bone marrow
contralto
dishallow
enwallow
eye shadow
foreshadow
Rialto
straight arrow
twifallow
unhallow
wheelbarrow
White Shadow

bow and arrow
overshadow
Palo Alto
straight and narrow

ALLOW 2 (see OTTO 1)
ALLOW 3 (see ELLO)
ALLOWER (see OGRAPHER)
ALLSY (see OCKEY)
ALLUM (see ALLION)
ALLUS (see ATIC 1)
ALLY 1 (see ALLEY)
ALLY 2 (see OLLY 1)

ALLYING

affying
caddying
dallying
rallying
sallying
tabbying
tallying
taxiing
waddying

dillydallying

ALM (see ON 1)
ALMER (see OLLAR)
ALMEST (see AWLESS)
ALMIEST (see OGGIEST)
ALMING 1 (see ALLING)
ALMING 2 (see ALLING)
ALMIST (see AWLESS)
ALMLY (see AWNY)
ALMNESS (see AWLESS)
ALMON (see ANSON 1)
ALMOND (see OTTEN)
ALMY (see AWNY)
ALO (see ADO 2)
ALOE (see ALLOW 1)
ALOGOUS (see ALYSIS)
ALOGY (see ALITY)
ALOM (see OTTEN)
ALON (see ALLON)
ALOR 1 (see ACKER)
ALOR 2 (see OLLAR)
ALORIE (see ALITY)

ALP

Alf
calc
palp

Ralph
scalp

ALPABLE (see ACTABLE)
ALPEL (see OUSAL)
ALPH (see ALP)
ALPHABETIZE (see ATURALIZE)
ALSA (see ADA 1)
ALSE (see AULT)
ALSELY (see OCKEY)
ALSO (see OTTO 1)
ALSY (see OCKEY)
ALT (see AULT)
ALTA (see ADA 1)
ALTAR (see ALTER)
ALTED (see AULTED)

ALTER

alder
altar
alter
balder
falter
faulter
golfer
halter
salter
scalder
solver
vaulter
Walter

absolver
assaulter
defaulter
dissolver
evolver
exalter
Gibraltar
pole-vaulter
resolver
revolver

somersaulter

Rock of Gibraltar

ALTERED (see OFFERED)

ALTIC (see OTIC)
ALTING (see OCKING)
ALTO (see ALLOW 1)
ALTY (see OCKEY)
ALTZ (see AULT)
ALTZING (see ALLING)

ALUE

baboon
backroom
bathroom
cashew
classroom
Matthew
statue
statute
vacuum
value

devalue
face value

absolute value

ALVAGE (see ATIC 1)
ALVARY (see ALITY)
ALVE (see ASS 1)
ALVO (see ALLOW 1)
ALY (see ADY)

ALYSIS

abacus
activist
additive
adequate
adjective
aggregate
agonist
alchemist
Arabic
avarice
average
blasphemous
calculus
catalyst
Catholic
classlessness

fabulous
habitus
hazardous
jacketless
laxative
massiveness
maverick
narrative
pacifist
passivist
placidness
ravenous
strategist

analogous
analysis
Annapolis
antagonist
dialysis
fantabulous
inadequate
miraculous
paralysis
protagonist
subaverage

Minneapolis
self-analysis
undergraduate

Indianapolis
psychoanalysis

AM 1 (see ON 1)
AM 2 (see AN 1)
AMA 1 (see ONNA)
AMA 2 (see ANA 1)
AMAGE (see ANISH 1)
AMAH (see ONNA)
AMAN (see OTTEN)
AMARA (see AMERA)
AMAS (see ADA 1)
AMATE (see ACATE)
AMATEUR (see AMETER)
AMB (see AN 1)
AMBER 1 (see AMMER)
AMBER 2 (see AINER)
AMBERED (see AMPERED)
AMBERING (see ANDERING 1)
AMBI (see ANDY)
AMBLE (see ANGLE)

AMBLED

ambled
anviled
brambled
canceled
candled
dandled
gambled
handled
mantled
rambled
sampled
scambled
scrambled
shambled
spanceled
trammeled
trampled

dismantled
exampled
manhandled
mishandled
panhandled
unscrambled

AMBLER (see AMMER)
AMBLING (see ANGLING)
AMBO 1 (see ONDO)
AMBO 2 (see ANGO 1)
AMBRIDGE (see ACES)
AMBULATE (see AMINATE)
AMBY (see ANDY)
AMCO (see ANGO 1)
AME 1 (see AIN 1)
AME 2 (see AN 1)
AMEDLY (see ACIOUSLY)
AMEFUL (see ABLE)
AMEL (see ANGLE)
AMELA (see AMERA)
AMELESS (see ACES)
AMELESSLY (see ACIOUSLY)
AMELY (see ADY)
AMEN 1 (see ATION 1)
AMEN 2 (see OTTEN)
AMENESS (see ACES)
AMEON (see ANIUM)
AMER 1 (see AINER)
AMER 2 (see OVER 1)

AMERA

Angela
anima
Ankara
camera
Canada
mandala
Pamela
stamina
Tamara

LaTamara

AMERATE (see AMINATE)
AMES (see ON 1)
AMEST (see ACES)

AMETER

amateur
bannister
canister
ganister
janitor
manager
tanager

diameter
dynameter
heptameter
hexameter
mismanager
octameter
parameter
peirameter
pentameter
pirameter
tetrameter
viameter
voltameter

myriameter
operameter
pluviameter
ureameter

haemadynameter
semidiameter

AMI 1 (see AWNY)
AMI 2 (see ANDY)
AMIC 1 (see ANIC)
AMIC 2 (see ONIC)
AMICALLY (see ANICALLY)
AMIE (see ADY)
AMIER (see AKIER)
AMILY (see ANITY)
AMINA (see AMERA)

AMINATE

ambulate
amputate
angulate
animate
annulate
antiquate
camerate
cancerate
candidate
laminate
strangulate

biangulate
concamerate
concatenate
contaminate
disanimate
examinate
reanimate
triangulate

decontaminate
incontaminate

AMINE (see ANSON 1)
AMING (see AINING)
AMINOUS (see ANIMOUS)
AMISH 1 (see ANISH 1)
AMISH 2 (see OLISH)
AMIST (see ACES)
AMITY (see ANITY)
AMMA (see ANA 1)
AMMABLE (see ANDABLE)
AMMAL (see ANGLE)
AMMAR (see AMMER)
AMMARY (see ANITY)
AMMEL (see ANGLE)
AMMELED (see AMBLED)

AMMER

amber
ambler
anchor
anger
angler
answer
antler
banger
banker
banner
banter
blancher
blander
camper
cancer
candor
canker
canner
canter
cantor
Chandler
chanter
clamber
clamor
clamper
clanger
clanker
crammer
cramper
cranker
damner
damper
dancer
dangler
danker
fanner
flanger
flanker
franker
gambler
gander
gangster
glamor
glamour
glancer
grammar
grander
grandeur

granter
hammer
hamper
hamster
hander
handler
hangar
hanger
hanker
jammer
jangler
lancer
mangler
manner
manor
pamper
pander
panner
panter
panther
planner
planter
prancer
pranker
rambler
rammer
rancher
rancor
ranker
ranter
sampler
sander
scamper
scanner
scanter
scrambler
scrammer
slammer
slander
slanter
spanker
spanner
stammer
stamper
stander
strangler
swanker
tamper
tanker
tanner

thanker
tramper
transfer
vamper
whammer
wrangler
yammer
yanker

advancer
Auslander
backhander
bystander
chancellor
cliffhanger
clothes hamper
clothes hanger
commander
day camper
deadpanner
decanter
demander
disbander
dismantler
drop anchor
enamor
encamper
enchanter
enhancer
entangler
entrancer
expander
financer
flimflammer
freelancer
grandslammer
grandstander
handstander
Icelander
implanter
jackhammer
manhandler
meander
mishandler
oil tanker
outlander
panhandler
philander
Pink Panther
programmer

recanter
replanter
revamper
righthander
romancer
sledgehammer
square dancer
suntanner
supplanter
tap dancer
transplanter
unhander
untangler

airplane hangar
Alexander
Arm and Hammer
bedside manner
belly dancer
city planner
coriander
countermander
Country Camper
disco dancer
disenchanter
disentangler
doppelganger
gallivanter
gerrymander
go-go dancer
high commander
M.C. Hammer
reprimander
salamander
understander

exotic dancer
lord of the manor
misunderstander
Star-Spangled Banner

Dr. David Bruce Banner

AMMERING (see ANDERING 1)
AMMERY (see ANITY)
AMMIE (see ANDY)
AMMING (see ANDING)
AMMO (see ANGO 1)
AMMOCK (see ANIC)
AMMON (see ANSON 1)
AMMONIZE (see ANDALIZE)

AMMY (see ANDY)
AMN (see AN 1)
AMNER (see AMMER)
AMNING (see ANDING)
AMO (see ANGO 1)
AMON (see ATION 1)
AMOR (see AMMER)
AMORING (see ANDERING 1)
AMORIZE (see ANDALIZE)
AMOROUS (see ANIMOUS)
AMORTIZE (see ANDALIZE)
AMORY (see ANITY)
AMOS (see ACES)
AMOUR (see AMMER)
AMOUS (see ACES)
AMOUSLY (see ACIOUSLY)
AMP 1 (see ANK)
AMP 2 (see ONT 2)
AMPANT (see ARENT)
AMPBELL (see ANGLE)
AMPEN (see ANSON 1)
AMPER (see AMMER)

AMPERED

answered
bannered
bantered
cantered
clambered
hampered
mannered
pampered
scampered
standard
tampered

gold standard
ill-mannered
substandard
well-mannered

double standard

AMPERING (see ANDERING 1)
AMPETT (see ARENT)
AMPI (see ANDY)
AMPIER (see AWNIER)
AMPINESS (see AWNINESS)
AMPING (see ANDING)

AMPION

Anakin
campion
champion
Flannigan
galleon
manakin
Mandarin
mandolin
manikin
mannequin
rampion
shenanigan
tampion
tannigen

AMPISH (see ANISH 1)
AMPLE (see ANGLE)
AMPLED (see AMBLED)
AMPLER (see AMMER)
AMPLING (see ANGLING)
AMPLY (see ANDY)
AMPNESS (see ANISH 1)
AMPRAS (see ANISH 1)
AMPUS (see ANISH 1)
AMPUTATE (see AMINATE)
AMPY 1 (see ANDY)
AMPY 2 (see AWNY)
AMSEL (see ANGLE)
AMSEY (see ANDY)
AMSTER (see AMMER)
AMUS 1 (see ACES)
AMUS 2 (see OLISH)
AMY (see ADY)

AN 1

am
an
and
Anne
bam
ban
band
bang
bland
bran
brand

cam
can
clam
clan
clang
cram
dam
damn
fam
fan
fang
flan
Fran
gang
glam
gland
graham
gram
grand
ham
hand
hang
jam
Jan
lamb
land
ma'am
man
Nan
Pam
pan
plan
ram
ran
rang
Sam
sand
sang
scam
scan
scram
sham
slam
slang
Spam
span
sprang
Stan
stand
strand

swam
swang
tam
tan
Tang
than
twang
van
Wang
wham
whang
yam
yang

Afghan
ape-man
armband
backhand
bagman
bandstand
Batman
bedpan
began
best man
big bang
brass band
by hand
cabstand
cancan
CAT scan
cave man
chain gang
Chopin
command
con man
dance band
deadpan
deck hand
defang
demand
disband
dishpan
door jamb
dreamland
dustpan
exam
expand
fan-tan
farmhand
firsthand

flat land
flight plan
flimflam
floor plan
forehand
free hand
front man
G-man
game plan
gang bang
gladhand
grandslam
grandstand
handstand
hangman
harangue
He-Man
headband
headman
health plan
hitman
homeland
hot damn
hour hand
house plan
iceman
Iran
Japan
kickstand
Koran
last stand
lawman
lead man
left hand
life span
longhand
madame
madman
main man
meringue
milkman
Moran
mustang
name brand
newsstand
oat bran
odd man
off-brand
offhand
oil can

oilman
old hand
on hand
Our Gang
outran
outrang
outswam
Pac-Man
Pearl Jam
point man
program
quicksand
Ray-Ban
remand
right hand
Roseanne
Saipan
sandman
saucepan
sedan
Shazam
shebang
shorthand
snowman
soup can
Spokane
sports fan
spray can
stagehand
stunt man
Sudan
suntan
taipan
Tarzan
the man
thirdhand
timespan
tin can
toe jam
Trans AM
trashcan
trashman
unhand
waistband
wasteland
watchband
webcam
wham bam
wild man
wise man

withstand	goal line stand	payment plan
Wolfgang	hand-in-hand	pension plan
wristband	handyman	Peter Pan
Wu-Tang	hat in hand	policeman
yes man	heavy hand	Promised Land
young man	helping hand	rack of lamb
	high command	Raisin Bran
Abraham	hit the fan	repairman
ampersand	hologram	reprimand
Amsterdam	Holy Land	right-hand man
anagram	hotdog stand	Rio Grande
anchorman	in a jam	roasting pan
at firsthand	in the can	rubberband
baby grand	Instagram	secondhand
beforehand	Iron Man	shortwave band
Birmingham	Jackie Chan	show your hand
body slam	kick the can	Silly Sand
Boogie Man	kilogram	sleight of hand
boomerang	Kool-Aid Man	spick-and-span
borderland	Krugerrand	Spider-Man
bottomland	Ku Klux Klan	Superman
brother man	ladies' man	take a stand
Buckingham	leading man	take in hand
cablegram	leg of lamb	take the stand
candied yam	lend a hand	taxi stand
Candy Land	mammogram	telegram
Candy Man	man-to-man	Toucan Sam
cap in hand	marching band	traffic jam
caravan	master plan	triggerman
close-at-hand	middleman	TV stand
contraband	milligram	Uncle Sam
countermand	minute hand	underhand
country twang	minuteman	understand
Dapper Dan	monogram	upper hand
diagram	motherland	weatherman
diaphragm	moving van	witness stand
Disneyland	Ms. Pac-Man	wonderland
Dixieland	Musicland	workingman
epigram	nanogram	yin and yang
exhaust fan	near at hand	
fairyland	no man's land	aerosol can
fatherland	on demand	Afghanistan
fellowman	on the lam	as best you can
force one's hand	one-night stand	attention span
four-in-hand	openhand	battering ram
frying pan	out of hand	bird in the hand
garbage can	overhand	Captain Caveman
garbageman	overland	chain of command
gerrymand	overran	company man
give a damn	Pakistan	confidence man

dirty old man
Dixieland band
Duran Duran
family man
fantasyland
flash-in-the-pan
generic brand
Get Along Gang
gingerbread man
Good Humor man
Green Eggs and Ham
hamburger stand
ideogram
installment plan
Invisible Man
law of the land
lay of the land
lemon meringue
medicine man
misunderstand
moo goo gai pan
newspaper stand
newspaperman
Omar Khayyam
oral exam
orangutan
pay on demand
Raggedy Ann
umbrella stand
watering can

after school program
Chico and The Man
deliveryman
eat out of your hand
go out with a bang
Howard Cunningham
Joanie Cunningham
Maytag repairman
never-never land
on the other hand
parallelogram
Richie Cunningham
second in command
second story man
Secret Agent Man
supply and demand
undercover man
Yosemite Sam

Chitty Chitty Bang Bang

Abominable Snowman
K.C. and The Sunshine Band

AN 2 (see ON 1)
AN'T (see ANK)

ANA 1

Anna
gamma
grandma
manna
panda
Sandra
Santa
stanza
Vanna

Amana
Amanda
Atlanta
banana
bandana
bonanza
cabana
Cassandra
Diana
Guiana
Guyana
Havana
hosanna
Miranda
Montana
organza
Samantha
savannah
Susana
Susanna
veranda

Africana
Alabama
Alexandra
French Guiana
Indiana
Mariana
memoranda

panorama
Pollyanna
propaganda
Santa Ana
Texarkana
Tropicana

Americana
British Guiana
Club Tropicana
extravaganza
Louisiana
Princess Diana
Tony Montana

Chiquita Banana

Napoleon and Samantha

ANA 2 (see ONNA)
ANABLE (see AINABLE)
ANACLE (see ANDABLE)
ANADA (see AMERA)
ANAGE (see ANISH 1)
ANAGER (see AMETER)
ANAH (see ONNA)
ANAKIN (see AMPION)
ANAL (see ABLE)
ANALIZE (see ANDALIZE)
ANALYST (see ANIMOUS)
ANALYZE (see ANDALIZE)
ANATE (see ANIC)
ANATEE (see ANITY)
ANC (see ANK)
ANCA (see ONNA)

ANCE 1

blanch
Blanche
branch
chance
dance
France
glance
lance
manse
pants
prance
ranch

stance
trance

advance
barn dance
breakdance
bromance
by chance
dude ranch
enhance
expanse
fat chance
finance
Flashdance
folk dance
freelance
last chance
no chance
off chance
perchance
rain dance
romance
side-glance
slim chance
square dance
sweatpants
tap dance
war dance

at a glance
avalanche
ballroom dance
belly dance
cattle ranch
chicken ranch
circumstance
even chance
fighting chance
game of chance
happenstance
hula dance
in a trance
in advance
olive branch
only chance
song and dance
sporting chance
stand a chance
take a chance
The Big Dance

hypnotic trance

ANCE 2 (see ONT 2)

ANCE 3

Andre
entrée
grande
hombre
Kanye

Beyoncé
fiancé
fiancée

ANCEABLE (see ANDABLE)
ANCEL (see ANGLE)
ANCELED (see AMBLED)
ANCELING (see ANDERING 1)
ANCELLING (see ANDERING 1)
ANCELLOR (see AMMER)
ANCEMENT (see ANIC)
ANCER (see AMMER)
ANCERATE (see AMINATE)
ANCEROUS (see ANIMOUS)
ANCET (see ARENT)
ANCH (see ANCE 1)
ANCHE 1 (see ANCE 1)
ANCHE 2 (see ANDY)
ANCHER (see AMMER)
ANCHING (see ANCING)
ANCHOR (see AMMER)
ANCHORING (see ANDERING 1)
ANCIAL (see ANGLE)
ANCID (see ANDED)
ANCIENT (see ATION 1)
ANCIFUL (see ANDABLE)

ANCING

blanching
branching
chancing
dancing
glancing
prancing
ranching

advancing
breakdancing

enhancing
entrancing
financing
freelancing
rain dancing
romancing
Slam Dancing
tap dancing

belly dancing
Dirty Dancing
high financing

ANCOR (see AMMER)
ANCORING (see ANDERING 1)
ANCY (see ANDY)
AND 1 (see AN 1)
AND 2 (see ON 1)
ANDA 1 (see ANA 1)
ANDA 2 (see ONNA)

ANDABLE

animal
annual
bandable
brandable
cannibal
canticle
danceable
fanciful
flammable
frangible
Hannibal
jammable
landable
manacle
mandible
manual
sandable
standable
tangible

biannual
bimanual
botanical
Britannical
commandable
demandable
Emanuel

expandable
infrangible
intangible
mechanical
organical
programmable
remandable
satanical
stuffed animal
tyranical
withstandable

countermandable
puritanical
reprimandable
semiannual
understandable

ANDAGE (see ANISH 1)
ANDAL (see ANGLE)
ANDALA (see AMERA)

ANDALIZE

amortize
analyze
anodize
canalize
canonize
cantonize
fantasize
glamorize
mammonize
maximize
sanitize
scandalize
strategize
vandalize

reanalyze
uncanonize

overanalyze
psychoanalyze

ANDALL (see ANGLE)
ANDALLESS (see ANIMOUS)
ANDALOUS (see ANIMOUS)
ANDARD (see AMPERED)
ANDARIN (see AMPION)

ANDARY (see AWNY)
ANDE 1 (see ANCE 3)
ANDE 2 (see AN 1)
ANDEAU (see ANGO 1)

ANDED

banded
branded
candid
canted
chanted
granted
handed
landed
panted
planted
rancid
ranted
sanded
slanted
stranded

backhanded
commanded
crash-landed
demanded
disbanded
enchanted
expanded
forehanded
high-handed
implanted
left-handed
offhanded
one-handed
recanted
remanded
righthanded
transplanted
two-handed

caught red-handed
countermanded
disenchanted
empty-handed
evenhanded
gallivanted
heavy-handed
openhanded

overhanded
overplanted
reprimanded
single-handed
take for granted
underhanded

ANDEM (see ANSON 1)
ANDENT (see ARENT)
ANDER 1 (see AMMER)
ANDER 2 (see ONOR 1)
ANDERED (see ONDERED)

ANDERING 1

anchoring
angering
answering
banishing
bantering
blandishing
brandishing
cambering
canceling
cancelling
cankering
cantering
chambering
channeling
clambering
clamoring
flanneling
gandering
hammering
hampering
hankering
jammering
pampering
pandering
paneling
planishing
rancoring
scampering
slandering
stammering
tampering
vanishing
yammering

enamoring
impaneling
inchambering
meandering
philandering

gerrymandering

ANDERING 2

conjuring
conquering
following
groveling
honoring
laundering
modeling
pondering
sponsoring
squandering
wandering

remodeling

ANDEUR (see AMMER)
ANDFUL (see ANGLE)
ANDIBLE (see ANDABLE)
ANDID (see ANDED)
ANDIDATE (see AMINATE)

ANDING

banding
banging
banning
branding
camping
canning
champing
Channing
chanting
clamming
clamping
clanging
cramming
cramping
damming
damning
fanning

ganging
granting
hamming
handing
hanging
jamming
landing
manning
panning
panting
planning
planting
ramming
ranting
sanding
scamming
scanning
scramming
slamming
slanting
spanning
stamping
standing
stranding
tanging
tanning
tramping
twanging
vamping
whamming
whanging

backhanding
bandstanding
commanding
crash-landing
deadpanning
decanting
defanging
demanding
disbanding
enchanting
expanding
forced landing
freestanding
grandstanding
implanting
longstanding
outstanding
programming

recanting
remanding
replanting
revamping
soft landing
supplanting
transplanting
unclamping
unhanding
upstanding
withstanding

belly-landing
boomeranging
countermanding
diagramming
disenchanting
gallivanting
last man standing
notwithstanding
overhanging
reprimanding
rubber-stamping
telegramming
three-point landing
understanding

misunderstanding

ANDISH (see ANISH 1)
ANDISHING (see ANDERING 1)
ANDIT (see ANIC)
ANDLE (see ANGLE)
ANDLED (see AMBLED)
ANDLELESS (see ANIMOUS)
ANDLER (see AMMER)
ANDLING (see ANGLING)
ANDLY (see ANDY)
ANDMA (see ANA 1)
ANDMENT (see ANIC)
ANDO 1 (see ANGO 1)
ANDO 2 (see ONDO)
ANDOLIN (see AMPION)
ANDOM (see ANSON 1)
ANDON (see ANSON 1)
ANDOR (see AMMER)
ANDRA (see ANA 1)
ANDRE (see ANCE 3)
ANDRO (see ONDO)
ANDSOME (see ANSON 1)
ANDT (see ANK)

ANDUM (see ANSON 1)
ANDWICH (see ANISH 1)
ANDWRIT (see ARENT)

ANDY

andy
Angie
angry
Annie
ante
anti
antsy
aunty
Bambi
banshee
blandly
blanky
brandy
campy
candy
canny
chancy
clammy
clanky
crampy
cranky
cranny
damply
dandy
Danny
Dante
fancy
fanny
Frankie
Grammy
grandly
granny
hammy
handy
hankie
jammie
lanky
mammy
Mandy
manly
Nancy
nanny
pansy
pantry

panty
randy
Sammy
sandy
scampi
scanty
shanty
slanty
Stanley
swanky
Tammy
tangy
tranny
twangy
whammy
Yankee

chimpanzee
Comanche
damnyankee
Dave Ramsey
Miami
rock candy
uncanny
unhandy

cotton candy
diaper dandy
double whammy
fancy-schmancy
fine and dandy
frangipani
hanky-panky
hootenanny
Mr. Hankey
namby-pamby
Orphan Annie
Pakistani
vigilante

tickle your fancy

Yankee Doodle Dandy

ANE 1 (see AIN 1)
ANE 2 (see AN 1)
ANEAN (see ANIUM)
ANEFUL (see ABLE)
ANEL (see ANGLE)
ANELING (see ANDERING 1)
ANELIST (see ANIMOUS)
ANELY (see ADY)

ANEOUS

achiest
atheist
cakiest
craziest
flakiest
gradient
haziest
laciest
laziest
patriot
quakiest
raciest
radiant
radius
sapient
shadiest
shakiest
snakiest
spaciest
waviest

Arabias
araneous
cutaneous
extraneous
irradiant
membraneous
spontaneous

consentaneous
instantaneous
miscellaneous
momentaneous
percutaneous
simultaneous
subterraneous
transcutaneous

ANER (see AINER)
ANERY (see AVERY)
ANET (see ANIC)
ANEY (see ADY)
ANG (see AN 1)
ANGAR (see AMMER)
ANGE (see AIN 1)
ANGEABLE (see AINABLE)
ANGEL (see ABLE)
ANGELA (see AMERA)
ANGELES (see ANIMOUS)

ANGELIST (see ANIMOUS)
ANGEMENT (see ATION 1)
ANGENESS (see ACES)
ANGENT (see ARENT)
ANGER 1 (see AINER)
ANGER 2 (see AMMER)
ANGER 3 (see AMMER)
ANGER 4 (see AMMER)
ANGERING (see ANDERING 1)
ANGEST (see ACES)
ANGIBLE (see ANDABLE)
ANGIE (see ANDY)
ANGINESS (see AKINESS)
ANGING 1 (see AINING)
ANGING 2 (see ANDING)

ANGLE

amble
ample
angle
ankle
bangle
camel
Campbell
cancel
candle
chancel
channel
crankle
damsel
dangle
Daniel
flannel
gamble
handful
handle
jangle
mammal
mangle
mantel
mantle
panel
ramble
Randall
rankle
sample
sandal
scandal
scramble

shamble
spangle
spaniel
strangle
tangle
tankful
thankful
trammel
trample
tranquil
vandal
wangle
wrangle
wrankle

ashamble
bojangle
dismantle
door handle
enamel
entangle
example
financial
floor sample
free sample
impanel
manhandle
mishandle
Nathaniel
panhandle
preamble
rectangle
right angle
substantial
triangle
unscramble
untangle
unthankful
wide-angle

circumstantial
cocker spaniel
disentangle
for example
intertangle
jingle jangle
jury panel
Roman candle
TV channel

ANGLED

angled
ankled
dangled
jangled
mangled
rankled
spangled
tangled
wangled
wrangled

entangled
quadrangled
star-spangled
untangled

disentangled
intertangled

ANGLER (see AMMER)

ANGLING

ambling
angling
bantling
brambling
brandling
candling
dandling
dangling
gambling
gangling
Grambling
handling
jangling
mangling
mantling
rambling
sampling
scambling
scantling
scrambling
shambling
strangling
tangling
trampling

wangling
wrangling

dismantling
entangling
exampling
manhandling
mishandling
panhandling
rehandling
unscrambling
untangling

ANGLISH (see ANISH 1)

ANGO 1

AAMCO
ammo
bandeau
banjo
Brando
camo
mango
Rambo
tango
whammo

commando
Durango
fandango
Fernando
glissando
Orlando
piano
soprano

Marlon Brando

accelerando
Tony Soprano

ANGO 2 (see ONDO)
ANGRAM (see ANSON 1)
ANGRY (see ANDY)
ANGSTER (see AMMER)
ANGUAGE (see ANISH 1)
ANGUE (see AN 1)
ANGUISH (see ANISH 1)

ANGULAR

angular
annular
granular

anagular
biangular
decangular
equangular
heptangular
hexangular
inangular
octangular
pentangular
quadrangular
quanquangular
rectangular
septangular
sexangular
subangular
surangular
triangular

acutangular
birectangular
equiangular
multiangular
obtusangular
subpentangular
subtriangular
trirectangular

ANGULATE (see AMINATE)
ANGY 1 (see ADY)
ANGY 2 (see ANDY)
ANHA (see ONNA)
ANI (see ANDY)

ANIA

mania
stadia

acadia
Albania
Arabia
Arcadia
Moldavia
Romania

Sylvania
Tasmania
titania

egomania
kleptomania
Lithuania
nymphomania
Pennsylvania
pyromania
Scandinavia
Transylvania

ANIAL (see ADIAL)
ANIAN (see ANIUM)

ANIC

anklet
antic
anxious
bandit
banquet
blanket
frantic
granite
hammock
Janet
mandment
manic
mantis
panic
planet
tannic
transit

advancement
Atlantic
Atlantis
botanic
Britannic
ceramic
commandment
disbandment
dynamic
enchantment
enhancement
entrancement
Germanic

gigantic
Hispanic
horseblanket
mechanic
organic
remandment
romantic
satanic
semantic
Titanic
tyrannic
volcanic
wet blanket

Captain Planet
disenchantment
inorganic
Messianic
oceanic
one-armed bandit
panoramic
pomegranate
praying mantis
puritanic
solid granite
transatlantic
unromantic

aerodynamic
Man from Atlantis
thermodynamic
transoceanic

make out like a bandit
security blanket

ANICAL (see ANDABLE)

ANICALLY

frantically
manically
transiently

dynamically
galvanically
gigantically
mechanically
organically

pedantically
romantically
satanically
semantically
volcanically

inorganically
nonmechanically
panoramically
puritanically
unromantically

aerodynamically
thermodynamically

ANIEL (see ANGLE)
ANIGAN (see AMPION)
ANIKIN (see AMPION)
ANILE (see ABLE)
ANIMA (see AMERA)
ANIMAL (see ANDABLE)
ANIMATE (see AMINATE)

ANIMOUS

amorous
analyst
animous
cancerous
candleless
cannabis
clamorous
glamorous
handleless
panelist
sandalless
scandalless
scandalous
vandalless

evangelist
examinous
flexanimous
Los Angeles
magnanimous
multanimous
unanimous
unglamorous

psychoanalyst
televangelist

ANINESS (see AKINESS)
ANING (see AINING)
ANION (see ANSON 1)

ANISH 1

anguish
bandage
banish
blandish
brandish
campus
canless
canvas
clanless
clannish
damage
dampness
famish
grandish
Kansas
language
languish
manage
mannish
manses
Manwich
planless
sandwich
scanless
slanguage
Spanglish
Spanish
trampish
vampish
vanish
vanquish

advantage
expanses
mismanage
off-campus
outlandish
Pete Sampras

disadvantage
hippocampus
knuckle sandwich

ANISH 2 (see ACES)
ANISHING (see ANDERING 1)
ANISTER (see AMETER)
ANITE (see ANIC)
ANITIZE (see ANDALIZE)
ANITOR (see AMETER)

ANITY

amity
Anthony
calamity
cannery
canopy
clamory
family
fantasy
Flannery
mammary
manatee
Sanity
scantily
stammery
tannery
vanity

humanity
inanity
insanity
Linsanity
philanthropy
profanity
urbanity

Christianity
inhumanity
Partridge Family
Sunshine Family
We Are Family

one big happy family

ANIUM

Adrian
alien
atrium
Australian
avian

cranium
Dameon
Fabian
stadium

Albanian
Arabian
Arcadian
Canadian
gymnasium
Moldavian
Romanian
Tasmanian
titanium
Ukranian
uranium

Lithuanian
Pennsylvanian
Scandinavian
subterranean

Episcopalian
Mediterranean
Saudi Arabian

ANJA (see ONNA)
ANJO (see ANGO 1)

ANK

amp
ant
aunt
bank
blank
camp
can't
champ
chant
clamp
clank
cramp
crank
damp
dank
drank
flank
franc

frank
grant
hank
lamp
lank
pant
plank
plant
prank
ramp
rank
rant
sank
scamp
scant
shank
shrank
slant
spank
stamp
stank
swank
tank
thank
tramp
vamp
yank

air tank
aslant
blood bank
bootcamp
decant
drunk tank
eggplant
embank
enchant
fish tank
food stamp
gas tank
handcrank
heatlamp
high rank
implant
Lou Grant
off-ramp
on-ramp
outdrank
outflank
outrank

point-blank
preshrank
pull rank
recant
Rembrandt
replant
revamp
sandbank
snowbank
sperm bank
sunlamp
supplant
think tank
transplant
unclamp

break the bank
data bank
disenchant
draw a blank
gallivant
hair transplant
heart transplant
holding tank
Lisa Frank
overdrank
play a prank
postage stamp
power plant
prison camp
pulling rank
riverbank
rubber-stamp
saddle tramp
septic tank
summer camp
trailer camp
Van de Kamp
walk the plank
water tank
writer's cramp

blankety-blank
Halloween prank
heavyweight champ
memory bank
surgical clamp

military rank

ANKA (see ONNA)
ANKARA (see AMERA)
ANKEE (see ANDY)
ANKER (see AMMER)
ANKERING (see ANDERING 1)
ANKET (see ANIC)
ANKEY (see ANDY)
ANKFUL (see ANGLE)
ANKIE (see ANDY)
ANKING (see ATING)
ANKLE (see ANGLE)
ANKLED (see ANGLED)
ANKLET (see ANIC)
ANKMENT (see ATION 1)
ANKY (see ANDY)
ANLESS (see ANISH 1)
ANLEY (see ANDY)
ANLY (see ANDY)
ANN (see AN 1)
ANNA 1 (see ANA 1)
ANNA 2 (see ONNA)
ANNABIS (see ANIMOUS)
ANNAH (see ANA 1)
ANNE (see AN 1)
ANNEL (see ANGLE)
ANNELING (see ANDERING 1)
ANNEQUIN (see AMPION)
ANNER 1 (see AMMER)
ANNER 2 (see ONOR 1)
ANNERED (see AMPERED)
ANNERY (see ANITY)
ANNI (see AWNY)
ANNIBAL (see ANDABLE)
ANNIC (see ANIC)
ANNICAL (see ANDABLE)
ANNIE (see ANDY)
ANNIGAN (see AMPION)
ANNIGEN (see AMPION)
ANNING (see ANDING)
ANNISH (see ANISH 1)
ANNISTER (see AMETER)
ANNON (see ANSON 1)
ANNUAL (see ANDABLE)
ANNULAR (see ANGULAR)
ANNULATE (see AMINATE)
ANNY (see ANDY)
ANO 1 (see OTTO 1)
ANO 2 (see ANGO 1)
ANO 3 (see ADO 2)
ANODIZE (see ANDALIZE)
ANON (see ANSON 1)
ANONIZE (see ANDALIZE)
ANOPY (see ANITY)

ANOR (see AMMER)
ANQUET (see ANIC)
ANQUIL (see ANGLE)
ANQUISH (see ANISH 1)
ANSAS (see ANISH 1)
ANSE (see ANCE 1)
ANSES (see ANISH 1)
ANSFUR (see AMMER)
ANSHEE (see ANDY)
ANSIENTLY (see ANICALLY)
ANSION (see ANSON 1)
ANSIT (see ANIC)
ANSOM (see ANSON 1)

ANSON 1

anthem
bantam
cannon
canon
canton
canyon
dampen
Dannon
famine
fandom
gammon
handsome
Hanson
mammon
mansion
pangram
phantom
random
ransom
salmon
Shannon
tandem
tantrum
transom

abandon
backgammon
companion
examine
expansion
Grand Canyon
king's ransom
smoked salmon
Ted Danson

cross-examine
feast or famine
Haunted Mansion
hold for ransom
memorandum
reexamine

ANSON 2 (see OTTEN)
ANSWER (see AMMER)
ANSWERED (see AMPERED)
ANSWERING (see ANDERING 1)
ANSY (see ANDY)
ANT 1 (see ANK)
ANT 2 (see ONT 2)
ANTA 1 (see ANA 1)
ANTA 2 (see ONNA)
ANTAGE (see ANISH 1)
ANTAM (see ANSON 1)
ANTASIZE (see ANDALIZE)
ANTASY (see ANITY)
ANTE 1 (see ANDY)
ANTE 2 (see ONT 2)
ANTE 3 (see AWNY)
ANTED 1 (see ANDED)
ANTED 2 (see AULTED)
ANTEL (see ANGLE)
ANTER (see AMMER)
ANTERED (see AMPERED)
ANTERING (see ANDERING 1)
ANTERN (see ATTERED)
ANTHA (see ANA 1)
ANTHEM (see ANSON 1)
ANTHER (see AMMER)
ANTHONY (see ANITY)
ANTHROPY (see ANITY)
ANTI 1 (see AWNY)
ANTI 2 (see ANDY)
ANTIAL (see ANGLE)
ANTIC (see ANIC)
ANTICALLY (see ANICALLY)
ANTICLE (see ANDABLE)
ANTILY (see ANITY)
ANTING 1 (see ANDING)
ANTING 2 (see ONNING)
ANTIQUATE (see AMINATE)
ANTIS (see ANIC)
ANTLE (see ANGLE)
ANTLED (see AMBLED)
ANTLER (see AMMER)
ANTLING (see ANGLING)
ANTMENT (see ANIC)
ANTO (see OTTO 1)

ANTOM (see ANSON 1)
ANTON (see ANSON 1)
ANTONIZE (see ANDALIZE)
ANTOR (see AMMER)
ANTRA (see ONNA)
ANTRO (see ONDO)
ANTRUM (see ANSON 1)
ANTRY (see ANDY)
ANTS (see ANCE 1)
ANTSY (see ANDY)
ANTY (see ANDY)
ANUAL (see ANDABLE)
ANUEL (see ANDABLE)
ANUKKAH (see ONICA)
ANULAR (see ANGULAR)
ANUS (see ACES)
ANVAS (see ANISH 1)
ANVILED (see AMBLED)
ANWICH (see ANISH 1)
ANXIOUS (see ANIC)
ANY 1 (see EMMY)
ANY 2 (see ADY)
ANYA (see ONNA)
ANYE (see ANCE 3)
ANYO (see ONDO)
ANYON (see ANSON 1)
ANZ (see ON 1)
ANZA (see ANA 1)
ANZEE (see ANDY)
AO (see OW 2)
AOIST (see OUTEST)
AOS 1 (see AYOFF)
AOS 2 (see OUT)
AP 1 (see ACK)
AP 2 (see OT)
APA (see ADA 1)
APABLE (see ADABLE)
APABLY (see AVERY)
APACY (see ACIOUSLY)
APAL (see ABLE)
APATHY (see ALITY)
APE 1 (see ACE 1)
APE 2 (see OCKEY)
APEABLE (see ADABLE)
APEL (see ACKLE)
APELY (see ADY)
APEMENT (see ATION 1)
APEN (see ATION 1)
APER (see ATOR)
APERED (see AVORED)
APERING (see AVORING)
APERS (see ATOR)
APERTURE (see ALENDAR)

APERY (see AVERY)
APH (see ASS 1)
APHIC (see ATIC 1)
APHICAL (see ACTABLE)
APHICALLY (see ATICALLY)
APHID (see ADED)
APHING (see ACKING)
APHNE (see ALLEY)
APID (see ATIC 1)
APIDLY (see ALITY)
APIENT (see ANEOUS)
APIER (see AKIER)
APIN (see ATTEN)
APING (see ATING)
APIR (see ATOR)
APIST (see ACES)
APITAL (see ACTABLE)
APITATE (see ACERATE)
APITOL (see ACTABLE)
APKIN (see ATTEN)
APLAIN (see ATTEN)
APLAN (see ATTEN)
APLE (see ABLE)
APLED (see ABLED)
APLER (see ATOR)
APLESS (see ASHES)
APLIN (see ATTEN)
APLING 1 (see ABLING)
APLING 2 (see ACKING)
APMENT (see ASSMENT)
APO (see OTTO 1)
APOLATE (see ACERATE)
APOLI (see ALITY)
APOLIS (see ALYSIS)
APON (see AYON)
APOR (see ATOR)
APORED (see AVORED)
APORY (see AVERY)
APP (see ACK)
APPA (see ASMA)
APPABLE 1 (see ACTABLE)
APPABLE 2 (see OGICAL)
APPEN (see ATTEN)
APPENED (see ASTENED)
APPER 1 (see ACKER)
APPER 2 (see OLLAR)
APPIC (see ATIC 1)
APPIER (see ABBIER)
APPIEST (see AGGIEST)
APPILY (see ALITY)
APPINESS (see ABBINESS)
APPING 1 (see ACKING)
APPING 2 (see OCKING)

APPLE (see ACKLE)
APPLED (see ADDLED)
APPLER (see ACKER)
APPLICANT (see ASSIONATE)
APPLING (see ACKING)
APPY (see ALLEY)
APRIO (see ACHIO)
APRON (see ATION 1)
APS (see AX)
APSE (see AX)
APSING (see ACKING)
APSODY (see ALITY)
APT (see ACK)
APTAIN (see ATTEN)
APTER (see ACKER)
APTERED (see ATTERED)
APTION (see ACTION)
APTIONED (see ASTENED)
APTIST (see ASHES)
APTIVATE (see ACERATE)
APTIVE (see ATIC 1)
APTLY (see ALLEY)
APTNESS (see ASHES)
APTON (see ATTEN)
APTOR (see ACKER)
APTURE (see ACKER)
APTURED (see ATTERED)
APTURING (see ATTERING)
APULA (see AFRICA)
AQ (see ACK)
AQI (see ALLEY)
AQUA (see ADA 1)
AQUE 1 (see ACK)
AQUE 2 (see ACE 1)

AR 1

are
bar
car
char
czar
far
gar
jar
mar
par
R
scar
spar
star

tar
tsar
yare

afar
ajar
all-star
armoire
attar
bazaar
bizarre
boudoir
boxcar
cigar
coaltar
costar
crossbar
crowbar
disbar
film star
five-star
flatcar
four-star
gold star
guitar
jaguar
lodestar
lone star
lumbar
memoir
North Star
pace car
polestar
PR
quasar
racecar
Renoir
sandbar
sidecar
sitar
snack bar
so far
sports car
stock car
streetcar
tartare
taskbar
track star
used car
Worldstar

armored car
au revoir
battlestar
below par
cable car
candy bar
cattle car
caviar
chocolate bar
Christmas star
cinnabar
compact car
cookie jar
CPR
evening star
fading star
falling star
football star
handlebar
Hershey bar
ice cream bar
insofar
isobar
lucky star
Mason jar
minibar
morning star
movie star
near and far
on a par
oyster bar
pass the bar
police car
R and R
railroad car
registrar
rent-a-car
repertoire
reservoir
rising star
salad bar
seminar
shooting star
singles bar
steak tartare
superstar
trolley car
VCR
wishing star
World Bazaar

Zanzibar
Zero Bar

bulletproof car
carry too far
hardy har har
mayonnaise jar
radio car
USSR

close but no cigar
wish upon a star

AR 2 (see ORE 1)

ARA

Cara
Clara
era
Sarah
terra
Vera

Ciara
Herrera
mascara
Sahara

aloe vera
riviera
Santa Clara

Hanna Barbera
Scarlett O'Hara

ARAB (see ARAT)
ARABIC (see ALYSIS)

ARABLE

aerial
airable
arable
Ariel
bearable
burial
clerical
darable

flairable
marital
pairable
parable
scarable
sharable
snarable
sparable
squarable
swearable
tearable
terrible
wearable

declarable
ensnarable
forebearable
generical
hysterical
impairable
imperical
numerical
repairable
unbearable
unwearable

actuarial
esoterical
secretarial

ARACTER (see ALENDAR)
ARAGE (see ARAT)
ARAGING (see ABLISHING)
ARAGUS (see ARIOUS)
ARAH (see ARA)
ARAKEET (see ARITY)
ARAMIE (see ARITY)
ARANTEE (see ARITY)
ARAOH (see ALLOW 1)

ARAT

Aaron
Arab
arid
baron
barren
carat
carriage
carrot

claret
Garret
Jared
karat
Karen
marriage
parrish
parrot
scarab
Sharon

disparage
miscarriage
mixed marriage
mozarab
muzarab

baby carriage
horseless carriage
Kelly Garrett
robber baron
Steve McGarrett

twenty-four carat

ARB (see ARD 1)
ARBAGE (see ARCTIC)
ARBARA (see ARTA)
ARBER (see ARTER 1)
ARBERING (see ARTERING 1)
ARBIE (see ARTY 1)
ARBING (see ARKING)
ARBINGER (see ARKENER)
ARBITAL (see ARGEABLE)
ARBITER (see ARKENER)
ARBLE (see ARTIAL)
ARBLING (see ARKING)
ARBLY (see ORY)
ARBON (see ARTEN)
ARBOR (see ARTER 1)
ARBORING (see ARTERING 1)
ARC (see ART 1)
ARCASS (see ARNISH)
ARCE (see ART 1)
ARCED (see ARKED)
ARCEL (see ARTIAL)
ARCH 1 (see ART 1)
ARCH 2 (see ART 1)
ARCHAL (see ARTIAL)
ARCHED (see ARKED)
ARCHER (see ARTER 1)
ARCHERY (see ARSITY)

ARCHIE (see ARTY 1)
ARCHING (see ARKING)
ARCHIST (see ARNISH)
ARCHY 1 (see ARTY 1)
ARCHY 2 (see ARTY 1)
ARCING (see ARKING)
ARCK (see ART 1)
ARCO (see ARGO)

ARCTIC

arctic
barrage
carnage
cartage
Carthage
cartridge
garbage
garlic
partridge
warpage

antarctic
Keith Partridge
lethargic
subarctic

anacartic
Danny Partridge
Laurie Partridge
Shirley Partridge

ARCUS (see ARNISH)
ARCY (see ARTY 1)

ARD 1

barb
bard
barge
carb
card
carve
chard
charge
garb
guard
hard
lard

large
Marge
Mars
Marv
sarge
SARS
shard
starve
yard

armed guard
at large
backyard
bank guard
barnyard
Bernard
blowhard
bombard
boneyard
canard
charge card
churchyard
Coast Guard
courtyard
cue card
depth charge
diehard
discard
discharge
dockyard
enlarge
face card
flash card
graveyard
green card
in charge
jail guard
junkyard
lifeguard
nose guard
off guard
old guard
on guard
placecard
playyard
postcard
rail guard
recharge
regard
retard

rhubarb
safeguard
scorecard
Scotchgard
shin guard
shipyard
stand guard
stockyard
surcharge
take charge
trump card
vanguard
wild card

avant-garde
baseball card
birthday card
bodyguard
boulevard
bumper guard
business card
by and large
calling card
Christmas card
color guard
cover charge
credit card
crossing guard
disregard
drawing card
extra-large
greeting card
Hallmark card
landing card
leotard
Master Card
overcharge
palace guard
prison guard
report card
Scotland Yard
St. Bernard
tub of lard
undercharge
union card
Visa card

library card
National Guard
Topps Baseball Card

security guard

ARD 2 (see OARD)
ARDABLE (see ORTABLE)
ARDE (see ARD 1)
ARDED (see ARTED)
ARDEN 1 (see ARTEN)
ARDEN 2 (see ORTION)
ARDENER (see ARKENER)

ARDENING

bargaining
cartoning
darkening
gardening
hardening
harkening
harshening
hearkening
margining
pardoning
sharpening

outbargaining
resharpening

ARDER 1 (see ARTER 1)
ARDER 2 (see ORDER)
ARDEST (see ARNISH)
ARDI (see ARTY 1)
ARDIAN (see ARTISAN)
ARDIGAN (see ARTISAN)
ARDINAL (see ARGEABLE)
ARDING 1 (see ARKING)
ARDING 2 (see ARKING)
ARDING 3 (see ORMING 1)
ARDIO (see ARIO 2)
ARDLESS (see ARNISH)
ARDLY (see ARTY 1)
ARDO (see ARGO)
ARDOM (see ARTEN)
ARDON (see ARTEN)
ARDONING (see ARDENING)
ARDOR (see ARTER 1)
ARDT (see ART 1)
ARDY (see ARTY 1)

ARE 1

air
bare

bear
blare
care
chair
Cher
dare
fair
fare
flair
flare
glare
hair
hare
heir
lair
mare
pair
pare
pear
rare
scare
share
snare
spare
square
stair
stare
swear
their
there
they're
ware
wear
where
yeah

affair
airfare
armchair
aware
Bel-Air
beware
bus fare
Care Bear
carfare
child care
compare
day care
declare
desk chair
despair

eclair
elsewhere
ensnare
fanfare
flatware
footwear
forbear
foursquare
fresh air
glassware
gray hair
hardware
health care
highchair
horsehair
hot air
impair
longhair
lounge chair
midair
nightmare
no fair
nowhere
outstare
outwear
Pierre
plane fare
plowshare
prepare
repair
software
somewhere
sportswear
take care
time share
Times Square
town square
train fare
unbare
unfair
warfare
welfare
wheelchair

angel hair
anywhere
barber chair
bill of fare
billionaire

bring to bear
bruin bear
camel hair
car repair
country fair
dance on air
debonair
Delaware
dentist chair
derriere
disrepair
doctrinaire
earthenware
easy chair
endowed chair
everywhere
fair and square
float on air
formalwear
Fred Astaire
Frigidaire
grizzly bear
here and there
Huggy Bear
laissez-faire
legionnaire
lion's share
love affair
maidenhair
Medicare
millionaire
nail repair
nom de guerre
not all there
on the air
open-air
over there
overbear
potty-chair
questionnaire
rocking chair
room to spare
silverware
solitaire
son and heir
Sugar Bear
swivel chair
take a chair
teddy bear
then and there
truth or dare

unaware
underwear
walk on air
wash and wear
wear and tear
when or where
women's wear
Yogi Bear
zillionaire

auto repair
beyond compare
breath of fresh air
concessionaire
devil-may-care
electric chair
full of hot air
intensive care
lighter-than-air
loaded for bear
long underwear
musical chairs
private affair
ready-to-wear
Smokey the Bear
Sonny and Cher
surface-to-air
up in the air

castles in the air
extraordinaire
Fresh Prince of Bel-Air
multimillionaire
neither here nor there

ARE 2 (see AR 1)
ARE 3 (see ARTY 1)

AREA

area
aria

Bavaria
Bay Area
Bulgaria
fringe area
hysteria
malaria
Vulgaria
wisteria

mass hysteria

disaster area

AREAN (see ARIAN 1)

ARED 1

aired
bared
blared
cared
chaired
dared
erred
fared
flaired
glared
paired
pared
scared
shared
snared
spared
squared
stared

compared
declared
despaired
ensnared
impaired
prepared
repaired
run scared

ill-prepared

hearing-impaired

ARED 2 (see ARAT)
AREL (see ARREL 1)
ARELESS (see ARENESS)
ARELY (see ARY)
AREM (see ERIC 1)
AREN (see ARAT)
ARENCE (see ARENT)
ARENCY (see ARITY)

ARENESS

airless
bareness
bearish
careless
chairless
fairness
glareless
hairless
heiress
heirless
prayerless
rareness
spareless
squareness
wareless
wearish

awareness
unfairness

debonairness
unawareness

ARENT

arrant
candent
Clarence
frangent
handwrit
lancet
parent
plangent
rampant
scandent
tangent

apparent
godparent
grandparent
Jed Clampett
transparent

foster parent
great-grandparent
heir apparent
single parent

unapparent
working parent

Elly May Clampett

ARENTING (see ABLISHING)
ARENTLY (see ARITY)
ARET (see ARAT)
AREY (see ARY)
ARF 1 (see ART 1)
ARF 2 (see ORSE 1)
ARFER (see ARTER 1)
ARFING (see ORMING 1)
ARGAIN (see ARTEN)
ARGAINING (see ARDENING)
ARGAL (see ARTIAL)
ARGE (see ARD 1)

ARGEABLE

arsenal
article
barbital
barnacle
cardinal
carnival
chargeable
particle

dischargeable
enlargeable
lethargical
nonchargeable
postcardinal
rechargeable
uncardinal

antiparticle

ARGELY (see ARTY 1)
ARGER (see ARTER 1)
ARGEST (see ARNISH)
ARGET (see ARNISH)
ARGIC (see ARCTIC)
ARGICAL (see ARGEABLE)
ARGICALLY (see ARSITY)
ARGIN (see ARTEN)
ARGING (see ARKING)
ARGINING (see ARDENING)
ARGLE (see ARTIAL)

ARGO

argot
Arlo
arno
arvo
borrow
cargo
Charo
Fargo
Harpo
Jarmo
largo
Marco
Margo
Marlo
morrow
parvo
sorrow

embargo
Key Largo
Lombardo
reborrow
Ricardo
tomorrow
Wells Fargo

beg, steal, or borrow
Kilimanjaro

Andrea del Sarto

ARGON (see ARTEN)
ARGOT (see ARGO)
ARGUS (see ARNISH)
ARI (see ARTY 1)
ARIA (see AREA)
ARIAL (see ARABLE)

ARIAN 1

arian
Aryan
barium
carrion
clarion
Marian
parian

agrarian
aquarian
aquarium
barbarian
Bavarian
Bulgarian
cesarean
cesarian
grammarian
gregarian
Hungarian
librarian
maidmarian
sectarian
statarian

honorarium
libertarian
planetarium
sanitarium
vegetarian

authoritarian
disciplinarian
humanitarian
totalitarian
utilitarian

Conan the Barbarian

ARIAN 2 (see ARTISAN)

ARIAT

chariot
Harriet
lariat

Iscariot
phanariot

commissariat
proletariat
secretariat

ARIC (see ERIC 1)
ARID (see ARAT)
ARIEL (see ARABLE)
ARIER (see ARRIER)
ARIFF (see ERIC 1)

ARILY (see ERITY1)
ARINER (see ALENDAR)

ARING

airing
baring
bearing
blaring
caring
daring
erring
faring
flaring
glaring
herring
pairing
paring
scaring
sharing
snaring
sparing
squaring
staring
swearing
wearing

comparing
declaring
despairing
ensnaring
forbearing
forswearing
impairing
long-wearing
outstaring
outwearing
preparing
red herring
repairing
seafaring
talebearing
uncaring
unerring

balibearing
Derry Daring
overbearing

revenue sharing

ARINGLY (see ARITY)

ARIO 1

Jericho
stereo

Ontario
scenario

impresario

worst-case scenario

ARIO 2

audio
barrio
cardio
Mario

Joe Dimaggio
Super Mario

ARION (see ARIAN 1)
ARIOT (see ARIAT)

ARIOUS

alias
Arius
various

Aquarius
asparagus
gregarious
hilarious
nefarious
precarious
vicarious

multifarious
Sagittarius
Stradivarius

ARIS (see ATIC 1)
ARISEE (see ARITY)
ARISH (see ATIC 1)

ARIST (see ARNISH)
ARITAL (see ARABLE)

ARIUM (see ARIAN 1)
ARIUS (see ARIOUS)
ARJORIE (see ARSITY)
ARK 1 (see ART 1)
ARK 2 (see ORK 1)
ARKA (see ARTA)

ARKEN (see ARTEN)

ARITY

blaringly
charity
clarity
daringly
flaringly
glaringly
guarantee
Laramie
parakeet
parity
parody
pharisee
rarity
sparingly
staringly

apparently
asperity
barbarity
disparity
forbearingly
hilarity
polarity
transparency
unsparingly
vulgarity

angularity
circularity
jocularity
overbearingly
popularity
regularity
secularity
similarity
singularity
solidarity

dissimilarity
faith, hope, and charity
familiarity
irregularity
particularity
peculiarity

ARKED

arced
barked
harked
marked
parked
sparked

benchmarked
birthmarked
black marked
bookmarked
check marked
debarked
Deutsche marked
earmarked
embarked
footmarked
hallmarked
landmarked
loan sharked
pockmarked
poolsharked
postmarked
quote marked
remarked
skid marked
smudge marked
stretch marked
trademarked

disembarked
doubleparked
fingermarked
matriarched
patriarched
question marked
valet parked
watermarked

exclamation marked
punctuation marked

ARKENER

arbiter
carpenter
darkener
gardener
harbinger
hardener
harkener
harvester
hearkener
sharpener

Karen Carpenter
pencil sharpener

ARKENING (see ARDENING)
ARKER (see ARTER 1)
ARKEST (see ARNISH)
ARKET (see ARNISH)
ARKEY (see ARTY 1)
ARKIE (see ARTY 1)

ARKING

arching
arcing
arming
barbing
barging
barking
barring
carbing
carding
carping
carting
carving
charging
charming
charring
charting
darling
darning
darting
farming
farting
gnarling

guarding
harking
harming
harping
jarring
marbling
marching
marking
marring
narcing
parching
parking
parsing
parting
scarring
smarting
snarling
sparking
sparring
starching
starling
starring
starting
starving
tarping
tarring

alarming
bombarding
co-starring
debarking
departing
disarming
disbarring
discarding
discharging
earmarking
embarking
enlarging
ensnarling
imparting
lifeguarding
my darling
no parking
outmarching
outsmarting
postmarking
recharging
regarding
remarking

restarting
retarding
safeguarding
surcharging
truck farming
unsnarling
woodcarving

disembarking
disregarding
doubleparking
overcharging
undercharging

ARKLE (see ARTIAL)
ARKLEY (see ARTY 1)
ARKLY (see ARTY 1)
ARKNESS (see ARNISH)
ARKSMAN (see ARTEN)
ARKY (see ARTY 1)

ARL

Carl
gnarl
snarl

ensnarl
unsnarl

ARLA (see ARTA)
ARLAND (see ARTEN)
ARLATAN (see ARTISAN)
ARLEM (see ARTEN)
ARLET (see ARNISH)
ARLEY (see ARTY 1)
ARLIC (see ARCTIC)
ARLIE (see ARTY 1)
ARLIN (see ARTEN)
ARLING (see ARKING)
ARLO (see ARGO)
ARLOR (see ARTER 1)
ARLOT (see ARNISH)
ARLOTTE (see ARNISH)
ARLY (see ARTY 1)

ARM 1

arm
barn

charm
darn
farm
harm
marm
yarn

alarm
disarm
fat farm
firearm
forearm
Red Barn
sidearm
strongarm
truck farm
unarm
unharm

arm in arm
chicken farm
dairy farm
false alarm
fire alarm
funny farm
give a darn
lucky charm
smoke alarm
snooze alarm
twist your arm
underarm

burglar alarm
cause for alarm
shot in the arm
silent alarm
travel alarm
twist someone's arm

ARM 2 (see ORN)
ARMA (see ARTA)
ARMACY (see ARSITY)
ARMAN (see ARTEN)
ARMEN (see ARTEN)
ARMENT (see ARTMENT)
ARMER 1 (see ORDER)
ARMER 2 (see ARTER 1)
ARMEST (see ORIST)
ARMFUL (see ARTIAL)
ARMING 1 (see ARKING)
ARMING 2 (see ORMING 1)

ARMINT (see ARTMENT)
ARMLESS (see ARNISH)
ARMLY (see ORY)
ARMO (see ARGO)
ARMONY (see ARSITY)
ARMOR (see ARTER 1)
ARMOT (see ARNISH)
ARMY (see ARTY 1)
ARN 1 (see ARM 1)
ARN 2 (see ORN)
ARNACLE (see ARGEABLE)
ARNAGE (see ARCTIC)
ARNAL (see ARTIAL)
ARNER 1 (see ARTER 1)
ARNER 2 (see ORDER)
ARNERING (see ARTERING 1)
ARNESS (see ARNISH)
ARNEST (see ARNISH)
ARNESTLY (see ERNITY)
ARNEY (see ARTY 1)
ARNIAN (see ARTISAN)
ARNING 1 (see ORMING 1)
ARNING 2 (see ARKING)

ARNISH

arcus
argus
armless
artist
barnish
carcass
cardless
carpet
carpus
Charlotte
charmless
darkest
darkness
darnest
farness
farthest
garnish
guardless
hardest
harlot
harmless
harness
harpist
harshest

harshness
harvest
heartless
Jarvis
largest
Marcus
market
marmot
scarlet
sharpest
sharpness
smartest
smartness
sparseness
sparsest
starkest
starkness
starlet
target
tarnish
tarsus
tartest
varnish
yardless

anarchist
bear market
bizarreness
bizarrest
blackmarket
bull market
con artist
flea market
guitarist
pygargus
regardless
revarnish
stock market
untarnish

matriarchist
Neiman-Marcus
patriarchist
supermarket

ARNIVAL (see ARGEABLE)
ARNO (see ARGO)
ARNY (see ARTY 1)
ARO 1 (see ARGO)
ARO 2 (see ERO 2)
ARODY (see ARITY)

AROL (see ARREL 1)
AROLD (see ARREL 1)
AROLE (see ARREL 1)
AROLING (see ABLISHING)
ARON (see ARAT)
AROT (see ALLOW 1)
ARP 1 (see ART 1)
ARP 2 (see ORP)
ARPAGE (see ARCTIC)
ARPAL (see ARTIAL)
ARPEN (see ARTEN)
ARPENER (see ARKENER)
ARPENING (see ARDENING)
ARPENT (see ARTMENT)
ARPENTER (see ARKENER)
ARPER (see ARTER 1)
ARPERING (see ARTERING 1)
ARPEST (see ARNISH)
ARPET (see ARNISH)
ARPIE (see ARTY 1)
ARPING 1 (see ARKING)
ARPING 2 (see ORMING 1)
ARPIST (see ARNISH)
ARPLY (see ARTY 1)
ARPNESS (see ARNISH)
ARPO (see ARGO)
ARPUS (see ARNISH)
ARRACK (see ATIC 1)
ARRACKING (see ABLISHING)
ARRAGE (see ARCTIC)
ARRANT 1 (see ORTION)
ARRANT 2 (see ARENT)
ARRANTY (see ORMITY)
ARRASS (see ATIC 1)
ARRASSING (see ABLISHING)
ARRATIVE (see ALYSIS)
ARRE (see AR 1)

ARREL 1

barrel
carol
Carole
carrel
Darrel
Harold

apparel

Christmas carol
cracker-barrel

double-barrel

lock, stock, and barrel

bottom of the barrel

ARREL 2 (see ORMAL)
ARRELING (see ABLISHING)
ARRELY (see ARTY 1)
ARREN 1 (see ARAT)
ARREN 2 (see ORTANCE)
ARRENESS (see ARNISH)
ARREST (see ARNISH)
ARRET (see ARAT)
ARRETT (see ARAT)
ARREY (see ARY)
ARRIAGE (see ARAT)
ARRIE (see ARY)

ARRIER

airier
barrier
carrier
glarier
hairier
marrier
merrier
scarier
tarrier
terrier
varier
warier

card carrier
fox terrier
germ carrier
mail carrier
miscarrier
sound barrier

aircraft carrier
letter carrier

the more the merrier

ARRIET (see ARIAT)
ARRING 1 (see ARKING)
ARRING 2 (see ORMING 1)
ARRIO (see ARIO 2)

ARRION (see ARIAN 1)
ARRIS (see ATIC 1)
ARRISH (see ARAT)
ARRISTER (see ALENDAR)
ARROT (see ARAT)
ARROTING (see ABLISHING)
ARROW (see ALLOW 1)
ARRY 1 (see ARY)
ARRY 2 (see ARTY 1)
ARRY 3 (see ORY)
ARRYING (see ABLISHING)
ARS (see ARD 1)
ARSAL (see ARTIAL)
ARSE (see ART 1)
ARSELY (see ARTY 1)
ARSEN (see ARTEN)
ARSENAL (see ARGEABLE)
ARSENESS (see ARNISH)
ARSER (see ARTER 1)
ARSEST (see ARNISH)
ARSH (see ART 1)
ARSHA (see ARTA)
ARSHAL (see ARTIAL)
ARSHALL (see ARTIAL)
ARSHEN (see ARTEN)
ARSHENING (see ARDENING)
ARSHEST (see ARNISH)
ARSHNESS (see ARNISH)
ARSING (see ARKING)

ARSITY

archery
artery
artistry
bartery
harmony
Marjorie
martially
martyry
partially
pharmacy
sparsity
varsity

cathartically
impartially
lethargically

intervarsity

ARSKY (see ARTY 1)
ARSLEY (see ARTY 1)
ARSON (see ARTEN)
ARSUS (see ARNISH)

ART 1

arc
arch
ark
art
barf
bark
carp
cart
chart
Clark
dark
dart
farce
fart
hark
harp
harsh
hart
heart
lark
marc
March
mark
marsh
mart
narc
parch
park
parse
part
scarf
shark
sharp
smart
spark
sparse
starch
stark
start
tarp
tart

aardvark
apart
ballpark
benchmark
Bernhardt
best part
birthmark
Bismarck
black mark
Bogart
bookmark
card shark
check mark
cornstarch
death march
debark
Denmark
depart
Deutsche mark
Dick Clark
dogcart
earmark
embark
eye chart
faint heart
false start
fine art
flow chart
folk art
footmark
fresh start
Get Smart
go-cart
golf cart
grand march
hallmark
hard heart
headstart
health chart
impart
jumpstart
K-Mart
kind heart
landmark
late start
light heart
loan shark
monarch
Mozart
outmarch

outsmart
Ozark
pitch-dark
pockmark
poolshark
pop art
Pop Tart
postmark
pushcart
quote mark
rampart
remark
restart
skid mark
skylark
smudge mark
soft heart
South Park
street smart
stretch mark
sweetheart
take heart
tea cart
theme park
trademark
upstart
Walmart

a la carte
abstract art
accent mark
baseball park
beauty mark
bleeding heart
Bonaparte
broken heart
Central Park
change of heart
counterpart
cross your heart
disembark
doublepark
easy mark
fall apart
fingermark
flower cart
flying start
from the heart
graphic art
great white shark

have a heart
heart to heart
in the dark
Joan of Arc
Jump the shark
killer shark
leave your mark
lonely heart
make your mark
martial art
matriarch
minimart
natal chart
Noah's ark
oligarch
on the mark
open heart
pastry cart
patriarch
pick apart
Purple Heart
question mark
razor sharp
running start
shopping cart
supermart
take apart
take to heart
trailer park
valet park
vital part
watermark
weatherchart
work of art

amusement park
break someone's heart
for the most part
Jurassic Park
Lewis and Clark
manual art
national park
performing art
replacement part
shot in the dark
state of the art
unkind remark
with all your heart

artificial heart

Dancing In the Dark
exclamation mark
punctuation mark
till death do you part

organization chart
Raiders of the Lost Ark

from the bottom of my heart
Jellystone National Park

ART 2 (see ORP)

ARTA

Barbara
Garza
karma
larva
Marla
Marsha
parka
Sparta

Magna Carta

ARTAGE (see ARCTIC)
ARTAL (see ARTIAL)
ARTAN (see ARTEN)
ARTE (see ART 1)

ARTED

bartered
carded
carted
charted
chartered
darted
farted
gartered
guarded
Hartford
Harvard
martyred
parted
smarted
started

blackhcarted
bombarded
departed
discarded
downhearted
fainthearted
good-hearted
halfhearted
hardhearted
imparted
jumpstarted
kindhearted
lifeguarded
lighthearted
outsmarted
rechartered
regarded
restarted
retarded
safeguarded
Scotchgarded
softhearted
stouthearted
uncharted
unguarded
warmhearted
wholehearted

brokenhearted
chickenhearted
disregarded
lionhearted
openhearted

ARTEN

arson
bargain
barman
carbon
Carmen
Carson
carton
chargin
darken
Darwin
garden
harden

harken
Harlem
harshen
hearten
jargon
Larsen
margin
marksman
marlin
Martian
Martin
Marvin
pardon
parson
sharpen
smarten
Spartan
squadron
stardom
tartan

dishearten
Doc Marten
milk carton
plea-bargain
postpartum
rose garden
Steve Martin

beg your pardon
Dolly Parton
Eric Cartman
Johnny Carson
Judy Garland
kindergarten

Elizabeth Arden

ARTER 1

arbor
archer
ardor
armor
Arthur
barber
barfer
barker

barter
carder
carper
carter
carver
charger
charmer
charter
darker
darner
darter
farmer
farter
farther
garner
garter
guarder
harbor
harder
Harper
larder
larger
marcher
marker
martyr
parcher
parker
parlor
parser
partner
scarfer
sharper
smarter
starcher
starker
starter
tarter
yarner

alarmer
Ann Arbor
bombarder
compartner
copartner
departer
departure
disarmer
discarder
discharger
enlarger

imparter
Kickstarter
Pearl Harbor
recharger
regarder
restarter
retarder
safe harbor
self-starter
slow starter
snake charmer
try harder

Charlie Parker
kindergartner
Peter Parker
silent partner
sparring partner
supercharger

point of departure

ARTER 2 (see ORDER)
ARTERED (see ARTED)

ARTERING 1

barbering
bartering
chartering
garnering
gartering
harboring
martyring
partnering
scarpering

rechartering

ARTERING 2 (see ORDERING)
ARTERLY (see ORMITY)
ARTERY (see ARSITY)
ARTEST (see ARNISH)
ARTFORD (see ARTED)
ARTH (see ORSE 1)
ARTHAGE (see ARCTIC)
ARTHER (see ARTER 1)
ARTHEST (see ARNISH)
ARTHUR (see ARTER 1)

ARTIAL

argal
armful
artal
carnal
carpal
charmful
dartle
garble
gargle
harmful
larval
marble
marshal
Marshall
martial
marvel
parcel
partial
sparkle
startle
tarsal

court-martial
fire marshal
grand marshal
impartial
unharmful
Will Marshall

hierarchal
matriarchal
metacarpal
metatarsal
oligarchal
part and parcel
patriarchal

fair and impartial
federal marshal

ARTIALLY (see ARSITY)
ARTIAN (see ARTEN)
ARTIC (see ARCTIC)
ARTICALLY (see ARSITY)
ARTICLE (see ARGEABLE)
ARTIN (see ARTEN)
ARTING 1 (see ARKING)
ARTING 2 (see ORMING 1)

ARTISAN

artisan
cardigan
charlatan
guardian
Marxian
Narnian
partisan
tarlatan

bipartisan
coguardian
Edwardian
nonpartisan

leptocardian
monocardian
perocardian
Rastafarian

ARTIST (see ARNISH)
ARTISTRY (see ARSITY)
ARTLE (see ARTIAL)
ARTLY (see ARTY 1)
ARTMAN (see ARTEN)

ARTMENT

arpent
garment
sergeant
varmint

apartment
compartment
department
disbarment

fire department
glove compartment
undergarment

luggage compartment

ARTNER (see ARTER 1)
ARTNERING (see ARTERING 1)
ARTNESS (see ARNISH)
ARTO (see ARGO)
ARTON 1 (see ARTEN)

ARTON 2 (see ORTION)
ARTONING (see ARDENING)
ARTRIDGE (see ARCTIC)

ARTS

arts
carts
charts
darts
farts
harts
hearts
parts
smarts
starts
tarts

departs
false starts
fine arts
flow charts
go-carts
golf carts
headstarts
imparts
jumpstarts
K-Marts
late starts
outsmarts
Pop-Tarts
pushcarts
ramparts
restarts
sweethearts
tea carts
upstarts

bleeding hearts
broken hearts
counterparts
graphic arts
heart of hearts
lonely hearts
martial arts
off the charts
private parts
queen of hearts
running starts
shopping carts

supermarts
weathercharts

bachelor of arts
liberal arts
performing arts
replacement parts

artificial hearts
patron of the arts

Associate of Arts

ARTUM (see ARTEN)
ARTURE (see ARTER 1)

ARTY 1

Archie
army
Barbie
Barkley
barley
barmy
Barney
blarney
carny
Charlie
Darcy
darkly
Farley
gnarly
hardly
hardy
Harley
harpie
harvey
hearty
largely
Markie
Marty
parley
parsley
partly
party
sari
scarvy
sharpie
sharply
smarmy

smartly
smarty
snarly
sorry
sparky
sparsely
starchy
starkly
starry
tardy

anarchy
Atari
autarchy
Bacardi
bizarrely
Bob Marley
Campari
Charles Barkley
curare
Daktari
Dave Starsky
Ferrari
foolhardy
Killarney
Lombardi
malarkey
monarchy
safari
search party
so sorry
tea party
third party

birthday party
calamari
cocktail party
guilty party
hierarchy
injured party
Marcy Darcy
Mata Hari
matriarchy
office party
oligarchy
patriarchy
slumber party
throw a party
Toga Party

Malibu Barbie
Salvation Army

writ of certiorari

ARTY 2 (see ORY)
ARTYR (see ARTER 1)
ARTYRED (see ARTED)
ARTYRING (see ARTERING 1)
ARTYRY (see ARSITY)
ARTZ (see ORSE 1)
ARV (see ARD 1)
ARVA (see ARTA)
ARVAL (see ARTIAL)
ARVARD (see ARTED)
ARVE (see ARD 1)
ARVEL (see ARTIAL)
ARVER (see ARTER 1)
ARVEST (see ARNISH)
ARVESTER (see ARKENER)
ARVEY (see ARTY 1)
ARVIN (see ARTEN)
ARVING (see ARKING)
ARVIS (see ARNISH)
ARVO (see ARGO)
ARVY (see ARTY 1)
ARWIN (see ARTEN)
ARXIAN (see ARTISAN)

ARY

aerie
airy
barely
Barry
berry
bury
Carrie
carry
cherry
dairy
fairly
fairy
ferry
Gary
Gerry
glary
hairy
Harry
Jerry

Kerry
Larry
marry
Mary
merry
parry
Perry
prairie
rarely
scary
sherry
squarely
tarry
Terry
vary
very
wary

bayberry
binary
blackberry
canary
Chuck Berry
contrary
cranberry
good fairy
gooseberry
hand-carry
Jim Carrey
library
make merry
miscarry
mulberry
primary
raspberry
remarry
rosemary
strawberry
tooth fairy
unfairly
unvary
unwary

actuary
adversary
antiquary
arbitrary
aviary
beriberi
bloody Mary

boysenberry
cackleberry
Canterbury
capillary
cautionary
cemetery
commentary
commissary
corollary
coronary
culinary
customary
dictionary
dietary
dignitary
Dirty Harry
emissary
February
fragmentary
Frankenberry
functionary
Halle Berry
Holy Mary
honorary
huckleberry
intermarry
January
lapidary
legendary
literary
loganberry
Londonderry
mercenary
military
missionary
momentary
monastery
monetary
mortuary
necessary
ordinary
Pictionary
planetary
pulmonary
salivary
salutary
sanctuary
sanitary
secondary
secretary

sedentary
seminary
solitary
stationary
stationery
statuary
sumptuary
temporary
tertiary
Tipperary
Tom and Jerry
topiary
tributary
Virgin Mary
visionary
voluntary

constabulary
contemporary
disciplinary
discretionary
extemporary
fiduciary
hereditary
imaginary
incendiary
involuntary
itinerary
Mariah Carey
obituary
pecuniary
precautionary
preliminary
probationary
proprietary
reactionary
subsidiary
Tom, Dick, and Harry
unnecessary
unordinary
unsanitary
veterinary
vocabulary

beneficiary
eat, drink, and be merry
extraordinary
intermediary
private secretary

Little House on the Prairie

By Any Means Necessary

ARYAN (see ARIAN 1)
ARYING (see ABLISHING)
ARZA (see ARTA)
AS 1 (see ASS 1)
AS 2 (see ASS 1)
AS 3 (see UG)
AS 4 (see A 1)
AS 5 (see AW)
ASA (see ASMA)
ASABLE (see ATIONAL 1)
ASAL (see ABLE)
ASBRO (see ACCO)
ASCAL (see ACKLE)
ASCENT (see ATION 1)
ASCHA (see ADA 1)
ASCINATE (see ACERATE)
ASCIST (see ASHES)
ASCO (see ACCO)
ASCULINE (see AFRICAN)
ASCUS (see ASHES)
ASE 1 (see ACE 1)
ASE 2 (see AVE 1)
ASELY (see ADY)
ASEMENT (see ATION 1)
ASER 1 (see ATOR)
ASER 2 (see ATOR)
ASES 1 (see ACES)
ASES 2 (see ACES)
ASEST (see ACES)
ASEY (see ADY)
ASH 1 (see ASS 1)

ASH 2

blotch
bosh
bosk
bosque
botch
cost
crotch
frosh
frost
gosh
josh
klatsch
loft

lost
mosque
nosh
notch
oft
posh
quash
Scotch
slosh
soft
splosh
splotch
squash
swash
swatch
waft
wash
watch

accost
aloft
backwash
birdwatch
brainwash
carwash
deathwatch
debauch
defrost
dishwash
exhaust
eyewash
get lost
goulash
hand wash
hayloft
hogwash
hopscotch
imbosk
kibosh
kiosk
low-cost
mouthwash
my gosh
nightwatch
stopwatch
topnotch
weight-watch
whitewash
wristwatch

abelmosk
coffee klatsch
holocaust
mackintosh
Pentecost
pocket watch

at any cost
Land of the Lost

ASHA (see ADA 1)
ASHABLE (see ACTABLE)
ASHEN (see ACTION)
ASHER 1 (see ACKER)
ASHER 2 (see OLLAR)

ASHES

abbess
access
actless
actress
aptness
ascus
ashes
atlas
axis
backless
badgeless
badness
bagless
baptist
bashes
batches
blackness
bractless
bragless
brashes
brashest
brashness
caches
cactus
capless
cashes
catches
catchless
chapless
clashes
classless
crashes

crassness
dashes
fascist
fastness
fatness
flagless
flapless
flashes
flatness
gashes
gastness
ghastness
gladness
gnashes
grassless
hapless
hashes
hatches
hatless
jagless
jazzes
klatches
lashes
latches
latchless
laxness
madness
mapless
mashes
massless
mastless
matches
matchless
matress
mattress
maxis
napless
pashes
passless
patches
patchless
patness
plashes
platness
practice
praxis
raptness
rashes
rashest
rashness

razzes
sadness
sapless
sashes
scatches
scratches
scratchless
slackness
slashes
smashes
snapless
snatches
splashes
stashes
strapless
tactless
taxless
thatches
thrashes
trashes
vastness
wrapless

abashes
abstractness
adaptness
attaches
backlashes
compactness
crosshatches
crosspatches
Damascus
despatches
detaches
detractress
disastrous
dispatches
exactness
exactress
eyelashes
gamashes
gramashes
hot flashes
inaptness
intactness
knee patches
love matches
malepractice
malpractice
mishmashes

mismatches
mispractice
molasses
moustaches
neuraxis
news flashes
nuthatches
overmatches
potashes
potlatches
reaccess
rehashes
rematches
repatches
steadfastness
synaxis
syntaxis
unlashes
unlatches
unsadness
whiplashes

aerotaxis
benefactress
boxing matches
calabashes
chiropraxis
coffee klatches
colorfastness
epistaxis
homotaxis
inexactness
interaxis
malefactress
out of practice
parataxis
phototaxis
phyllotaxis
prophylaxis
reattaches
rhizotaxis
semiaxis
shouting matches
spatterdashes
tennis matches
thermotaxis
thigmotaxis
unattaches

chemiotaxis
parasynaxis

ASHEST (see ASHES)
ASHEW (see ALUE)
ASHFUL (see ACKLE)
ASHIAN (see AFRICAN)
ASHIE (see ALLEY)
ASHIER 1 (see ABBIER)
ASHIER 2 (see OGGIER)
ASHIES (see ADDIES)
ASHIEST (see AGGIEST)
ASHILY (see ALITY)
ASHINESS 1 (see ABBINESS)
ASHINESS 2 (see OCKINESS)
ASHING 1 (see ACKING)
ASHING 2 (see OCKING)
ASHINGTON (see OCCASIN)
ASHION (see ACTION)
ASHIONING (see ABLISHING)
ASHLEY (see ALLEY)
ASHLY (see ALLEY)
ASHMENT (see ASSMENT)
ASHNESS (see ASHES)
ASHY 1 (see ALLEY)
ASHY 2 (see OCKEY)
ASI (see OCKEY)

ASIA

Ada
Asia
beta
data
eta
gala
geisha
Layla
mesa
playa
Sega
strata
theta
Vega

abasia
acacia
aphagia
aphasia
astasia
Australia
azalea
bodega

Consuela
Croatia
dysplasia
fantasia
Grenada
Isaiah
Jamaica
Malaya
Malaysia
Omega
pro rata
regalia
sub strata

Alpha Beta
Anastasia
euthanasia
Himalaya
rutabaga
Southeast Asia
Venezuela

Alpha Omega
paraphernalia

ASIAN (see ATION 1)
ASIC (see ATIVE)
ASICS (see ACES)
ASIE (see ADY)
ASIL (see ABLE)
ASIN (see ATION 1)
ASING 1 (see ATING)
ASING 2 (see ATING)
ASINGLY (see AKINGLY)
ASION (see ATION 1)
ASIONAL (see ATIONAL 1)
ASIS (see ACES)
ASIUM (see ANIUM)
ASIVE (see ATIVE)
ASK (see ASS 1)
ASKA (see ASMA)
ASKAN (see ATTEN)
ASKELL (see ACKLE)
ASKER (see ACKER)
ASKET (see ATIC 1)
ASKETRY (see ALITY)
ASKING (see ACKING)
ASLOW (see ACCO)

ASM

Adam
atom
chasm
fathom
madam
magnum
maxim
plasm
sacrum
spasm
sphagnum

orgasm
phantasm
platinum
sarcasm

pleonasm
protoplasm

enthusiasm
iconoclasm

ASMA

Abba
asthma
bassa
kappa
massa
NASA
phasma
plasma
quagga
Shasta

Alaska
canasta
chiasma
dynasta
melasma
miasma
Nebraska
onagga
oquassa
phantasma

Cleopatra
endoplasma
kyptoplasma
ovoplasma
protoplasta
spermoplasma
xanthelasma

idioplasma
karyoplasma
Phi Beta Kappa

ASMINE (see ATTEN)
ASN'T (see ATTEN)
ASO (see ACCO)
ASON (see ATION 1)
ASONRY (see ACIOUSLY)
ASP 1 (see AX)
ASP 2 (see OX)
ASPEN (see ATTEN)
ASPER (see ACKER)
ASPHEMOUS (see ALYSIS)
ASPHEMY (see ALITY)
ASPIEST (see AGGIEST)
ASPIN (see ATTEN)
ASPING (see ACKING)
ASPIRIN (see ATTEN)
ASPORA (see AFRICA)
ASPY (see ALLEY)

ASS 1

aft
as
ash
ask
ass
bash
bask
batch
bath
blast
brash
brass
cache
calf
calve
cash
cask
cast

caste
catch
chaff
clash
class
craft
crash
crass
daft
dash
draft
fast
flash
flask
gaffe
gas
gash
glass
gnash
graft
graph
grass
half
halve
has
hash
hatch
hath
have
jazz
lash
lass
last
latch
laugh
mash
mask
mass
mast
match
math
pass
past
patch
path
plash
raft
rash
razz
salve

sash
sass
scratch
shaft
slash
smash
snatch
spaz
splash
staff
staph
stash
Taft
task
thatch
thrash
trash
vast
wrath

abaft
abash
aghast
aircraft
alas
amass
at last
attach
avast
backlash
behalf
big brass
bike path
birdbath
bloodbath
bluegrass
bombast
broadcast
bypass
bypath
cold cash
contrast
crabgrass
crankshaft
crevasse
crosshatch
crosspatch
cut glass
decaf
detach

dispatch
door latch
downcast
downdraft
eyeglass
eyelash
facemask
fat ass
first class
first draft
flagstaff
flight path
footbath
footpath
forecast
from scratch
full blast
gas mask
gate crash
giraffe
glide path
half caste
half past
half-staff
halfmast
harass
hard cash
high class
hip flask
hold fast
hot flash
hourglass
impasse
jackass
jive-ass
Jordache
knee patch
lardass
last laugh
life raft
love match
low class
mine shaft
miscast
mishmash
mismatch
moustache
nerve gas
new math
news flash

newscast
no match
one-half
outcast
outclass
outlast
outmatch
panache
pizazz
play cast
podcast
potlatch
press pass
rehash
rematch
repast
repatch
rescratch
riffraff
sandblast
seabass
ski mask
skin graft
smart ass
sour mash
spacecraft
splish splash
sponge bath
spun glass
spyglass
stained glass
stand fast
steadfast
steam bath
surpass
tear gas
third class
tonguelash
top brass
topaz
trespass
typecast
unlash
unlatch
unmask
updraft
warpath
whereas
whiplash
wine cask

wise-ass
witchcraft
woodcraft
world class

aftermath
Alcatraz
all that jazz
all-star cast
at long last
autograph
balderdash
belly laugh
better half
boarding pass
boxing match
bring to pass
bubble bath
cabbage patch
cabin class
Calabash
chief of staff
clump of grass
cocktail glass
colorcast
colorfast
come to pass
cook with gas
corned beef hash
demitasse
diaper rash
down the hatch
elbow patch
epitaph
escape hatch
false eyelash
fiberglass
flabbergast
get the shaft
Grapes of Wrath
half-and-half
hard and fast
heart bypass
holograph
homograph
Hovercraft
Johnny Cash
laughing gas
lithograph
looking glass

lower-class
make a pass
make a splash
middle-class
mix and match
monograph
mountain pass
out of gas
overcast
overdraft
overmatch
overpass
overstaff
paragraph
parking pass
perfect match
petty cash
phonograph
photograph
poison gas
polo match
polygraph
psychopath
razzmatazz
reattach
safety catch
second class
seismograph
shooting match
shouting match
simulcast
sleeping gas
smooth as glass
succotash
take a bath
take to task
telecast
telegraph
tennis match
Turkish bath
unattach
underpass
understaff
up to scratch
upper-class
water flask
watercraft
working-class

antiaircraft

cardiograph
choreograph
get nowhere fast
Halloween mask
head of the class
mimeograph
natural gas
not up to scratch
osteopath
pain in the ass
run out of gas
snake in the grass
sociopath
step on the gas
strawberry patch
time and a half
while supplies last

Geoffrey the Giraffe
magnifying glass
off the beaten path

coronary bypass

ASS 2 (see ACE 1)
ASSA (see ASMA)
ASSACRE (see ALENDAR)
ASSADOR (see ALENDAR)
ASSAGE (see ATIC 1)
ASSAIL (see OTTLE)
ASSAL (see ACKLE)
ASSE (see ASS 1)
ASSEE (see ALLEY)
ASSEL (see ACKLE)
ASSELED (see ADDLED)
ASSELING (see ABLISHING)
ASSENGER (see ALENDAR)
ASSER (see ACKER)
ASSERBY (see ASSIFY)
ASSES (see ASHES)
ASSETT (see ATIC 1)
ASSIC (see ATIC 1)
ASSICAL (see ACTABLE)
ASSICALLY (see ALITY)
ASSIDY (see ALITY)
ASSIE (see ALLEY)
ASSIER (see ABBIER)
ASSIEST (see AGGIEST)

ASSIFY

abaci
Adonai
classify
dragonfly
gratify
magnify
Malachi
pacify
passerby
ratify
satisfy
stratify

beatify
capacify
declassify
dissatisfy
misclassify
opacify
reclassify
repacify
subclassify

interstratify
overmagnify

ASSILY (see ALITY)
ASSIN (see ATTEN)
ASSINATE (see ACERATE)
ASSINESS (see ABBINESS)
ASSING (see ACKING)
ASSION (see ACTION)

ASSIONATE

accident
accurate
adamant
applicant
cabinet
fractionate
habitant
passionate
rabinet
saginate
tabinet
vaginate

compassionate
dispassionate
empassionate
establishment
evaginate
extravagant
imaginate
impassionate
inaccurate
inhabitant
invaginate
unaccurate
unpassionate

incompassionate
uncompassionate

overcompassionate

ASSIS (see ALLEY)
ASSIST 1 (see ATIC 1)
ASSIST 2 (see ACES)
ASSIUM (see ALIUM)
ASSIVE (see ATIC 1)
ASSIVELY (see ALITY)
ASSIVENESS (see ALYSIS)
ASSIVIST (see ALYSIS)
ASSLE (see ACKLE)
ASSLED (see ADDLED)
ASSLESS (see ASHES)
ASSLESSNESS (see ALYSIS)
ASSLING (see ACKING)
ASSLY (see ALLEY)

ASSMENT

blastment
shaftment

abashment
amassment
dismastment
enactment
encashment
engraffment
engraftment
entassment
entrapment
enwrapment
harassment

impackment
ingraftment

deculassment
reenactment

ASSNESS (see ASHES)
ASSO 1 (see ACCO)
ASSO 2 (see OTTO 1)
ASSOCK (see ATIC 1)
ASSROOM (see ALUE)
ASSY (see ALLEY)
AST (see ASS 1)
ASTA 1 (see ASMA)
ASTA 2 (see ADA 1)
ASTARD (see ATTERED)
ASTARDLY (see ALITY)
ASTE 1 (see ACE 1)
ASTE 2 (see ASS 1)
ASTED 1 (see ATIC 1)
ASTED 2 (see ADED)
ASTEFUL (see ABLE)
ASTEFULLY (see ACIOUSLY)
ASTELESS (see ACES)
ASTELY (see ADY)
ASTEN 1 (see ATTEN)
ASTEN 2 (see ATION 1)

ASTENED

battened
blackened
captioned
challenged
fastened
fattened
flattened
happened
slackened

closed captioned
refastened
unchallenged
unfastened

ASTENER (see ALENDAR)
ASTENESS (see ACES)
ASTENING (see ABLISHING)
ASTER 1 (see ACKER)
ASTER 2 (see ATOR)
ASTERED (see ATTERED)

ASTERING (see ATTERING)
ASTERY (see ALITY)
ASTEST (see ATIC 1)
ASTHMA (see ASMA)
ASTI (see ALLEY)
ASTIC (see ATIC 1)
ASTICALLY (see ATICALLY)
ASTICATE (see ACERATE)
ASTIER (see ABBIER)
ASTIES (see ADDIES)
ASTIEST (see AGGIEST)
ASTIKA (see ONICA)
ASTILY 1 (see ALITY)
ASTILY 2 (see AVERY)
ASTINATE (see ACERATE)
ASTINESS 1 (see AKINESS)
ASTINESS 2 (see ABBINESS)
ASTING 1 (see ACKING)
ASTING 2 (see ATING)
ASTITY (see ALITY)
ASTLE (see ACKLE)
ASTLED (see ADDLED)
ASTLESS (see ASHES)
ASTLING (see ACKING)
ASTLY (see ALLEY)
ASTMENT (see ASSMENT)
ASTNESS (see ASHES)
ASTOR (see ACKER)
ASTORED (see ATTERED)
ASTORING (see ATTERING)
ASTRAL (see ACKLE)
ASTRIC (see ATIC 1)
ASTRO (see ACCO)
ASTROPHE (see ALITY)
ASTROUS (see ASHES)
ASTRY (see ADY)
ASTURBATE (see ACERATE)
ASTURE (see ACKER)
ASTY 1 (see ALLEY)
ASTY 2 (see ADY)
ASUAL (see ACTABLE)
AT 1 (see ACK)
AT 2 (see OT)
AT 3 (see UP)
AT 4 (see AW)
ATA 1 (see ADA 1)
ATA 2 (see ASIA)

ATABLE 1

cratable
datable

flavorful
gratable
slatable
statable

abatable
collatable
creatable
crematable
debatable
deflatable
dilatable
elatable
equatable
frustratable
inflatable
ligatable
locatable
mandatable
narratable
negatable
placatable
relatable
rotatable
sedatable
translatable
updatable
vacatable
vibratable

activatable
advocatable
aggravatable
agitatable
allocatable
amputatable
annotatable
arbitratable

ATABLE 2 (see ACTABLE)
ATAL (see ABLE)
ATALLY (see ACIOUSLY)
ATALYST (see ALYSIS)
ATAN (see ATION 1)
ATANT 1 (see ATION 1)
ATANT 2 (see ATTEN)
ATANTLY (see ACIOUSLY)
ATCH 1 (see ASS 1)
ATCH 2 (see ASH 2)

ATCHABLE (see ACTABLE)
ATCHER 1 (see ACKER)
ATCHER 2 (see OLLAR)
ATCHERY (see ALITY)
ATCHES (see ASHES)
ATCHET (see ATIC 1)
ATCHFUL (see OTTLE)
ATCHIEST (see AGGIEST)
ATCHINESS (see ABBINESS)
ATCHING 1 (see ACKING)
ATCHING 2 (see OCKING)
ATCHLESS (see ASHES)
ATCHMAN (see OTTEN)
ATCHMENT (see ACHMENT)
ATCHY 1 (see ALLEY)
ATCHY 2 (see OCKEY)

ATE 1

ate
bait
bate
crate
date
eight
fate
freight
gait
gate
grate
great
hate
Kate
late
mate
plait
plate
rate
sate
skate
slate
state
straight
strait
trait
wait
weight

abate
aerate

Allstate
await
bedmate
berate
birth date
birthrate
birthweight
blind date
bookplate
breastplate
cakeplate
castrate
cellmate
cheapskate
checkmate
classmate
clean slate
Colgate
collate
court date
create
cremate
cut-rate
dead weight
death rate
debate
deflate
donate
due date
elate
equate
estate
filtrate
first date
first mate
first-rate
fixate
flat rate
floodgate
flyweight
frustrate
gold plate
helpmate
home plate
home state
hot plate
ice skate
inflate
ingrate
inmate

innate
jailbait
Jean Nate
Kuwait
lactate
ligate
lightweight
live bait
locate
mandate
misstate
narrate
negate
orate
ornate
out late
outdate
outwait
Phi Bete
postdate
predate
prime rate
probate
prom date
prorate
prostate
prostrate
pulsate
rebate
relate
rotate
sedate
serrate
shipmate
sleep state
soulmate
stagnate
stalemate
tailgate
third rate
translate
update
upstate
V-eight

808
abdicate
abnegate
abrogate
acerbate

act of fate
actuate
advocate
aggravate
agitate
allocate
annotate
antedate
arbitrate
aspirate
boiler plate
calculate
capsulate
carbonate
castigate
celebrate
chief of state
circulate
cogitate
complicate
concentrate
confiscate
conjugate
constipate
contemplate
correlate
culminate
cultivate
cumulate
decorate
demonstrate
deprecate
dinner date
dislocate
double-date
duplicate
educate
elongate
emanate
emigrate
enervate
escalate
exchange rate
fabricate
federate
figure skate
fluctuate
fluoridate
formulate
fornicate

fourth estate
fumigate
Golden Gate
graduate
guesstimate
heavy date
heavyweight
hibernate
hyphenate
imitate
immigrate
implicate
impregnate
in a state
incubate
infiltrate
instigate
insulate
interstate
inundate
irrigate
irritate
isolate
liberate
license plate
liquidate
litigate
Lone Star State
lubricate
menstruate
middleweight
mitigate
modulate
motivate
Mr. Slate
mutilate
nauseate
navigate
obfuscate
obligate
orchestrate
osculate
out-of-date
out-of-state
overrate
overstate
overweight
palpitate
paper plate
paperweight

pass the plate
perorate
perpetrate
police state
pollinate
postulate
potentate
procreate
profligate
promulgate
propagate
pull your weight
punctuate
re-create
real estate
reinstate
relocate
renovate
replicate
reprobate
rollerskate
running mate
scintillate
second-rate
section eight
segregate
separate
silverplate
situate
solid-state
speculate
starting gate
stipulate
subjugate
sublimate
suffocate
syncopate
tabulate
target date
tolerate
twitterpate
underrate
understate
underweight
undulate
up to date
upper plate
vacillate
validate
ventilate

violate
Watergate
welfare state

accentuate
accommodate
accumulate
adulterate
annihilate
appropriate
articulate
asphyxiate
assimilate
at any rate
authenticate
capitulate
coagulate
cohabitate
collection plate
commiserate
communicate
congratulate
consolidate
cross-ventilate
deliberate
delineate
dilapidate
ejaculate
elucidate
emancipate
encapsulate
equivocate
eradicate
evacuate
evaluate
evaporate
exacerbate
exaggerate
exasperate
exhilarate
felicitate
gesticulate
Gonzo The Great
hallucinate
impersonate
incarcerate
indoctrinate
infatuate
ingeniate
inoculate

insinuate
interrogate
intoxicate
invalidate
invigorate
luxuriate
manipulate
matriculate
miscalculate
miscegenate
orientate
participate
peregrinate
perpetuate
pontificate
precipitate
premediate
prevaricate
prognosticate
proliferate
public debate
pull your own weight
recaptivate
reciprocate
redecorate
refrigerate
regurgitate
remunerate
repudiate
resuscitate
retaliate
reverberate
substantiate

ameliorate
catatonic state
differentiate
hyperventilate
misappropriate
overcompensate
reinvigorate

political debate
Secretary of State

ATE 2 (see OCKEY)
ATEABLE (see ADABLE)

ATED

baited
grated
hated
mated
plaited
plated
rated
sated
skated
slated
stated
waited

abated
berated
castrated
collated
created
cremated
debated
deflated
dilated
donated
elated
equated
frustrated
gyrated
ice-skated
inflated
located
migrated
misstated
negated
orated
outdated
placated
prorated
prostrated
pulsated
related
rotated
sedated
stagnated
tailgated
translated
updated
vacated
vibrated

acclimated
activated
advocated
aggravated
agitated
allocated
amputated
animated
annotated
arbitrated
calculated
calibrated
captivated
carbonated
celebrated
circulated
compensated
complicated
concentrated
confiscated
conjugated
constipated
contemplated
copulated
culminated
cultivated
decimated
decorated
dedicated
defecated
dehydrated
delegated
demonstrated
deprecated
designated
detonated
devastated
deviated
dislocated
dissipated
dominated
duplicated
educated
elevated
elongated
emanated
emigrated
emulated
escalated
extricated

fabricated
fascinated
federated
fluctuated
formulated
fornicated
fumigated
generated
germinated
graduated
gravitated
hesitated
hibernated
hyphenated
illustrated
imitated
immigrated
implicated
impregnated
incubated
indicated
infiltrated
instigated
insulated
integrated
intimated
inundated
irrigated
irritated
isolated
iterated
lacerated
laminated
liberated
liquidated
litigated
lubricated
masticated
masturbated
mediated
medicated
meditated
menstruated
mitigated
moderated
modulated
motivated
mutilated
nauseated
navigated

obfuscated
obligated
operated
oscillated
overrated
overstated
penetrated
percolated
perforated
permeated
pollinated
postulated
predicated
procreated
profligated
propagated
radiated
recreated
regulated
reinstated
relegated
relocated
renovated
roller-skated
salivated
satiated
saturated
segregated
separated
silver-plated
simulated
speculated
stimulated
stipulated
strangulated
subjugated
suffocated
syndicated
tabulated
terminated
titillated
tolerated
underrated
understated
undulated
vacillated
validated
venerated
ventilated
vindicated
violated

abbreviated
accelerated
accentuated
accommodated
accumulated
adulterated
affiliated
alienated
alleviated
annihilated
anticipated
appreciated
appropriated
articulated
asphyxiated
assassinated
associated
authenticated
capitulated
commemorated
commiserated
communicated
congratulated
consolidated
contaminated
cooperated
coordinated
debilitated
decaffeinated
deliberated
depreciated
dilapidated
discriminated
domesticated
ejaculated
elaborated
eliminated
elucidated
emaciated
emancipated
encapsulated
equivocated
eradicated
evacuated
evaporated
exacerbated
exaggerated
exasperated

exhilarated
exterminated
extrapolated
facilitated
felicitated
hallucinated
impersonated
incarcerated
indoctrinated
infatuated
ingratiated
initiated
inoculated
insinuated
interrogated
intimidated
intoxicated
invalidated
investigated
invigorated
irradiated
manipulated
matriculated
miscalculated
necessitated
negotiated
officiated
orientated
participated
perpetuated
pontificated
precipitated
prevaricated
procrastinated
prognosticated
proliferated
recaptivated
reciprocated
recuperated
redecorated
refrigerated
regurgitated
reiterated
rejuvenated
repudiated
resuscitated
retaliated
reverberated

Sports Illustrated
substantiated
well-educated

ameliorated
differentiated
discombobulated
hyperventilated
misappropriated
rehabilitated
reinvigorated

ATEFUL (see ABLE)
ATEFULLY (see ACIOUSLY)
ATEGIST (see ALYSIS)
ATEGIZE (see ANDALIZE)
ATEGORIZE (see ATURALIZE)
ATEGY (see ALITY)
ATELESS (see ACES)
ATELY (see ADY)
ATEMENT (see ATION 1)

ATEMENTS

agents
cadence
fragrance
latents
pagans
patience
pavements
payments
statements

abatements
acquaintance
coagents
covalence
engravements
enslavements
impatience
maintenance
misstatements
prepayments
reagents
repayments
restatements
subagents
surveillance
unpatience

demicadence
overstatements
reinstatements
Secret Agents
understatements

ATEN 1 (see ATTEN)
ATEN 2 (see OTTEN)
ATENATE (see AMINATE)
ATENCY (see ACIOUSLY)
ATENESS (see ACES)
ATENT 1 (see ATTEN)
ATENT 2 (see ATION 1)
ATENTS (see ATEMENTS)
ATER 1 (see ATOR)
ATER 2 (see OLLAR)
ATERAL (see ACTABLE)
ATERED 1 (see AVORED)
ATERED 2 (see OFFERED)
ATERING 1 (see AVORING)
ATERING 2 (see OTTERING)
ATERY (see OMETRY)
ATES (see ACE 1)
ATESMAN (see ATION 1)
ATEST (see ACES)
ATEY (see ADY)
ATH 1 (see ASS 1)
ATH 2 (see OFF)
ATHAN (see ATION 1)
ATHE (see AVE 1)
ATHEIST (see ANEOUS)
ATHER 1 (see OLLAR)
ATHER 2 (see ACKER)
ATHERED 1 (see ATTERED)
ATHERED 2 (see OFFERED)
ATHERING (see ATTERING)
ATHERLY (see OMETRY)
ATHIC (see ATIC 1)
ATHICALLY (see ATICALLY)
ATHIEST (see AGGIEST)
ATHING (see ATING)
ATHINGLY (see AKINGLY)
ATHOLIC (see ALYSIS)
ATHOM (see ASM)
ATHROOM (see ALUE)
ATHY (see ALLEY)
ATI 1 (see OCKEY)
ATI 2 (see ALLEY)
ATIA (see ASIA)
ATIABLE (see ATIONAL 1)
ATIAL (see ABLE)
ATIAN (see ATION 1)

ATIATE

aviate
glaciate
gladiate
radiate
satiate
spatiate

conglaciate
corradiate
emaciate
eradiate
expatiate
ingratiate
insatiate
irradiate
reradiate
unsatiate

reingratiate

ATIBLE (see ACTABLE)

ATIC 1

abbot
Abbott
acid
acted
active
adage
added
addict
agate
Alec
Alex
Alice
attic
avid
badded
baddest
baggage
ballad
ballot
barrack
basket
Bassett
batted

blasted
brackage
bracket
bracted
cabbage
calid
callid
callous
callus
captive
casket
chalice
chatted
classic
classist
crafted
Dallas
drafted
drastic
fabric
facet
fasted
fastest
fattest
flaccid
flasket
flattest
fracted
gadded
gadget
Gallic
gallop
garish
gasket
gastric
gavage
gladded
grafted
graphic
habit
hafted
Harris
hassock
hatchet
havoc
jacket
Lappic
lasket
lasted
latchet

lavage
lavish
madded
maddest
maggot
magic
magnet
malice
mallet
Maris
marish
massive
masted
matted
package
packet
padded
palace
palate
pallet
pallid
Paris
parish
passage
passive
Patrick
patted
phallic
placid
plastic
rabbit
rabid
racket
racquet
radish
rafted
rapid
ratchet
ratted
ravage
ravish
Sabbath
sackage
saddest
salad
salvage
sapid
savage
scallop
scavage

shafted
shallop
slackage
spastic
stackage
static
status
stratus
tabid
tablet
tacit
tactic
tatted
trackage
traffic
tragic
valid
vapid
wafted

abstracted
abstractive
air traffic
antacid
asthmatic
attracted
attractive
bad habit
black magic
Black Sabbath
bombastic
breadbasket
broadcasted
chitchatted
chromatic
climatic
coacted
cohabit
combatted
compacted
contacted
contracted
contractive
contrasted
detracted
didactic
diffracted
distracted
distractive
dogmatic

dramatic
drug habit
ecstatic
elastic
embarrass
emphatic
enacted
enactive
engrafted
erratic
establish
exacted
extracted
fanatic
fantastic
Fitzpatrick
flight jacket
forecasted
fruit salad
fur jacket
galactic
Greg Maddux
gymnastic
handcrafted
horseradish
Illmatic
impacted
impallid
impassive
inactive
infracted
ingrafted
inhabit
invalid
italic
jackrabbit
Lake Placid
lifejacket
love ballad
lymphatic
metallic
misadded
monastic
outlasted
playacted
pragmatic
prepackage
proactive
protracted
protractive

quadratic
reacted
reactive
redacted
redrafted
refracted
refractive
repackage
retracted
sandblasted
sarcastic
schematic
scholastic
smart alec
Socratic
somatic
sporadic
stigmatic
straitjacket
subtracted
subtractive
theatric
thematic
tossed salad
transacted
traumatic
wall bracket
wastebasket
whipgrafted
workbasket

abreacted
acrobatic
apparatus
aromatic
Asiatic
autocratic
automatic
biographic
blow a gasket
bureaucratic
Calvin Harris
cast a ballot
cataphracted
charismatic
cinematic
counteracted
counteractive
democratic
demographic

dinner jacket
diplomatic
disestablish
Easter basket
Easter rabbit
emblematic
enigmatic
flabbergasted
force of habit
geographic
geriatric
holographic
hyperactive
inabstracted
incoacted
incompacted
incontracted
infographic
interacted
interactive
kick the habit
lithographic
mathematic
neoclassic
one-way traffic
operatic
out of habit
overacted
overactive
pancreatic
pediatric
phonographic
photographic
plutocratic
pornographic
precontracted
problematic
psychiatric
psychopathic
recontracted
reenacted
reestablish
retroacted
retroactive
retrofracted
riding habit
Roger Rabbit
secret ballot
seismographic
smoking jacket

stenographic
subcontracted
superadded
symptomatic
systematic
telegraphic
telepathic
tennis racket
Thriller Jacket
unattracted
underacted
undramatic
unretracted
yellowjacket

aristocratic
axiomatic
bury the hatchet
choreographic
creature of habit
Debbie Does Dallas
ecclesiastic
enthusiastic
iconoclastic
idiomatic
Inspector Gadget
interscholastic
Jessica Rabbit
melodramatic
Mr. Fantastic
overreacted
psychosomatic
radioactive
undiplomatic

a tisket, a tasket
autobiographic
hell in a handbasket
idiosyncratic
Members Only jacket
semiautomatic
Who Framed Roger Rabit?

National Geographic

Super Elastic Bubble Plastic

ATIC 2 (see OTIC)
ATICA (see AFRICA)
ATICAL (see ACTABLE)

ATICALLY

actually
drastically
factually
gradually
graphically
magically
naturally
practically
radically
statically
tragically

aristocratically
dogmatically
dramatically
ecstatically
emphatically
enigmatically
erratically
fanatically
fantastically
grammatically
nomadically
pragmatically
sporadically

autocratically
automatically
charismatically
democratically
diplomatically
mathematically
systematically
telepathically
ungrammatically

melodramatically
undiplomatically

idiosyncratically

ATICAN (see AFRICAN)
ATIE (see ADY)
ATIENCE (see ATEMENTS)
ATIENT (see ATION 1)
ATIENTLY (see ACIOUSLY)
ATIFY (see ASSIFY)
ATIM (see ATION 1)
ATIN 1 (see ATTEN)
ATIN 2 (see OTTEN)

ATING

aching
acing
aging
aiding
aping
baiting
baking
banking
basing
basting
bathing
blanking
blazing
bracing
braiding
braising
braking
breaking
caging
caking
casing
chafing
chasing
clanking
cranking
craving
dazing
draping
facing
fading
fainting
faking
fazing
feinting
flaking
freighting
gaping
gauging
gazing
glazing
gracing
grading
grating
grazing
hating
hazing
lacing
lading

lathing
lazing
making
mating
pacing
paging
painting
pasting
paving
phasing
phrasing
placing
plaiting
plating
praising
quaking
racing
raging
raiding
raising
raking
ranking
raping
rating
raving
razing
sating
saving
scathing
scraping
shading
shaking
shaping
shaving
skating
slating
slaving
snaking
spacing
spading
spanking
staging
staking
stating
tainting
taking
tanking
taping
tasting
thanking

tracing
trading
wading
waging
waiting
waiving
waking
wasting
waving
yanking

abating
abrading
acquainting
amazing
appraising
assuaging
awaking
backaching
backbreaking
behaving
berating
blockading
breathtaking
cake baking
cascading
castrating
charading
checkmating
collating
creating
cremating
crusading
debasing
debating
defacing
deflating
degrading
depraving
dilating
disgracing
displacing
dissuading
donating
downgrading
earthshaking
elating
embracing
engaging
engraving

enlacing
enraging
enslaving
equating
erasing
escaping
evading
face-saving
fixating
flag waving
floodgating
forsaking
freebasing
frustrating
fund-raising
groundbreaking
gyrating
handcranking
handshaking
heartaching
heartbreaking
high-ranking
horseracing
ice-skating
inflating
invading
jailbreaking
landscaping
leavetaking
locating
lovemaking
mandating
migrating
misplacing
misshaping
misstating
mistaking
muckraking
negating
orating
outdating
outflanking
outpacing
outraging
outranking
painstaking
parading
partaking
persuading
pervading

placating
probating
prorating
prostrating
pulsating
rampaging
rebating
relating
remaking
repainting
repaving
rephrasing
replacing
reshaping
retaking
retracing
rotating
Scotch taping
sedating
serrating
stagnating
stalemating
stargazing
sunbathing
tailgating
tirading
trailblazing
translating
unfading
unlacing
upbraiding
updating
upgrading
upraising
upstaging
vacating
vibrating
winetasting

abdicating
abnegating
abrogating
acclimating
acerbating
activating
actuating
adulating
advocating
aggravating
agitating

allocating
amputating
animating
annotating
arbitrating
aspirating
barricading
bellyaching
bifurcating
calculating
calibrating
captivating
carbonating
castigating
celebrating
circulating
cogitating
compensating
complicating
concentrating
confiscating
congregating
conjugating
constipating
contemplating
copulating
correlating
credit rating
culminating
cultivating
cumulating
decimating
decorating
dedicating
defecating
dehydrating
delegating
demarcating
demonstrating
deprecating
designating
detonating
devastating
deviating
disengaging
dislocating
dissipating
dominating
doublespacing
duplicating

educating
elevating
elongating
emanating
emigrating
emulating
enervating
escalating
escapading
extricating
fabricating
fascinating
federating
finger waving
fingerpainting
fluctuating
fluoridating
formulating
fornicating
freshman hazing
fumigating
generating
germinating
graduating
gravitating
hesitating
hibernating
hyphenating
illustrating
imitating
immigrating
implicating
impregnating
incubating
indicating
infiltrating
insulating
integrating
interfacing
interlacing
intimating
inundating
irrigating
irritating
isolating
iterating
jubilating
laborsaving
lacerating

laminating
legislating
liberating
liquidating
litigating
lubricating
masquerading
masticating
masturbating
mediating
medicating
meditating
menstruating
microwaving
misbehaving
mitigating
moderating
modulating
motivating
movie making
mutilating
nauseating
navigating
obfuscating
obligating
operating
oscillating
overpraising
overrating
overstating
overtaking
palpitating
pantyraiding
paraphrasing
penetrating
percolating
perforating
permeating
perorating
pillowcasing
pollinating
postulating
predicating
procreating
profligating
promulgating
propagating
radiating
reacquainting
reappraising

recreating
regulating
reinstating
relegating
relocating
remonstrating
renovating
retrograding
roller-skating
ruminating
salivating
satiating
saturating
scintillating
segregating
self-effacing
separating
serenading
silver-plating
simulating
single-spacing
speculating
steeplechasing
stimulating
stipulating
stock-car racing
strangulating
subjugating
sublimating
suffocating
syndicating
tabulating
terminating
titillating
tolerating
underrating
understating
undertaking
undulating
vacillating
validating
venerating
ventilating
vindicating
violating

abbreviating
abominating
accelerating
accentuating

accommodating
accumulating
adjudicating
adulterating
affiliating
alienating
alleviating
annihilating
anticipating
appreciating
appropriating
articulating
asphyxiating
assassinating
associating
authenticating
capitulating
chariot racing
coagulating
commemorating
commiserating
communicating
conciliating
congratulating
consolidating
contaminating
cooperating
coordinating
cross-ventilating
debilitating
decaffeinating
deliberating
delineating
depopulating
depreciating
discriminating
domesticating
ejaculating
elaborating
eliminating
elucidating
emaciating
emancipating
encapsulating
equivocating
eradicating
evacuating
evaporating
exacerbating
exaggerating

exasperating
excruciating
exhilarating
exterminating
extrapolating
facilitating
felicitating
gesticulating
hallucinating
illuminating
impersonating
incarcerating
indoctrinating
infatuating
ingratiating
initiating
inoculating
insider trading
insinuating
interrogating
intimidating
intoxicating
invalidating
investigating
investment banking
invigorating
irradiating
luxuriating
manipulating
matriculating
miscalculating
necessitating
negotiating
officiating
orientating
participating
perpetuating
pontificating
precipitating
prevaricating
procrastinating
prognosticating
proliferating
ranting and raving
recaptivating
reciprocating
recriminating
recuperating
redecorating
refrigerating

regurgitating
reiterating
rejuvenating
remunerating
repudiating
resuscitating
retaliating
reverberating
subordinating
substantiating
videotaping

ameliorating
differentiating
discombobulating
hyperventilating
misappropriating
rehabilitating
reinvigorating

ATINGLY

gratingly
pratingly
waitingly

debatingly
frustratingly
inflatingly

aggravatingly
alternatingly
calculatingly
deprecatingly
devastatingly
hesitatingly
instigatingly
irritatingly
nauseatingly
penetratingly
ruminatingly
scintillatingly
stimulatingly
suffocatingly
supplicatingly
titillatingly

accommodatingly
appreciatingly

depreciatingly
exacerbatingly
excruciatingly
humiliatingly
illuminatingly
infuriatingly
insinuatingly
preponderatingly
undeviatingly
unhesitatingly

undescriminatingly

ATINUM (see ASM)

ATIO 1

Maceo
radio
ratio

clock radio
fellatio
Horatio
loss ratio

ATIO 2 (see ACHIO)

ATION 1

Abram
agent
ancient
apron
Asian
avum
bacon
basement
basin
batement
blatant
blazon
brazen
Cajun
casement
Caymen
chasten
claimant
Clayton

craven
Creighton
Damon
datum
Dayton
flagrant
flamen
fragrant
graven
Haitian
hasten
haven
Jason
laden
latent
layman
maiden
mason
matron
mayhem
nascent
Nathan
nation
pagan
patient
patron
pavement
payment
placement
raiment
raisin
raven
Reagan
reagent
Salem
Satan
scapement
shaken
shapen
shaven
stamen
statement
statesman
station
straighten
straiten
stratum
taken
vacant
vagrant
waken

abasement
abatement
abrasion
abstainment
adjacent
amazement
arraignment
arrangement
Art Tatum
assailant
assuagement
attainment
awaken
backpayment
bank statement
beratement
betrayment
Carl Sagan
carnation
castration
Caucasion
causation
cessation
citation
coagent
cognation
collation
complacent
complaisant
constrainment
contagion
containment
creation
cremation
crustacean
Dalmatian
damnation
debasement
defacement
deflatement
deflation
defrayment
depravement
derangement
detainment
dictation
dilation
disclaimant
displacement
dissuasion

donation
down payment
duration
effacement
elatement
elation
embankment
emblazon
embracement
encasement
engagement
enragement
enslavement
equation
escapement
estrangement
Eurasian
evasion
exhalant
filtration
fire station
fixation
flirtation
flotation
formation
forsaken
foundation
free-agent
frustration
gas station
gestation
gradation
gyration
highwayman
hydration
impatient
inflatement
inflation
inhalant
invasion
Jamaican
libation
location
Matt Damon
migration
misplacement
misstatement
mistaken
mutation
narration

Nick Saban
notation
occasion
oration
ordainment
ovation
partaken
persuasion
pervasion
plantation
Playstation
portrayment
prepayment
probation
prostration
pulsation
quotation
relation
renascent
repavement
repayment
replacement
retainment
retaken
rotation
salvation
sensation
smooth-shaven
space station
stagnation
starvation
stonemason
subagent
substation
substratum
summation
surveillant
sustainment
tarnation
taxation
temptation
translation
unshaken
unshaven
untaken
vacation
verbatim
vexation
vibration
vocation

washbasin
weigh station
well-taken
workstation

abdication
aberration
acclamation
accusation
adaptation
admiration
adoration
adulation
affectation
affirmation
aggravation
agitation
allegation
allocation
alteration
altercation
amputation
animation
annexation
annotation
appellation
application
arbitration
ascertainment
aspiration
augmentation
aviation
avocation
bargain basement
calculation
calibration
cancellation
capitation
captivation
carbonation
castigation
celebration
circulation
cogitation
combination
commendation
compensation
compilation
complication
condemnation

condensation
confirmation
conflagration
conformation
confrontation
conjugation
consecration
conservation
consolation
constellation
consternation
consultation
contemplation
conversation
convocation
Copenhagen
coronation
corporation
correlation
crop rotation
culmination
cultivation
declaration
decoration
dedication
defamation
degradation
dehydration
delegation
demarcation
demonstration
denotation
deportation
deprivation
derivation
desecration
designation
desolation
desperation
destination
detonation
devastation
deviation
disarrangement
disengagement
dislocation
dispensation
dissertation
dissipation
distillation

duplication
education
edutainment
eggs and bacon
elevation
entertainment
estimation
exaltation
excavation
excitation
expectation
expiration
explanation
exploitation
exploration
exportation
exultation
fabrication
fascination
federation
fermentation
figuration
filling station
fluctuation
fomentation
formulation
fornication
fumigation
generation
godforsaken
graduation
gravitation
habitation
heavy-laden
hesitation
hibernation
hyphenation
importation
inclination
indentation
indication
indignation
infestation
inflammation
information
inhalation
inspiration
installation
intimation
iron maiden

irritation
isolation
jubilation
laceration
lamentation
lamination
legislation
levitation
liberation
liquidation
litigation
lubrication
lumination
machination
malformation
masturbation
maturation
mediation
medication
meditation
menstruation
ministration
mitigation
moderation
molestation
motivation
mutilation
navigation
noise abatement
obligation
observation
on occasion
orchestration
overladen
overtaken
palpitation
penetration
perforation
peroration
perpetration
perspiration
pollination
pound the pavement
prearrangement
preengagement
preparation
presentation
preservation
procreation
propagation

provocation
publication
punctuation
radiation
rearrangement
reawaken
recitation
recreation
reformation
registration
regulation
relaxation
renovation
reparation
reputation
reservation
resignation
respiration
restoration
retardation
revelation
riboflavin
salivation
salutation
sanitation
saturation
Secret Agent
segmentation
segregation
separation
service station
simulation
situation
somnifacient
speculation
stimulation
stipulation
syncopation
syndication
tabulation
termination
Third World Nation
toleration
transformation
transplantation
transportation
trepidation
ultimatum
undertaken
undulation

unforsaken
unladen
usurpation
vaccination
validation
valuation
variation
vegetation
veneration
ventilation
vindication
violation
visitation

abbreviation
acceleration
accentuation
accommodation
accreditation
accumulation
adjudication
administration
adulteration
affiliation
alienation
alleviation
alliteration
amplification
analyzation
annihilation
anticipation
appreciation
appropriation
approximation
argumentation
articulation
asphyxiation
assassination
assimilation
association
authentication
authorization
beautification
bring home the bacon
canonization
capitulation
centralization
certification
civilization
clarification

classification
co-education
collaboration
colonization
columnization
commemoration
commensuration
commiseration
communication
conciliation
confederation
configuration
conglomeration
congratulations
consideration
consolidation
contamination
continuation
coordination
corroboration
crystallization
debilitation
decapitation
deceleration
defoliation
degeneration
deliberation
delineation
denunciation
depreciation
determination
dignification
discoloration
discrimination
dissemination
documentation
domestication
dramatization
edification
ejaculation
elimination
emaciation
emancipation
emasculation
enumeration
enunciation
equivocation
eradication
evaluation
exacerbation

exaggeration
examination
exasperation
exhilaration
exoneration
expropriation
extenuation
extermination
facilitation
falsification
felicitation
fertilization
flower arrangement
formalization
fortification
fraternization
gentrification
gesticulation
glorification
gratification
habituation
hallucination
harmonization
humanization
humiliation
idealization
idolization
illumination
imagination
impersonation
implementation
improvisation
inauguration
incarceration
incineration
incorporation
incrimination
indoctrination
inebriation
infuriation
ingratiation
inhabitation
initiation
insemination
insinuation
instrumentation
interpretation
interrelation
interrogation
intimidation

intoxication
invalidation
investigation
invigoration
irradiation
justification
legalization
Lost Generation
luxuriation
magnetization
magnification
manifestation
manipulation
matriculation
minimization
misapplication
miscalculation
misinformation
modernization
modification
mortification
multiplication
necessitation
negotiation
neutralization
normalization
notification
nullification
obliteration
officiation
opening statement
organization
orientation
origination
ornamentation
paralyzation
participation
pasteurization
patronization
penalization
perambulation
polarization
precipitation
predestination
premeditation
pressurization
prevarication
procrastination
prognostication
proliferation

pronunciation
purification
qualification
radio station
ramification
ratification
realization
reciprocation
recommendation
recrimination
recuperation
refrigeration
regeneration
regimentation
regurgitation
reiteration
rejuvenation
remuneration
renunciation
repatriation
representation
repudiation
resuscitation
retaliation
reverberation
sanctification
sedimentation
Serbo-Croatian
signification
simplification
socialization
solemnization
solicitation
sophistication
specification
stabilization
standardization
standing ovation
sterilization
substantiation
summarization
summer vacation
suplementation
symbolization
synchronization
tranquilization
transfiguration
unification
urbanization
utilization

vandalization
verbalization
verification
versification
victimization
vilification
vocalization

adult education
alphabetization
amelioration
antagonization
capitalization
categorization
characterization
college education
commercialization
covert operation
cross-examination
decentralization
demobilization
demoralization
deodorization
deterioration
differentiation
discontinuation
disorganization
disqualification
diversification
electrification
excommunication
exemplification
experimentation
familiarization
generalization
high school education
identification
immortalization
inconsideration
inside information
insubordination
intensification
intermediation
liberalization
militarization
mispronunciation
misrepresentation
monopolization
nationalization
naturalization

no-win situation
parks and recreation
personification
popularization
recapitulation
reconciliation
reconsideration
rehabilitation
reorganization
revitalization
self-determination
solidification
under obligation
visualization
women's liberation
workman's compensation

Americanization
contract negotiation
double-digit inflation
intercommunication
liberal education
materialization
physical education
spiritualization

artifical respiration
guilty by association
individualization
intellectualization
National Lampoon's Vacation

Articles of Confederation
artificial insemination

ATION 2 (see ATION 1)
ATION 3 (see ACTION)

ATIONAL 1

chasable
faceable
paceable
placeable
satiable
stational
traceable

creational
defaceable
displaceable
durational
embraceable
equational
erasable
foundational
gestational
gradational
lactational
migrational
misplaceable
mutational
notational
oblational
occasional
outpaceable
probational
quotational
replaceable
retraceable
rotational
salvational
sensational
taxational
unlaceable
vibrational
vocational

aberrational
aggregational
annexational
arbitrational
avocational
calculational
computational
conformational
confrontational
congregational
conjugational
conservational
conversational
convocational
declarational
dedicational
demonstrational
deputational
derivational
deviational

dissertational
educational
emigrational
federational
fluctuational
generational
gravitational
ideational
imitational
incubational
informational
innervational
inspirational
interlaceable
invitational
invocational
irreplaceable
irrotational
maturational
mediational
motivational
navigational
nonrelational
nonvocational
obligational
observational
occupational
operational
perturbational
prevocational
propagational
recreational
reformational
registrational
respirational
revelational
situational
terminational
transformational
transpertational
valuational
variational
vegetational
visitational

accommodational
acculturational
administrational
associational
co-educational

configurational
consociational
denominational
descriminational
hallucinational
imaginational
improvisational
interpretational
interrogational
investigational
multiplicational
noneducational
organizational
representational

nondenominational
nonrepresentational
undenomenational

interdenominational

ATIONAL 2 (see ACTABLE)
ATIONALIZE (see ATURALIZE)
ATIONING (see ABLISHING)
ATIOUS (see ACES)
ATISFY (see ASSIFY)
ATIST (see ACES)

ATIVE

bailiff
basic
bracelet
dative
laic
native
stative

abrasive
archaic
bumbailiff
creative
debative
dilative
dissuasive
elative
evasive
favorite
frustrative
invasive
Judaic

mosaic
mutative
persuasive
pervasive
prosaic
rotative
translative

affidavit
agitative
algebraic
altercative
animative
calculative
circulative
cogitative
compensative
complicative
connotative
contemplative
copulative
cumulative
decorative
deprecative
designative
dominative
duplicative
educative
emanative
emulative
explicative
federative
friendship bracelet
generative
gubernative
hesitative
imitative
implicative
innovative
irrigative
irritative
iterative
judicative
lacerative
legislative
meditative
motivative
palliative
penetrative
procreative

qualitative
quantitative
recreative
regulative
segregative
simulative
speculative
stimulative
suffocative
terminative
uncreative
vegetative
ventilative

accelerative
accumulative
administrative
anticipative
appreciative
associative
authoritative
collaborative
commemorative
communicative
discriminative
elucidative
enumerative
exonerative
illuminative
incriminative
investigative
manipulative
opinionative
premeditative
recriminative
recuperative
remunerative
retaliative

Macaroni Mosaic

ATLAS (see ASHES)
ATLESS (see ASHES)
ATLY (see ALLEY)
ATNER (see ACKER)
ATNESS (see ASHES)
ATO 1 (see ADO 2)
ATO 2 (see OTTO 1)
ATOM (see ASM)
ATOMY (see ALITY)

ATOR

acre
ager
aider
aper
baiter
baker
blazer
bracer
braider
braiser
braver
breaker
caper
cater
chafer
chaser
chaster
crater
craver
dater
dazer
draper
facer
fader
faker
favor
fazer
flavor
Frazer
freighter
gaper
gator
gauger
gazer
glacier
glazer
grader
grater
graver
grazer
greater
hater
labor
lacer
Laker
laser
later
macer

major
maker
nature
neighbor
pacer
pager
paper
paster
paver
phaser
phraser
placer
praiser
quaker
quaver
racer
rager
raider
raiser
raker
raper
rater
raver
razor
saber
safer
sager
sapor
saver
savior
savor
Schaefer
scraper
shaker
shaper
shaver
skater
slater
slaver
spacer
stager
staker
stapler
stater
strafer
straighter
tabor
taker
taper
tapir

taster
tater
tracer
trader
traitor
vapor
wader
wafer
wager
waiter
waiver
waker
waster
waver

abaser
abater
amazer
appraiser
assuager
awaker
backbreaker
backstager
behaver
behavior
behaviour
belabor
blockader
blue blazer
bone-breaker
bookmaker
boy chaser
car racer
caretaker
castrator
charader
collator
creator
cremator
crepe paper
crusader
curator
Darth Vader
day labor
deal maker
debaser
debater
Decatur
defacer
deflator

degrader
dictator
dilator
disfavor
disgracer
displacer
dissuader
donator
drag racer
dreammaker
dressmaker
drum major
earthshaker
effacer
embracer
engager
engraver
enlacer
enrager
enslaver
equator
eraser
evader
face-saver
filmmaker
filtrator
find favor
fixator
flag-waver
flypaper
forsaker
freebaser
frustrater
fund-raiser
girl chaser
good nature
good neighbor
grubstaker
gyrator
hair-raiser
handshaker
hard labor
haymaker
headwaiter
heartbreaker
hell-raiser
homebreaker
homemaker
horseracer
ice breaker

ice skater	sedator	back to nature
icemaker	self-praiser	barricader
inflator	shoemaker	boilermaker
invader	skin bracer	cabinetmaker
jawbreaker	skirt chaser	calculator
lambaster	skygazer	call of nature
landscaper	skyscraper	captivator
lawbreaker	slave labor	celebrator
lawmaker	slave trader	census taker
lifesaver	spectator	circuit breaker
locator	stargazer	circulator
lovemaker	stock trader	coffeemaker
man chaser	straight razor	commentator
man hater	tailgater	compensator
mandator	tar paper	concentrator
matchmaker	teenager	confiscator
migrator	theater	congregator
misplacer	tiebreaker	conjugator
misshaper	timesaver	consecrator
muckraker	trailblazer	contemplator
mythmaker	translator	Corey Baker
narrator	unchaster	correlator
negator	unlacer	crystal gazer
newsmaker	updater	culminator
newspaper	upgrader	cultivator
noisemaker	upstager	decorator
notepaper	vibrator	dedicator
outpacer	wallpaper	defecator
outrager	watchmaker	dehydrator
pacemaker	white paper	delegator
parader	windbreaker	demonstrator
partaker	winemaker	deprecator
peacemaker	winetaster	desecrater
persuader		designator
place saver	abdicator	detonator
playmaker	abnegator	devastator
pulsator	acclimater	deviator
rampager	activator	disengager
remaker	actuator	dominator
repaver	adulator	doublespacer
replacer	advocator	duplicator
reshaper	agitator	educator
retracer	alligator	elevator
rice paper	allocator	emigrator
risk taker	animator	emulator
rotator	annotator	escalator
rule breaker	applicator	escapader
salt shaker	arbitrator	estimator
sandpaper	aspirator	excavator
scratch paper	aviator	explicator

extricator
fabricator
fascinator
fluctuator
formulator
fornicator
fumigator
funny papers
generator
gladiator
good behavior
gravitator
hesitater
hibernator
Hit Parader
human nature
illustrator
image maker
imitator
immigrator
implicator
impregnator
incubator
indicator
infiltrator
innovator
instigator
insulator
integrator
inundater
irrigator
irritator
isolator
Kelly Slater
lacerator
laminator
legislator
legislature
liberator
liquidator
litigator
lubricator
masquerader
masticator
masturbator
mediator
medicator
meditator
misbehaver
misbehavior

mischiefmaker
mitigator
moderator
modulator
moneymaker
Mother Nature
motivator
moviemaker
nauseator
navigator
next-door neighbor
nominator
numerator
obligator
operator
orchestrator
out of favor
overtaker
paraphraser
penetrator
pepper shaker
percolator
perforator
permeater
perpetrator
player hater
pollinator
postulator
predicator
procreator
promulgator
propagator
radiator
recreator
regulator
reinstater
relay racer
relegator
relocater
renovator
respirator
revelator
roller skater
safety razor
salivater
saturater
second nature
see you later
segregator
self-effacer

separator
serenader
simulator
speculator
stimulater
stipulator
Studebaker
subjugator
suffocater
syndicator
tabulator
terminator
titillater
toilet paper
tolerator
troublemaker
undertaker
vacillator
ventilator
vindicator
violator
walking papers
wild-goose chaser
woman chaser
woman hater

accelerator
accentuator
accommodator
accumulator
administrator
adulterator
affiliator
alienator
alleviator
ambulance chaser
amphitheater
annihilator
anticipator
appreciator
appropriator
articulator
asphyxiator
assassinator
associator
authenticator
collaborator
commiserator
communicator
conciliator

congratulator
consolidator
contaminator
cooperator
coordinator
corroborator
debilitator
decision-maker
defibrillator
deliberator
delineator
denominator
depreciator
discriminator
domesticator
drive-in theater
ejaculator
elaborator
eliminator
elucidator
emaciator
emancipator
equivocator
eradicator
evacuator
evaluator
evaporator
exacerbator
exaggerator
exhilarator
exterminator
extrapolator
facilitator
gesticulator
hallucinator
humiliator
illuminator
impersonator
incinerator
indoctrinator
infatuator
ingratiator
initiator
insinuator
interrogator
intimidator
intoxicator
invalidator
investigator
invigorator

manipulator
miscalculator
mover and shaker
necessitator
negotiator
officiator
orientator
participator
perpetuator
policymaker
pontificator
precipitator
prevaricator
procrastinator
prognosticator
proliferator
recaptivator
reciprocator
recuperator
refrigerator
regurgitator
reiterator
rejuvenator
repudiator
resuscitator
retaliator
reverberator
smooth operator
Suzy Homemaker
vanilla wafer
videotaper

ameliorator
Arnold Schwarzenegger
differentiator
discombobulator
hyperventilator
misappropriator
rehabilitator
reinvigorator

common denominator
telephone operator

elevator operator
interior decorator

ATRA 1 (see ADA 1)
ATRA 2 (see ASMA)
ATRED (see ADED)
ATRESS (see ASHES)

ATRIC (see ATIC 1)
ATRICK (see ATIC 1)
ATRIOT (see ANEOUS)
ATRIUM (see ANIUM)
ATRIX (see ACES)
ATRON (see ATION 1)
ATSBY (see ALLEY)
ATSCH (see ASH 2)
ATSCHY (see OCKEY)
ATSIES (see ADDIES)
ATSUN (see OTTEN)
ATSY (see ALLEY)
ATT (see OT)
ATTAGE (see OTIC)
ATTAN (see ATTEN)
ATTED 1 (see ATIC 1)
ATTED 2 (see OLID)

ATTEN

accent
Aspen
aspirin
batten
blacken
cabin
captain
chaplain
Chaplin
fasten
fatten
flatten
gallant
gladden
happen
hasn't
haven't
Jasmine
Kaplan
lapin
Latin
napkin
padden
pageant
patent
Patton
platen
raspin
sadden
satin

scadden
slacken
talent

Aladdin
Alaskan
assassin
combatant
imagine
John Madden
Manhattan
Nebraskan
pig latin
refasten
unfasten

Charlie Chaplin
Eric Clapton
Princess Jasmine

ATTENED (see ASTENED)
ATTENER (see ALENDAR)
ATTENING (see ABLISHING)
ATTER 1 (see ACKER)
ATTER 2 (see OLLAR)

ATTERED

badgered
bastard
battered
blabbered
captured
cavern
chaptered
chattered
clattered
dastard
factored
flattered
fractured
gathered
haggard
hazard
jabbered
laggard
lantern
lathered
mastered
mattered

mazzard
pastored
pattered
pattern
placard
plastered
Saturn
shattered
slattern
splattered
tattered
tavern
tractored

haphazard

Dukes of Hazzard
Hewlard Packard

ATTERING

badgering
blabbering
blathering
cadgering
capturing
chattering
clattering
factoring
flattering
fracturing
gathering
jabbering
lathering
mastering
mattering
pastoring
pattering
plastering
rapturing
shattering
slathering
smattering
splattering
staggering
swaggering

enrapturing
recapturing
regathering
unflattering
woolgathering

benefactoring
chiropractoring
manufacturing

ATTERN (see ATTERED)
ATTERY (see ALITY)
ATTEST (see ATIC 1)
ATTHEW (see ALUE)
ATTI (see OCKEY)
ATTIC (see ATIC 1)
ATTICA (see AFRICA)
ATTIER (see ABBIER)
ATTIES (see ADDIES)
ATTIEST (see AGGIEST)
ATTILY (see ALITY)
ATTINESS (see ABBINESS)
ATTING 1 (see ACKING)
ATTING 2 (see OCKING)
ATTLE (see ACKLE)
ATTLED (see ADDLED)
ATTLER (see ACKLER)
ATTLING (see ACKLING)
ATTO (see OTTO 1)
ATTON (see ATTEN)
ATTRESS (see ASHES)
ATTY 1 (see ALLEY)
ATTY 2 (see OCKEY)
ATUE (see ALUE)
ATULA (see AFRICA)
ATUM (see ATION 1)
ATUR (see ATOR)
ATURAL (see ACTABLE)

ATURALIZE

actualize
alphabetize
categorize
fractionalize
magicalize
nationalize
naturalize
practicalize
radicalize
rationalize

connaturalize
denationalize

denaturalize
disnaturalize
misalphabetize
unnaturalize

internationalize
supernaturalize

ATURALLY (see ATICALLY)
ATURATE (see ACERATE)
ATURE 1 (see ATOR)
ATURE 2 (see ACKER)
ATURED (see AVORED)
ATURN (see ATTERED)
ATUS 1 (see ATIC 1)
ATUS 2 (see ACES)
ATUTE (see ALUE)
ATZAH (see ADA 1)
AU (see OW 2)
AUB (see OD)
AUBLE (see OTTLE)
AUBLY (see OCKEY)
AUBREY (see OCKEY)
AUBURN (see OFFERED)
AUCE (see OFF)
AUCER (see OLLAR)
AUCET (see OCKET)
AUCH (see ASH 2)
AUCHER (see OVER 1)
AUCHERIES (see OLOGIES)
AUCHERY (see OMETRY)
AUCHING (see OCKING)
AUCIEST (see OGGIEST)
AUCILY (see OMETRY)
AUCINESS (see OCKINESS)
AUCITY (see OMETRY)
AUCOUS (see AWLESS)
AUCRACY (see OMETRY)
AUCTION (see OTTEN)
AUCUS (see AWLESS)
AUCY (see OCKEY)
AUD (see OD)
AUDABLE (see OGICAL)
AUDE 1 (see OWDY)
AUDE 2 (see OD)
AUDED (see OLID)
AUDER (see OLLAR)
AUDI (see OWDY)
AUDIA (see AFIA)

AUDIBLE (see OGICAL)
AUDIENCE (see OMINENCE)
AUDILY (see OMETRY)
AUDINESS (see OCKINESS)
AUDING (see ALLING)
AUDIO (see ARIO 2)
AUDIST (see OLISH)
AUDIT (see OCKET)
AUDITIVE (see OSITIVE)
AUDITOR (see OGRAPHER)
AUDREY (see OCKEY)
AUDRON (see ARTEN)
AUDRY (see OCKEY)
AUDY (see OCKEY)
AUER (see OWER 1)
AUFFEUR (see OVER 1)
AUGE (see ADE 1)
AUGER (see ATOR)
AUGH (see ASS 1)
AUGHABLE (see ACTABLE)
AUGHER (see ACKER)
AUGHERTY (see ORY)
AUGHING (see ACKING)
AUGHLIN (see OTTEN)
AUGHN (see ON 1)
AUGHT (see OT)
AUGHTER 1 (see OLLAR)
AUGHTER 2 (see ACKER)
AUGHTERED (see OFFERED)
AUGHTERING (see OTTERING)
AUGHTERLY (see OMETRY)
AUGHTFUL (see OTTLE)
AUGHTILY (see OMETRY)
AUGHTINESS (see OCKINESS)
AUGHTLY (see OCKEY)
AUGHTY (see OCKEY)
AUGING (see ATING)
AUGUR (see OLLAR)
AUGUST (see AWLESS)
AUI (see OWDY)
AUK (see OT)
AUKEE (see OCKEY)
AUL (see ALL 1)
AULA (see ADA 1)
AULAGE (see OTIC)
AULER (see OLLAR)
AULETTE (see OBJECT)
AULIC (see OTIC)
AULING (see ALLING)

AULK (see OT)
AULKING (see ALLING)
AULO (see OTTO 1)

AULT

bald
false
fault
halt
malt
salt
scald
schmaltz
solve
vault
waltz

absolve
asphalt
assault
at fault
bank vault
cobalt
default
dissolve
evolve
exalt
find fault
gestalt
gevalt
involve
no fault
pole-vault
resolve
revolve
rock salt

by default
double fault
earthquake fault
grain of salt
Morton Salt
pinch of salt
somersault
to a fault
true or false

Molly Ringwald

San Andreas Fault

aggravated assault

AULTED

Achmed
daunted
faulted
flaunted
halted
haunted
malted
salted
taunted
vaulted
wanted

assaulted
defaulted
exalted
gestalted
gevalted
help wanted
most wanted
pole-vaulted
undaunted

AULTER (see ALTER)
AULTING (see OCKING)
AULTY (see OCKEY)
AUM (see ON 1)
AUMA (see ONNA)
AUN (see ON 1)
AUNA (see ONNA)
AUNCH (see ONT 2)
AUNCHABLE (see OGICAL)
AUNCHES (see AWLESS)
AUNCHIER (see AWNIER)
AUNCHIEST (see OGGIEST)
AUNCHINESS (see AWNINESS)
AUNCHING (see ONNING)
AUNCHLY (see AWNY)
AUNCHNESS (see AWLESS)
AUNCHY (see AWNY)
AUNCIER (see AWNIER)
AUNCY (see AWNY)
AUNDER (see ONOR 1)

AUNDERING (see ANDERING 2)
AUNDRY (see AWNY)
AUNT 1 (see ONT 2)
AUNT 2 (see ANK)
AUNTABLE (see OGICAL)
AUNTED (see AULTED)
AUNTIE (see AWNY)
AUNTIER (see AWNIER)
AUNTIEST (see OGGIEST)
AUNTINESS (see AWNINESS)
AUNTING (see ONNING)
AUNTLET (see ONIC)
AUNTY 1 (see ANDY)
AUNTY 2 (see AWNY)
AUPE (see OAT)
AUPER (see OLLAR)
AUQUA (see ADA 1)
AUR (see ORE 1)
AURAL (see ORMAL)
AUREL (see ORMAL)
AURIE (see ORY)
AURUS (see ORIST)
AUS (see OFF)
AUSABLE (see OGICAL)
AUSAGE (see OTIC)
AUSAL (see OTTLE)
AUSATIVE (see OSITIVE)
AUSE (see OFF)
AUSEA (see AFIA)
AUSEOUS (see AWLESS)
AUSES (see AWLESS)
AUSIBLE (see OGICAL)
AUSING (see ALLING)
AUSS (see OUT)
AUSSIE (see OCKEY)
AUST 1 (see ASH 2)
AUST 2 (see OUT)
AUSTED (see OLID)
AUSTIBLE (see OGICAL)
AUSTIC (see OTIC)
AUSTIN (see OTTEN)
AUSTING (see OCKING)
AUSTRIA (see AFIA)
AUT 1 (see OT)
AUT 2 (see OUT)
AUTEN (see OTTEN)
AUTER (see OLLAR)
AUTEST (see OLISH)
AUTHOR (see OLLAR)
AUTHORED (see OFFERED)
AUTHORING (see OTTERING)
AUTIC (see OTIC)
AUTICAL (see OGICAL)

AUTION (see OTTEN)
AUTIOUS (see AWLESS)
AUTIOUSLY (see OMETRY)
AUTIST (see OUTEST)
AUTLY (see OCKEY)
AUTO (see OTTO 1)
AUTOMATE (see OPULATE)
AUTOMATION (see OPERA-
TION)
AUTRY (see OCKEY)
AUTUMN (see OTTEN)
AUVE (see OFF)
AUX (see OW 1)
AUZE (see OFF)
AUZER (see OWSER)
AUZY (see OCKEY)
AV (see OFF)
AVA (see ADA 1)
AVABLE (see ADABLE)
AVAGANT (see ASSIONATE)
AVAGE (see ATIC 1)
AVAL (see ABLE)
AVALRY (see ALITY)
AVARICE (see ALYSIS)
AVATE (see ACATE)

AVE 1

bathe
beige
blaze
braise
brave
cave
crave
craze
daze
fave
faze
gave
gaze
glaze
grave
graze
haze
knave
lathe
lave
laze
maze
nave

pave
phase
phrase
praise
raise
rave
raze
save
scathe
shave
slave
stave
they've
waive
wave

ablaze
airwave
amaze
appraise
behave
brainwave
buzzphrase
catch phrase
close shave
cold wave
concave
conclave
deprave
enclave
engrave
enslave
forgave
heat wave
malaise
new wave
repave
rephrase
self-praise
shockwave
shortwave
skygaze
soundwave
stargaze
sunbathe
trailbiaze
unfaze
upraise

aftershave
body wave
bouillabaise
coin a phrase
fingerwave
galley slave
hollandaise
lyonnaise
mayonnaise
microwave
misbehave
overpraise
paraphrase
rant and rave
reappraise
scrimp and save
tidal wave
underpraise

one foot in the grave

prepositional phrase
turn over in his grave

AVE 2 (see ASS 1)
AVEL 1 (see ACKLE)
AVEL 2 (see ABLE)
AVELED (see ADDLED)
AVELESS (see ACES)
AVELIN (see AFRICAN)
AVELING (see ABLISHING)
AVELY 1 (see ADY)
AVELY 2 (see OCKEY)
AVEMENT (see ATION 1)
AVEMENTS (see ATEMENTS)
AVEN (see ATION 1)
AVENDER (see ALENDAR)
AVENESS 1 (see ACES)
AVENESS 2 (see OLISH)
AVENGER (see ALENDAR)
AVENOUS (see ALYSIS)
AVENT (see ATTEN)
AVER 1 (see ATOR)
AVER 2 (see ACKER)
AVERAGE (see ALYSIS)
AVERAL (see ACTABLE)
AVERED (see AVORED)
AVERICK (see ALYSIS)
AVERING (see AVORING)
AVERLY (see AVERY)
AVERN (see ATTERED)

AVERY

avery
bakery
bravery
capably
crazily
drapery
fakery
flavory
hastily
hazily
knavery
lacily
lazily
mazily
napery
papery
quavery
racily
savory
slavery
tapery
vapory
wafery
Waverly
wavery

chicanery
depravery
mistakably
pro-slavery
sandpapery
unsavory

anti-slavery

AVEST (see ACES)
AVESTY (see ALITY)
AVIA (see ANIA)
AVIAL (see ADIAL)
AVIAN (see ANIUM)
AVIATE (see ATIATE)
AVIC (see OTIC)
AVID 1 (see ADED)
AVID 2 (see ATIC 1)
AVIDLY (see ALITY)
AVIER (see AKIER)
AVIES (see ADIES)
AVIEST (see ANEOUS)
AVIL (see ACKLE)

AVILA (see AFRICA)
AVIN (see ATION 1)
AVINESS (see AKINESS)
AVING 1 (see ATING)
AVING 2 (see ACKING)
AVINGLY (see AKINGLY)
AVIOR (see ATOR)
AVIS (see ACES)
AVISH (see ATIC 1)
AVISHING (see ABLISHING)
AVISHLY (see ALITY)
AVIT (see ATIVE)
AVITATE (see ACERATE)
AVITY (see ALITY)
AVO (see OTTO 1)
AVOC (see ATIC 1)
AVON (see AYON)
AVOR (see ATOR)

AVORED

capered
catered
cratered
favored
flavored
hayward
labored
layered
majored
natured
nayward
papered
quavered
savored
slavered
tabored
tailored
tapered
vapored
wafered
wagered
wavered
wayward

awayward
belabored
beslavered
denatured
disfavored

disnatured
repapered
sandpapered
tarpapered
unfavored
unlabored
unsavored
wallpapered

deminatured
multilayered
overlabored

AVORFUL (see ATABLE 1)

AVORING

capering
catering
favoring
flavoring
laboring
majoring
neighboring
papering
quavering
razoring
savoring
tailoring
tapering
trailering
wagering
waitering
wavering

belaboring
disfavoring
unwavering
wallpapering

AVORITE (see ATIVE)
AVORY (see AVERY)
AVUM (see ATION 1)
AVVIER (see ABBIER)
AVVY (see ALLEY)
AVY (see ADY)

AW

aw
awe
caw
chaw
claw
craw
daw
draw
flaw
gnaw
jaw
law
naw
paw
pshaw
raw
saw
Shaw
slaw
straw
taw
thaw

bear claw
buzz saw
by-law
case law
cat's-paw
chainsaw
Choctaw
coleslaw
Crenshaw
foresaw
gewgaw
glass jaw
guffaw
hacksaw
hawkshaw
hee-haw
in awe
in-law
jackdaw
jigsaw
last straw
leash law
lockjaw
lynch law
macaw

old saw
outdraw
outlaw
quickdraw
rickshaw
ripsaw
scrimshaw
seesaw
southpaw
state law
Warsaw
withdraw

Arkansas
canon law
Chickasaw
civil law
common law
coup d'etat
court of law
five-card draw
Jabberjaw
lower jaw
Mackinac
martial law
Murphy's Law
overawe
overdraw
oversaw
power saw
sunshine law

above the law
brother-in-law
father-in-law
federal law
lay down the law
luck of the draw
mother-in-law
Quick Draw McGraw
quick on the draw
sister-in-law
unwritten law

attorney-at-law
letter of the law
long arm of the law

AWA (see ADA 1)
AWCETT (see OCKET)
AWDILY (see OMETRY)

AWDINESS (see OCKINESS)
AWDLE (see OTTLE)
AWDLER (see OBBLER)
AWDLING (see OBBLING)
AWDRY (see OCKEY)
AWDUST (see OLISH)
AWDY (see OCKEY)
AWE (see AW)
AWELESS (see AWLESS)
AWER (see ORE 1)
AWESOME (see OTTEN)
AWESOMELY (see OMETRY)
AWFISH (see AWLESS)
AWFORD (see OFFERED)
AWFUL (see OTTLE)
AWFULLY (see OCKEY)
AWG (see OD)

AWING

aahing
awing
bahing
cawing
chawing
clawing
drawing
gnawing
jawing
pawing
pshawing
sawing
thawing

guffawing
hee-hawing
hurrahing
oompahing
outdrawing
outlawing
seesawing
withdrawing

overawing
overdrawing

AWK (see OT)
AWKABLE (see OGICAL)
AWKER (see OLLAR)
AWKILY (see OMETRY)

AWKINESS (see OCKINESS)
AWKING (see OCKING)
AWKISH (see AWLESS)
AWKWARD (see OFFERED)
AWKWARDLY (see OMETRY)
AWKY (see OCKEY)
AWL (see ALL 1)
AWLER (see OLLAR)

AWLESS

August
aweless
Bacchus
braless
calmest
calmness
caucus
causes
cautious
clauses
clawless
coccus
crawfish
doggish
flawless
gawkish
haunches
hawkish
hoggish
jawless
launches
lawless
nauseous
noxious
office
offish
palmist
paunches
pauses
pawless
raucous
rawness
shockus
softness
solace
songstress
spoffish
staunchness
Wallace

Caracas
Cornwallis
incautious
innoxious
lost causes
maracas
obnoxious
Post Office
standoffish

common clauses
escape clauses
overcautious
unobnoxious

grandfather clauses
probable causes

political caucus

AWLING (see ALLING)
AWLY (see OLLY 1)
AWN (see ON 1)
AWNABLE (see OGICAL)
AWNER (see ONOR 1)
AWNESS (see AWLESS)
AWNEST (see OLISH)

AWNIER

brawnier
dauncier
fawnier
flauntier
jauntier
paunchier
raunchier
sauncier
scrawnier
swampier
tawnier
wonkier

AWNINESS

brawniness
jauntiness
paunchiness
raunchiness

scrawniness
swampiness
tawniness

AWNING (see ONNING)

AWNY

auntie
balmy
blondie
bondly
Bonnie
bonny
brawny
calmly
calmy
Chauncy
commie
Connie
donkey
fawny
fondly
jaunty
Johnny
konky
laundry
mommy
Monte
palmy
paunchy
promptly
qualmy
quandary
raunchy
scrawny
staunchly
strongly
swami
swampy
tawny
Tommy
wrongly
zombie

Ashanti
Chianti
ophthalmy
pastrami
salami

tatami
tsunami

Abercrombie
exophthalmy
Giovanni
honky-tonky
in a quandary
microphthalmy
origami
xerophthalmy

Asti Spumante

pin the tail on the donkey

AWRENCE (see ORTANCE)
AWYER (see ORDER)

AX

apse
asp
ax
axe
clasp
fax
gasp
grasp
hasp
lapse
lax
Max
rasp
sax
tax
wax

Ajax
beeswax
chillax
climax
collapse
earwax
elapse
Ex-Lax
floorwax
hand clasp
last gasp
Mad Max

perhaps	**AY**	amscray
pickax		archway
poll tax	A	array
relapse	bae	ashtray
relax	bay	astray
sales tax	bray	at bay
surtax	clay	away
syntax	day	aweigh
thorax	fay	b-day
time lapse	Faye	backpay
unclasp	fray	ballet
	gay	beret
battle-ax	gray	betray
candle wax	grey	bidet
city tax	hay	birthday
income tax	hey	blasé
moustache wax	J	bluejay
overtax	jay	Bombay
parallax	K	bouquet
sealing wax	Kay	breath spray
to the max	lay	breezeway
	lei	Broadway
memory lapse	Mae	cachet
mind your beeswax	May	café
property tax	nay	Camay
withholding tax	neigh	causeway
	pay	chalet
inheritance tax	play	child's play
	pray	cliché
AXABLE (see ACTABLE)	prey	convey
AXATIVE (see ALYSIS)	ray	crochet
AXE (see AX)	say	croquet
AXEN (see ACTION)	Shea	decay
AXER (see ACKER)	slay	deejay
AXI (see ALLEY)	sleigh	defray
AXIE (see ALLEY)	spay	delay
AXIING (see ALLYING)	spray	dismay
AXIM (see ASM)	stay	display
AXIMA (see AFRICA)	stray	doomsday
AXIMIZE (see ANDALIZE)	sway	doorway
AXINESS (see ABBINESS)	they	downplay
AXING (see ACKING)	tray	driveway
AXIS (see ASHES)	way	essay
AXLE (see ACKLE)	weigh	fair play
AXLED (see ADDLED)	whey	fairway
AXLESS (see ASHES)	yea	feng shui
AXLY (see ALLEY)		field day
AXNESS (see ASHES)		filet
AXON (see ACTION)	affray	foreplay
AXTER (see ACKER)	all-day	foul play
AXY (see ALLEY)	allay	

frappé
freeway
Friday
gainsay
gangway
gateway
give way
glacé
gourmet
Green Bay
gunplay
hair spray
halfway
hallway
headway
hearsay
heyday
highway
hooray
horseplay
ice tray
inlay
inveigh
leeway
long-play
mainstay
make way
Mayday
melee
midday
Midway
mislay
misplay
Monday
Monet
my way
nae nae
no way
Norway
obey
olé
one-way
outlay
outré
outweigh
parfait
parlay
parquet
passé
pathway

payday
Pelé
per se
Pompeii
portray
prepay
puree
purvey
raceway
railway
relay
repay
replay
risqué
roadway
role-play
runway
sachet
sashay
sauté
screenplay
segue
sick pay
soiree
someway
soufflé
stairway
stingray
subway
sundae
Sunday
survey
Taipei
Thursday
today
touché
toupee
Tuesday
two-way
valet
veejay
walkway
waylay
Wednesday
weekday
wordplay
workday
x-ray

A-OK
all the way
alleyway
attaché
blow away
blue Monday
break of day
breakaway
by the way
cabaret
castaway
Chevrolet
chipotle
Christmas Day
CIA
come what may
cosmic ray
CPA
créme brulée
cutaway
day by day
day-to-day
die away
disarray
disobey
divorcée
DNA
DOA
double play
Dr. Dre
easy way
entranceway
every way
everyday
exposé
expressway
fadeaway
faraway
Father's Day
fire away
gamma ray
getaway
giveaway
go away
Hemingway
here to stay
hideaway
hit the hay
holiday
in the way

interplay
IRA
Judgment Day
Kid 'n' Play
Labor Day
lackaday
latter-day
layaway
lead astray
lead the way
lingerie
lump of clay
M.I.A.
macramé
Mandalay
Marvin Gaye
matinee
Milky Way
modern-day
Monterey
Mother's Day
nasal spray
NBA
negligee
New Year's Day
night and day
off Broadway
on display
only way
out of play
pass away
passageway
pave the way
play-by-play
popinjay
power play
present-day
PTA
résumé
ricochet
right away
right-of-way
RNA
runaway
San Jose
Santa Fe
Saturday
silver tray
straightaway
take-away

thataway
time of day
tooth decay
touchdown play
Triple A
triple play
underplay
underway
USA
vajayjay
walkaway
waste away
waterway
wedding day
yea or nay
yesterday

anchors away
any which way
April Fools' Day
born yesterday
bridal bouquet
cabriolet
café au lait
call it a day
carried away
catch of the day
children at play
day after day
dead giveaway
deodorant spray
Dr. Bombay
Dylan McKay
every which way
far and away
Freaky Friday
games people play
go all the way
happy birthday
hot-fudge sundae
in a bad way
in the worst way
instant replay
late in the day
Lazy Sunday
LL Cool J
out of the way
overtime pay
papier-maché
roll in the hay

rub the wrong way
St. Patrick's Day
UCLA
vitamin A
water ballet
YMCA

American way
be that as it may
Billie Holiday
go out of your way
look the other way
TWA
up up and away

any given Sunday

AYA 1 (see ASIA)
AYA 2 (see IAH)
AYABLE (see ADABLE)
AYAL (see ABLE)
AYBE (see ADY)
AYE (see AY)
AYER (see AILER)
AYERED (see AVORED)
AYFUL (see ABLE)
AYHEM (see ATION 1)
AYLA (see ASIA)
AYLOR (see AILER)
AYMAN (see ATION 1)
AYMATE (see ACATE)
AYMEN (see ATION 1)
AYMENT (see ATION 1)
AYMENTS (see ATEMENTS)
AYNE (see AIN 1)
AYO 1 (see ADO 2)

AYOFF

Adolph
caos
layoff
payoff
playoff

AYON

Avon
capon

crayon
radon
rayon

liaison
portcrayon

AYOR (see AILER)
AYS (see ESS)
AYSIA (see ASIA)
AYTON (see ATION 1)
AYWARD (see AVORED)
AYZ (see ADY)
AZ (see ASS 1)
AZA (see ADA 1)
AZARD (see ATTERED)
AZARDOUS (see ALYSIS)
AZDA (see ADA 1)
AZE 1 (see AVE 1)
AZE 2 (see OCKEY)
AZEABLE (see ADABLE)
AZEFUL (see ABLE)
AZEL (see ABLE)
AZEMENT (see ATION 1)
AZEN (see ATION 1)
AZER (see ATOR)
AZES (see ACES)
AZEY (see ADY)
AZI 1 (see OCKEY)
AZI 2 (see OCKEY)
AZIER (see AKIER)
AZIES (see ADIES)
AZIEST (see ANEOUS)
AZILY (see AVERY)
AZINESS (see AKINESS)
AZING (see ATING)
AZINGLY (see AKINGLY)
AZON (see ATION 1)
AZOR (see ATOR)
AZORING (see AVORING)
AZS (see OFF)
AZY (see ADY)
AZZ (see ASS 1)
AZZA (see ADA 1)
AZZARD (see ATTERED)
AZZER (see ACKER)
AZZES (see ASHES)
AZZI (see OCKEY)
AZZIER (see ABBIER)
AZZIEST (see AGGIEST)
AZZILY (see ALITY)
AZZINESS (see ABBINESS)

AZZING (see ACKING)
AZZLE (see ACKLE)
AZZLED (see ADDLED)
AZZLING (see ACKING)
AZZO (see OTTO 1)
AZZY (see ALLEY)

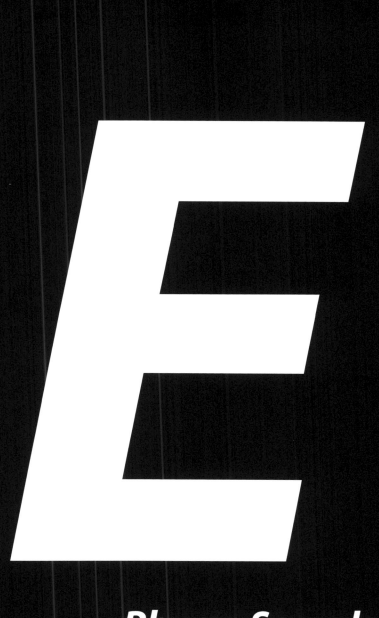

Rhyme Sounds

E 1

B
be
bee
C
D
E
fee
flea
flee
free
gee
glee
he
key
knee
lea
Lee
me
mi
oui
pea
pee
plea
sea
see
she
si
ski
spree
tea
tee
thee
three
ti
tree
vee
we
wee
whee
ye

A.D.
A.P.
agree
at sea
B.C.
Bruce Lee
Capri

card-key
carefree
CB
Chablis
Chee-Chee
chick-pea
D.C.
Dead Sea
debris
decree
deep-sea
degree
Dundee
emcee
feel free
foresee
goatee
Grand Prix
he-she
Hi-C
home free
look-see
low-key
M. D.
Marie
marquee
marquis
MP
must-see
off-key
oui, oui
P. E.
PC
peewee
queen bee
Red Sea
rent-free
RV
salt-free
scot-free
sightsee
stud fee
sweet pea
tab key
tax-free
TB
TD
tehee
three-D
toll-free

TP
turnkey
TV
VP
wee wee
would-be

ABC
abductee
absentee
addressee
amputee
apogee
assignee
attendee
awardee
BBC
blackeyed pea
BLT
bumblebee
busy bee
C.O.D.
c'est la vie
Cherokee
chickadee
Christmas tree
cop a plea
cup of tea
DDT
departee
devotee
disagree
DMV
do re mi
dungaree
duty-free
employee
escapee
excuse me
F.O.B.
fancy free
FCC
finder's fee
first-degree
fricassee
GOP
herbal tea
honeybee
honoree
if need be

jamboree
jubilee
let it be
licensee
LSD
minor key
MIT
money tree
Mr. T
MSG
MTV
MVP
NBC
nominee
OMG
oversee
pardon me
PCP
pedigree
Ph.D.
potpourri
R.I.P.
referee
refugee
repartee
Rosemarie
Sara Lee
shivaree
shopping spree
so help me
spelling bee
sugar-free
Tennessee
third-degree
Twiddledee
undersea
up a tree
USC
used to be
user's fee
VIP
Waikiki
water ski
worker bee
worry-free
XYZ

admission fee
ASAP
AT&T

bon appetit
BYOB
Chef Boyardee
college degree
consent decree
evacuee
family tree
General Lee
land of the free
long time no see
maintenance fee
master's degree
ROTC
RSVP
Run D.M.C.
Run DMC
to a degree
vitamin B
VSOP
your cup of tea

between you and me
chicken fricassee
Chicken of The Sea
Crocodile Dundee
Donny and Marie
repeat after me
under lock and key
Washington, D.C.

agree to disagree
easy as ABC
moneyback guarantee
NAACP
you ain't the boss of me

E 2 (see AY)
E 3 (see UH)
E'LL (see EAL 1)
E'RE (see EAR 1)
E'VE (see EED 1)
EA 1 (see E 1)
EA 2 (see IA)
EA 3 (see AY)
EACABLE (see IEVABLE)
EACE (see EAT 1)
EACEFUL (see EGAL)
EACH (see EAT 1)
EACHABLE (see IEVABLE)
EACHABLY (see EITY)
EACHER (see EATER 1)

EACHIER (see EEDIER)
EACHIEST (see EAKIEST)
EACHING (see EATING 1)
EACHMENT (see EQUENT)
EACHY (see EASY)
EACON (see ESIAN)
EACONING (see EASONING)

EAD 1

wed
bed
beg
Bev
bled
bread
bred
Craig
dead
deb
dread
dredge
dreg
ebb
Ed
edge
egg
fed
fled
fledge
Greg
head
hedge
kedge
keg
lead
led
ledge
leg
med
Meg
neb
Ned
peg
pled
pledge
read
reb
red
rev

said
sedge
shed
shred
sled
sledge
sped
spread
stead
Ted
thread
tread
veg
web
wedge
zed

abed
ahead
airhead
allege
bald head
beachhead
bedspread
beer keg
behead
big head
Big Red
blackhead
blockhead
bloodshed
bobsled
boiled egg
bonehead
bootleg
break bread
bulkhead
bum leg
bunkbed
car bed
celeb
Club Med
co-ed
cobweb
cokehead
corn bread
cornfed
cowshed
daybed

deadhead
deathbed
dog sled
dopehead
drop dead
egghead
embed
fathead
flatbed
forehead
French bread
goose egg
hard-edge
hardhead
highbred
homestead
hot head
hotbed
ill-bred
inbred
instead
jughead
knife edge
lunkhead
meth head
misread
moosehead
moped
nest egg
on edge
Op-Ed
outspread
pegleg
pinhead
point spread
pothead
premed
proofread
purebred
redhead
retread
rewed
see red
shortbread
sickbed
skinhead
spearhead
spoonfed
stone dead
straightedge

sweetbread
swellhead
unread
unsaid
unwed
warhead
well-bred
well-fed
well-read
widespread
wingspread
woodshed

acid-head
arrowhead
baby bed
bottlefed
break a leg
Charlotte's Web
city-bred
copperhead
country-bred
cutting edge
daily bread
Diamond Head
Easter egg
empty head
featherbed
figurehead
flower bed
fountainhead
garlic bread
gingerbread
go ahead
Grateful Dead
hammerhead
in the red
infrared
keep your head
king-sized bed
knock 'em dead
knucklehead
lay an egg
leading edge
letterhead
lose your head
maidenhead
Mr. Ed
newlywed
on the edge

overfed
overhead
powder keg
pull your leg
razor's edge
riverbed
scrambled egg
shake a leg
sleepyhead
sneakerhead
soft-boiled egg
sortilege
sourdough bread
straight-ahead
Sudafed
thoroughbred
underfed
use your head
waterbed
watershed
window ledge
Winnipeg
Wonder Bread
wooden leg

Dawn of the Dead
early to bed
full speed ahead
go to your head
hole in the head
hospital bed
over the edge
over your head
paint the town red
Radiohead
that's what she said
turn someone's head

in over your head
Sweet polly purebred
wrong side of the bed

cost an arm and a leg
hit the nail on the head
Mr. Potato Head
Mrs. Potato Head
off the top of the head

EAD 2 (see EED 1)
EADABLE (see IEVABLE)
EADABLY (see EITY)

EADED 1

bedded
breaded
dreaded
fetid
fretted
headed
jetted
netted
petted
shedded
shredded
sledded
sweated
threaded
wedded
wetted
whetted

abetted
airheaded
beheaded
bigheaded
bullheaded
embedded
hard-headed
homesteaded
hot-headed
indebted
lightheaded
regretted
retreaded
spearheaded
subletted
unleaded

bayonetted
levelheaded
pirouetted
silhouetted

EADED 2 (see EASTED 1)
EADEN (see ESSION)
EADER 1 (see EATER 1)
EADER 2 (see ECTOR)
EADFUL (see EVEL)
EADFULLY (see ETICALLY)
EADIER (see EEDIER)
EADIEST (see EAKIEST)
EADILY (see ETICALLY)

EADINESS (see EAKINESS)
EADING 1 (see ESSING)
EADING 2 (see EEDING)
EADLE (see EVEL)
EADLESS (see ECTLESS)
EADLIER (see EDGIER)
EADLY (see ELLY)
EADNESS (see ECTLESS)
EADOW (see ELLO)
EADTH (see ESS)
EADY 1 (see ELLY)
EADY 2 (see EASY)
EAF 1 (see EAT 1)
EAF 2 (see ESS)
EAFEN (see ESSION)
EAFENING (see EDITING)
EAFER (see ECTOR)
EAFIEST (see EAKIEST)
EAFING (see EATING 1)
EAFLESS (see ESIS)
EAFLY (see ELLY)
EAFY (see EASY)
EAGER (see EATER 1)
EAGLE (see EGAL)
EAGUE (see EED 1)
EAGUER (see EATER 1)
EAGUING (see EATING 1)
EAGULL (see EGAL)
EAH (see ARE 1)
EAK 1 (see EAT 1)
EAK 2 (see ACE 1)
EAKABLE (see IEVABLE)
EAKABLY (see EITY)
EAKE (see EAT 1)
EAKEN (see ESIAN)
EAKENING (see EASONING)
EAKER (see EATER 1)
EAKEST (see EANEST)
EAKFAST (see ETIC)
EAKIER (see EEDIER)

EAKIEST

beachiest
beadiest
beakiest
beastliest
beechiest
beefiest
breeziest
cheekiest

creakiest
creamiest
creepiest
dreamiest
easiest
freakiest
gleamiest
greasiest
greediest
leachiest
leafiest
leakiest
measliest
meatiest
neediest
peachiest
peakiest
peatiest
preachiest
queasiest
reediest
screechiest
seamiest
seediest
sleepiest
sleetiest
sneakiest
sneeziest
speediest
squeakiest
steamiest
streakiest
streamiest
tedious
teensiest
tweakiest
tweediest
weediest
weensiest
weepiest
wheeziest

tragedious
uneasiest

allogeneous
extrageneous
homogeneous
intermedious
overtedious

heterogeneous
nonhomogeneous

EAKINESS

beadiness
beefiness
breeziness
cheekiness
clinginess
creakiness
creepiness
easiness
freakiness
geekiness
greediness
leakiness
meatiness
neediness
queasiness
seediness
sleepiness
sneakiness
speediness
squeakiness
stinkiness
weepiness
wheeziness

uneasiness

EAKING (see EATING 1)
EAKLING (see EATING 1)
EAKLY (see EASY)
EAKNESS (see ESIS)
EAKS (see EAT 1)
EAKY (see EASY)

EAL 1

deal
eel
feel
field
he'll
heal
heel
kneel
meal

peel
real
reel
seal
she'll
shield
squeal
steal
steel
teal
veal
we'll
wheel
wield
yield
zeal

afield
airfield
appeal
backfield
big deal
big wheel
Camille
cartwheel
conceal
cornfield
cornmeal
fair deal
fifth wheel
for real
four-wheel
freewheel
Garfield
genteel
good deal
high heel
ideal
infield
midfield
minefield
misdeal
New Deal
newsreel
O'Neill
oatmeal
ordeal
outfield
raw deal
redeal

repeal
reseal
reveal
Springfield
square meal
surreal
unreal
unseal
windshield

at the wheel
Bakersfield
balance wheel
battlefield
bookmobile
camomile
Christmas seal
cop a feel
cut a deal
dirty deal
double-deal
eye appeal
Ferris wheel
glockenspiel
Happy Meal
lemon peel
Marshall Field
movie reel
no big deal
Oldsmobile
package deal
paddlewheel
pimpmobile
play the field
sex appeal
snowmobile
spinning wheel
stainless steel
steering wheel
wagonwheel
wheel and deal

Achilles' heel
automobile
official seal
Quaker Oatmeal
Tatum O'neal

Captain and Tennille
real recognize real

Love is a Battlefield

EAL 2 (see ALL 1)
EALABLE (see IEVABLE)

EALER

dealer
feeler
fielder
healer
kneeler
pealer
peeler
realer
reeler
sealer
shielder
spieler
squealer
stealer
steeler
wheeler
wielder
yielder

appealer
brickfielder
concealer
faith healer
freewheeler
infielder
misdealer
outfielder
paint sealer
repealer
revealer
scene-stealer
two-wheeler

used-car dealer
wheeler-dealer

EALEST (see EANEST)

EALING

ceiling
dealing
feeling
healing

kneeling
pealing
peeling
reeling
sealing
squealing
stealing
steeling
wheeling

appealing
cartwheeling
concealing
Darjeeling
freewheeling
gut feeling
misdealing
redealing
repealing
resealing
revealing

dirty dealing
double-dealing
hit the ceiling
sinking feeling

once more with feeling
wheeling and dealing

EALIST (see EANEST)
EALLY (see EASY)
EALM (see ELT)
EALMS (see ELVES)
EALOT (see ELFISH)

EALOUS

beverage
jealous
lettuce
leverage
message
precious
premise
presage
severage
vestige
zealous

miszealous
nonprecious
unzealous

get the message
overjealous
overzealous
semiprecious

EALOUSY (see ETICALLY)
EALT (see ELT)
EALTH (see ELT)
EALTHY (see ELLY)
EALTY (see ILKY)
EALY (see EASY)
EAM (see EEN 1)
EAMAN (see ESIAN)
EAMER (see EATER 1)
EAMIEST (see EAKIEST)

EAMING

beaming
beaning
breaming
cleaning
creaming
deeming
dreaming
evening
gleaming
gleaning
greening
leaning
meaning
preening
reaming
scheming
screaming
screening
seaming
seeming
steaming
streaming
teaming
teeming
weaning

blaspheming
careening

convening
daydreaming
demeaning
dry-cleaning
mainstreaming
pipedreaming
recleaning
redeeming
well-meaning

contravening
intervening
reconvening

EAMINGLY

beamingly
creepingly
dreamingly
leapingly
pleasingly
screamingly
seemingly
seethingly
sweepingly
teasingly
weepingly

beseechingly
decreasingly
exceedingly
increasingly
unceasingly

overweeningly

EAMISH (see ESIS)
EAMLESS (see ESIS)
EAMSTRESS (see EANEST)
EAMT (see ENT)
EAMY (see EASY)
EAN 1 (see EATEN 1)
EAN 2 (see EEN 1)
EANER (see EATER 1)

EANEST

bleakest
cheapest

chicest
cleanest
deepest
deist
elix
Felix
freest
greenest
helix
keenest
leanest
meanest
meekest
Phoenix
premix
realest
realist
remix
seamstress
secret
sleekest
steepest
theist
weakest

amnesics
anthelix
collegiate
extremist
hygeist
hygienist
idealist
kinesics
machinist
nonsecret
obscenest
serenest
strategic
surrealist
tritheist
unsecret
vaccinist

analgesics
antihelix
antitheist
autotheist
double helix
geodesics
hylotheist
magazinist

Manicheist
monotheist
paraplegic
polytheist
quadriplegic
supersecret
trampolinist

antivaccinist
intercollegiate

Victoria Secret

EANIE (see EASY)
EANING (see EAMING)
EANLY (see EASY)
EANNESS (see ESIS)
EANNIE (see EASY)
EANOR (see EATER 1)
EANSE (see ENCH)
EANSER (see ENDER)
EANSING (see ENDING)
EANT (see ENT)
EANY (see EASY)
EAP (see EAT 1)
EAPEN (see ESIAN)
EAPENING (see EASONING)
EAPER (see EATER 1)
EAPEST (see EANEST)
EAPIE (see EASY)
EAPING (see EATING 1)
EAPINGLY (see EAMINGLY)
EAPLY (see EASY)
EAPO (see IO 1)
EAPON (see ESSION)
EAPONING (see EDITING)
EAPT (see ET 1)

EAR 1

beer
blear
cheer
clear
dear
deer
drear
ear
fear
gear

hear
here
jeer
leer
mere
near
peer
pier
queer
rear
schmear
sear
seer
shear
sheer
smear
sneer
spear
sphere
steer
tear
tier
veer
we're
year

adhere
all clear
appear
arrear
brassiere
career
cashier
cashmere
cohere
dog-ear
draft beer
emir
endear
fakir
first gear
frontier
headgear
high gear
inhere
King Lear
last year
leap year
light-year
mid-year

near beer
new year
next year
Pam Grier
Pap smear
pierced ear
premier
reindeer
revere
root beer
severe
Shakespeare
sincere
steer clear
stripped gear
tin ear
unclear
veneer
Zaire

atmosphere
auctioneer
bombardier
boutonniere
brigadier
buccaneer
cavalier
chandelier
coast is clear
commandeer
crystal-clear
disappear
domineer
ear-to-ear
engineer
far and near
financier
free and clear
gadgeteer
ginger beer
hemisphere
in the clear
inner ear
insincere
interfere
landing gear
lend an ear
loud and clear
lunar year
mountaineer

mouseketeer
musketeer
mutineer
never fear
nowhere near
out of fear
overhear
overseer
Paul Revere
peer-to-peer
persevere
pioneer
play by ear
profiteer
racketeer
reappear
Richard Gere
souvenir
stratosphere
to the rear
volunteer
world premier
yesteryear

bring up the rear
calendar year
election year
Happy New Year

academic year
blow it out your ear
cauliflower ear

A&W Root Beer

EAR 2 (see ARE 1)
EARANCE (see ERENCE)
EARCH (see IRST)
EARCHER (see URNER)
EARCHING (see ERTING)
EARD 1 (see ORD 2)
EARD 2 (see EARED)
EARDLESS (see EARLESS)
EARE (see EAR 1)

EARED

beard
cheered
cleared

eared
feared
geared
jeered
leered
neared
peered
reared
seared
sheared
smeared
sneered
speared
steered
teared
tiered
veered
weird

adhered
appeared
besmeared
Blackbeard
Bluebeard
cashiered
dog-eared
endeared
graybeard
inhered
premiered
revered
two-tiered
uncleared
veneered

disappeared
domineered
engineered
interfered
persevered
pioneered
racketeered
reappeared
volunteered

EARER

cheerer
clearer

dearer
drearer
fearer
gearer
hearer
jeerer
leerer
nearer
queerer
rearer
searer
shearer
sheerer
smearer
sneerer
spearer
steerer

adherer
appearer
coherer
reverer
severer
sincerer
unclearer

insincerer
interferer
overhearer

EAREST

clearest
dearest
fiercest
nearest
queerest
sheerest
weirdest

severest
sincerest

Mommy Dearest

EARFUL

cheerful

earful
fearful
jeerful
sneerful
tearful

unfearful

EARIER (see ERIOR)

EARINESS

bleariness
cheeriness
dreariness
eeriness
leeriness
teariness
weariness

EARING (see EERING)
EARISH (see ARENESS)
EARL (see IRL)

EARLESS

beardless
cheerless
clearness
dearness
fearless
fierceness
peerless
queerness
sheerness
spearless
tearless
weirdness

brassiereless
careerless
severeness
sincereness

EARLIER (see URLIER)
EARLY 1 (see EARY)
EARLY 2 (see IRTY)
EARN (see URN)
EARNER (see URNER)

EARNESS (see EARLESS)
EARNEST (see ERVICE)
EARNING (see ERTING)
EARNT (see ORK 1)
EARP (see ORK 1)
EARRING (see EERING)
EARSABLE (see URTABLE)
EARSAL (see URTLE)
EARSE (see IRST)
EARSING (see ERTING)
EARST (see IRST)
EARTH (see IRST)
EARTHING (see ERTING)
EARTHLY (see IRTY)
EARTLESS (see ARNISH)

EARY

bleary
cheery
clearly
Cleary
dearly
dreary
eerie
fiercely
jeery
leery
merely
nearly
queerly
query
Siri
smeary
sneery
teary
theory
weary
yearly

severely
sincerely
unclearly
war-weary

big bang theory
cavalierly
Einstein's theory
hara-kiri
insincerely

trickle-down theory

EAS (see EED 1)
EASABLE 1 (see IEVABLE)
EASABLE 2 (see IEVABLE)
EASANT (see ESCENT)
EASE 1 (see EAT 1)
EASE 2 (see EED 1)
EASEL (see EGAL)
EASEMENT (see EQUENT)
EASER (see EATER 1)
EASH (see EAT 1)
EASHING (see EATING 1)
EASIBLE (see IEVABLE)
EASIBLY (see EITY)
EASIER (see EEDIER)
EASIEST (see EAKIEST)
EASILY (see EITY)
EASINESS (see EAKINESS)
EASING 1 (see EATING 1)
EASING 2 (see EATING 1)
EASINGLY 1 (see EAMINGLY)
EASINGLY 2 (see EAMINGLY)
EASIVE (see ESIS)
EASLEY (see EASY)
EASLIEST (see EAKIEST)
EASLY (see EASY)
EASON (see ESIAN)
EASONAL (see IEVABLE)

EASONING

beaconing
cheapening
deepening
reasoning
seasoning
steepening
sweetening
weakening

outreasoning
unreasoning

EAST 1 (see EAT 1)
EAST 2 (see ESS)

EASTED 1

beaded
ceded
cheated
deeded

feasted
greeted
heated
heeded
kneaded
needed
pleaded
pleated
seated
seeded
sleeted
treated
tweeted
weeded

acceded
competed
completed
conceded
conceited
deepseated
defeated
deleted
depleted
entreated
exceeded
excreted
impeded
maltreated
mistreated
preceded
proceeded
receded
reheated
repeated
reseated
reseeded
retreated
seceded
secreted
stampeded
steam-heated
succeeded
unseated

anteceded
incompleted
interceded
overheated
superseded
trick-or-treated

EASTED 2 (see ECTED)
EASTER (see EATER 1)
EASTIES (see EATIES)
EASTING (see EATING 1)
EASTLIEST (see EAKIEST)
EASURABLE (see EPARABLE)
EASURE (see ECTOR)
EASUREMENT (see ELEGANT)

EASURER

fetterer
gesturer
measurer
pepperer
pleasurer
treasurer

admeasurer
archtreasurer
subtreasurer

undertreasurer

EASURING (see ESTERING)
EASURY (see ETICALLY)

EASY

beady
beamy
beanie
beefy
bleakly
blini
breezy
briefly
cheapie
cheaply
cheeky
cheesy
chiefly
cleanly
creaky
creamy
creepy
deeply
dreamy
easy

eensy
eeny
Fifi
Fiji
fleety
freaky
freebie
freely
geeky
genie
Gigi
gleamy
greedy
greenly
ichi
Jeanie
keenly
kiwi
leafy
leaky
meany
measly
meaty
meekly
Mimi
neatly
needy
ouija
peachy
peaty
Peavey
PG
Phoebe
preachy
preemie
queasy
queenie
queenly
really
reedy
screamy
screechy
Sealy
seamy
seedy
seemly
seepy
sheenly
sleazy
sleekly

sleepy
sneaky
sneezy
specie
speedy
squeaky
squeegee
steamy
steely
steeply
Stevie
streaky
sweetie
sweetly
teensy
teeny
tepee
tiki
treaty
tweety
Vichy
weakly
weedy
weekly
weensy
weepy
wheelie
wheezy
wienie
Yeezy

be easy
bi- weekly
bikini
completely
concretely
discreetly
entreaty
extremely
graffiti
Houdini
ideally
Lil Weezy
linguine
martini
obliquely
obscenely
Parcheesi
peace treaty
Puccini

sashimi
serenely
speakeasy
supremely
Swahili
Tahiti
uneasy
uniquely
unseemly
zucchini

eeny meeny
fettuccine
George and Weezy
heebie-jeebie
incompletely
indiscretely
Mrs. Beasley
Mussolini
over easy
pop a wheelie
scaloppine
teeny weeny
tetrazzini
tortellini
Toscanini
touchy-feely
yes indeedy

I Dream of Jeannie
Jambi the Genie

Sylvester and Tweety

EAT 1

beach
beak
beast
beat
beech
beef
beep
beet
bleach
bleak
bleep
breach
brief
cease

cheap
cheat
cheek
cheep
chic
chief
cleat
clique
creak
crease
creek
creep
deep
deke
each
east
eat
eek
feast
feat
feep
feet
fleece
fleet
freak
geek
geese
grease
Greece
Greek
greet
grief
heap
heat
heath
jeep
keep
Keith
leaf
leak
leap
lease
leash
least
leech
leek
meat
meek
meet
neat

niece	tweet	decrease
peace	weak	deep sleep
peach	week	defeat
peak	weep	delete
peek	wheat	deplete
peep	wreak	dirt cheap
Pete	wreath	discreet
pic	yeast	discrete
piece		dog leash
pique	aesthete	downbeat
pleat	antique	drumbeat
preach	apiece	elite
priest	artiste	entreat
quiche	asleep	excrete
reach	at least	fact sheet
reap	athlete	false teeth
reef	back street	Far East
reek	backseat	fig leaf
screech	batik	fire chief
seat	bedsheet	flat feet
seek	belief	flyleaf
seep	beneath	for lease
sheaf	bequeath	free speech
sheep	beseech	front seat
sheesh	bespeak	gold leaf
sheet	black sheep	good grief
sheik	blue streak	hairpiece
Sheikh	Bo Peep	hashish
shriek	boutique	heartbeat
skeet	buck teeth	hell week
sleek	buckwheat	hot seat
sleep	caprice	housekeep
sleet	car seat	impeach
sneak	car thief	increase
speak	cerise	Jones Beach
speech	Clarisse	jump seat
squeak	clean sweep	knee-deep
steep	Cochise	loose-leaf
streak	cold feet	loveseat
street	compete	lunchmeat
suite	complete	Main Street
sweep	conceit	make peace
sweet	concrete	Maurice
teach	corned beef	mesquite
teak	critique	Mideast
teat	dead heat	midweek
teeth	deadbeat	mincemeat
thief	debrief	mine sweep
treat	decease	misspeak
tweak	deceit	mistreat

motif
mouthpiece
mystique
newsbeat
Newsweek
northeast
O'Keefe
obese
oblique
off-beat
outreach
petite
physique
pipsqueak
police
proof sheet
rap sheet
receipt
reheat
release
relief
repeat
replete
reseat
reseek
retreat
retweet
rime riche
roast beef
scrapheap
secrete
shopkeep
short-sheet
showpiece
side street
skin-deep
South Beach
southeast
spreadsheet
steam heat
sublease
swapmeet
sweetmeat
technique
Teen Beat
time sheet
timekeep
timepiece
trackmeet
Twin Peaks

two-piece
unchic
unique
unleash
upbeat
upkeep
upsweep
valise
waist-deep
Wall Street
wild geese
worksheet
workweek
world peace

ankle-deep
balance sheet
Battle Creek
beauty sleep
bittersweet
body heat
bucketseat
centerpiece
cheek-to-cheek
Chesapeake
chimneysweep
Christmas wreath
city street
cloverleaf
coral reef
county seat
disbelief
driver's seat
easy street
elbow grease
expertise
flying leap
Georgia peach
Golden Fleece
grit your teeth
handkerchief
have a seat
hide-and-seek
hold your peace
Holy Week
hotel suite
incomplete
indiscrete
keep the peace
keynote speech

leitmotif
magnifique
make ends meet
mantelpiece
Martinique
masterpiece
microfiche
Middle East
misbelief
Mozambique
Muscle Beach
neckerchief
obsolete
one-way street
overeat
overheat
overreach
oversleep
part of speach
petty thief
piece by piece
piece of meat
police sweep
potty seat
predecease
prerelease
press release
prickly heat
put to sleep
quantum leap
rest in peace
ringside seat
rosy cheek
senate seat
short and sweet
shredded wheat
so to speak
sound asleep
speak your piece
spring a leak
sugar sweet
take a leak
take a peek
talk is cheap
Tiger Beat
time-release
toilet seat
tongue in cheek
trick or treat
twilight sleep

two left feet
unbelief
underneath
up the creek
Where's The Beef?
widow's peak
wildebeest
window seat
yellow streak

all in one piece
aperitif
barrier reef
bicycle seat
comic relief
companion piece
fashion police
figure of speech
freedom of speech
gaggle of geese
Hail to the Chief
honeymoon suite
Indian chief
land on your feet
last but not least
like pulling teeth
mark of the beast
Miami Beach
Papa Don't Preach
peck on the cheek
period piece
pickled pigs' feet
quarterback sneak
read 'em and weep
red as a beet
secret police
Sesame Street
set in concrete
to say the least

21 Jump Street
Beauty and the Beast
Commander-in-Chief
conversation piece
justice of the peace
Nightmare on Elm Street

James and The Giant Peach
turn over a new leaf

EAT 2 (see ET 1)
EAT 3 (see ATE 1)

EATABLE (see IEVABLE)
EATABLY (see EITY)
EATED 1 (see EASTED 1)
EATED 2 (see EADED 1)

EATEN 1

beaten
cretin
eaten
Eden
Eton
freedom
neaten
paean
Sweden
sweeten
vegan
wheaten

Achaean
Achean
Aegean
Argean
browbeaten
Chaldean
Judean
Korean
moth-eaten
Norwegian
petrean
Sabaean
tempean
Thomaean
unbeaten
uneaten

European
galilean
herculean
overeaten
Tennesseean
weatherbeaten

Garden of Eden
Jennifer Keaton
Mallory Keaton
Pythagorean

Indo-European

EATEN 2 (see ESSION)
EATENING (see EDITING)

EATER 1

beacher
beader
beaker
beamer
beater
beaver
beefer
beeper
bleacher
bleaker
bleeder
bleeper
breacher
breather
briefer
Caesar
cedar
cheaper
cheater
cleaner
cleaver
creamer
creature
creeper
deeder
deemer
deeper
dreamer
eager
easer
Easter
eater
either
feature
feeder
femur
fever
fleeter
freezer
geezer
gleamer
greener
greeter
griever
heaper

heater
heaver
heeder
Keebler
keener
keeper
keister
leader
leaner
leaper
leaver
leecher
leisure
lemur
liter
meager
meaner
meeker
meester
meter
neater
needer
neither
peeker
peeper
peever
Peter
pleader
pleaser
preacher
preener
reacher
reader
reamer
reaper
reefer
schemer
screamer
screecher
screener
seater
seeker
seeper
seether
seizer
seizure
senior
shrieker
sleeker
sleeper

sneaker
sneezer
speaker
speeder
squeaker
squeezer
steamer
steeper
streaker
streamer
sweeper
sweeter
teacher
teeter
teether
treater
tweaker
weaker
weaner
weaver
weeder
weeper
wheezer

acceder
achiever
anteater
appeaser
bandleader
Beefeater
beleaguer
believer
bequeather
beseecher
big leaguer
blasphemer
born leader
car heater
careener
cheerleader
child beater
competer
conceder
conceiver
convener
critiquer
crossbreeder
Dance Fever
Dawn Wiener
daydreamer

debriefer
deceiver
deep freezer
defeater
deleter
demeanor
depleter
discreter
displeaser
doorkeeper
dry cleaner
egg beater
entreater
exceeder
gang leader
gate keeper
goalkeeper
grim reaper
group leader
hay fever
housecleaner
housekeeper
impeacher
impeder
inbreeder
innkeeper
Jet Screamer
June Cleaver
loudspeaker
man-eater
meat cleaver
mind reader
minesweeper
misleader
misreader
mistreater
obscener
old geezer
outreacher
palm reader
perceiver
pipe cleaner
pipedreamer
preceder
prescreener
procedure
proceeder
proofreader
receder
receiver

redeemer
reliever
repeater
repriever
retriever
ringleader
saltpeter
scout leader
secretor
serener
shopkeeper
song leader
sound sleeper
speed reader
spot-cleaner
spring fever
St. Peter
stampeder
steam cleaner
street cleaner
succeeder
swamp fever
team leader
timekeeper
tramp steamer
two-seater
unseater
upheaver
wife-beater
zookeeper

at your leisure
basketweaver
cabin fever
carpet sweeper
centimeter
disbeliever
double feature
eager beaver
facial feature
grass is greener
heavy breather
interceder
intervener
interweaver
Justin Bieber
little leaguer
major leaguer
milliliter
misdemeanor

overeager
overeater
overheater
oversleeper
parking meter
record keeper
search and seizure
Stanley Steamer
superseder
trick-or-treater
vacuum cleaner
Wally Cleaver
wide receiver
window cleaner
yellow fever

follow the leader
golden retriever
Leave it to Beaver
Nebuchadnezzar
overachiever
take to the cleaner
underachiever

graduation speaker
Saturday Night Fever

EATER 2 (see ECTOR)
EATEST (see ESIS)
EATH 1 (see ESS)
EATH 2 (see EAT 1)
EATHABLE (see IEVABLE)
EATHAL (see EGAL)
EATHE (see EED 1)
EATHEN (see ESIAN)
EATHER 1 (see ECTOR)
EATHER 2 (see EATER 1)
EATHERING (see ESTERING)
EATHERWEIGHT (see ESTI-GATE)
EATHERY (see ETICALLY)
EATHING (see EATING 1)
EATIER 1 (see EEDIER)
EATIER 2 (see EDGIER)

EATIES

beasties
feces
species

sweeties
treaties
weeklies
Wheaties
wheelies

entreaties
peace treaties

diabetes

EATIEST (see EAKIEST)
EATILY 1 (see EITY)
EATILY 2 (see ETICALLY)
EATINESS (see EAKINESS)

EATING 1

beaching
beating
beefing
beeping
bleaching
bleeping
breaching
breathing
breezing
briefing
ceasing
cheating
cheeping
cleaving
creaking
creasing
creeping
easing
eating
feasting
fleecing
fleeting
freaking
freezing
greasing
greeting
grieving
heaping
heating
heaving
keeping
leafing

leaguing
leaking
leaping
leashing
leasing
leaving
meeting
peaking
peeking
peeping
peeving
piecing
pleasing
pleating
preaching
reaching
reaping
reefing
reeking
screeching
seating
seeking
seeping
seething
seizing
sheeting
shrieking
sieging
sleeping
sleeting
sneaking
sneezing
speaking
squeaking
squeezing
steeping
streaking
sweeping
teaching
teasing
teething
treating
tweaking
tweeting
weakling
weaving
weeping
wheezing
wreaking
yeasting

achieving
aggrieving
appeasing
believing
bequeathing
bereaving
beseeching
besieging
bespeaking
chance meeting
child-beating
competing
completing
conceiving
critiquing
debriefing
deceiving
decreasing
defeating
deleting
depleting
displeasing
entreating
excreting
fatiguing
housekeeping
impeaching
in keeping
increasing
misspeaking
mistreating
perceiving
policing
receiving
reheating
releasing
relieving
repeating
retreating
retrieving
reweaving
safekeeping
secreting
self-seeking
shopkeeping
subleasing
timekeeping
town meeting
unleashing
upkeeping

business meeting
disbelieving
interweaving
misconceiving
overeating
overheating
overreaching
oversleeping
prayer meeting
preconceiving
prereleasing
public speaking
strictly speaking
take a beating
trick or treating
undereating

manner of speaking
overachieving
underachieving

EATING 2 (see ESSING)
EATISE (see ESIS)
EATIST (see ESIS)
EATLESS (see ESIS)
EATLY 1 (see ADY)
EATLY 2 (see EASY)
EATMENT (see EQUENT)
EATNESS 1 (see ACES)
EATNESS 2 (see ESIS)
EATON (see EATEN 1)
EATURE (see EATER 1)
EATY 1 (see EASY)
EATY 2 (see ELLY)
EAU (see OW 1)
EAUS (see OSE 1)
EAUT (see UTE)
EAUX (see OSE 1)
EAVABLE (see IEVABLE)
EAVAL (see EGAL)
EAVE (see EED 1)
EAVELESS (see ESIS)
EAVEMENT (see EQUENT)
EAVEN (see ESSION)
EAVENLY (see ETICALLY)
EAVER (see EATER 1)
EAVEY (see EASY)
EAVIER (see EDGIER)
EAVILY (see ETICALLY)
EAVING (see EATING 1)
EAVOR (see ECTOR)
EAVORED (see EPHERD)

EAVORING (see ESTERING)
EAVY (see ELLY)
EAZE (see EED 1)
EAZY (see EASY)
EB (see EAD 1)
EBA (see IA)
EBB (see EAD 1)
EBBIE (see ELLY)
EBBING (see ESSING)
EBBLE (see EVEL)
EBE (see EED 1)
EBEL (see EVEL)
EBIAN (see EDIAN)
EBIT (see ETIC)
EBITED (see ECTIONIST)
EBITING (see EDITING)
EBLE (see EVEL)
EBLER (see EATER 1)
EBLO (see ERO 2)
EBO (see IO 1)
EBONY (see ETICALLY)
EBRA 1 (see IA)
EBRA 2 (see ELLA)
EBRAL (see EGAL)
EBRIATE (see EDIENT)
EBRITY (see ETICALLY)
EBT (see ET 1)
EBTED (see EADED 1)
EBTOR (see ECTOR)
EC (see ET 1)
ECADENT (see ELEGANT)
ECCA (see ELLA)
ECCABLE (see ECTABLE)
ECEDENCE (see EMINENCE)
ECEDENT (see ELEGANT)

ECENCY

decency
decently
frequency
frequently
leniently
recency
recently
regency

conveniently
indecency
indecently
infrequently

precedently
undecency
vehemently

antecedently
inconveniently
interregency

ECENT (see EQUENT)
ECENTLY (see ECENCY)
ECES (see EATIES)
ECH 1 (see ET 1)
ECH 2 (see ESS)
ECHER (see ECTOR)
ECHEROUS (see ECTIONIST)
ECHIE (see ELLY)
ECHNICAL (see ECTABLE)
ECHNO (see ELLO)
ECHO (see ELLO)
ECIAL (see EVEL)
ECIALIST (see ECTIONIST)
ECIATE (see EVIATE)
ECIBEL (see ECTABLE)
ECIE (see EASY)
ECIES (see EATIES)
ECIFY (see ECTIFY)
ECIL (see EGAL)
ECILY (see ETICALLY)
ECIMAL (see ECTABLE)
ECIMATE (see ESTIGATE)
ECIMEN (see ELEGANT)
ECIOUS 1 (see EALOUS)
ECIOUS 2 (see ESIS)
ECIPE (see ETICALLY)
ECIPICE (see ECTIONIST)
ECK (see ET 1)
ECKABLE (see ECTABLE)
ECKER (see ECTOR)
ECKIER (see EDGIER)
ECKING (see ESSING)
ECKLACE (see ECTLESS)
ECKLE (see EVEL)
ECKLER (see ETTLER)
ECKLESS (see ECTLESS)
ECKLESSLY (see ETICALLY)
ECKLIER (see EDGIER)
ECKLING (see ESSING)
ECKON (see ESSION)
ECKONING (see EDITING)
ECKY (see ELLY)
ECO (see ELLO)
ECOMPENSE (see EMINENCE)

ECON (see EON)
ECOND (see ESSION)
ECORD (see EPHERD)
ECRET (see EANEST)
ECSTACY (see ETICALLY)
ECSTASY (see ETICALLY)
ECT (see ET 1)

ECTABLE

beggable
bettable
blessable
cessible
checkable
credible
decibel
decimal
dredgeable
dressable
edible
effable
epical
equinal
etchable
ethical
federal
fellable
festival
flexible
general
guessable
hedgeable
hexable
legible
medical
nexible
peccable
peckable
pectinal
pectoral
pedestal
pedistal
peggable
pettable
pressable
rectoral
sceptical
sectional
sectoral

sellable
septical
several
sexual
skeletal
skeptical
sketchable
spectacle
spellable
stressable
stretchable
technical
tellable
temporal
testable
testicle
textual
trekkable
vestibule
vexable
wreckable

abjectional
acceptable
accessible
addressable
aesthetical
affectable
affectible
affectional
allegible
annexable
apellable
arrestable
aseptical
asexual
aspectable
assessable
attestable
bimestrial
bisectable
bisectional
bisexual
caressable
centesimal
collectable
collectible
collectional
comestible
compellable

compressible
conceptible
conceptional
conceptual
confectional
confessable
confessional
congestable
congressional
connectable
connectional
contestable
contextual
correctable
correctible
correctional
cross-sectional
deceptible
defectible
deflectable
dejectional
delectable
depectible
depressable
detectable
detectible
detestable
digestible
digressible
directable
directional
discresional
dissectable
dissectible
dissectional
distressable
divestible
dyspeptical
effectible
effectual
ejectable
ejectional
electable
electional
electoral
electrical
erectable
exceptional
expectable
expellable

expressible
expressional
finessible
forgettable
genetical
heretical
illegible
impeccable
impressible
impressional
incessable
incredible
indelible
indexable
ineffable
infectable
infectible
infectional
infestable
inflectional
inflexible
ingestible
injectional
inspectional
intestinal
investible
majestical
mid-sectional
millesimal
nonethical
nonflexible
objectable
objectional
offsettable
oppressible
pathetical
pedestrial
perceptible
perceptual
perfectable
perfectible
perfectional
perpetual
perplexable
phonetical
poetical
possessable
processional
professional
progressional

projectable
projectional
proleptical
protectable
protectional
protectoral
protestable
protreptical
receptacle
receptible
recessional
redressible
refectional
reflectable
reflectible
reflectional
reflexible
regrettable
rejectable
repressible
requestable
resettable
respectable
selectable
selectional
semestrial
subjectable
suggestible
suppressible
susceptible
suspectable
sylleptical
synthetical
terrestrial
trajectional
transgressible
transsexual
trimestrial
undwellable
unethical
unflexible
upsettable
vigesimal

alphabetical
antiseptical
arithmetical
disrespectable
epileptical
homosexual
hypothetical

imperceptible
imperfectible
imperfectional
inaccessible
inapellable
incompressable
inconceptible
indefectible
indelectable
indigestible
ineffectible
ineffectual
inexpectable
inexpressible
infinitesimal
insuppressible
insurrectional
insusceptible
intellectual
interjectable
interjectional
intersectable
intersectional
intransgressible
introspectional
irrejectable
irrepressible
manifestable
metaleptical
misdirectional
noncollectible
nonsusceptible
orthoepical
overskeptical
parenthetical
planetesimal
quadragesimal
reassessible
recollectional
redirectional
reelectable
repossessible
resurrectable
resurrectional
sexagesimal
subterrestrial
superethical
theoretical
unacceptable
unaccessible
undetectable

undigestible
unexceptional
unexpressible
unforgettable
unimpressible
unprofessional
unsupressible
unsusceptible
vivisectional

apologetical
extraterrestrial
heterosexual
semiprofessional
semirejectable
semirespectable
superterrestrial

closet homosexual
pseudo intellectual

E.T. The Extra Terrestrial

ECTABLY (see ETICALLY)
ECTACLE (see ECTABLE)
ECTAL (see EVEL)
ECTANT (see ESCENT)
ECTAR (see ECTOR)

ECTED

bested
crested
jested
method
nested
quested
rested
sexist
tepid
tested
vested
wettest
wrested

accepted
affected
arrested
attested
bisected

collected
congested
connected
contested
corrected
defected
deflected
dejected
detected
detested
digested
directed
dissected
divested
effected
ejected
elected
erected
expected
infected
infested
inflected
ingested
injected
inspected
intrepid
invested
molested
neglected
objected
perfected
projected
prospected
protected
protested
reflected
rejected
requested
respected
selected
suggested
suspected
trajected

barrel-crested
dark-complected
decongested
disconnected
disinfected
double-breasted

genuflected
intercepted
interjected
intersected
light-complected
manifested
misdirected
recollected
redirected
reelected
resurrected
unaffected
undetected
undirected
unexpected
unreflected
unsuspected

ECTER (see ECTOR)
ECTFUL (see EVEL)
ECTIBLE (see ECTABLE)
ECTIC (see ETIC)
ECTICUT (see ECTIONIST)

ECTIFY

edify
rectify
specify
terrify
testify
verify

celestify
correctify
disedify
electrify
objectify
reedify
subjectify

ECTIN (see ESSION)
ECTINAL (see ECTABLE)
ECTING (see ESSING)
ECTION (see ESSION)
ECTIONAL (see ECTABLE)
ECTIONATE (see ECTIONIST)

ECTIONIST

celibate
cleverest
credited
debited
deficit
definite
desolate
desperate
edifice
edited
effortless
etiquette
Everest
exited
exodus
fetterless
letterless
nepotist
Oedipus
pessimist
precipice
specialist
terrorist
therapist
treacherous

accredited
affectionate
concessionist
confessionist
Connecticut
defectionist
discredited
expressionist
impressionist
incredited
inedited
nonspecialist
perfectionist
progressionist
projectionist
protectionist
receptionist
recessionist
reedited
secessionist
selectionist
successionist
unedited

insurrectionist
introspectionist
reaccredited
resurrectionist
unaccredited

ECTIOUS (see ECTLESS)
ECTIOUSLY (see ETICALLY)
ECTIVE (see ESSIVE)

ECTLESS

bedless
checkless
chefless
chestless
deadness
deckless
edgeless
fleckless
guestless
headless
Lexus
necklace
neckless
Netflix
nexus
peckless
plexus
reckless
redness
refless
restless
sectless
sedgeless
sexless
speckless
stressless
tetris
Texas
trekless
wedless
wreckless
Xmas

abjectless
affectless
Alexis
apexless
bisectless

complexus
connectless
detectless
directness
effectless
ejectless
erectness
infectious
infectless
inflectless
injectless
insectless
objectless
perfectless
projectless
protectless
subjectless

ambidextrous
shark-tooth necklace
young and restless

ECTLY (see ELLY)
ECTNESS (see ECTLESS)
ECTO (see ELLO)
ECTOMY (see ETICALLY)

ECTOR

Becker
beggar
better
checker
cheddar
Cheshire
Chester
clever
deafer
debtor
decker
dredger
edger
effort
error
Esther
etcher
ever
expert
feather
fester

fetcher
fetter
Fletcher
fresher
fretter
gesture
getter
header
heather
Hector
hedger
heifer
jester
leather
lecher
lecture
ledger
leper
Lester
letter
lever
measure
mesher
nectar
nester
Nestor
never
pecker
pepper
pester
petter
pleasure
pledger
prepper
pressure
rector
redder
refresher
rester
retcher
scepter
sector
setter
sever
shedder
shredder
sketcher
specter
stepper
stretcher
sweater

terror
tester
tether
texture
threader
thresher
treader
treasure
trekker
Trevor
vector
weather
wedger
western
wetter
whether
whetter
wrecker
zephyr

abettor
air pressure
ancestor
arrester
attester
bedwetter
begetter
beheader
bisector
blood pressure
chain letter
collector
congester
conjecture
connector
contester
corrector
court jester
defector
deflector
detector
detester
director
displeasure
dissector
divestor
elector
endeavor
erector
fairweather

fan letter
forever
forgetter
form letter
foul weather
go-getter
goal setter
green pepper
hat checker
high-stepper
homewrecker
however
infestor
inflector
ingester
injector
inspector
investor
jet setter
love letter
McGregor
midwestern
molestor
my pleasure
newsletter
night terror
northwestern
objector
pacesetter
peer pressure
perfecter
projector
protector
protestor
receptor
red pepper
reflector
selector
semester
sequester
sidestepper
southwestern
tape measure
taste tester
together
trendsetter
trimester
typesetter
whatever
whenever

wherever
whichever
whoever
whomever
with pleasure
woodpecker

altogether
architecture
beyond measure
Black and Decker
cayenne pepper
change of weather
chief inspector
countermeasure
disconnector
disinfector
double-decker
doubleheader
Dr. Pepper
English Leather
genuflector
get-together
go one better
hidden treasure
howsoever
interjector
intersector
Irish Setter
last forever
lie detector
overstepper
paper shredder
patent leather
polyester
private sector
public sector
recollector
red-hot pepper
resurrector
salt and pepper
smoke detector
stage director
stormy weather
system error
tar and feather
to the letter
trial and error
TV Western
whatsoever

wheresoever
whomsoever
whosoever

birds of a feather
cardigan sweater
get it together
light as a feather
metal detector
under the weather

get your act together
pull yourself together

conscientious objector
put two and two together
typographical error

ECTORAL (see ECTABLE)
ECTORY (see ETICALLY)
ECTRA (see ELLA)
ECTRAL (see EVEL)
ECTRIC (see ETIC)
ECTRICAL (see ECTABLE)
ECTRIFY (see ECTIFY)

ECTRUM

Belgium
Ephron
plectrum
rectum
seldom
skellum
spectrum
vellum
welcome

unwelcome

antebellum
cerebellum
very seldom

ECTUAL (see ECTABLE)
ECTUM (see ECTRUM)
ECTURE (see ECTOR)
ECTURED (see EPHERD)

ECULAR

cellular
creditor
editor
messeneger
predator
register
regular
secular
specular

co-editor
competitor
discreditor
molecular
nonsecular

bimolecular
submolecular
supersecular

intermolecular
intramolecular
monomolecular
multimolecular
orthomolecular
supermolecular

ECUTIVE

expletive
negative
relative
sedative

abnegative
appetitive
competitive
consecutive
executive
imperative
irrelative
prosecutive
repetitive
subsecutive

inconsecutive
noncompetitive

nonconcsecutive
photonegative
uncompetitive

overcompetitive

ED (see EAD 1)
EDA (see IA)
EDABLE (see IEVABLE)
EDAL (see EVEL)
EDAR (see EATER 1)
EDATIVE (see ECUTIVE)
EDATOR (see ECULAR)
EDDAR (see ECTOR)
EDDED (see EADED 1)
EDDEN (see ESSION)
EDDENING (see EDITING)
EDDER (see ECTOR)
EDDIE (see ELLY)
EDDING (see ESSING)
EDDISH (see ETIC)
EDDLE (see EVEL)
EDDLER (see ETTLER)
EDDLING (see ESSING)
EDDON (see ESSION)
EDDY (see ELLY)
EDE 1 (see EED 1)
EDE 2 (see ADE 1)
EDED (see EASTED 1)
EDEN (see EATEN 1)

EDENCE

chievance
credence
egence
frequence
grievance
regence
sequence

accedence
achievance
aggrievance
allegiance
convenience
decedents
infrequence
lenience
precedents

subsequence
vehemence

antecedence
antecedents
inconvenience
intercedence
supersedence

EDENT (see EQUENT)
EDENTLY (see ECENCY)
EDENTS (see EDENCE)
EDER (see EATER 1)
EDERAL (see ECTABLE)
EDES (see ADIES)
EDESTAL (see ECTABLE)
EDGE (see EAD 1)
EDGEABLE (see ECTABLE)
EDGELESS (see ECTLESS)
EDGER (see ECTOR)
EDGERED (see EPHERD)
EDGIE (see ELLY)

EDGIER

deadlier
dreggier
dressier
edgier
eggier
fledgier
frecklier
heavier
hedgier
heftier
hellier
ledgier
leggier
messier
peckier
peppier
pettier
sedgier
sexier
shellier
smellier
sweatier
tressier
wedgier

EDGILY (see ETICALLY)
EDGING (see ESSING)
EDGLING (see ESSING)
EDGY (see ELLY)
EDIA (see ENIA)
EDIAL (see IEVABLE)

EDIAN

median
plebian

bohemian
comedian
submedian
tragedian

academian

encyclopedian

EDIANT (see EDIENT)
EDIATE 1 (see EDIENT)
EDIATE 2 (see EVIATE)
EDIBLE 1 (see ECTABLE)
EDIBLE 2 (see IEVABLE)
EDIBLY (see ETICALLY)
EDIC 1 (see ETIC)
EDIC 2 (see ESIS)
EDICAL (see ECTABLE)
EDICALLY (see ETICALLY)
EDICATE (see ESTIGATE)
EDICINE (see ELEGANT)

EDIENT

deviant
lenient
mediant

convenient
expedient
immediate
inebriate
ingredient
obedient

disobedient
inconvenient

inexpedient
intermediate

EDIFICE (see ECTIONIST)
EDIFY (see ECTIFY)
EDIMENT (see ELEGANT)
EDING (see EEDING)
EDIOUS (see EAKIEST)
EDIPUS (see ECTIONIST)
EDISH (see ESIS)
EDISON (see ELEGANT)
EDISTAL (see ECTABLE)
EDIT (see ETIC)
EDITATE (see ESTIGATE)
EDITED (see ECTIONIST)

EDITING

beckoning
cherishing
crediting
deafening
debiting
destining
editing
exiting
lessening
leveling
meriting
perishing
questioning
reckoning
reddening
relishing
threatening
weaponing

accrediting
demeriting
discrediting
disheriting
embellishing
embezzling
inheriting
processioning

copyediting
day of reckoning
disinheriting

EDITOR (see ECULAR)
EDITY (see ETICALLY)
EDIUM (see ELIUM)
EDLESS (see ECTLESS)
EDLEY (see ELLY)
EDN'T (see EQUENT)
EDNA (see ELLA)
EDNESS (see ECTLESS)
EDO 1 (see IO 1)
EDO 2 (see ADO 2)
EDRAL (see EGAL)
EDRO (see ERO 2)
EDURE (see EATER 1)
EE 1 (see E 1)
EE 2 (see AY)
EEABLE (see IEVABLE)
EEABLY (see EITY)
EEB (see EED 1)
EEBIE (see EASY)
EEBLE (see EGAL)
EECE (see EAT 1)
EECH (see EAT 1)
EECHABLE (see IEVABLE)
EECHER (see EATER 1)
EECHIEST (see EAKIEST)
EECHING (see EATING 1)
EECHINGLY (see EAMINGLY)
EECHLESS (see ESIS)
EECHY (see EASY)
EECING (see EATING 1)

EED 1

bead
bleed
breathe
breed
breeze
cede
cheese
cleave
creed
deed
dweeb
ease
Eve
feed
flees
freed
freeze
geez

geeze
greed
grieve
heave
heed
keyed
knead
kneed
lead
league
leave
liege
mead
need
peed
peeve
plead
please
plebe
read
reed
screed
seas
seed
seethe
seize
siege
skied
skis
sleaze
sleeve
sneeze
speed
squeeze
steed
Steve
Swede
teas
tease
teethe
these
thieve
tweed
tweeze
we've
weave
weed
wheeze

accede
achieve
aggrieve
agreed
appease
at ease
believe
Belize
besiege
big cheese
big league
birdseed
blue cheese
Chinese
colleague
concede
conceive
cream cheese
crossbreed
deceive
decreed
deep freeze
degrees
disease
displease
exceed
fatigue
force-feed
full speed
Godspeed
good deed
hair weave
halfbreed
hand-feed
hayseed
high seas
high speed
impede
inbreed
indeed
intrigue
knock-kneed
lipread
Lockheed
Louise
main squeeze
misdeed
mislead
misread
naive

nosebleed
perceive
pet peeve
precede
prestige
proceed
proofread
ragweed
recede
receive
relieve
reprieve
retrieve
sea breeze
seaweed
secede
shirt sleeve
sick leave
speedread
spoonfeed
stampede
succeed
sweet peas
ten-speed
three-speed
top seed
top speed
trapeze
trust deed
unfreeze
upheave
weak-kneed
whoopeed

ABCs
antecede
antifreeze
apple seed
basketweave
black-eyed peas
Cantonese
centipede
chickenfeed
Christmas Eve
Chuck E. Cheese
cottage cheese
cottonseed
disagreed
disbelieve
dungarees

go to seed
guaranteed
gum disease
if you please
intercede
interweave
Ivy League
Japanese
Lebanese
legalese
Little League
locoweed
love and leave
major leage
make-believe
misconceive
Monchichis
New Year's Eve
overfeed
overseas
pedigreed
Pekingese
preconceive
pretty please
Pyrenees
refereed
Seven Seas
shoot the breeze
Siamese
supersede
take one's leave
third-degreed
title deed
tumbleweed
underfeed
up to speed
water skis

Adam and Eve
archdiocese
Florida Keys
overachieve
overfatigue
underachieve
Vietnamese

maternity leave

macaroni and cheese
wear your heart on your sleeve

EED 2 (see ADE 1)
EEDABLE (see IEVABLE)
EEDED (see EASTED 1)
EEDER (see EATER 1)
EEDFUL (see EGAL)

EEDIER

beadier
beefier
creepier
easier
greasier
greedier
meatier
meteor
needier
preachier
seedier
sneakier
speedier
weedier

EEDIEST (see EAKIEST)
EEDILY (see EITY)
EEDINESS (see EAKINESS)

EEDING

beading
being
bleeding
breeding
ceding
feeding
fleeing
freeing
heeding
keying
kneeing
leading
needing
peeing
pleading
reading
seeding
seeing
skiing
speeding

teeing
treeing
weeding

acceding
agreeing
breast-feeding
conceding
crossbreeding
decreeing
exceeding
foreseeing
good breeding
impeding
inbreeding
lipreading
mind reading
misleading
misreading
preceding
proceeding
proofreading
receding
reseeding
seceding
spoon-feeding
stampeding
succeeding
well-being

human being
interceding
overfeeding
overseeing
refereeing
superseding
underfeeding
water skiing

EEDINGLY (see EAMINGLY)
EEDLE (see EGAL)
EEDLESS (see ESIS)
EEDOM (see EATEN 1)
EEDY (see EASY)
EEF (see EAT 1)
EEFER (see EATER 1)
EEFIER (see EEDIER)
EEFIEST (see EAKIEST)
EEFILY (see EITY)
EEFINESS (see EAKINESS)
EEFING (see EATING 1)

EEFLESS (see ESIS)
EEFY (see EASY)
EEGEE (see EASY)
EEING (see EEDING)
EEK (see EAT 1)
EEKABLE (see IEVABLE)
EEKEND (see ESIAN)
EEKER (see EATER 1)
EEKEST (see EANEST)
EEKIEST (see EAKIEST)
EEKILY (see EITY)
EEKINESS (see EAKINESS)
EEKING (see EATING 1)
EEKLIES (see EATIES)
EEKLY (see EASY)
EEKNESS (see ESIS)
EEKY (see EASY)
EEL (see EAL 1)
EELABLE (see IEVABLE)
EELER (see EALER)
EELESS (see ESIS)
EELIE (see EASY)
EELIES (see EATIES)
EELING (see EALING)
EELY (see EASY)
EEM (see EEN 1)
EEMABLE (see IEVABLE)
EEMABLY (see EITY)
EEMAN (see ESIAN)
EEMENT (see EQUENT)
EEMER (see EATER 1)
EEMING (see EAMING)
EEMINGLY (see EAMINGLY)
EEMLESS (see ESIS)
EEMLY (see EASY)

EEN 1

beam
bean
clean
cream
dean
deem
deme
dream
fiend
gene
gleam
glean
green

Jean
keen
lean
lien
mean
meme
mien
queen
ream
scene
scheme
scream
screen
seam
seem
seen
sheen
spleen
steam
stream
team
teem
teen
theme
tween
wean

abeam
agleam
airstream
archfiend
between
blaspheme
bloodstream
caffeine
canteen
careen
chlorine
Christine
codeine
cold cream
come clean
convene
crime-scene
crossbeam
cuisine
Darlene
daydream
demean
dentine

Dentyne
door screen
dope fiend
downstream
drag queen
dream team
drill team
dry-clean
eighteen
esteem
Eugene
extreme
fifteen
flat-screen
foreseen
fourteen
gangrene
greenbean
high beam
home team
hygiene
ice cream
inseam
Irene
jet stream
Joaquin
Kathleen
latrine
machine
mainstream
marine
Marlene
Maxine
midstream
mob scene
moonbeam
morpheme
morphine
nineteen
obscene
on-screen
pea green
pipedream
praline
prescreen
preteen
pristine
prom queen
protein
Racine

ravine
reclean
redeem
regime
routine
saline
sardine
sateen
sea green
serene
silkscreen
Sistine
sixteen
smokescreen
soybean
spot-clean
spring-clean
stringbean
sunbeam
sunscreen
supreme
tag team
thirteen
touch-screen
track team
umpteen
unclean
unkeen
unseen
upstream
vaccine
vitrine
wet dream
whipped cream
wide-screen

academe
amandine
Argentine
Augustine
balance beam
baseball team
blow off steam
bowling green
Bruce Springsteen
Byzantine
coffee bean
color scheme
come between
Constantine

contravene
Cotton Dream
Dairy Queen
Dancing Queen
debate team
double-team
epicene
Ernestine
evergreen
fall between
fax machine
figurine
Florentine
football team
gasoline
get between
go-between
Green Machine
guillotine
gum machine
Halloween
in-between
intervene
jellybean
Josephine
Juan Epstein
kerosene
kidney bean
lean and mean
libertine
lima bean
limousine
Listerine
magazine
Magic Screen
make the scene
Maybelline
mezzanine
movie screen
Mr. Clean
mustard green
Nazarene
nectarine
never seen
nicotine
on the beam
on the scene
Ovaltine
overseen
peachy-keen

philistine
pick up steam
putting green
quarantine
reconvene
self-esteem
serpentine
seventeen
sex machine
sight unseen
silver screen
slot machine
sour cream
squeaky clean
submarine
sweet sixteen
tambourine
tangerine
time machine
trampoline
unforeseen
Vaseline
velveteen
village green
wintergreen
wolverine
wrinkle cream

adding machine
amphetamine
aquamarine
basketball team
carbon 14
emerald green
expansion team
flying machine
Jethro Bodine
keep your nose clean
Mad Magazine
merchant marine
no I in team
peaches and cream
pyramid scheme
rowing machine
see and be seen
sewing machine
St. Bernadine
U.S. Marine
vanishing cream
vending machine

visiting team
washing machine

American Dream
answering machine
few and far between
impossible dream
Playgirl Magazine
Yellow Submarine

Swedish Bikini Team

EEN 2 (see IN 1)
EENAN (see ESIAN)
EENER (see EATER 1)
EENEST (see EANEST)
EENIE (see EASY)
EENING (see EAMING)
EENINGLY (see EAMINGLY)
EENLESS (see ESIS)
EENLY (see EASY)
EENNESS (see ESIS)
EENSIEST (see EAKIEST)
EENSY (see EASY)
EENY (see EASY)
EEP (see EAT 1)
EEPEN (see ESIAN)
EEPENING (see EASONING)
EEPER (see EATER 1)
EEPEST (see EANEST)
EEPIER (see EEDIER)
EEPIEST (see EAKIEST)
EEPILY (see EITY)
EEPINESS (see EAKINESS)
EEPING (see EATING 1)
EEPINGLY (see EAMINGLY)
EEPLE (see EGAL)
EEPLESS (see ESIS)
EEPLY (see EASY)
EEPNESS (see ESIS)
EEPSIE (see ITTY)
EEPY (see EASY)
EER (see EAR 1)
EERED (see EARED)
EERER (see EARER)
EEREST (see EAREST)
EERFUL (see EARFUL)
EERIEST (see ERIOUS)
EERINESS (see EARINESS)

EERING

cheering
clearing
earring
fearing
hearing
jeering
leering
nearing
peering
shearing
smearing
sneering
spearing
steering
tearing
veering

adhering
appearing
cohering
dog-earing
endearing
inhering
premiering
revering
veneering

buccaneering
disappearing
domineering
engineering
hard of hearing
interfering
overhearing
persevering
pioneering
profiteering
racketeering
reappearing
volunteering

Congressional Hearing

EERLESS (see EARLESS)
EERLY (see EARY)
EERNESS (see EARLESS)
EERY (see EARY)
EES (see EED 1)

EESE 1 (see EED 1)
EESE 2 (see EAT 1)
EESH (see EAT 1)
EESI (see EASY)
EEST 1 (see EAT 1)
EEST 2 (see EANEST)
EESTER (see EATER 1)
EESY (see EASY)
EET (see EAT 1)
EETABLE (see IEVABLE)
EETAH (see IA)
EETED (see EASTED 1)
EETEN (see EATEN 1)
EETENING (see EASONING)
EETER (see EATER 1)
EETEST (see ESIS)
EETH (see EAT 1)
EETHABLE (see IEVABLE)
EETHE (see EED 1)
EETHER (see EATER 1)
EETHING (see EATING 1)
EETHINGLY (see EAMINGLY)
EETIES (see EATIES)
EETIEST (see EAKIEST)
EETING (see EATING 1)
EETLE (see EGAL)
EETLESS (see ESIS)
EETLY (see EASY)
EETNESS (see ESIS)
EETOH (see IO 1)
EETY (see EASY)
EEVABLE (see IEVABLE)
EEVE (see EED 1)
EEVELESS (see ESIS)
EEVER (see EATER 1)
EEVING (see EATING 1)
EEZ (see EED 1)
EEZABLE (see IEVABLE)
EEZE (see EED 1)
EEZER (see EATER 1)
EEZIEST (see EAKIEST)
EEZINESS (see EAKINESS)
EEZING (see EATING 1)
EEZY (see EASY)
EF (see ESS)
EFACE (see ETIC)
EFE (see EAT 1)
EFECATE (see ESTIGATE)
EFER (see ATOR)
EFERENCE (see ESCENCE)
EFF (see ESS)
EFFABLE (see ECTABLE)
EFFING (see ESSING)

EFFORT (see ECTOR)
EFFORTLESS (see ECTIONIST)
EFICIT (see ECTIONIST)
EFINITE (see ECTIONIST)
EFLESS (see ECTLESS)
EFT (see ESS)
EFTIER (see EDGIER)
EFTY (see ELLY)
EFUL (see ITLE)
EG 1 (see EAD 1)
EG 2 (see EAD 1)
EGA 1 (see ASIA)
EGA 2 (see ELLA)
EGACY (see ETICALLY)

EGAL

beagle
beetle
betel
Cecil
deedful
diesel
eagle
easel
equal
evil
feeble
fetal
greedful
heedful
legal
lethal
needful
needle
peaceful
penal
people
regal
renal
seagull
Segal
sequel
steeple
tweedle
venal
weasel
Weevil
wheedle

adrenal
bald eagle
bequeathal
boat people
cathedral
cerebral
church steeple
deceitful
illegal
medieval
retrieval
spread-eagle
unequal
unregal
upheaval

chosen people
Dr. Evil
extralegal
paralegal
Village People
we the people

Evel Knievel
separate but equal
Volkswagen Beetle

EGALLY (see EITY)
EGAN (see EATEN 1)
EGAS (see ACES)
EGATIVE (see ECUTIVE)
EGE 1 (see EAD 1)
EGE 2 (see ID)
EGENCE (see EDENCE)
EGENCY (see ECENCY)
EGEND (see ESSION)
EGETABLE (see EPARABLE)
EGETATE (see ESTIGATE)
EGG (see EAD 1)
EGGABLE (see ECTABLE)
EGGAR (see ECTOR)
EGGER (see ATOR)
EGGIE (see ELLY)
EGGIER (see EDGIER)
EGGING (see ESSING)
EGGLER (see ETTLER)
EGGO (see ELLO)
EGGY (see ELLY)
EGIAN 1 (see EDIAN)
EGIAN 2 (see ESIAN)
EGIANCE (see EDENCE)

EGIATE (see EANEST)
EGIBLE (see ECTABLE)
EGIBLY (see ETICALLY)
EGIC (see EANEST)
EGIMEN (see ELEGANT)
EGING 1 (see ESSING)
EGING 2 (see ESSING)
EGION (see ESIAN)
EGIONAL (see IEVABLE)
EGIOUS (see ESIS)
EGISLATE (see ESTIGATE)
EGISTER (see ECULAR)
EGISTRY (see ETICALLY)
EGIUM (see ELIUM)
EGLIGENT (see ELEGANT)
EGM (see EN)
EGMENT (see ESCENT)
EGMY (see EMMY)
EGNANCY (see ETICALLY)
EGNANT (see ESCENT)
EGO 1 (see IO 1)
EGO 2 (see ELLO)
EGON (see EON)
EGOR (see ECTOR)
EGRITY (see ETICALLY)
EGRO 1 (see ELLO)
EGRO 2 (see ERO 1)
EGULAR (see ECULAR)
EGULATE (see ESTIGATE)
EHICLE (see IEVABLE)
EI (see AY)
EIDER (see IZER)
EIFER (see ECTOR)
EIGE (see AVE 1)
EIGH (see AY)
EIGHABLE (see ADABLE)
EIGHBOR (see ATOR)
EIGHBORING (see AVORING)
EIGHER (see AILER)
EIGHT (see ATE 1)
EIGHTER (see ATOR)
EIGHTH (see ACE 1)
EIGHTING (see ATING)
EIGHTLESS (see ACES)
EIGHTON (see ATION 1)
EIGHTY (see ADY)
EIGLE (see ABLE)
EIGLED (see ABLED)
EIGN (see AIN 1)
EIGNABLE (see AINABLE)
EIGNER (see AINER)

EIGNING (see AINING)
EII (see AY)
EIK (see EAT 1)
EIKH (see EAT 1)
EIL (see AIL)
EILA (see IA)
EILER (see AILER)
EILING 1 (see EALING)
EILING 2 (see AILING)
EILL (see EAL 1)
EILLANCE (see ATEMENTS)
EILLANT (see ATION 1)
EIN 1 (see AIN 1)
EIN 2 (see INE 1)
EIN 3 (see EEN 1)
EINE (see EEN 1)
EINER (see AINER)
EING (see EEDING)
EINING (see AINING)
EINLESS (see ACES)
EINOUS (see ACES)
EINT (see AINT)
EINTED (see AINTED)
EINTER (see AINER)
EINTING (see ATING)
EINY (see ADY)
EIPT (see EAT 1)
EIR (see ARE 1)
EIRD (see EARED)
EIRDEST (see EAREST)
EIRDNESS (see EARLESS)
EIRDO (see ERO 1)
EIRESS (see ARENESS)
EIRLESS (see ARENESS)
EIRO (see ERO 2)
EISHA (see ASIA)
EIST 1 (see EANEST)
EIST 2 (see ICE 1)
EISTER (see EATER 1)
EISTIER (see INIER)
EISTINESS (see IGHTLINESS)
EISTING (see INDING)
EISURE (see EATER 1)
EIT 1 (see EAT 1)
EIT 2 (see IGHT)
EITED (see EASTED 1)
EITFUL (see EGAL)
EITH (see EAT 1)
EITHER (see EATER 1)
EITING (see ITTING)

EITY

beefily
cheekily
creepily
deity
easily
equally
evilly
feasibly
fevery
greasily
greedily
greenery
legally
meatily
needily
penally
queasily
readably
regally
scenery
seedily
sleepily
speedily
thievery
treatably
venally
weedily
weevilly

agreeably
believably
coequally
gaseity
illegally
machinery
multeity
obesity
uneasily
unequally
unspeakably
velleity

corporeity
disagreeably
extraneity
femineity
indefeasibly
irredeemably
irretrievably

spontaneity
unbelievably
unimpeachably

EIVABLE (see IEVABLE)
EIVE (see EED 1)
EIVER (see EATER 1)
EIVING (see EATING 1)
EIZABLE (see IEVABLE)
EIZE (see EED 1)
EIZER (see EATER 1)
EIZING (see EATING 1)
EIZURE (see EATER 1)
EJO (see ADO 2)
EK (see ET 1)
EKA (see IA)
EKE (see EAT 1)
EKEL (see EVEL)
EKKABLE (see ECTABLE)
EKKER (see ECTOR)
EKKIE (see ELLY)
EKKING (see ESSING)
EKLESS (see ECTLESS)
EKYLL (see EVEL)
EL (see ELL)
ELAGH (see ADY)
ELANIE (see ETICALLY)
ELATIN (see ELEGANT)
ELATIVE (see ECUTIVE)
ELBA (see ELDA)
ELBOW (see ELLO)
ELBY (see ELLY)
ELCH (see ELVES)
ELCHER (see ELTER)
ELCHING (see ELLING)
ELCO (see ELLO)
ELCOME (see ECTRUM)
ELCRO (see ELLO)
ELD (see ELT)

ELDA

delta
Elba
Elga
Elma
Elsa
Elva
Shelta
Zelda

Esmerelda

Legend of Zelda

ELDER (see ELTER)
ELDEST (see ELFISH)
ELDING (see ELLING)
ELDOM (see ECTRUM)
ELDON (see ELLION)
ELDS (see ELVES)
ELE 1 (see ADY)
ELE 2 (see ELL)
ELEGANCE (see EMINENCE)

ELEGANT

decadent
delegant
detriment
devilment
Edison
elegant
element
elephant
eloquent
Evelyn
evident
excellent
excrement
exigent
gelatin
heroin
heroine
hesitant
measurement
medicine
negligent
pediment
pelican
precedent
president
prevalent
regimen
relevant
resident
retriment
reverent
sediment
settlement
Sheraton

skeleton
specimen
terapin
veteran

American
bedevilment
benevolent
development
dissettlement
embellishment
embezzlement
expediment
impediment
inelegant
ineloquent
inevident
irrelevant
irreverent
malevolent
nonresident
resettlement
self-evident
unelegant
unreverent
unsettlement
vice president

biomedicine
David Letterman
dermoskeleton
endoskeleton
exoskeleton
French American
geomedicine
neuroskeleton
omniprevalent
overelegant
pneumoskeleton
scleroskeleton
superexcellent
Thai American
Welsh American

Chinese American
Cuban American
German American
Irish American
Latin American
Native American

Polish American
Russian American
Scottish American
Spanish American
Swedish American

African American
Italian American
Korean American
Mexican American

Filipino American
Vietnamese American

ELEGATE (see ESTIGATE)
ELEMENT (see ELEGANT)
ELEMENTS (see EMINENCE)
ELEN (see ESSION)
ELEPHANT (see ELEGANT)
ELEPHANTS (see EMINENCE)
ELERATE (see ESTIGATE)
ELERY (see ETICALLY)
ELET (see IET)
ELETAL (see ECTABLE)
ELETON (see ELEGANT)
ELEVANCE (see EMINENCE)
ELEVANT (see ELEGANT)
ELEVATE (see ESTIGATE)
ELF (see ELT)
ELFIE (see ELLY)
ELFING (see ELLING)

ELFISH

Belgic
celtic
crevice
deltic
eldest
elfish
Ellis
Elvis
hellish
helmet
helpless
keltic
pelfish
pellet
pelvic
pelvis

relish
selfish
selfless
shellfish
velvet
zealot

appellate
disrelish
embellish
unselfish

catapeltic
Jerome Bettis

ELFLESS (see ELFISH)
ELGA (see ELDA)
ELGIAN (see ELLION)
ELGIC (see ELFISH)
ELGIN (see ELLION)
ELGIUM (see ECTRUM)
ELHI (see ELLY)
ELI (see ELLY)
ELIA (see ENIA)
ELIBATE (see ECTIONIST)
ELIBLE (see ECTABLE)
ELIC (see ETIC)
ELICA (see ERICA)
ELICAN (see ELEGANT)
ELIGIBLE (see EPARABLE)
ELING (see ELLING)
ELISH (see ELFISH)
ELISHING (see EDITING)
ELITY (see ETICALLY)

ELIUM

helium
medium
premium

collegium
elysium
magnesium
Norwegium

happy medium
intermedium
manganesium

ELIX (see EANEST)

ELK (see ELT)
ELKS (see ELVES)

ELL 1

bell
belle
cell
dell
dwell
fell
gel
hell
jell
L
Nell
quell
sell
shell
smell
spell
swell
tell
well
yell

Adele
blood cell
bombshell
brain cell
cartel
catch hell
Chanel
clamshell
compel
Cornell
cowbell
dispel
do tell
doorbell
dumbbell
eggshell
excel
expel
farewell
foretell
gazelle
halfshell
hard-shell
hardsell

hotel
impel
ink well
jail cell
lapel
Maxwell
misspell
motel
noel
nutshell
oh well
oil well
pastel
propel
raise hell
rappel
Raquel
repel
resell
retell
schoolbell
sea shell
sleighbell
soft-shell
softsell
stairwell

bagatelle
cancer cell
caramel
caravel
carousel
cast a spell
clientele
dinner bell
diving bell
Gargamel
infidel
Isabel
Jezebel
jingle bell
kiss and tell
magic spell
muscatel
NFL
oversell
Packard Bell
padded cell
parallel
personnel
prison cell

Raphael
red blood cell
show and tell
Southern belle
Taco Bell
Tinker Bell
tortoise shell
undersell
very well
William Tell
wishing well
Zinfandel

artesian well
cold day in hell
Liberty Bell
mademoiselle
Pacific Bell
Saved By The Bell

all's well that ends well
isolation cell

like a bat out of hell

ELL 2 (see OLE 1)

ELLA

Bella
cuesta
Debra
Decca
Edna
ella
Etta
extra
Ezra
fella
feta
Greta
Jetta
Mecca
mega
plectra
spectra
Stella
Tesla
testa
Vesta

avesta
celesta
contessa
Daniella
egesta
electra
fiesta
Francesca
ingesta
Odessa
podesta
Rebecca
rubella
siesta
umbrella
Vanessa
vendetta

a cappella
Cinderella
Isabella
Marietta
mozzarella
salmonella
tarantella

Tony Baretta

ELLABLE (see ECTABLE)
ELLAR (see ELLER)
ELLATE (see ELFISH)
ELLE (see ELL)
ELLEN (see ESSION)
ELLENCE (see ESCENCE)

ELLER

cellar
dweller
feller
Keller
queller
seller
sheller
smeller
speller
stellar
sweller
teller
yeller

bank teller
bestseller
cave dweller
compeller
dispeller
exceller
expeller
foreteller
impeller
old yeller
propeller
storm cellar
wine cellar

cellar dweller
fortuneteller
Helen Keller
interstellar
Rockefeller
storyteller

ELLET (see ELFISH)
ELLEY (see ELLY)
ELLFISH (see ELFISH)
ELLI (see ELLY)
ELLIE (see ELLY)
ELLIER (see EDGIER)
ELLIES (see ELLY)

ELLING

belching
belting
delving
dwelling
elding
felting
gelding
helming
helping
helving
jelling
kelping
melding
melting
pelting
quelling
selfing
selling
shelling

shelving
smelling
smelting
spelding
spelling
squelching
swelling
telling
welching
welding
welshing
welting
whelming
whelping
yelling
yelping
yelting

best-selling
compelling
dispelling
excelling
expelling
foretelling
foul smelling
impelling
misspelling
no telling
propelling
rappelling
rebelling
remelting
repelling
reselling
retelling
rewelding
softselling
sweet smelling

overselling
overwhelming
paralleling
Tori Spelling
underselling

ELLION

Belgian
Elgin

elsin
hellion
Kelvin
Melton
Melvin
Nelson
Sheldon
Shelton
stellion

rebellion

ELLIS (see ELFISH)
ELLISH (see ELFISH)
ELLISHING (see EDITING)
ELLISHMENT (see ELEGANT)

ELLO

bellow
cello
deco
echo
eggo
elbow
Elmo
exo
expo
fellow
fresco
ghetto
Greco
hello
Jell-O
Jethro
Lego
meadow
mellow
metro
mezzo
pesto
presto
recto
retro
techno
velcro
yellow
zesto

alfresco
allegro
art deco
bordello
convexo
El Greco
espresso
falsetto
Gepetto
good fellow
libretto
Longfellow
marshmallow
Modesto
Norelco
Othello
palmetto
perfecto
stiletto
tenesco

amaretto
Donatello
intermezzo
manifesto
Monticello
Pocatello
Rigoletto

L'Eggo My Eggo

ELLOW (see ELLO)
ELLULAR (see ECULAR)
ELLUM (see ECTRUM)

ELLY

Becky
belly
bestie
Betty
bevy
bready
celly
Chelsea
chesty
Chevy
deadly
deafly
Debbie

Delhi
deli
dreggy
dressy
Eddie
eddy
edgy
eggy
Elfie
Elsie
Espy
every
fleshy
healthy
heavy
hedgy
hefty
Jellies
jelly
Jessie
Kelly
Kelsey
ketchy
lefty
leggy
lessee
levee
levy
medley
meshy
Messi
messy
Nellie
Nestle
Peggy
peppy
Pepsi
pesky
pesty
petty
preppie
prexy
ready
Reggie
selfie
sexy
Shelby
Shelley
sketchy
smelly
steady

stealthy
stretchy
sweaty
techie
teddy
telly
testy
tetchy
Trekkie
veggie
vestry
vetchy
wealthy
wedgie
Wesley
wetly
zesty

abjectly
already
ancestry
Andretti
beer belly
burlesquely
confetti
correctly
directly
erectly
expressly
get ready
go steady
machete
New Delhi
pork belly
potbelly
spaghetti
top-heavy
unhealthy
Wayne Gretzgy

apoplexy
arabesquely
Botticelli
circumspectly
Elvis Presley
hot and heavy
I'm too Sexy
incorrectly
indirectly
Jelly Belly
Little Debbie

overwealthy
picturesquely
statuesquely
Welch's Jelly
yellow-belly

all right already
Dizzy Gillespie
Machiavelli

peanut butter and jelly

ELM (see ELT)
ELMA (see ELDA)
ELMER (see ELTER)
ELMET (see ELFISH)
ELMING (see ELLING)
ELMO (see ELLO)
ELMS (see ELVES)
ELODY (see ETICALLY)
ELON (see ESSION)
ELONY (see ETICALLY)
ELOPE (see ETICALLY)
ELOPMENT (see ELEGANT)
ELOQUENCE (see EMINENCE)
ELOQUENT (see ELEGANT)
ELP (see ELT)
ELPER (see ELTER)
ELPFUL (see EVEL)
ELPING (see ELLING)
ELPLESS (see ELFISH)
ELPS (see ELVES)
ELSA (see ELDA)
ELSE (see ELVES)
ELSEA (see ELLY)
ELSEY (see ELLY)
ELSH (see ELVES)
ELSHING (see ELLING)
ELSIE (see ELLY)
ELSIN (see ELLION)
ELSON (see ELLION)

ELT

belt
Celt
dealt
delve
dwelt
elf
elk

elm
felt
health
held
helm
help
knelt
meld
melt
pelt
realm
self
shelf
shelve
smelt
stealth
svelte
twelve
wealth
weld
welt
whelm
whelp
yelp

beheld
black belt
bookshelf
Corn Belt
fan belt
handheld
heartfelt
herself
himself
itself
misdealt
misspelt
myself
oneself
ourself
redealt
seatbelt
self-help
sunbelt
thyself
unfelt
upheld
withheld
yourself

board of health
commonwealth
Cotton Belt
garter belt
hired help
mental health
on the shelf
overwhelm
patty melt
Roosevelt
underwhelm

clean bill of health
do-it-yourself

ELTA (see ELDA)
ELTE (see ELT)

ELTER

belcher
belter
elder
Elmer
helper
melder
melter
seltzer
shelter
smelter
swelter
welder
welter
whelper
yelper

bomb shelter

Alka-Seltzer
helter skelter

animal shelter
Hamburger Helper

Santa's Little Helper

ELTIC (see ELFISH)
ELTING (see ELLING)
ELTON (see ELLION)
ELTS (see ELVES)

ELTZER (see ELTER)
ELVA (see ELDA)
ELVE (see ELT)

ELVES

belch
belts
delves
elks
elms
else
elves
gelds
helms
helps
melts
pelts
Phelps
realms
selves
shelves
welch
Welsh
welts
whelps

bookshelves
fan belts
ourselves
seatbelts
theirselves
themselves
yourselves

garter belts
patty melts
someone else

everything else
somebody else

ELVET (see ELFISH)
ELVIC (see ELFISH)
ELVIN (see ELLION)
ELVING (see ELLING)
ELVIS (see ELFISH)
EM (see EN)
EMA (see IA)
EMACY (see ENDENCY)

EMANE (see ENDENCY)
EMANENCE (see EMINENCE)
EMBASSY (see ENDENCY)
EMBER (see ENDER)
EMBERED (see ENTERED)

EMBERING

centering
entering
membering
rendering
tendering

dismembering
engendering
remembering

EMBLE (see ENTAL)
EMBLEM (see ENTUM)
EMBLY (see EMMY)
EME 1 (see EEN 1)
EME 2 (see EN)
EMEDY (see ENDENCY)
EMELESS (see ESIS)
EMELY (see EASY)
EMEN 1 (see ESIAN)
EMEN 2 (see ESSION)
EMENCE (see EDENCE)
EMENCY (see ENDENCY)
EMENT (see ENDENT)
EMENTLY (see ECENCY)
EMER (see EATER 1)
EMESIS (see ENEROUS)
EMI (see EMMY)
EMIA (see ENIA)
EMIAN (see EDIAN)
EMIC 1 (see ENTIOUS)
EMIC 2 (see ESIS)
EMICAL (see ENDABLE)
EMICALLY (see ENDENCY)
EMIE (see EASY)
EMIGRATION (see IMITATION)
EMINATE (see ENERATE)

EMINENCE

detriments
elegance
elements

elephants
eloquence
eminence
evidence
excellence
hesitance
pestilence
precedence
prevalence
recompense
relevance
remanence
resonance
reverence
severance

inelegance
inevidence
irrelevance
irreverence
preeminence

supereminence

EMING 1 (see EAMING)
EMING 2 (see ENDING)
EMINIST (see ENEROUS)
EMISE (see EALOUS)
EMISH (see ENTIOUS)
EMIST (see EANEST)
EMISTRY (see ENDENCY)
EMITE (see ENDENCY)
EMITIST (see ENEROUS)
EMITY (see ENDENCY)
EMIUM (see ELIUM)
EMIX (see EANEST)
EMLIN (see ENTION)
EMMA (see ENTA)
EMME (see EN)
EMMING (see ENDING)
EMMITT (see ENDENT)

EMMY

any
bendy
Benji
benny
Bentley
blenny

centry
demi
emmy
empty
entry
envy
fenny
frenzy
friendly
gemmy
gently
gentry
Hemi
Henry
jemmy
jenny
Kenny
Lenny
many
penny
phlegmy
plenty
semi
sentry
stemmy
tempty
trendy
twenty
Wendy
wenny

aplenty
assembly
attently
catchpenny
contently
fourpenny
halfpenny
intently
Jack Benny
lickpenny
McKenzie
misentry
nonempty
not any
outsentry
pickpenny
pinchpenny
postentry
reentry

scrapepenny
sixpenny
subentry
tenpenny
threepenny
tupenny
twelvepenny
twopenny
unendly
unfriendly

consequently
continently
discontently
evidently
Freckles Friendly
horn of plenty
incidently
J. C. Penney
lucky penny
overempty
point of entry
pretty penny
Spuds Mackenzie
subsequently
twenty-twenty

coincidently

EMN (see EN)
EMNANT (see ENDENT)
EMNING (see ENDING)
EMO 1 (see ENTO)
EMO 2 (see IO 1)
EMON 1 (see ESIAN)
EMON 2 (see ESSION)
EMONY (see ENDENCY)
EMORABLE (see EPARABLE)
EMORATE (see ENERATE)
EMORIST (see ENEROUS)
EMORY (see ENDENCY)
EMP (see ENT)
EMPATHY (see ENDENCY)
EMPER (see ENCHER)
EMPERATURE (see ENTURER)
EMPERED (see ENTERED)
EMPEREDLY (see ENDENCY)
EMPEROR (see ENTURER)
EMPHASIS (see ENEROUS)
EMPING (see ENDING)
EMPLARY (see ENDENCY)

EMPLE (see ENTAL)
EMPO (see ENTO)
EMPORAL (see ECTABLE)
EMPT (see ENT)
EMPTABLY (see ENDENCY)
EMPTER (see ENDER)
EMPTIEST (see ENEROUS)
EMPTING (see ENDING)
EMPTION (see ENTION)
EMPTIVE (see ENTIOUS)
EMPTY (see EMMY)
EMU (see ENU)
EMULATE (see ENERATE)
EMUR (see EATER 1)

EN

'em
Ben
bend
blend
den
end
femme
fend
friend
gem
glen
hem
hen
ken
lend
M
men
mend
N
pen
phlegm
rend
send
spend
stem
ten
tend
them
then
trend
vend
wend
when

wren
yen
Zen

a.m.
again
ahem
amen
amend
append
ascend
attend
bartend
befriend
best friend
Big Ben
Big Ten
boyfriend
bullpen
cayenne
Cheyenne
commend
condemn
contend
day's end
dead-end
defend
depend
descend
distend
expend
extend
firemen
FM
girlfriend
godsend
hang ten
has-been
he-men
high-end
impend
intend
kneebend
land's end
loose end
offend
p.m.
Pac Ten
pig pen
playpen

portend
pretend
rear end
RN
split end
suspend
tag end
tail end
take ten
the end
transcend
unbend
upend
wit's end
X-men
year-end

apprehend
ATM
ballpoint pen
Bethlehem
bitter end
born again
bosom friend
comprehend
condescend
count to ten
diadem
dividend
Eminem
end-to-end
fountain pen
IBM
lady friend
lion's den
man's best friend
MGM
might have been
mother hen
now and then
off-again
on the mend
on-again
once again
open-end
overspend
poison pen
R.E.M.
recommend
reprehend

requiem
round the bend
RPM
stratagem
supermen
theorem
three wise men
where or when

around the bend
creme de la creme
ESPN
fair-weather friend
family friend
gentleman friend
hold up one's end
misapprehend
now and again
off the deep end
over again
overextend
receiving end
slip of the pen
superintend
time and again
world without end

every now and then
OB-GYN
time and time again

ENA (see IA)
ENACE (see ENTIOUS)
ENAL (see EGAL)
ENALLY (see EITY)
ENALTY (see ENDENCY)
ENANCE (see ENDENCE)
ENANCY (see ENDENCY)
ENANT (see ENDENT)
ENATE (see ENDENT)
ENATOR (see ENTURER)
ENCE (see ENT)
ENCER (see ENDER)
ENCES (see ENTIOUS)

ENCH

bench
Benz
cleanse

clench
drench
French
quench
stench
trench
wench
wrench

avenge
entrench
park bench
revenge
Stonehenge
unclench
work bench

monkeywrench
warm the bench

Mercedez-Benz

Montezuma's revenge

ENCHANT (see ENDENT)
ENCHANTLY (see ENDENCY)

ENCHER

clencher
denture
drencher
quencher
temper
tenner
tenor
venture
yenner

adventure
distemper
entrencher
fist clencher
gut-wrencher
indenture
joint venture
teeth clencher

misadventure

ENCHES (see ENTIOUS)
ENCHIEST (see IPPIEST)
ENCHING (see ENDING)
ENCIA (see ILIA)
ENCIL (see ENTAL)
ENCING (see ENDING)
ENCO (see ENTO)
END (see EN)
ENDA (see ENTA)

ENDABLE

bendable
blendable
chemical
endable
genital
lendable
mendable
pentacle
plentiful
sendable
sensible
sensual
spendable
tentacle
wendable

accentual
amendable
ascendable
attendable
authentical
biennial
centennial
commendable
condensible
consensual
conventical
conventional
decennial
defendable
defensible
dependable
dimensional
dispensable
eventual
expendable

extendable
identical
insensible
intentional
millennial
novennial
octennial
ostensible
perennial
pretendable
quadrennial
quadriennial
quinquennial
septennial
sexennial
suspendable
sustentacle
tricennial
triennial
unbendable
vicennial

academical
bicentennial
comprehensible
epidemical
indefensible
indispensable
postmillennial
premillennial
recommendable
recompensable
reprehensible
tercentennial
three-dimensional
unconventional
undependable
unintentional

incomprehensible
irreprehensible
multidimensional

ENDABLY (see ENDENCY)
ENDAGE (see ITIOUS)
ENDANCE (see ENDENCE)
ENDANCY (see ENDENCY)
ENDANT (see ENDENT)

ENDED

blended
dented
ended
fended
mended
pended
rented
scented
splendid
tended
tented
vended
vented
wended

airvented
amended
appended
ascended
assented
attended
augmented
bartended
befriended
cemented
commended
consented
contended
contented
dead-ended
defended
demented
depended
descended
dissented
distended
expended
extended
fermented
fomented
impended
indented
intended
invented
lamented
offended
percented
portended

presented
pretended
prevented
rear-ended
relented
repented
resented
suspended
tormented
transcended
upended

apprehended
circumvented
complemented
complimented
comprehended
condescended
discontented
implemented
malcontented
open-ended
recommended
reprehended
represented
supplemented

experimented
misapprehended
misrepresented
overextended
superintended

ENDENCE

engine
ensign
entrance
penance
penguin
penman
sentence
vengeance

ascendance
attendance
dependence
malengine
relentence

repentence
resplendence
transcendence

independence

interdependence

ENDENCY

century
chemically
chemistry
clemency
demency
denimy
density
dentistry
embassy
emory
empathy
enemy
energy
enmity
entity
Kennedy
lemony
memory
mentally
penalty
pendency
pendently
remedy
sensibly
sensory
slenderly
temperedly
tenancy
tendency
tenderly
tensity
trenchantly
venomy

appendency
archenemy
ascendancy
ascendency
attendancy

compensary
contemptably
death penalty
defensibly
dependably
dependancy
dependency
dependently
descendancy
discrepancy
dispensary
exemplary
extremity
Gethsemane
hegemony
identity
ill-temperedly
immensity
impendency
inclemency
intendancy
intensity
lieutenancy
nonentity
ostensibly
parentally
prevenancy
propendency
propensity
resplendency
resplendently
subtenancy
supremacy
transcendency
transcendently
transplendency
vehemency
Yosemite

accidentally
complementary
complimentary
comprehensibly
condescendency
departmentally
detrimentally
dissapendency
documentary
elementary
equipendency

fundamentally
governmentally
hypertensity
incidentally
incrementally
independency
independently
instrumentally
John F. Kennedy
monumentally
parliamentary
penitentiary
reprehensibly
rudimentary
sentimentally
supplementary
temperamentally
undertenancy
vilipendency

coincidentally
environmentally
experimentally
incomprehensibly
interdependency
semidependently
superintendency

chemical dependency

ENDENT

Bennett
clement
Emmitt
genet
penchant
pendant
pennant
remnant
senate
sentient
tenant
tenet
trenchant

ascendant
assentment
attendant

contentment
cotenant
defendant
dependent
descendant
indentment
intrenchant
lieutenant
presentment
relentment
resentment
resplendent
subtenant
transcendent
untenant

appurtenant
co-defendant
co-dependent
discontentment
independent
malcontentment
representment
sublieutenant
U. S. Senate
undertenant

interdependent
superintendent

ENDENTLY (see ENDENCY)

ENDER

bender
blender
censor
censure
center
cleanser
denser
Denver
ember
ender
enter
fencer
fender
gender
lender

member
mender
prender
render
renter
sender
sensor
slender
Spencer
spender
splendor
tempter
tender
tenser
tensor
trender
vender
vendor

amender
appender
ascender
ascenter
attender
avenger
bartender
befriender
big spender
book lender
cementer
commencer
commender
condenser
contender
dead center
dead-ender
December
defender
degender
depender
descender
descenter
dismember
dispender
dispenser
dissenter
distender
ear bender
emender
engender

entender
extender
fermenter
frequenter
gang member
goaltender
hellbender
ingender
intender
inventor
John Denver
lamenter
mind bender
misrender
misspender
muckender
November
off center
offender
perpender
portender
presenter
pretender
provender
reenter
relenter
remember
repenter
resenter
September
SportsCenter
surrender
suspender
tormentor
trade center
transcender
upender
weekender

apprehender
big-time spender
circumventer
civic center
complementer
complimenter
comprehender
condescender
control center
discommender
do not enter

documenter
epicenter
fender bender
first offender
five-percenter
front and center
implementor
legal tender
moneylender
recommender
reprehender
representor
sex offender
shopping center
supplementer
trauma center
World Trade Center

medical center
misapprehender
overextender
public defender
superintender
Toxic Avenger

ENDERED (see ENTERED)
ENDERING (see EMBERING)
ENDERLESS (see ENEROUS)
ENDERLY (see ENDENCY)
ENDID (see ENDED)
ENDIEST (see ENEROUS)

ENDING

benching
bending
blending
cleansing
clenching
denting
drenching
ending
fencing
fending
Fleming
hemming
hemping
lemming
lending
mending

pending
penning
quenching
rending
renting
scenting
sending
sensing
spending
stemming
temping
tempting
tending
tensing
tenting
vending
venting
wending
wrenching
yenning

amending
appending
ascending
assenting
attempting
attending
augmenting
avenging
bartending
befriending
cementing
commencing
commending
condemning
condensing
consenting
contending
dead-ending
defending
defensing
depending
descending
dispensing
dissenting
distending
entrenching
exempting
expending
fermenting

fomenting
frequenting
gut-wrenching
impending
indenting
intending
inventing
lamenting
misspending
offending
portending
preempting
presenting
pretending
preventing
rehemming
relenting
repenting
resenting
suspending
tormenting
transcending
unbending
unclenching
upending

apprehending
circumventing
complementing
complimenting
comprehending
condescending
implementing
never-ending
overspending
patent pending
recommending
recompensing
representing
unrelenting

deficit spending
experimenting
misrepresenting
missapprehending
overextending
storybook ending

ENDITURE (see ENTURER)
ENDIX (see ENTIOUS)
ENDLESS (see ENTIOUS)

ENDLIEST (see ENEROUS)
ENDLY (see EMMY)
ENDO (see ENTO)
ENDON (see ENTION)
ENDOR (see ENDER)
ENDOUS (see ENTIOUS)
ENDRA (see ENTA)
ENDRE (see ONNA)
ENDRICK (see ENTIOUS)
ENDRIX (see ENTIOUS)
ENDUM (see ENTUM)
ENDY (see EMMY)
ENE (see EEN 1)
ENEFIT (see ENEROUS)
ENELY (see EASY)
ENEMY (see ENDENCY)
ENEOUS (see EAKIEST)
ENER (see EATER 1)
ENERAL (see ECTABLE)

ENERATE

emulate
fenereate
geminate
generate
memorate
penetrate
remorate
seminate
venerate

commemorate
degenerate
disseminate
effeminate
ingenerate
inseminate
intenerate
progenerate
regenerate
rememorate
reseminate

interpenetrate
unregenerate

ENEREATE (see ENERATE)
ENERGY (see ENDENCY)

ENEROUS

benefit
centurist
emphasis
emptiest
feminist
friendliest
genderless
generous
genesis
memorist
mentalist
nemesis
plentiest
seminist
Semitist
strenuous
tenuous
trendiest
venerous
venomous

congenerous
degenerous
ingenuous
nonvenomous
profeminist
ungenerous

disingenuous
fundamentalist
instrumentalist
multigenerous
orientalist
overemphasis
overgenerous
sacramentalist
sentimentalist
transcendentalist

environmentalist
experimentalist

antienvironmentalist

ENERY (see EITY)
ENESIS (see ENEROUS)
ENESS 1 (see ESIS)
ENESS 2 (see ITIS)
ENEST (see EANEST)

ENET (see ENDENT)
ENETRATE (see ENERATE)
ENGE (see ENCH)
ENGEANCE (see ENDENCE)
ENGER (see ENDER)
ENGINE (see ENDENCE)
ENGING (see ENDING)
ENGLAND (see ITION)
ENGLISH (see ITIOUS)
ENGTH (see ENT)
ENGTHEN (see ENTION)
ENGUIN (see ENDENCE)

ENIA

Celia
media

Alicia
Amelia
anemia
Armenia
asthenia
Bohemia
bulimia
Cecelia
gardenia
leukemia
mass media
Ophelia
toxemia

academia
multimedia
paraphelia
schizophrenia

encyclopedia
hypoglycemia

sickle cell anemia

ENIAL (see IEVABLE)
ENIC (see ESIS)
ENICE (see ENTIOUS)
ENIE (see EASY)
ENIENCE (see EDENCE)
ENIENT (see EDIENT)
ENIENTLY (see ECENCY)
ENIM (see ENTUM)

ENIMY (see ENDENCY)
ENING (see EAMING)
ENIOR (see EATER 1)
ENIOUS (see ESIS)
ENIS (see ESIS)
ENISH (see ENTIOUS)
ENITAL (see ENDABLE)
ENITH (see ESIS)
ENITOR (see ENTURER)
ENITY (see ILITY)
ENIUS (see ESIS)
ENJI (see EMMY)
ENMAN (see ENDENCE)
ENMITY (see ENDENCY)
ENNA (see ENTA)
ENNAGE (see ITIOUS)
ENNANT (see ENDENT)
ENNE 1 (see EN)
ENNE 2 (see IN 1)
ENNEDY (see ENDENCY)
ENNER (see ENCHER)
ENNETT (see ENDENT)
ENNEY (see EMMY)
ENNIAL (see ENDABLE)
ENNIFER (see ENTURER)
ENNING (see ENDING)
ENNIS (see ENTIOUS)
ENNOX (see ENTIOUS)
ENNY (see EMMY)
ENO 1 (see INO 3)
ENO 2 (see ERO 2)
ENO 3 (see ENTO)
ENOM (see ENTUM)
ENOMOUS (see ENEROUS)
ENOMY (see ENDENCY)
ENON (see EON)
ENOR (see ENCHER)
ENOS (see ESIS)
ENOUS (see ESIS)
ENRE (see ONNA)
ENRY (see EMMY)
ENSABLE (see ENDABLE)
ENSARY (see ENDENCY)
ENSATIVE (see ENSITIVE)
ENSE (see ENT)
ENSELESS (see ENTIOUS)
ENSER (see ENDER)
ENSES (see ENTIOUS)
ENSIBLE (see ENDABLE)
ENSIBLY (see ENDENCY)
ENSICS (see ENTIOUS)
ENSIGN (see ENDENCE)
ENSIL (see ENTAL)

ENSING (see ENDING)
ENSION (see ENTION)
ENSIONAL (see ENDABLE)

ENSITIVE

pensative
sensitive
tentative

augmentative
fermentative
frequentative
insensitive
intensative
intensitive
nonsensitive
presentative
preventative
sustentative
unsensitive

argumentative
complimentative
hypersensitive
hyposensative
oversensitive
photosensitive
representative
supersensitive

experimentative
misrepresentative
nonrepresentative
radiosensitive
unrepresentative

ENSITY (see ENDENCY)
ENSIVE (see ENTIOUS)
ENSOR (see ENDER)
ENSORED (see ENTERED)
ENSORY (see ENDENCY)
ENSUAL (see ENDABLE)
ENSURE (see ENDER)
ENSURED (see ENTERED)
ENSUS (see ENTIOUS)

ENT

bent
cent
dense
dent
dreamt
Ent.
fence
gent
hemp
hence
kemp
length
lent
meant
rent
scent
sense
sent
Spence
spent
strength
temp
tempt
tense
tent
tenth
thence
vent
went
whence

against
airvent
assent
at length
attempt
augment
brute stength
cement
Clark Kent
commence
condense
consent
contempt
content
defense
descent
dispense

dissent
event
exempt
expense
extent
ferment
foment
for rent
full strength
full-length
good sense
hellbent
horse sense
ill-spent
immense
incense
indent
intense
intent
invent
lament
make sense
misspent
nonsense
offence
offense
past tense
percent
preempt
present
pretense
prevent
relent
repent
resent
sixth sense
suspense
unbent
unspent
wavelength
well spent

came and went
chain-link fence
circumvent
common sense
complement
compliment
consequence
consequent

discontent
false pretense
frankincense
future tense
heart's content
heaven sent
hypertense
implement
in a sense
make a dent
malcontent
no nonsense
on the fence
Pepsodent
picket fence
present tense
reinvent
represent
self-defense
tax-exempt
underwent

age of consent
biblical sense
civil defense
experiment
misrepresent
over the fence
sit on the fence
tower of stength

criminal contempt
go to any length
in any event
national defense
one hundred percent
truth or consequence

out-of-pocket expense

ENTA

Brenda
Emma
Jenna
Kendra

addenda
agenda

antenna
credenza
dilemma
magenta
placenta
polenta

hacienda
influenza
referenda

Oscar de la Renta

ENTACLE (see ENDABLE)
ENTAGE (see ENTIOUS)

ENTAL

central
dental
gentle
lentil
mental
pencil
rental
scentful
stencil
temple
tensil
tremble

assemble
contentful
credential
essential
eventful
fragmental
inventful
judgmental
parental
placental
potential
prudential
regental
relentful
repentful
resemble
resentful
segmental

sequential
tormentful
torrential
utensil

accidental
compartmental
complemental
confidential
consequential
continental
deferential
departmental
detrimental
differential
documental
elemental
existential
fundamental
governmental
implemental
incidental
incremental
inessential
influential
instrumental
monumental
oriental
ornamental
preferential
presidential
providential
quintessential
reassemble
referential
regimental
residential
reverential
sacramental
sentimental
Shirley Temple
summer rental
supplemental
unessential
uneventful

coincidental
developmental
environmental
experimental

inconsequential
temperamental

intercontinental
interdepartmental

ENTALIST (see ENEROUS)
ENTALLY (see ENDENCY)
ENTARY (see ENDENCY)
ENTATIVE (see ENSITIVE)
ENTE (see ONT 2)
ENTED (see ENDED)
ENTENCE (see ENDENCE)
ENTER (see ENDER)

ENTERED

censored
censured
centered
entered
fendered
gendered
membered
mentored
rendered
tempered
tendered
ventured

dismembered
distempered
engendered
foremembered
reentered
remembered
self-centered
surrendered
uncensored
unentered

misadventured
unremembered

ENTERING (see EMBERING)
ENTFUL (see ENTAL)
ENTH (see ENT)
ENTIAL (see ENTAL)
ENTIARY (see ENDENCY)
ENTIC (see ENTIOUS)

ENTICAL (see ENDABLE)
ENTICE (see ENTIOUS)
ENTIENT (see ENDENT)
ENTIEST (see ENEROUS)
ENTIFUL (see ENDABLE)
ENTIL (see ENTAL)
ENTING (see ENDING)

ENTION

gremlin
lengthen
mention
pension
strengthen
tendon
tension

abstention
ascension
attention
contention
convention
descension
detention
dimension
dissension
exemption
extension
indention
intention
invention
pretension
prevention
redemption
retension
subvention
suspension

apprehension
circumvention
comprehension
condescension
hypertension
inattention
intervention
not to mention
reprehension
three dimension

misapprehension

honorable mention
retirement pension

ENTIONAL (see ENDABLE)

ENTIOUS

benches
bendless
blemish
blendous
census
centric
Dennis
dentist
dentless
endless
Ennis
fences
friendless
Kendrick
Lennox
lentic
menace
pensive
plenish
rhenish
scentless
senseless
senses
tennis
tenses
tentless
trendless
Venice
ventage
ventless

abstentious
acentric
adventist
appendix
apprentice
attentive
augmentive
authentic
commences

concentric
condenses
condensive
consensus
contentious
contentless
defenseless
defenses
defensive
dementive
dispenses
displenish
dissentious
eccentric
eccentrics
eventless
excentric
expenses
expensive
extensive
forensics
horrendous
incentive
intensive
intentness
inventious
inventive
lamentive
licentious
momentous
offenseless
offenses
offensive
percentage
portentous
preemptive
pretenses
pretentious
preventive
relentive
relentless
repentive
repentless
replenish
retentive
stupendous
suspenseless
systemic
tormentive
tremendous

academic
apprehensive
circumventive
comprehensive
conscientious
consequences
egocentric
epidemic
hypertensive
implementive
incedentless
inexpensive
Jimi Hendrix
precedentless
recompenses
recompensive
reprehensive
representive
table tennis
unauthentic
unoffensive
unrepentive

business expenses
come to your senses
Dennis The Menace
experimentive
hyperglycemic
hypoglycemic
incomprehensive
labor-intensive

overconscientious
truth or consequences

ENTIST (see ENTIOUS)
ENTISTRY (see ENDENCY)
ENTITY (see ENDENCY)
ENTIVE (see ENTIOUS)
ENTLE (see ENTAL)
ENTLESS (see ENTIOUS)
ENTLEY (see EMMY)
ENTLY (see EMMY)
ENTMENT (see ENDENT)
ENTNESS (see ENTIOUS)

ENTO

cento
demo

kempo
lento
memo
MO
tempo

crescendo
flamenco
Jay Leno
Lorenzo
memento
Nintendo
pimento
up-tempo

innuendo
Sacramento

diminuendo
Dr. Demento

ENTOR (see ENDER)
ENTORED (see ENTERED)
ENTOUS (see ENTIOUS)
ENTRAL (see ENTAL)
ENTRANCE (see ENDENCE)
ENTREE (see ANCE 3)
ENTRIC (see ENTIOUS)
ENTRICS (see ENTIOUS)
ENTRY (see EMMY)
ENTUAL (see ENDABLE)

ENTUM

denim
emblem
venom

addendum
agendum
blue denim
credendum
envenom
momentum
outvenom
snake venom

referendum

ENTURE (see ENCHER)
ENTURED (see ENTERED)

ENTURER

emperor
Jennifer
senator
venturer

adventurer
expenditure
progenitor
temperature

coadventurer

ENTURIST (see ENEROUS)
ENTURY (see ENDENCY)
ENTY (see EMMY)

ENU

emu
genu
menu
venue

parvenu

change of venue

ENUE (see ENU)
ENUOUS (see ENEROUS)
ENUS (see ESIS)
ENVER (see ENDER)
ENVY (see EMMY)
ENZ (see ENCH)
ENZA (see ENTA)
ENZIE (see EMMY)
ENZO (see ENTO)
ENZY (see EMMY)
EO (see IO 1)

EON

aeon
Egon
eon
freon
Leon
neon

Nissan
paeon
peon
pheon
recon
xenon

EOPARD (see EPHERD)
EOPARDY (see ETICALLY)
EOPLE (see EGAL)
EORY (see EARY)
EP (see ET 1)
EPANCY (see ENDENCY)

EPARABLE

eligible
inseparable
irreparable
measurable
memorable
pleasurable
preparable
reparable
separable
severable
treasurable
unseparable
vegetable

displeasurable
immeasurable
inevitable

EPE (see ACE 1)
EPEE (see EASY)
EPER (see ECTOR)
EPHEN (see ESIAN)

EPHERD

bettered
festered
fettered
gestured
lectured
ledgered
leopard
lettered

peppered
pressured
record
severed
shepherd
tethered

endeavored
track record
unfettered
unlettered

broken record
German shepherd
off-the-record
salt-and-peppered

EPHRON (see ECTRUM)
EPHYR (see ECTOR)
EPIC (see ETIC)
EPICAL (see ECTABLE)
EPICALLY (see ETICALLY)
EPID (see ECTED)
EPITATE (see ESTIGATE)
EPLICA (see ERICA)
EPO (see IO 1)
EPOT (see IO 1)
EPOTIST (see ECTIONIST)
EPP (see ET 1)
EPPELIN (see ESSION)
EPPER (see ECTOR)
EPPERED (see EPHERD)
EPPERER (see EASURER)
EPPIE (see ELLY)
EPPIER (see EDGIER)
EPPING (see ESSING)
EPPY (see ELLY)
EPROSY (see ETICALLY)
EPSI (see ELLY)
EPT (see ET 1)
EPTABLE (see ECTABLE)
EPTACLE (see ECTABLE)
EPTED (see ECTED)
EPTER (see ECTOR)
EPTH (see ESS)
EPTIBLE (see ECTABLE)
EPTIC (see ETIC)
EPTICAL (see ECTABLE)
EPTING (see ESSING)
EPTION (see ESSION)
EPTIONAL (see ECTABLE)
EPTIONIST (see ECTIONIST)

EPTIVE (see ESSIVE)
EPTOR (see ECTOR)
EPTUAL (see ECTABLE)
EPUTY (see ETICALLY)
EQUAL (see EGAL)
EQUALLY (see EITY)
EQUE (see ET 1)
EQUEL (see EGAL)
EQUENCE (see EDENCE)
EQUENCY (see ECENCY)

EQUENT

decedent
decent
easement
frequent
indecent
needn't
preachment
precent
recent
sequent
treatment

achievement
agreement
appeachment
appeasement
bereavement
diseasement
entreatment
impeachment
infrequent
maltreatment
mistreatment
obsequent
posttreatment
relievement
retreatment
retrievement
undecent
unfrequent

disagreement
nonagreement
overfrequent

overachievement
underachievement

EQUENTLY (see ECENCY)
EQUIN (see ESIAN)
EQUINAL (see ECTABLE)
EQUITY (see ETICALLY)

ER 1

blur
burr
cur
err
fir
fur
her
Kerr
myrrh
per
purr
sir
slur
spur
stir
were
whir

astir
aver
Ben Hur
bestir
Big Sur
concur
confer
defer
demur
deter
incur
infer
inter
occur
prefer
recur
refer
yessir

as it were
disinter
him and her

ER 2 (see ARE 1)
ERA (see ARA)

ERAL (see EVEL)
ERALD (see EVEL)
ERANCE (see ERENCE)
ERAPIN (see ELEGANT)
ERAPIST (see ECTIONIST)
ERAPY (see ERITY1)
ERATIVE (see ECUTIVE)
ERATON (see ELEGANT)
ERB (see ORD 2)
ERBAGE (see ERVICE)
ERBAL (see URTLE)
ERBALLY (see ERNITY)
ERBIAGE (see ERVICE)
ERBIAL (see URTABLE)
ERBICIDE (see ERSIFY)
ERBIE (see IRTY)
ERBIL (see URTLE)
ERBOLE (see ERNITY)
ERBY (see IRTY)
ERCE (see IRST)
ERCER (see URNER)
ERCERY (see ERNITY)
ERCH (see IRST)
ERCHANT (see ERSION)
ERCHER (see URNER)
ERCHERY (see ERNITY)
ERCHING (see ERTING)
ERCIAL (see URTLE)
ERCIALLY (see ERNITY)
ERCIBLE (see URTABLE)
ERCIFUL (see URTABLE)
ERCING (see ERTING)
ERCION (see ERSION)
ERCIVE (see ERVICE)
ERCIVELY (see ERNITY)
ERCOLATE (see ERMINATE)
ERCURY (see ERNITY)
ERCY (see IRTY)
ERD (see ORD 2)
ERDED (see URDED)
ERDER (see URNER)
ERDICT (see ERVICE)
ERDING (see ERTING)
ERDURE (see URNER)
ERDY (see IRTY)
ERE 1 (see EAR 1)
ERE 2 (see ARE 1)
ERE 3 (see ER 1)
EREAL (see ERIAL 1)
ERED (see EARED)
EREK (see ERIC 1)
ERELESS (see EARLESS)
ERELY (see EARY)

EREMY (see ERITY1)
EREN'T (see ERSION)

ERENCE

clearance

adherence
appearance
coherence
inherence

disappearance
domineerance
incoherence
interference
perseverance
reappearance

ERENESS (see EARLESS)
ERENT (see ARENT)
EREO (see ARIO 1)
ERER (see EARER)
EREST (see EAREST)
ERESY (see ERITY1)
ERF (see IRST)
ERFECT (see ERVICE)
ERFORATE (see ERMINATE)
ERG (see ORD 2)
ERGABLE (see URTABLE)
ERGE (see ORD 2)
ERGEANT (see ARTMENT)
ERGENCE (see ERSION)
ERGENCY (see ERNITY)
ERGENT (see ERSION)
ERGER (see URNER)
ERGIC (see ERVICE)
ERGING (see ERTING)
ERGO (see ERNO)
ERGY (see IRTY)
ERI (see ARY)

ERIA 1

Syria

Algeria
bacteria
criteria
diphtheria

Iberia
Liberia
Nigeria
Siberia

cafeteria

ERIA 2 (see AREA)

ERIAL 1

cereal
serial

bacterial
boxed cereal
ethereal
imperial
impirial
material
venereal

immaterial
managerial
raw material

ERIAL 2 (see ARABLE)

ERIAN

Syrian

Algerian
criterion
Iberian
Liberian
Nigerian
Siberian

Presbyterian

ERIC 1

cherish
cleric
Derek
derrick
Eric

ferret
ferrous
harem
merit
perish
sheriff
sherriff
tariff
terrace

barbaric
Bo Derek
demerit
generic
Homeric
hysteric
inherit
numeric
oil derrick

badge of merit
esoteric

ERIC 2 (see ISTIC)

ERICA

Erica
plethora
replica
retina

America
Angelica
etcetera

Miss America

Captain America

Justice League of America

ERICAL 1 (see ARABLE)
ERICAL 2 (see ITTABLE)
ERICAN (see ELEGANT)
ERICHO (see ARIO 1)
ERIE 1 (see EARY)
ERIE 2 (see ARY)
ERIER (see ERIOR)
ERIFF (see ERIC 1)

ERIFY (see ECTIFY)
ERIL (see EVEL)
ERILE (see EVEL)
ERILY (see ERITY1)
ERING (see EERING)
ERIOD (see ERIOUS)
ERION (see ERIAN)

ERIOR

blearier
cheerier
drearier
eerier
leerier
smearier
sneerier
tearier
wearier

exterior
inferior
interior
posterior
superior
ulterior

Lake Superior

ERIOUS

cheeriest
eeriest
leeriest
myriad
period
serious

delirious
imperious
materious
mysterious

semiserious

ERISH (see ERIC 1)
ERISHING (see EDITING)
ERIT (see ERIC 1)
ERITING (see EDITING)

ERITY 1

airily
heresy
Jeremy
merrily
scarily
terribly
therapy
verily
verity
warily

austerity
dexterity
posterity
prosperity
severity
sincerity
temerity

insincerity

ambidexterity

ERITY 2 (see ARITY)
ERJURE (see URNER)
ERJURY (see ERNITY)
ERK (see ORK 1)
ERKER (see URNER)
ERKING (see ERTING)
ERKY (see IRTY)
ERLATIVE (see ERVATIVE)
ERLESS (see ARENESS)
ERLIN (see ERSION)
ERLING (see ERTING)
ERLOT (see ERNO)
ERM (see URN)
ERMAL (see URTLE)
ERMAN (see ERSION)
ERMANENT (see OURAGEMENT)
ERMEATE (see ERMINATE)
ERMENT (see ERSION)
ERMIN (see ERSION)
ERMINAL (see URTABLE)

ERMINATE

germinate
percolate
perforate

permeate
terminate

exterminate
imperforate

predeterminate

ERMINE (see ERSION)
ERMING (see ERTING)
ERMIS (see ERVICE)
ERMON (see ERSION)
ERMOS (see ERVICE)
ERMY (see IRTY)
ERN (see URN)
ERNAL (see URTLE)
ERNALIZE (see ERSIFY)
ERNALLY (see ERNITY)
ERNATIVE (see ERVATIVE)
ERNE (see URN)
ERNEL (see URTLE)
ERNER (see URNER)
ERNEST (see ERVICE)
ERNIBLY (see ERNITY)
ERNIE (see IRTY)
ERNING (see ERTING)

ERNITY

burglary
burgundy
certainly
certainty
circuitry
courtesy
currency
currently
cursively
cursory
curtesy
earnestly
fervently
firmity
furmity
furtively
herbally
hurtfully
mercery
mercury
nervously
nursery

perjury
purgery
surdity
surgery
tersory
urgency
urgently
verbally
vernally
vertically

absurdity
adversity
alternity
assertively
assurgency
coercery
coercively
commercially
concurrency
concurrently
convergency
decursively
discernibly
discourtesy
discursively
discursory
divergency
diversity
diversory
emergency
eternally
eternity
excursively
externally
fraternally
fraternity
hyperbole
incertainty
infernally
infirmity
insurgency
internally
internity
maternally
maternity
modernity
nocturnally
observably
observantly

paternally
paternity
percursory
perversity
precursory
recurrency
recurrently
recursively
resurgency
reversibly
superchery
uncertainty

anniversary
chemosurgery
coeternity
controversary
cryosurgery
Freddie Mercury
irreversibly
microsurgery
multiversity
neurosurgery
nonassertively
noncommercially
nonconcurrently
preeternity
undiscernibly
university
unobservantly

counterinsurgency
electrosurgery
overassertively
overdiversity
uncontroversory

interuniversity

ERNLY (see IRTY)

ERNO

borough
burro
burrow
ergo
furrow
Merlot

Sterno
thorough
turbo
Virgo

Alberto
concerto
inferno
Marlborough
Umberto
unthorough

Towering Inferno

ERNON (see ERSION)
ERNY (see IRTY)

ERO 1

hero
negro
Nero
weirdo
zero

ground zero
Shapiro
subzero
war hero

below zero
Less then Zero
superhero

Robert De Niro

ERO 2

beso
faro
Pedro
peso
pueblo
queso

bolero
Camaro
dinero

ranchero
Romero
sombrero
torero

jalapeño

Pinky Tuscadero
Rio de Janeiro

EROIN (see ELEGANT)
EROINE (see ELEGANT)
ERP (see ORK 1)
ERPENT (see ERSION)
ERPING (see ERTING)
ERPT (see ORK 1)
ERQUE (see IRTY)
ERR (see ER 1)
ERRA (see ARA)
ERRABLE (see URTABLE)
ERRACE (see ERIC 1)
ERRAL (see URTLE)
ERRANT (see ARENT)
ERRE (see ARE 1)
ERRED (see ARED 1)
ERRENT (see ERSION)
ERRET (see ERIC 1)
ERRIBLE (see ARABLE)
ERRIBLY (see ERITY1)
ERRICK (see ERIC 1)
ERRIER (see ARRIER)
ERRIFF (see ERIC 1)
ERRIFY (see ECTIFY)
ERRILL (see EVEL)
ERRILY (see ERITY1)
ERRING 1 (see ERTING)
ERRING 2 (see ARING)
ERROL (see EVEL)
ERROR (see ECTOR)
ERRORIST (see ECTIONIST)
ERROUS (see ERIC 1)
ERRY (see ARY)
ERSABLE (see URTABLE)
ERSAL (see URTLE)
ERSARY (see ERNITY)
ERSATIVE (see ERVATIVE)
ERSCHEL (see URTLE)
ERSE (see IRST)
ERSELY (see IRTY)
ERSER (see URNER)
ERSEY (see IRTY)
ERSHEY (see IRTY)

ERSHWIN (see ERSION)
ERSIAL (see URTLE)
ERSIAN (see ERSION)
ERSIBLE (see URTABLE)
ERSIBLY (see ERNITY)

ERSIFY

certify
herbicide
journalize
vernalize
versify

diversify
eternalize
externalize
internalize

subdiversify

overdiversify

ERSING (see ERTING)

ERSION

Berman
bourbon
burden
burgeon
Burton
certain
currant
current
curtain
ermine
fervent
German
Herman
merchant
mergence
Merlin
merman
Persian
person
sermon
serpent
servant

Sherman
sturgeon
surgeon
turban
urban
urchin
urgent
vermin
Vernon
version
virgin
weren't
worsen

abstergent
alertin
aspersion
assertion
aversion
chairperson
coercion
concurrent
confirmance
convergence
convergent
conversion
convertin
crosscurrent
deferment
desertion
detergent
determent
determine
deterrent
dispersion
disturbance
divergence
divergent
diversion
emergence
emergent
emersion
excursion
exertion
for certain
immersion
incursion
insertion
insurgence
insurgent

interment
inversion
layperson
maidservant
make certain
manservant
Mt. Vernon
nonperson
observant
perversion
recurrent
recursion
resurgence
resurgent
reversion
short version
smoked sturgeon
spokesperson
Steve Irwin
submergence
submersion
suburban
subversion
unburden
uncertain

anchor person
bamboo curtain
beast of burden
blackout curtain
civil servant
disconcertion
displaced person
extroversion
final curtain
introversion
Ira Gershwin
iron curtain
overburden
Pee-wee Herman
people person
plastic surgeon
predetermine
undercurrent
unobservant
vestal virgin

overexertion
person-to-person
ring down the curtain

holiday excursion

ERSITY (see ERNITY)
ERSIVE (see ERVICE)
ERSON (see ERSION)
ERSONAL (see URTABLE)
ERSORY (see ERNITY)
ERST (see IRST)
ERSUS (see ERVICE)
ERSY (see IRTY)
ERT (see ORK 1)
ERTABLE (see URTABLE)
ERTAIN (see ERSION)
ERTAINLY (see ERNITY)
ERTAINTY (see ERNITY)
ERTED (see URDED)
ERTER (see URNER)
ERTH (see IRST)
ERTIAL (see URTLE)
ERTIBLE (see URTABLE)
ERTICAL (see URTABLE)
ERTICALLY (see ERNITY)
ERTIE (see IRTY)
ERTIFY (see ERSIFY)
ERTIGO (see URTABLE)
ERTILE (see URTLE)
ERTIN (see ERSION)

ERTING

birthing
blurring
blurting
burning
burping
burring
bursting
chirping
churning
clerking
curbing
curding
curling
cursing
curving
during
earning
firming
flirting
furling
girding
herding
hurling

hurting
irking
Irving
jerking
learning
lurching
luring
lurking
merging
mooring
nursing
perching
perking
perming
purging
purling
purring
pursing
searching
serving
shirking
skirting
slurping
slurring
smirking
splurging
spurning
spurring
spurting
squirming
squirting
sterling
stirring
surfing
surging
swerving
terming
thirsting
touring
turning
twerping
urging
verging
versing
whirling
whirring
wording
working
worming
yearning

adjourning
affirming
alluring
asserting
assuring
averting
besmirching
book-learning
chauffeuring
coercing
concerning
concurring
conferring
confirming
conserving
contouring
converging
conversing
converting
cross-burning
curdling
deferring
demurring
deserting
deserving
deterring
detouring
deworming
disbursing
discerning
dispersing
disturbing
diverging
diverting
emerging
enduring
everting
exerting
girdling
hair curling
hurdling
immersing
incurring
inferring
inserting
interning
interring
inverting
maturing
networking

not working
observing
occurring
perturbing
perverting
preferring
preserving
recurring
referring
rehearsing
researching
reserving
resurging
returning
reversing
reverting
rewording
reworking
self-serving
sojourning
soul-searching
strip-searching
submerging
submersing
subverting
sunburning
tearjerking
transversing
traversing
uncurling
unearthing
unfurling
unlearning
unnerving
upsurging

bloodcurdling
body-searching
disaffirming
disconcerting
disinterring
interspersing
overturning
reaffirming
reassuring
reconfirming
reemerging
reimbursing
resubmerging
undiscerning

overexerting

ERTION (see ERSION)
ERTIVE (see ERVICE)
ERTIVELY (see ERNITY)
ERTLY (see IRTY)
ERTO (see ERNO)
ERTY (see IRTY)
ERVABLY (see ERNITY)
ERVANT (see ERSION)
ERVANTLY (see ERNITY)

ERVATIVE

acervative
adversative
affirmative
alternative
confirmative
conservative
conversative
infirmative
observative
preservative
reservative
superlative

ERVE (see ORD 2)
ERVENT (see ERSION)
ERVENTLY (see ERNITY)
ERVER (see URNER)
ERVES (see ORD 2)
ERVICAL (see URTABLE)

ERVICE

blurbish
burnish
cervix
circuit
circus
courage
cursive
Curtis
dermis
earnest
Ernest
firmest
furnace
furnish
furtive

nervous
nourish
perfect
purchase
purpose
service
skirmish
sternest
surface
thermos
Turkish
verbage
verbiage
verdict
versus
worship
worthless

all-purpose
allergic
assertive
aversive
blast furnace
coercive
concertive
conversive
cross-purpose
decursive
discourage
discursive
disservice
diversive
divertive
encourage
excursive
exertive
inversive
invertive
lip service
maid service
on purpose
perversive
recursive
refurbish
refurnish
revertive
room service
self-service
subversive
unfurtive

unnervous
wire service

badge of courage
civil service
epidermis
extrovertive
introvertive
multipurpose
out of service
secret service
self-assertive
three-ring circus
undernourish

Jamie Lee Curtis
practice makes perfect

ERVING (see ERTING)
ERVIX (see ERVICE)
ERVOR (see URNER)
ERVOUS (see ERVICE)
ERVOUSLY (see ERNITY)
ERVY (see IRTY)
ERY (see ARY)
ERYL (see EVEL)
ES (see ESS)
ESA 1 (see IA)
ESA 2 (see ASIA)
ESAGE (see EALOUS)
ESAME (see ETICALLY)
ESANT (see ESCENT)
ESBIAN (see ESTRIAN)
ESCA (see ELLA)
ESCE (see ESS)

ESCENCE

crescents
essence
nescience
preference
presence
reference

cross-reference
depressants
fluorescence
oppressants
quiescence

quintessence
repellence

acquiescence
adolescence
convalescence
effervescence
frame of reference
iridescence
luminescence
obsolescence
omnipresence
phosphorescence

ESCENT

cessant
cessment
crescent
extant
gestant
jessant
peasant
pheasant
pleasant
pregnant
questant
restant
segment
sextant
vestment

arrestment
ascessant
assessment
attestant
bisegment
candescent
confessant
congestant
contestant
depressant
digestant
divestment
fluorescent
impressment
incessant
investment
malfeasant

nonextant
oppressant
quiescent
redressment
refreshment
subsegment
suggestment
suppresant
uncessant
unpleasant

acquiescent
adolescent
convalescent
decongestant
disinfectant
disinfestant
effervescent
evanescent
incandescent
iridescent
juvenescent
obsolescent
reassessment
reinvestment

antidepressant
beauty contestant
overassessment
underassessment

immunosuppressant

ESCENTS (see ESCENCE)
ESCER (see ESSOR)
ESCIENCE (see ESCENCE)
ESCING (see ESSING)
ESCO (see ELLO)
ESE 1 (see EED 1)
ESE 2 (see EAT 1)
ESECRATE (see ESTIGATE)
ESENCE (see ESCENCE)
ESENT (see ETIC)
ESH (see ESS)
ESHEN (see ESSION)
ESHER (see ECTOR)
ESHING (see ESSING)
ESHIRE (see ECTOR)
ESHMAN (see ESSION)
ESHMENT (see ESCENT)
ESHY (see ELLY)

ESIA (see IA)

ESIAN

beacon
cheapen
deacon
deepen
demon
Ethan
even
heathen
Keenan
legion
lesion
reason
region
seaman
season
semen
sequin
steepen
Stephen
Steven
treason
weaken
weekend

adhesion
artesian
break even
Cartesian
cohesion
collegian
completion
deletion
depletion
excretion
get even
high treason
Mohican
Parisian
Rhodesian
secretion
speed demon
Tunisian
uneven
Venetian

even-steven
foreign legion
incompletion
Indonesian
Jackie Gleason
Morgan Freeman
out of season
Polynesian
stand to reason

no rhyme or reason

American Legion

ESICS 1 (see EANEST)
ESICS 2 (see EANEST)
ESIDENT (see ELEGANT)
ESIGNATE (see ESTIGATE)
ESIMAL (see ECTABLE)
ESIN (see ESSION)
ESION (see ESIAN)
ESIONAL (see ECTABLE)

ESIS

beamless
bleakness
briefless
chiefless
cleanness
creamless
creedless
dreamless
Enos
feeless
feetless
fetus
freeness
genius
genus
greenness
grievous
heatless
heedless
Jesus
keenness
keyless
kneeless
leafless

leanness
meanness
meatless
meekness
memeless
neatest
neatness
needless
penis
reefless
scenic
schemeless
schesis
screamless
seamless
seatless
seedless
seemless
sleekness
sleepless
sleeveless
specious
speechless
spleenless
squeamish
steedless
steepness
streamless
Swedish
sweetest
sweetness
teamless
teetless
themeless
thesis
treatise
treeless
Venus
weakness
weaveless
weedless
zenith

adhesive
aesthesis
anemic
anthesis
appeasive
auxesis
bejesus

bulimic
cohesive
comedic
completeness
concreteness
deesis
defeatist
discreetness
discreteness
egregious
eliteness
elitist
facetious
illesive
ingenious
kinesis
mathesis
Miletus
mimesis
noesis
obliqueness
ochlesis
orthopedic
paresis
petiteness
prestigious
prosthesis
uniqueness
upbeatness

coenesthesis
intravenous
nonadhesive
noncohesive
senior thesis

telekinesis

ESITANCE (see EMINENCE)
ESITANT (see ELEGANT)
ESITATE (see ESTIGATE)
ESITY (see EITY)
ESIUM (see ELIUM)
ESIVE (see ESIS)
ESK (see ESS)
ESKY (see ELLY)
ESLA (see ELLA)
ESLEY (see ELLY)
ESO (see ERO 2)
ESOLATE (see ECTIONIST)
ESONANCE (see EMINENCE)

ESONATE (see ESTIGATE)
ESPERATE (see ECTIONIST)
ESPIAN (see ESTRIAN)
ESPIE (see ELLY)
ESPY (see ELLY)
ESQUE (see ESS)
ESQUELY (see ELLY)

ESS

best
bless
blest
breadth
breast
breath
chef
chess
chest
clef
cleft
cress
crest
deaf
death
def
deft
depth
desk
dress
eft
etch
F
fest
fetch
fez
flesh
fresh
guess
guest
Jeff
jest
ketch
lech
left
less
lest
mesh
mess
meth

nest
pest
Pez
press
prez
quest
ref
rest
retch
S
says
sketch
stress
stretch
Tess
test
theft
thresh
vest
west
wretch
yes
zest

abreast
address
afresh
armrest
arrest
assess
at best
attest
B.S.
backrest
bad breath
bed rest
bench-press
bereft
bird nest
blood test
burlesque
caress
Celeste
compress
confess
congest
conquest
contest
Cortez
depress

detest
digest
digress
distress
divest
duress
egress
excess
express
far west
finesse
footrest
free press
French chef
front desk
funfest
gabfest
grand theft
grotesque
headdress
headrest
homestretch
hope chest
housedress
houseguest
ice chest
impress
in jest
in-depth
incest
infest
ingest
ingress
inquest
invest
largess
life vest
Loch Ness
Macbeth
midwest
molest
Mos Def
noblesse
northwest
obsess
oppress
out west
outstretch
P.S.
possess

profess
protest
recess
redress
refresh
regress
repress
request
screen test
slugfest
songfest
southwest
stress test
success
suggest
sundress
suppress
talkfest
tone deaf
transgress
undress
unless
unrest
war chest
who says
Wild West

acid test
acquiesce
air express
all the rest
Alvarez
arabesque
Bangladesh
baroness
beauty rest
Budapest
by request
catch your breath
cause of death
CBS
chicken breast
cocktail dress
come to rest
convalesce
dairy fresh
day of rest
decompress
decongest
driver's test

effervesce
empty nest
Etch-A-Sketch
evening dress
false arrest
fancy dress
for the best
formal dress
full-court press
garlic press
hairy chest
hang a left
hold your breath
hornet's nest
house arrest
in excess
in the flesh
ink blot test
IRS
Jonny Quest
kiss of death
L.D.S.
last request
lay to rest
litmus test
manifest
master chef
more or less
nonetheless
nothing left
nothing less
out of breath
overdress
overstress
party dress
petty theft
picturesque
printing press
put to death
RAF
reassess
repossess
retrogress
right and left
S.O.S.
save your breath
second best
second-guess
short of breath
Simon Says

starve to death
statuesque
sudden death
take a breath
talk to death
treasure chest
underdress
UNICEF
UPS
watercress
wedding dress
Wild Wild West
wrongful death

anyone's guess
aptitude test
bulletproof vest
change of address
christening dress
Community Chest
direct address
dress for success
Elizabeth
farewell address
form of address
in the same breath
keynote address
medicine chest
nevertheless
overnight guest
permanent press
pony express
pregnancy test
put to the test
Readers Digest
scared half to death
tickled to death
under arrest
under duress
under your breath

accidental death
anybody's guess
cardiac arrest
citizen's arrest
Dr. Benton Quest
freedom of the press
Gettysburg Address
ladder of success
say it with your chest

American Express
Associated Press
matter of life and death

ESSA (see ELLA)
ESSABLE (see ECTABLE)
ESSAGE (see EALOUS)
ESSANT (see ESCENT)
ESSANTS (see ESCENCE)
ESSE (see ESS)
ESSEE (see ELLY)
ESSEL (see EVEL)
ESSEN (see ESSION)
ESSENCE (see ESCENCE)
ESSENEGER (see ECULAR)
ESSENING (see EDITING)
ESSER (see ESSOR)
ESSFUL (see EVEL)
ESSI (see ELLY)
ESSIBLE (see ECTABLE)
ESSIBLY (see ETICALLY)
ESSIE (see ELLY)
ESSIER (see EDGIER)
ESSILY (see ETICALLY)
ESSIMIST (see ECTIONIST)

ESSING

bedding
begging
besting
betting
blessing
breading
checking
cheffing
cresting
decking
dreading
dredging
dressing
ebbing
edging
egging
etching
exing
fetching
fledgling
fleshing
freckling

freshing
fretting
getting
guessing
heading
heckling
heddling
hexing
jesting
jetting
legging
meddling
meshing
messing
necking
nesting
nestling
netting
pecking
peddling
pegging
pepping
petting
pledging
prepping
pressing
reffing
repping
resting
retching
revving
setting
shedding
shredding
sledding
speckling
spreading
stepping
stressing
stretching
sweating
testing
texting
threading
threshing
treading
trekking
vexing
webbing
wedding

wedging
wetting
whetting
wrecking
wresting
wrestling

abetting
abscessing
accepting
accessing
addressing
affecting
alleging
annexing
arresting
assessing
bedwetting
begetting
beheading
benchpressing
besetting
bisecting
bobsledding
bs-ing
caressing
cobwebbing
collecting
compressing
concepting
confessing
connecting
contesting
correcting
defecting
deflecting
depressing
detecting
detesting
digesting
digressing
directing
dissecting
distressing
divesting
effecting
ejecting
electing
enmeshing
erecting

excepting
expecting
expressing
finessing
forgetting
homesteading
immeshing
impressing
indexing
infecting
infesting
inflecting
ingesting
injecting
inmeshing
inspecting
investing
jet setting
misstepping
mixed blessing
molesting
neglecting
objecting
obsessing
offsetting
oppressing
perfecting
perplexing
place setting
possessing
pretexting
professing
progressing
projecting
prospecting
protecting
protesting
recessing
reflecting
refreshing
regressing
regretting
rejecting
reneging
repressing
requesting
resetting
respecting
selecting
settling

sidestepping
snow-sledding
spearheading
subjecting
subletting
suggesting
suppressing
suspecting
transgressing
undressing
upsetting

acquiescing
bodychecking
bottlenecking
coalescing
contracepting
convalescing
decompressing
decongesting
disconnecting
disinfecting
dispossessing
doublechecking
effervescing
genuflecting
heavy petting
intercepting
interjecting
intermeddling
intermeshing
intersecting
manifesting
misdirecting
off-track betting
overdressing
overmeddling
overstressing
reassessing
recollecting
redirecting
reelecting
repossessing
resurrecting
retrogressing
rubbernecking
shotgun wedding
silhouetting
unsettling

idyllic setting
mosquito netting

Nice Day For A White Wedding

ESSION

beckon
cession
deaden
deafen
destine
Devon
Ellen
felon
flexion
freshen
freshman
heaven
Helen
Heston
jetson
Kevin
leaden
leaven
legend
lemon
lessen
lesson
Levin
melon
pectin
question
reckon
redden
resin
second
section
session
seven
seventh
Stetson
Texan
threaten
weapon
Weston
Yemen

abjection
accession
affection
aggression
annexion
bisection
C-section
clandestine
collection
complexion
compression
conception
concession
confection
confession
congestion
connection
connexion
correction
cross-section
deception
defection
deflection
deflexion
dejection
depression
detection
digestion
digression
direction
discretion
dissection
ejection
election
eleven
eleventh
erection
exception
expression
hog heaven
implexion
impression
inception
infection
inflection
inflexion
ingestion
injection
inspection
intestine

jam session
Jane Jetson
Led Zeppelin
mid-section
misreckon
objection
obsession
oppression
outreckon
perception
perfection
possession
predestine
procession
profession
progression
projection
protection
rap session
reception
recession
refection
reflection
reflexion
refreshen
regression
rejection
repression
secession
selection
split second
subjection
succession
suggestion
suppression
thank heaven
Tibetan
trajection
transgression

anteflexion
Armageddon
art collection
beg the question
beyond question
chest congestion
circumflexion
circumspection
contraception
deadly weapon

decongestion
depth perception
disaffection
discomplexion
disconnection
disinfection
false impression
fuel injection
genuflection
imperfection
indigestion
indirection
indiscretion
insurrection
interception
interjection
intersection
introspection
Judy Jetson
lame-duck session
learn your lesson
learned profession
Love Connection
lucky seven
microsecond
millisecond
misconception
misdirection
move the question
nanosecond
object lesson
overreckon
pop the question
preconception
predilection
recollection
redirection
reelection
repossession
resurrection
retroflexion
retrogression
retrospection
rhythm section
right direction
self-deception
self-expression
sense perception
seventh heaven
Smith and Wesson

smoking section
summer session
take exception
take possession
underreckon
Urban Legend
use discretion
vivisection
watermelon
wrong direction

24/7
7-Eleven
bundle from heaven
convicted felon
delicatessen
house of correction
make an impression
nonsmoking section
out of the question
sense of direction
Stairway to Heaven
stink to high heaven
traffic congestion
wedding reception
without exception

acid indigestion
executive session
natural selection
sensory perception
under the impression
world's oldest profession

Immaculate Conception

environmental protection

ESSIONAL (see ECTABLE)
ESSIONING (see EDITING)
ESSIONIST (see ECTIONIST)
ESSITATE (see ESTIGATE)
ESSITY (see ETICALLY)

ESSIVE

festive
restive

abjective

accessive
affective
aggressive
collective
congestive
connective
contestive
corrective
deceptive
defective
deflective
depressive
detective
digestive
digressive
directive
effective
elective
excessive
expressive
impressive
infective
inflective
objective
obsessive
oppressive
perceptive
perspective
possessive
processive
progressive
prospective
protective
receptive
recessive
reflective
regressive
repressive
respective
selective
subjective
successive
suggestive
suppressive
susceptive

circumspective
contraceptive
disinfective
imperceptive

ineffective
insurrective
interceptive
interjective
introspective
irrespective
retrospective
unprotective

manic-depressive
overprotective
passive-aggressive
private detective

oral contraceptive

ESSLESS (see ECTLESS)
ESSLY (see ELLY)
ESSMENT (see ESCENT)
ESSO (see ELLO)
ESSON (see ESSION)

ESSOR

dresser
guesser
lesser
messer
presser
stressor

accessor
addressor
aggressor
assessor
benchpresser
caresser
compressor
confessor
cross-dresser
digresser
expressor
finesser
hairdresser
impresser
obsessor
oppressor
possessor
processor
professor

successor
suppressor
transgressor

acquiescer
convalescer
decompressor
fancy dresser
food processor
overdresser
predecessor
reassessor
repossessor
second-guesser
tongue depressor
word processor

ESSORY (see ETICALLY)
ESSURE (see ECTOR)
ESSURED (see EPHERD)
ESSY (see ELLY)
EST (see ESS)
ESTA (see ELLA)
ESTABLE (see ECTABLE)
ESTANT (see ESCENT)
ESTE (see ESS)
ESTED (see ECTED)
ESTER (see ECTOR)
ESTERED (see EPHERD)

ESTERING

bettering
feathering
festering
fettering
gesturing
lettering
levering
measuring
pestering
pleasuring
severing
tethering
tettering
treasuring
weathering
westering
whethering

dissevering
endeavoring
relettering
remeasuring
sequestering

ESTERN (see ECTOR)
ESTFUL (see EVEL)
ESTHER (see ECTOR)
ESTIAL (see EVEL)
ESTIAN (see ESTRIAN)
ESTIBLE (see ECTABLE)
ESTIBULE (see ECTABLE)
ESTIC (see ETIC)
ESTICAL (see ECTABLE)
ESTICATE (see ESTIGATE)
ESTICLE (see ECTABLE)
ESTIE (see ELLY)
ESTIFY (see ECTIFY)

ESTIGATE

crepitate
decimate
dedicate
defecate
delegate
desecrate
designate
destinate
detonate
devastate
elevate
estimate
evocate
excavate
explicate
extricate
featherweight
hesitate
legislate
levitate
medicate
meditate
predicate
regulate
relegate
resonate
revocate
vegetate

accelerate
decelerate
deregulate
domesticate
expeditate
investigate
irregulate
misestimate
misregulate
necessitate
predesignate
predestinate
preestimate
premeditate
rededicate
revegetate
subdelegate

overestimate
reinvestigate
underestimate
undomesticate

ESTIGE (see EALOUS)
ESTILENCE (see EMINENCE)
ESTIMATE (see ESTIGATE)
ESTINAL (see ECTABLE)
ESTINATE (see ESTIGATE)
ESTINE (see ESSION)
ESTING (see ESSING)
ESTINING (see EDITING)
ESTION (see ESSION)
ESTIONING (see EDITING)
ESTIVAL (see ECTABLE)
ESTIVE (see ESSIVE)
ESTLE 1 (see EVEL)
ESTLE 2 (see ELLY)
ESTLER (see ETTLER)
ESTLESS (see ECTLESS)
ESTLING (see ESSING)
ESTMENT (see ESCENT)
ESTO (see ELLO)
ESTON (see ESSION)
ESTOR (see ECTOR)
ESTRAL (see EVEL)
ESTRIAL (see ECTABLE)

ESTRIAN

lesbian
Mexican
thespian

campestrian
equestrian
orchestian
palestrian
pedestrian
sylvestrian

ESTRY (see ELLY)
ESTURE (see ECTOR)
ESTURED (see EPHERD)
ESTURER (see EASURER)
ESTURING (see ESTERING)
ESTY (see ELLY)
ESUS (see ESIS)

ET 1

beck
bet
check
Chex
crept
Czech
debt
deck
ex
fleck
flex
fret
get
heck
hep
hex
jet
kept
leapt
let
met
neck
net
next
peck
pep
pet
prep
rep
Rex
sec
sect
set

sex
slept
spec
speck
step
strep
sweat
swept
tech
text
threat
trek
vet
vex
wept
wet
whet
wreck
X
yep
yet

abet
abject
accept
adept
affect
all set
all wet
annex
apex
as yet
asset
Aztec
bad check
bad debt
baguette
bedwet
beget
beset
bicep
bisect
blank check
Brand X
breakneck
briquette
brochette
brunette
cadet
Cal. Tech.

cassette
claim check
coat check
cold sweat
collect
connect
correct
Corvette
crew neck
croquette
cross check
dead set
death threat
defect
deflect
detect
dinette
direct
dissect
doorstep
dragnet
effect
eject
elect
erect
except
exec
expect
fair sex
fanjet
first step
flight deck
footstep
forget
gazette
Gillette
goose step
hair net
half-step
hat check
headset
high-tech
in debt
in step
index
inept
infect
inflect
inject
inkjet

insect
inspect
Jeanette
jet set
kismet
latex
marked deck
mind-set
misstep
neglect
no sweat
not yet
nymphet
on deck
OPEC
parsec
paycheck
perplex
poop deck
precept
prefect
pretext
protect
quartet
Quebec
quintet
raincheck
rainswept
redneck
reflect
reflex
regret
reject
reset
respect
Rosette
roughneck
safe sex
sales check
same-sex
select
septet
sextet
shipwreck
side bet
sidestep
Smurfette
spell check
Star Trek
subject

sublet
sunset
suspect
tape deck
tea set
Tibet
toilette
trainwreck
traject
two-step
typeset
unkept
unmet
upset
vertex
vignette
vortex

alphabet
amulet
Antoinette
architect
bachelorette
bassinet
bayonet
Bernadette
better yet
birth defect
body check
bottleneck
call collect
calumet
cashier's check
castanet
Chiang Kai-Shek
cigarette
circumflex
circumspect
clarinet
contracept
coronet
countercheck
dial direct
dialect
diaper set
dinette set
disconnect
discotheque
disinfect
disrespect

DMX
double-check
dripping wet
epithet
fairer sex
genuflect
heavyset
hedge a bet
hit the deck
in effect
incorrect
indirect
intellect
intercept
interject
intersect
introspect
Johnny Depp
Juliet
keep in check
Lafayette
leatherneck
majorette
Malcolm X
Margaret
martinet
matching set
minuet
misdirect
neck and neck
oral sex
out of debt
overslept
overstep
pirouette
place a bet
quarterdeck
recollect
redirect
reelect
resurrect
retrospect
rubber check
rubberneck
safety net
save your neck
self-respect
side effect
silhouette
sobriquet

sound effect
Soviet
stack the deck
statuette
string quartet
super jet
take effect
teacher's pet
total wreck
traveler's check
triple threat
turbojet
turtleneck
unisex
vinaigrette
what the heck
wringing wet

Carol Burnett
cause-and-effect
certified check
Chemistry Set
Doppler effect
in retrospect
marionette
mosquito net
national debt
pain in the neck
religious sect
ripple effect
security check
special effect
take a rain check
Toulouse-Lautrec
up to your neck
win by a neck

audio cassette
domino effect
forgive and forget
Generation X
play with a full deck
video cassette

Romeo and Juliet

ETAL 2 (see EGAL)
ETAN (see ESSION)
ETCH (see ESS)
ETCHABLE (see ECTABLE)
ETCHER (see ECTOR)
ETCHING (see ESSING)
ETCHY (see ELLY)
ETE 1 (see EAT 1)
ETE 2 (see ELLY)
ETE 3 (see ATE 1)
ETED (see EASTED 1)
ETEL 1 (see EGAL)
ETEL 2 (see EVEL)
ETELY (see EASY)
ETENESS (see ESIS)
ETEOR (see EEDIER)
ETER (see EATER 1)
ETERA (see ERICA)
ETERAN (see ELEGANT)
ETES (see EATIES)
ETFUL (see EVEL)
ETH (see ESS)
ETHA (see IA)
ETHAL (see EGAL)
ETHAN (see ESIAN)
ETHEL (see EVEL)
ETHER (see ECTOR)
ETHERED (see EPHERD)
ETHERING (see ESTERING)
ETHIC (see ETIC)
ETHICAL (see ECTABLE)
ETHICALLY (see ETICALLY)
ETHNIC (see ETIC)
ETHOD (see ECTED)
ETHOL (see EVEL)
ETHORA (see ERICA)
ETHRO (see ELLO)
ETHYL (see EVEL)
ETIAN (see ESIAN)

ETIC

breakfast
credit
debit
eddish
edit
epic
ethic
ethnic
exit

fetish
gestic
hectic
medic
melic
metric
pectic
peptic
preface
reddish
relic
sceptic
septic
skeptic
telic
wettish

accredit
aesthetic
angelic
ascetic
athletic
co-edit
cosmetic
dietic
dipsetic
discredit
domestic
dyslectic
dyslexic
eclectic
electic
electric
esthetic
fire exit
genetic
kinetic
magnetic
majestic
no exit
pathetic
phonetic
planetic
poetic
prophetic
prosthetic
recredit
reedit
smart aleck
symmetric

synthetic
uncredit
unhectic

alphabetic
analectic
anorexic
archangelic
diabetic
dialectic
diametric
emphathetic
epileptic
evangelic
everpresent
for the present
geometric
isometric
multipresent
narcoleptic
nonelectric
nonpoetic
omnipresent
orthoepic
paramedic
parathetic
psychedelic
psychodelic
sympathetic
synergetic
theoretic

apologetic
biogenetic
unsympathetic

emergency exit

ETICAL (see ECTABLE)

ETICALLY

brevity
Cecily
celery
deputy
dreadfully
dressily
ebony

ecstacy
ecstasy
edgily
edibly
epically
equity
ethically
feathery
felony
flexibly
heavenly
heavily
jealousy
jeopardy
leathery
legacy
legibly
leprosy
levity
medically
Melanie
melody
messily
pregnancy
readily
recipe
recklessly
registry
sesame
seventy
sexily
steadily
sweatily
treasury
weathery

accessory
aesthetically
celebrity
complexity
concessory
confessibly
directory
duplexity
fidelity
heredity
infectiously
integrity
longevity
mastectomy

necessity
pathetically
Penelope
perplexity
poetically
possessory
professory
projectory
prophetically
respectably
synthetically
trajectory
vasectomy

alphabetically
ambidextrously
appendectomy
high fidelity
hypothetically
hysterectomy
infidelity
intercessory
parenthetically
theoretically
tonsillectomy

apologetically
hemorrhoidectomy

ETID (see EADED 1)
ETIE (see EASY)
ETIN (see EATEN 1)
ETINA (see ERICA)
ETING (see EATING 1)
ETION 1 (see ESIAN)
ETION 2 (see ESSION)
ETIOUS (see ESIS)
ETIQUETTE (see ECTIONIST)
ETISH (see ETIC)
ETITIVE (see ECUTIVE)
ETITOR (see ECULAR)
ETLY (see ELLY)
ETO (see IO 1)
ETON (see EATEN 1)
ETONATE (see ESTIGATE)
ETOR (see EATER 1)
ETRIC (see ETIC)
ETRIMENT (see ELEGANT)
ETRIMENTS (see EMINENCE)
ETRIS (see ECTLESS)
ETRO (see ELLO)

ETSON (see ESSION)
ETT (see ET 1)
ETTA (see ELLA)
ETTABLE (see ECTABLE)
ETTE (see ET 1)
ETTED (see EADED 1)
ETTER (see ECTOR)
ETTERED (see EPHERD)
ETTERER (see EASURER)
ETTERING (see ESTERING)
ETTERLESS (see ECTIONIST)
ETTERMAN (see ELEGANT)
ETTEST (see ECTED)
ETTI (see ELLY)
ETTIER 1 (see EDGIER)
ETTIER 2 (see ITTIER)
ETTIEST (see IPPIEST)
ETTINESS (see IPPIEST)
ETTING (see ESSING)
ETTIS (see ELFISH)
ETTISH (see ETIC)
ETTLE (see EVEL)
ETTLEMENT (see ELEGANT)

ETTLER

eggler
heckler
meddler
nestler
nettler
peddler
settler
wrestler

backsettler
embezzler
outsettler

intermeddler

ETTLING (see ESSING)
ETTO (see ELLO)
ETTOR (see ECTOR)
ETTUCE (see EALOUS)
ETTY 1 (see ELLY)
ETTY 2 (see ITTY)
ETUAL (see ECTABLE)
ETUM (see EUM 1)
ETUS (see ESIS)
ETZEL (see EVEL)

ETZGY (see ELLY)
EU (see EW 1)
EUCE (see OOSE 1)
EUCING (see UTING 1)
EUCY (see UTY)
EUD 1 (see OOM)
EUD 2 (see OID)
EUDABLE (see OOTABLE)
EUDAL (see OODLE)
EUDALLY (see UITY 1)
EUE (see EW 1)
EUEING (see UING)
EULAH (see UNA)

EUM 1

Librium
museum
per diem

arboretum
art museum
carpe diem
coliseum
mausoleum
wax museum

equilibrium

EUM 2 (see OOM)
EUMY (see UTY)
EUNUCH (see EWISH)
EUR 1 (see ORE 1)
EUR 2 (see EWER 1)
EURISH (see ORIST)
EURLY (see URELY)
EURO (see UNO)
EUS 1 (see USE 1)
EUS 2 (see OOSE 1)
EUSABLE (see OOTABLE)
EUSE (see OOSE 1)
EUSEL (see OODLE)
EUSS (see OOSE 1)
EUTER (see UTER)
EUTERING (see UTORING)
EUTHER (see UTER)
EUTHFUL (see OODLE)
EUTHING (see UTING 1)
EUTIAN (see UTION)
EUTRAL (see OODLE)
EUVER (see UTER)

EV 1 (see EAD 1)
EV 2 (see OFF)
EVA (see IA)
EVALENCE (see EMINENCE)
EVALENT (see ELEGANT)
EVANCE (see EDENCE)
EVASTATE (see ESTIGATE)
EVE 1 (see EED 1)
EVE 2 (see ID)
EVEE (see ELLY)

EVEL

bestial
Bethel
bevel
Cheryl
chestful
deckle
devil
dreadful
Errol
ethel
ethol
ethyl
feral
festful
fettle
freckle
fretful
Gerald
Gretel
heckle
helpful
herald
Jekyll
jestful
keckle
kettle
level
medal
meddle
Merrill
metal
mettle
nestful
nettle
Neville
pebble
pedal

peddle
peril
pestful
pestle
petal
pretzel
rebel
rectal
restful
revel
settle
shekel
special
speckle
spectral
sterile
stressful
treadle
treble
tressful
trestle
vessel
wrestle
zestful

ancestral
arm wrestle
backpedal
base metal
bespeckle
blood vessel
celestial
daredevil
distressful
embezzle
eye level
Fitzgerald
forgetful
gold medal
gun metal
high-level
imperil
kenspeckle
low-level
molestful
neglectful
orchestral
pot metal
reflectful
regretful

respectful
rose petal
sea level
selectful
semestral
sequestral
she-devil
sheet metal
soft pedal
soup kettle
split level
successful
suggestful
suspectful
teakettle
top level
trimestral
unblestful
unlevel
unsettle

disrespectful
Dr. Jekyll
entry-level
heavy metal
introspectful
on the level
raise the devil
retrospectful
unrespectful
unsuccessful

go to the devil
poverty level

Tasmanian Devil

EVELING (see EDITING)
EVELYN (see ELEGANT)
EVEN 1 (see ESIAN)
EVEN 2 (see ESSION)
EVENING (see EAMING)
EVENTH (see ESSION)
EVENTY (see ETICALLY)
EVER 1 (see ECTOR)
EVER 2 (see EATER 1)
EVERABLE (see EPARABLE)
EVERAGE (see EALOUS)
EVERAL (see ECTABLE)
EVERANCE (see EMINENCE)
EVERED (see EPHERD)

EVERENCE (see EMINENCE)
EVERENT (see ELEGANT)
EVEREST (see ECTIONIST)
EVERING (see ESTERING)
EVERY 1 (see ELLY)
EVERY 2 (see EITY)
EVIANT (see EDIENT)

EVIATE

breviate
deviate
mediate

abbreviate
alleviate
appreciate
depreciate
remediate

EVICE (see ELFISH)
EVIDENCE (see EMINENCE)
EVIDENT (see ELEGANT)
EVIE (see EASY)
EVIL 1 (see EVEL)
EVIL 2 (see EGAL)
EVILLE (see EVEL)
EVILLY (see EITY)
EVILMENT (see ELEGANT)
EVIN (see ESSION)
EVITABLE (see EPARABLE)
EVITATE (see ESTIGATE)
EVITY (see ETICALLY)
EVOCATE (see ESTIGATE)
EVOLENT (see ELEGANT)
EVON (see ESSION)
EVOR (see ECTOR)
EVVING (see ESSING)
EVY (see ELLY)

EW 1

blew
blue
boo
brew
chew
clue
crew
cue

dew
do
drew
due
ewe
few
flew
flu
flue
glue
gnu
goo
grew
hue
Jew
knew
lieu
loo
moo
new
nu
ooh
pew
phew
pooh
Q
queue
roux
rue
screw
shoe
shrew
slew
slue
spew
stew
sue
threw
through
to
too
true
two
U
view
whew
who
woo
you
zoo

accrue
add to
adieu
ado
ah-choo
all through
anew
askew
bamboo
Bantu
beaucoup
big do
bless you
blue flu
brand new
breakthrough
can-do
canoe
choo-choo
church pew
come through
come to
come true
construe
corkscrew
cuckoo
curfew
debut
dim view
dog-doo
doo-doo
drive-through
ensue
eschew
fall through
fondue
froufrou
goo-goo
GQ
ground crew
gumshoe
hairdo
hereto
home-brew
horseshoe
how-to
I do
imbue
in lieu
IQ

kazoo
kung fu
lean-to
love to
me too
milieu
miscue
misdo
muumuu
old shoe
on cue
on view
outdo
outgrew
pass-through
past due
perdu
Peru
pooh-pooh
PU
pull through
Purdue
purlieu
pursue
ragout
Ragu
rearview
redo
renew
review
revue
says who?
see-through
shampoo
skiddoo
sky-blue
snafu
snowshoe
soft-shoe
subdue
taboo
tattoo
thank you
thereto
thumbscrew
to-do
too too
true blue
U2
undo

undue
unglue
unscrew
unto
untrue
walk-through
whereto
who's who
withdrew
woo-woo
work crew
worldview
yahoo

avenue
baby shoe
ballyhoo
barbecue
Big League Chew
bird's-eye view
black and blue
boogaloo
book review
break in two
BTU
buckaroo
bugaboo
caribou
cleaning crew
cockapoo
cockatoo
cordon bleu
countercoup
countersue
curlicue
deja vu
derring-do
dipsy-doo
doodle-oo
double U
dream come true
entre vous
field of view
flopperoo
follow through
Great Gazoo
hitherto
honeydew
I love you
impromptu

in a stew
in full view
in situ
ingenue
interview
Irish stew
jujitsu
kangaroo
Katmandu
kickapoo
law review
looky-loo
Malibu
marabou
midnight blue
misconstrue
Mountain Dew
much ado
Naboombu
Nancy Drew
navy blue
no can do
ocean view
overdo
overdue
overshoe
overthrew
overview
oyster stew
PDQ
peek-a-boo
petting zoo
Pikachu
point of view
postage due
quite a few
rendezvous
residue
retinue
revenue
royal blue
Scooby-Doo
Scrappy-Doo
shiatsu
Sigma Nu
smackeroo
sockeroo
stinkaroo
Super Glue
Swiss fondue

switcheroo
tennis shoe
through and through
Timbuktu
tried and true
two-by-two
W
Waterloo
well-to-do
whoop-de-do
witches brew
wooden shoe
World War II
worm's-eye view
wrecking crew
Xanadu
Yucca-Dew

ACLU
Bartholomew
bolt from the blue
brand spanking new
bully for you
catch-22
corrective shoe
Honey Boo Boo
how do you do?
hullabaloo
Kalamazoo
merci beaucoup
Mr. Magoo
mulligan stew
out of the blue
pass in review
poo poo pee doo
R2-D2
red, white, and blue
room with a view
skeleton crew
Tippecanoe
up the kazoo
We Will Rock You
Winnie the Pooh

cock-a-doodle-doo
drop the other shoe
judicial review
Maya Angelou
musical review
panoramic view

Saks Fifth Avenue
VFW

Internal Revenue
win a few, lose a few

EW 2 (see OW 1)
EWABLE (see OOTABLE)

EWAL

crewel
cruel
dual
duel
fuel
gruel
jewel

accrual
bejewel
crown jewel
pursual
renewal
subdual
uncruel

family jewel
license renewal
urban renewal

EWAN (see UTION)
EWART (see UTER)
EWB (see OOM)
EWBIE (see UTY)
EWD (see OOM)
EWDER (see UTER)
EWDEST (see OONEST)
EWDITY (see UITY 1)
EWDLY (see UTY)
EWDNESS (see UTENESS)
EWE (see EW 1)
EWEL (see EWAL)
EWELER (see OOLER)
EWELRY (see UITY 1)

EWER 1

bluer
brewer

chewer
cooer
doer
ewer
fewer
gluer
newer
ruer
screwer
sewer
shoer
skewer
stewer
suer
truer
viewer
who're
wooer

construer
ensuer
horseshoer
manure
outdoer
pursuer
redoer
revewer
reviewer
shampooer
subduer
tattooer
undoer
unscrewer
wrongdoer

barbecuer
countersuer
evildoer
horse manure
interviewer
misconstruer
overdoer
revenuer

entrepreneur

EWER 2 (see OVER 1)
EWERY (see UITY 1)
EWEY (see EWY)
EWING 1 (see UING)
EWING 2 (see OWING 1)
EWIS (see UENESS)

EWISH

bluish
cubic
cufic
cumic
eunuch
foolish
ghoulish
humic
Jewish
kufic
moonish
mulish
Munich
music
mutic
newish
pubic
pudic
punic
rheumic
Rubik
rutic
shrewish
stewish
tunic
unit
zumic

acoustic
baboonish
buffoonish
poltroonish
pound foolish

pharmaceutic
Sound of Music
therapeutic

EWLESS (see UENESS)
EWLY (see UTY)
EWMAN (see UTION)
EWN 1 (see OOM)
EWN 2 (see ONE 1)
EWNESS (see UENESS)
EWPIE (see UTY)
EWS (see USE 1)
EWSTER (see UTER)
EWSY (see UTY)
EWT (see UTE)

EWTER (see UTER)
EWTON (see UTION)

EWY

buoy
chewy
Dewey
dewy
gooey
hooey
Huey
phooey
screwy
sooey

chop suey
Drambuie
kerflooey
mildewy
unchewy

Hong Kong Phooey
ratatouille

Huey, Dewey, and Louie

EX (see ET 1)
EXABLE (see ECTABLE)
EXAN (see ESSION)
EXAS (see ECTLESS)
EXCAVATE (see ESTIGATE)
EXCELLENCE (see EMINENCE)
EXCELLENT (see ELEGANT)
EXCREMENT (see ELEGANT)
EXIBLE (see ECTABLE)
EXIBLY (see ETICALLY)
EXIC (see ETIC)
EXICAN (see ESTRIAN)
EXIER (see EDGIER)
EXIGENT (see ELEGANT)
EXILY (see ETICALLY)
EXING (see ESSING)
EXION (see ESSION)
EXIS (see ECTLESS)
EXIST (see ECTED)
EXIT (see ETIC)
EXITED (see ECTIONIST)
EXITING (see EDITING)
EXITY (see ETICALLY)
EXLESS (see ECTLESS)

EXMAS (see ECTLESS)
EXO (see ELLO)
EXODUS (see ECTIONIST)
EXPERT (see ECTOR)
EXPLETIVE (see ECUTIVE)
EXPLICATE (see ESTIGATE)
EXPO (see ELLO)
EXT (see ET 1)
EXTANT (see ESCENT)
EXTING (see ESSING)
EXTRA (see ELLA)
EXTRICATE (see ESTIGATE)
EXTROUS (see ECTLESS)
EXTROUSLY (see ETICALLY)
EXTUAL (see ECTABLE)
EXTURE (see ECTOR)
EXUAL (see ECTABLE)
EXUS (see ECTLESS)
EXY (see ELLY)
EY 1 (see AY)
EY 2 (see E 1)
EY'D (see ADE 1)
EY'LL (see AIL)
EY'RE (see ARE 1)
EY'VE (see AVE 1)
EYABLE (see ADABLE)
EYED 1 (see IDE)
EYED 2 (see EED 1)
EYELID (see IET)
EYER (see AILER)
EYES (see IZE 1)
EYING (see EEDING)
EYLESS (see ESIS)
EYOR (see AILER)
EYS (see EED 1)
EYSER (see IZER)
EZ (see ESS)
EZE (see EED 1)
EZRA (see ELLA)
EZZAR (see EATER 1)
EZZLE (see EVEL)
EZZLEMENT (see ELEGANT)
EZZLER (see ETTLER)
EZZLING (see EDITING)
EZZO (see ELLO)

Rhyme Sounds

I 1 (see Y)
I 2 (see E 1)
I'LL (see ILE 1)
I'M (see INE 1)
I'S (see IZE 1)
I'VE (see IZE 1)

IA

cheetah
diva
Eva
FEMA
FIFA
Gila
Gina
Leda
Leila
Lena
Libra
Lima
Lisa
mia
Nina
Pima
Pisa
pita
pizza
Prima
Reba
Rita
schema
Sheba
Sheila
Tina
via
visa
viva
Xena
zebra

Aida
amnesia
amoeba
arena
Aretha
arriba
Athena
Bathsheba
Christina

eczema
edema
eureka
fajita
Fatima
Garcia
Geneva
Georgina
hyena
idea
Juanita
Judea
Korea
Latina
Lolita
Louisa
Maria
marina
Medea
Medina
novena
Noxzema
paprika
Rhodesia
sangria
Sophia
subpoena
tequila
Teresa
Topeka
tortilla
Tunisia

Alameda
analgesia
anesthesia
aphrodesia
Argentina
ballerina
bright idea
Catalina
Chick Corea
concertina
Costa Rica
diarrhea
emphysema
galleria
gonorrhea
Hiroshima
Indonesia

Iwo Jima
Magdalena
Mamma Mia!
margarita
Micronesia
Mona Lisa
panacea
Pasadena
pizzeria
Polynesia
Queen Latifah
ratafia
senorita
Taco Via

anaphrodesia
Domino's Pizza
Jerry Garcia
laughing hyena
Milk of Magnesia
Mother Teresa

prima ballerina

IABLE 1 (see ITABLE 1)
IABLE 2 (see IEVABLE)
IACAL (see ITABLE 1)

IAH

China

angina
Delilah
Elvira
Godiva
Josiah
Messiah
pariah
saliva
vagina

Aunt Jemima
Indochina
jambalaya
Jeremiah
Nehemiah
Zachariah

North Carolina
South Carolina

IAL (see ITLE)
IALER (see IZER)
IALING (see INDING)
IAMOND (see IGHTEN)
IAN (see ION 1)
IANCE (see ITIS)
IANT (see ION 1)
IANTLY (see IETY)
IAPER (see IZER)
IAR (see IER 1)
IARY (see IETY)
IAS (see ITIS)
IATH (see IET)
IATRIST (see IVALIST)
IB (see ID)
IBA (see IA)
IBABLE (see ITABLE 1)
IBABLY (see IETY)
IBAL (see ITLE)

IBBEAN

Crimean
Gideon
gillian
Libyan
simian
Vivian

amphibian
Arminian
Bolivian
Caribbean
czarinian
darwinian
Floridian
meridian
oblivion

postmeridian
Vaudevillian

Pirates of the Caribbean

IBBER (see ITTER)
IBBERED (see ITTERED)
IBBERISH (see ITIONIST)
IBBEST (see ITIOUS)
IBBING (see ITTING)
IBBLE (see ITTLE)

IBBLER

crippler
dibbler
diddler
dribbler
fiddler
fribbler
giggler
higgler
littler
middler
nibbler
piddler
quibbler
quiddler
riddler
riffler
rippler
scribbler
sniffler
stippler
tippler
triddler
twiddler
whiffler
whistler
wiggler
wriggler

belittler
brittler
epistler
unriddler

IBBLING (see ITTING)
IBE (see IDE)
IBEL (see ITLE)
IBELESS (see ITIS)
IBELIST (see IVALIST)
IBER (see IZER)
IBERAL (see ITTABLE)
IBERALLY (see ISTICALLY)
IBERTY (see ILITY)
IBERY (see IETY)
IBIA (see ILIA)
IBIAN (see IBBEAN)
IBIAS (see IPPIEST)
IBID (see ITTED)
IBING (see INDING)

IBIS (see ITIS)
IBIT (see ISTIC)
IBITED (see IVALENT)
IBITER (see ITIONER)

IBITING

cricketing
fidgeting
gimmicking
limiting
picketing
pivoting
ticketing
visiting

cohibiting
delimiting
eliciting
exhibiting
inhibiting
prelimiting
prohibiting
revisiting
soliciting

reexhibiting

IBITIVE (see IBUTIVE)
IBITOR (see ITIONER)
IBLE (see ITLE)
IBLESS (see ITIOUS)
IBLET (see ISTIC)
IBLICAL (see ITTABLE)
IBLICALLY (see ISTICALLY)
IBLING (see ITTING)
IBRA (see IA)
IBRATE (see YDRATE)
IBRILLATE (see IMINATE)
IBSON (see ITION)
IBULAR (see ITIONER)
IBUTE (see ISSUE)
IBUTER (see ITIONER)

IBUTIVE

fixative
limitive
primitive

privative
acquisitive
attributive
contributive
definitive
derivative
disquisitive
distributive
exhibitive
exquisitive
infinitive
inhibitive
inquisitive
prohibitive
requisitive
retributive

nonattributive
semiprimitive
subderivative

IBUTOR (see ITIONER)
IBYA (see ILIA)
IBYAN (see IBBEAN)
IBYL (see ITTLE)
IC 1 (see IP)
IC 2 (see EAT 1)
IC 3 (see IST 1)
IC 4 (see IGHT)
ICA (see IA)
ICABLE (see ITTABLE)
ICABLY (see ILITY)
ICAN (see ESIAN)
ICAR (see ITTER)

ICCUP

bishop
hiccup
hyssop
pickup
situp

ICE 1

Christ
dice
fife
heist

ice
knife
lice
life
mice
nice
price
rice
rife
slice
spice
splice
strife
thrice
twice
vice
wife

advice
allspice
concise
crushed ice
deice
device
dog's life
dry ice
entice
ex-wife
good life
head lice
high life
housewife
jackknife
list price
love life
low-life
mid-life
midwife
nightlife
no dice
on ice
pen knife
precise
preslice
pro life
sale price
shelf life
shoot dice
still life

suffice
think twice
true-life
wild rice
wildlife
afterlife
Antichrist
asking price
awful nice
before Christ
block of ice
break the ice
carving knife
Church of Christ
Facts of Life
Fisher-Price
imprecise
Jesus Christ
loaded dice
man and wife
merchandise
on thin ice
once or twice
overprice
paradise
pocketknife
poltergeist
pull a heist
right to life
sacrifice
sticker price
three blind mice
underprice
way of life

at any price
common-law wife
fair market price
fool's paradise
husband and wife
larger-than-life
legal advice
Miami Vice
My So-called Life
new lease on life
not on your life
self-sacrifice
sensing device
skate on thin ice
sugar and spice

Uncle Ben's Rice
You Light Up My Life

trouble in paradise

ICE 2 (see EAT 1)
ICEE (see IGHTLY)
ICELESS (see ITIS)
ICELY (see IGHTLY)
ICEMENT (see ILEMENT)
ICENESS (see ITIS)
ICENSE (see ITIS)
ICER (see IZER)
ICEST (see EANEST)
ICEY (see IGHTLY)
ICH (see IST 1)
ICHAEL (see ITLE)
ICHARD (see ITTERED)
ICHE 1 (see EAT 1)
ICHE 2 (see IST 1)
ICHEN (see ITION)
ICHENING (see ITIONING)
ICHER (see ITTER)
ICHES (see ITIOUS)
ICHI (see EASY)
ICHIE (see ITTY)
ICHING (see ITCHING)
ICHLY (see ITTY)
ICHTER (see ITTER)
ICHY (see EASY)
ICIA 1 (see ILLA 1)
ICIA 2 (see ENIA)
ICIAL (see ITTLE)
ICIAN (see ITION)
ICIATE (see IMINATE)
ICIENCY (see ILITY)
ICIENT (see INGENT)
ICIER (see INIER)
ICILY (see ILITY)
ICINESS (see IGHTLINESS)
ICING 1 (see INDING)
ICING 2 (see EATING 1)
ICION (see ITION)
ICIOUS (see ITIOUS)
ICIOUSLY (see ILITY)
ICIPATE (see IMINATE)
ICIT (see ISTIC)
ICITED (see IMITED)
ICITER (see ITIONER)
ICITING (see IBITING)
ICITLY (see ILITY)
ICITOR (see ITIONER)

ICITY (see ILITY)
ICK (see IP)
ICKABLE (see ITTABLE)
ICKED (see ITTED)
ICKEDLY (see ILITY)
ICKEE (see ITTY)
ICKEL (see ITTLE)
ICKEN (see ITION)
ICKENING (see ITIONING)
ICKER (see ITTER)
ICKERED (see ITTERED)
ICKERING (see ITTERING)
ICKERLESS (see ITIONIST)
ICKERY (see ILITY)
ICKEST (see ITIOUS)
ICKET (see ISTIC)
ICKETED (see IMITED)
ICKETING (see IBITING)
ICKETY (see ILITY)
ICKEY (see ITTY)
ICKI (see ITTY)
ICKIE (see ITTY)
ICKIER (see ITTIER)
ICKIEST (see IPPIEST)
ICKILY (see ILITY)
ICKINESS (see IPPIEST)
ICKING (see ITTING)
ICKLE (see ITTLE)
ICKLESS (see ITIOUS)
ICKLIER (see ITTIER)
ICKLIEST (see IPPIEST)
ICKLING (see IDDLING)
ICKLY (see ITTY)
ICKMENT (see INGENT)
ICKNESS (see ITIOUS)
ICKO (see ILLOW)
ICKORY (see ILITY)
ICKRY (see ILITY)
ICKSTER (see ITTER)
ICKUP (see ICCUP)
ICKY (see ITTY)
ICLE (see ITTLE)
ICNIC (see ITIOUS)
ICO (see IO 1)
ICON (see YLON)
ICORY (see ILITY)
ICRON (see YLON)
ICT 1 (see IP)
ICT 2 (see IGHT)
ICTABLE 1 (see ITTABLE)
ICTABLE 2 (see ITABLE 1)
ICTED (see ITED 1)
ICTER 1 (see ITTER)

ICTER 2 (see IZER)
ICTIM (see ITION)
ICTING 1 (see ITTING)
ICTING 2 (see INDING)
ICTION (see ITION)
ICTIONAL (see ITTABLE)
ICTIONALLY (see ISTICALLY)
ICTIVE (see ITIOUS)
ICTLY (see ITTY)
ICTMENT (see ION 1)
ICTOR (see ITTER)
ICTORY (see ILITY)
ICTUAL (see ITTLE)
ICTUM (see ITION)
ICTURE (see ITTER)
ICTURED (see ITTERED)
ICULAR (see ITIONER)
ICULOUS (see IVOROUS)
ICUS (see ITIS)
ICUTRED (see ITTERED)
ICY (see IGHTLY)
ICYCLE (see ITABLE 1)

ID

bib
bid
big
biz
bridge
brig
cig
crib
did
dig
fib
fig
fizz
fridge
frig
frizz
gig
give
glib
grid
hid
his
is
jib
Jig

kid
lib
lid
live
Liz
mid
Midge
Ms.
nib
pig
quid
quiz
rib
rid
ridge
rig
sib
Sid
sieve
skid
slid
smidge
sprig
squib
squid
swig
tizz
trig
twig
Whig
whiz
wig
zig

abridge
ad lib
amid
as is
backslid
bigwig
drawbridge
footbridge
forbid
forgive
gee whiz
gin fizz
high bid
low bid
Madrid
misgive

nonskid
oil rig
outbid
outdid
outlive
pop quiz
prime rib
redid
relive
renege
shindig
showbiz
sparerib
talk big
toll bridge
whiz kid

Adam's rib
baby bib
Captain Kidd
flip your lid
flip your wig
guinea pig
highest bid
latchkey kid
London Bridge
lowest bid
make it big
overbid
overdid
Porky Pig
pyramid
toilet lid
underbid
women's lib

Billy the Kid
chauvinist pig
Garbage Pail Kid
initiative
Karate Kid
live and let live
thingamajig

it is what it is

IDABLE (see ITABLE 1)
IDAL (see ITLE)
IDALLY (see IETY)
IDANCE (see ITIS)
IDAS (see ITIS)

IDD (see ID)
IDDABLE (see ITTABLE)
IDDED (see ITTED)
IDDEN (see ITION)
IDDER (see ITTER)
IDDIE (see ITTY)
IDDIER (see ITTIER)
IDDIEST (see IPPIEST)
IDDILY (see ILITY)
IDDINESS (see IPPIEST)
IDDING (see ITTING)
IDDISH (see ITIOUS)
IDDITY (see ILITY)
IDDLE (see ITTLE)
IDDLED (see ITTLED)
IDDLER (see IBBLER)
IDDLEY (see ITTY)

IDDLING

bristling
chittling
crippling
diddling
drizzling
dwindling
fiddling
fizzling
giggling
griddling
jiggling
kindling
Kipling
middling
pickling
piddling
prickling
quiddling
riddling
rippling
sizzling
sniggling
spindling
stippling
stripling
swindling
tickling
tippling
trickling
tripling

twiddling
whistling
whittling
widdling
wiggling
belittling
enkindling
rekindling
unriddling

IDDO (see ILLOW)
IDDY (see ITTY)

IDE

bide
bribe
bride
chide
Clyde
cried
died
dried
dyed
eyed
fried
gibe
glide
guide
hide
hyde
jibe
lied
plied
pride
pried
ride
scribe
shied
side
sighed
slide
snide
spied
stride
tide
tied
tribe

tried
vibe
vied
wide

abide
allied
applied
ascribe
aside
astride
backside
backslide
bedside
beside
black-eyed
blindside
blue-eyed
bright-eyed
broadside
brown-eyed
bug-eyed
child bride
chloride
cockeyed
collide
complied
confide
conscribe
courtside
cowhide
cross-eyed
decide
decried
deep-fried
defied
denied
deride
describe
divide
downside
dry-eyed
elide
false pride
fireside
fisheyed
flip side
free ride
freeze-dried
green-eyed

hawkeyed
high tide
hillside
hogtied
horsehide
implied
inscribe
inside
joyride
lakeside
landslide
low tide
misguide
mud slide
oblige
outride
outside
oxhide
poolside
prescribe
preside
proscribe
provide
rawhide
red tide
red-eyed
relied
replied
reside
ringside
riptide
roadside
seaside
shanghaied
spin-dried
stateside
statewide
stir-fried
subscribe
subside
sulfide
sun-dried
supplied
tongue-tied
topside
tour guide
transcribe
untied

wall-eyed
wayside
wide-eyed
worldwide
yuletide
alibied
alongside
amplified
beady-eyed
beautified
bona fide
brush aside
buggy ride
bum a ride
certified
chicken-fried
circumscribe
citywide
clarified
classified
coincide
countryside
crucified
cut and dried
cyanide
deified
diatribe
dignified
edified
eventide
evil-eyed
falsified
far and wide
fortified
fratricide
freedom ride
genocide
glorified
glossy-eyed
gratified
hit your stride
homicide
horrified
horseback ride
justified
liquefied
magnified
misapplied
modified
mollified

mortified
mountainside
multiplied
mummified
mystified
nationwide
notified
nullified
occupied
oceanside
on the side
ossified
other side
override
pacified
pesticide
petrified
prophesied
purified
qualified
quantified
ramified
ratified
reapplied
rectified
regicide
resubscribe
riverside
rockabyed
sanctified
satisfied
set aside
side-by-side
signified
simplified
slip and slide
specified
spermicide
starry-eyed
step aside
stupefied
subdivide
suicide
take in stride
teary-eyed
terrified
testified
travel guide
turn the tide
TV Guide

typified
underside
unified
up and died
verified
vilified
wave aside

declassified
deep down inside
disqualified
dissatisfied
electrified
exemplified
formaldehyde
here comes the bride
identified
indemnified
Indian tribe
industry-wide
insecticide
intensified
Jekyll and Hyde
mail-order bride
Mary J. Blige
personified
preoccupied
refortified
self-satisfied
solidified
take for a ride
tyrannicide
unoccupied
unsatisfied
unverified

along for the ride
father of the bride
mother of the bride
overqualified
roller-coaster ride

IDED (see ITED 1)
IDEFUL (see ITLE)
IDELESS (see ITIS)
IDELY (see IGHTLY)
IDEMENT (see ILEMENT)
IDEN (see IGHTEN)
IDENCE (see ITIS)
IDENER (see IGHTENER)
IDENESS (see ITIS)

IDENING (see IGHTENING)
IDEON (see IBBEAN)
IDEOUS (see IPPIEST)
IDER 1 (see IZER)
IDER 2 (see ITTER)
IDER 3 (see IZER)
IDERANCE (see IVALENCE)
IDERATE (see IVALENT)
IDERED (see ITTERED)
IDERING (see ITTERING)
IDGE (see ID)
IDGEMENT (see INGENT)
IDGEN (see ITION)
IDGEON (see ITION)
IDGES (see ITIOUS)
IDGET (see ISTIC)
IDGETED (see IMITED)
IDGETING (see IBITING)
IDGETY (see ILITY)
IDGIN (see ITION)
IDI 1 (see ITTY)
IDI 2 (see IGHTLY)
IDIAN (see IBBEAN)
IDIC (see ISTIC)
IDICAL (see ITTABLE)
IDIER (see INIER)
IDIFY (see IGNIFY)
IDINESS (see IGHTLINESS)
IDING (see INDING)
IDIOT (see IPPIEST)
IDIOUS (see IPPIEST)
IDITY (see ILITY)
IDLE (see ITLE)
IDLING (see INDING)
IDLY (see IGHTLY)
IDNEY (see ITTY)
IDO 2 (see IO 1)
IDOL (see ITLE)
IDOLIST (see IVALIST)
IDON (see IGHTEN)
IDOW (see ILLOW)
IDT (see IP)
IDTH (see IST 1)
IDUAL (see ITTABLE)
IDUALIST (see IGAMIST)
IDY (see IGHTLY)
IDYLL (see ITLE)
IE 1 (see Y)
IE 2 (see E 1)
IE 3 (see AY)
IEBER (see EATER 1)
IECE (see EAT 1)
IECING (see EATING 1)

IED 1 (see IDE)
IED 2 (see EED 1)
IEF (see EAT 1)
IEFER (see EATER 1)
IEFING (see EATING 1)
IEFLESS (see ESIS)
IEFLY (see EASY)
IEGE (see EED 1)
IEGING (see EATING 1)
IEGO (see ADO 2)
IEK (see EAT 1)
IEKER (see EATER 1)
IEKING (see EATING 1)
IEL (see EAL 1)
IELD (see EAL 1)
IELDABLE (see IEVABLE)
IELDER (see EALER)
IELDING (see ILLING)
IELER (see EALER)
IEM (see EUM 1)
IEN 1 (see EEN 1)
IEN 2 (see ION 1)
IENCE (see ITIS)
IEND (see EEN 1)
IENER (see EATER 1)
IENIE (see EASY)
IENIST (see EANEST)
IENT (see ION 1)

IER 1

briar
buyer
crier
drier
dryer
dyer
eyer
flier
flyer
friar
fryer
higher
iron
liar
plyer
prior
pryer
shyer
sigher
slyer

spyer
trier
tyer
vier
wrier

applier
belier
cast iron
clothes dryer
complier
defier
denier
gridiron
hair dryer
high flyer
pump iron
supplier
sweetbrier
town crier
untier

amplifier
beautifier
calcifier
certifier
classifier
codifier
crucifier
curling iron
dignifier
falsifier
fortifier
glorifier
horrifier
justifier
magnifier
modifier
mollifier
multiplier
mystifier
notifier
nullifier
occupier
Oscar Mayer
pacifier
petrifier
prophesier
purifier
putrefier
qualifier

ratifier
rectifier
Richard Pryor
sanctifier
satisfier
signifier
simplifier
specifier
stupefier
terrifier
testifier
unifier
verifier
versifier
vilifier

declassifier
disqualifier
electrifier
identifier
intensifier
personifier
solidifier

IER 2 (see EAR 1)
IERCELY (see EARY)
IERCENESS (see EARLESS)
IERCEST (see EAREST)
IERED (see EARED)
IERING (see EERING)
IERKY (see IRTY)
IERLY (see EARY)
IERRE (see ARE 1)
IERY (see IETY)
IES (see IZE 1)
IESEL (see EGAL)
IEST (see EAT 1)

IET

climate
diet
eyelet
eyelid
hybrid
pilot
pirate
private
quiet
riot

Wyatt

co-pilot
crash diet
disquiet
Goliath
run riot
test pilot

automatic pilot

IETER (see IGHTENER)
IETOR (see IGHTENER)

IETY

bribery
diary
dinery
dynasty
entirety
fiery
finally
finery
irony
ivory
jibery
piety
piracy
pliantly
priory
privacy
rivalry
spinally
vinery
winery

advisory
anxiety
connivery
defiantly
Duck Dynasty
impiety
propriety
provisory
refinery
sobriety
society

variety

high society
homicidally
impropriety
indescribably
insobriety
notoriety
supervisory

cafe society
garden variety
irreconcilably

IEU (see EW 1)

IEVABLE

beachable
beatable
bleachable
breachable
breathable
breedable
ceasable
cheatable
creasable
dealable
easable
eatable
feasible
feedable
feelable
fleeable
freeable
freezable
genial
greasable
grievable
healable
heatable
heavable
heedable
leadable
leakable
leasable
leavable
lenial
meetable

menial
peacable
peelable
peevable
pleasable
preachable
reachable
readable
regional
screechable
sealable
seasonal
seatable
seeable
seekable
seizable
skiable
sneezable
speakable
squeakable
squeezable
stealable
teachable
teasable
teethable
treatable
vehicle
venial
weedable
wheelable
yieldable

achievable
agreeable
appealable
appeasable
believable
beseechable
completable
concealable
conceivable
congenial
critiqueable
deceivable
decreasable
decreeable
defeatable
deletable
displeasable
exceedable

foreseeable
impeachable
impedible
increasable
perceivable
recedable
receivable
redeemable
releasable
relievable
remedial
repealable
repeatable
reprievable
resealable
retrievable
revealable
stampedable
unbeatable
unfreezable
ungenial
unreachable
unspeakable
unteachable

disagreeable
guaranteeable
inconceivable
interweavable
irretrievable
unbelievable
unforeseeable

accounts receivable

IEVABLY (see EITY)
IEVAL (see EGAL)
IEVE (see EED 1)
IEVEL (see EGAL)
IEVEMENT (see EQUENT)
IEVER (see EATER 1)
IEVERY (see EITY)
IEVING (see EATING 1)
IEVOUS (see ESIS)
IEW (see EW 1)
IF 1 (see IST 1)
IF 2 (see EAT 1)
IFA (see IA)
IFAH (see IA)
IFE (see ICE 1)
IFELESS (see ITIS)

IFELY (see IGHTLY)
IFENESS (see ITIS)
IFER (see IZER)
IFEY (see IGHTLY)
IFF (see IST 1)
IFFANY (see ILITY)
IFFE (see IST 1)
IFFEL (see ITLE)
IFFEN (see ITION)
IFFER (see ITTER)
IFFERED (see ITTERED)
IFFERENCE (see IVALENCE)
IFFERENT (see IVALENT)
IFFERENTLY (see ILITY)
IFFERING (see ITTERING)
IFFEST (see ITIOUS)
IFFIER (see ITTIER)
IFFIEST (see IPPIEST)
IFFIN (see ITION)
IFFINESS (see IPPIEST)
IFFING (see ITTING)
IFFLE (see ITTLE)
IFFLER (see IBBLER)
IFFNESS (see ITIOUS)
IFFY (see ITTY)
IFI (see EASY)
IFIC (see ISTIC)
IFICATE (see IVALENT)
IFIE (see IGHTLY)
IFING (see INDING)
IFLE (see ITLE)
IFLING (see INDING)
IFT (see IST 1)
IFTER (see ITTER)
IFTH (see IST 1)
IFTIER (see ITTIER)
IFTIEST (see IPPIEST)
IFTINESS (see IPPIEST)
IFTING (see ITTING)
IFTLY (see ITTY)
IFTNESS (see ITIOUS)
IFTY (see ITTY)
IG (see ID)
IGAMENT (see IVALENT)

IGAMIST

bigamist
bitterest
brittlest
digamist
imageless

infamous
inquirist
littlest
ministress
symphonist
trigamist
calligraphist
epigraphist
epitomist
polygamist
quadrigamist
ubiquitist

individualist

IGAMY (see ILITY)
IGATE (see ISTIC)
IGE 1 (see EED 1)
IGE 2 (see IDE)
IGEL (see ITLE)
IGEON (see ITION)
IGER 1 (see IZER)
IGER 2 (see IZER)
IGERENCE (see IVALENCE)
IGERENT (see IVALENT)
IGGER (see ITTER)
IGGERED (see ITTERED)
IGGERING (see ITTERING)
IGGERLESS (see ITIONIST)
IGGEST (see ITIOUS)
IGGIE (see ITTY)
IGGIER (see ITTIER)
IGGIEST (see IPPIEST)
IGGING (see ITTING)
IGGITY (see ILITY)
IGGLE (see ITTLE)
IGGLER (see IBBLER)
IGGLEY (see ITTY)
IGGLIER (see ITTIER)
IGGLIEST (see IPPIEST)
IGGLING (see IDDLING)
IGGLY (see ITTY)
IGGY (see ITTY)
IGH (see Y)
IGHABLE (see ITABLE 1)
IGHED (see IDE)
IGHER (see IER 1)
IGHFILL (see ITLE)

IGHFUL (see ITLE)
IGHING (see INDING)
IGHLAND (see IGHTEN)
IGHLY (see IGHTLY)
IGHNESS (see ITIS)
IGHS (see IZE 1)

IGHT

bike
bite
blight
bright
byte
cite
dike
Dwight
fight
flight
fright
gripe
height
hike
hype
Ike
kite
knight
light
like
lite
mic
might
Mike
mite
night
ninth
pike
pint
pipe
plight
psych
quite
right
ripe
rite
shrike
sight
sike
site

Skype
sleight
slight
smite
snipe
spike
spite
sprite
strike
stripe
swipe
tight
trike
tripe
trite
tyke
type
white
wight
wipe
write

airtight
alight
alike
all right
all-night
alright
backbite
bagpipe
birthright
blood type
blowpipe
bombsight
bug bite
bullfight
catfight
catlike
childlike
cockfight
contrite
crash site
daylight
delight
despite
dislike
dogfight
downright
drain pipe
dreamlike
excite
eyesight

finite
firelight
first strike
fistfight
flashlight
floodlight
footlight
foresight
forthright
fortnight
frostbite
Fruit Stripe
gang fight
gaslight
ghostwrite
godlike
good night
graphite
green light
gun fight
hand-wipe
handwrite
headlight
Heartlight
heat light
highlight
hindsight
hitchhike
ignite
in-flight
incite
indict
insight
invite
Klondike
lamplight
last night
late-night
lifelike
limelight
Lite-Brite
lovelight
midnight
mike fright
Miss Right
moonlight
night-light
not quite
off-white
on strike

on-site
outpsych
outright
peace pipe
penlight
pinstripe
pitch pipe
playwright
polite
porchlight
prizefight
recite
red light
requite
retype
Schwinn bike
searchlight
Semite
sideswipe
sit tight
skintight
skylight
skywrite
snakebite
Snow White
soundbite
spotlight
stage fright
starlight
Starlite
stoplight
stovepipe
streetlight
strobe light
sunlight
taillight
tailpipe
take flight
termite
tonight
top flight
torchlight
turnpike
twilight
twinight
typewrite
unite
unlike
unripe
upright

uptight
Van Dyke
warlike
website
white knight
windpipe
appetite
archetype
at first sight
black and white
bring to light
broad daylight
candlelight
cellulite
charter flight
civil right
come to light
copyright
day and night
Dick Van Dyke
disunite
divine right
down the pike
dynamite
erudite
expedite
extradite
Fahrenheit
featherlight
fight or flight
flight-or-fright
fly-by-night
gazuntite
gigabyte
Gladys Knight
go on strike
guttersnipe
Handi Wipe
honor bright
Hoss Cartwright
hunger strike
impolite
in the right
Inner Light
Israelite
know by sight
ladylike
legal right
linotype
look-alike

Lucky Strike
megabyte
motorbike
Mr. Right
Muscovite
neon light
neophyte
not quite right
out-of-sight
overbite
overheight
overnight
overripe
oversight
parasite
pearly white
pillow fight
pilot light
plebiscite
Price is Right
proselyte
prototype
Rainbow Brite
recondite
reignite
reunite
satellite
second sight
see the light
serve one right
shining light
signal light
socialite
sound alike
spend the night
sportsmanlike
stalactite
stalagmite
stenotype
take a bite
take a hike
tandem bike
teletype
traffic light
transvestite
tripartite
unalike
underripe
underwrite

waterpipe
watertight
wedding night
yellow light
yellow stripe

dawn's early light
Dudley Do-Right
electrolyte
electrotype
go fly a kite
hermaphrodite
high as a kite
indirect light
infrared light
love at first sight
media hype
meteorite
natural light
not wrapped too tight
opening night
out like a light
Rappers Delight
red light, green light
starlight, starbright
stereotype
sweetness and light
tomorrow night
Turkish delight

by cover of night
higher than a kite
idiot's delight
lady-of-the-night
Little Joe Cartwright
middle of the night
supersonic flight
ultraviolet light

straighten up and fly right
Uptown Saturday Night

IGHTABLE (see ITABLE 1)
IGHTED (see ITED 1)

IGHTEN

Bison
brighten

Brighton
Byron
Byrum
crinum
diamond
Dryden
frighten
heighten
highland
hydron
hymen
hyphen
hyphened
island
item
Ivan
lighten
liken
linum
liven
Myron
phylum
ripen
siphon
siphoned
siren
Thailand
tighten
Titan
Triton
Tyson
vinum
whiten
widen
wisemen
wisen

asylum
enlighten
enliven
environ
horizon
hot item
Long Island
Mike Tyson
Neil Diamond
Poseidon
Rhode Island
subitem

subphylum

aconitum
Dancing Island
infinitum
sempervivum
Fantasty Island
Gilligan's Island
Gloria Steinem
insane asylum
mediastinum
on the horizon
Paradise Island

political asylum

IGHTENER

brightener
dieter
frightener
heightener
lightener
livener
quieter
rioter
ripener
tightener
whitener
widener

proprietor
sole proprietor

IGHTENING

brightening
frightening
heightening
hyphening
lightening
likening
livening
ripening
siphoning
tightening
whitening
widening

enlightening
enlivening

IGHTEOUS (see ITIS)
IGHTER (see IZER)
IGHTFUL (see ITLE)
IGHTIE (see IGHTLY)
IGHTIER (see INIER)
IGHTINESS (see IGHTLINESS)
IGHTING (see INDING)

IGHTLINESS

feistiness
flightiness
griminess
iciness
knightliness
likeliness
liminess
liveliness
mightiness
shininess
sightliness
sliminess
spiciness
spikiness
spininess
sprightliness
tidiness
timeliness
tininess
wiliness

almightiness
unlikeliness
unsightliness
untidiness
untimeliness

IGHTLY

blimey
blindly
brightly
briny
childly
crikey
dicey
direly

dryly
feisty
finely
flighty
grimy
Heidi
heinie
highly
Icee
icy
ID
idly
IV
ivy
kindly
lifely
lightly
likely
lively
mighty
Mikie
mildly
miry
nicely
nightie
nightly
Nike
ninety
piny
pricey
primely
psyche
rhymy
rifely
rightly
rimy
ripely
shiny
shyly
signee
slightly
slimy
slyly
smiley
snidely
spicy
spiky
spindly
spiny
spritely

stymie
tidy
tightly
timely
tiny
tritely
twiny
viny
whiny
whitey
widely
wifely
wifey
wifie
wildly
Wiley
winy
wiry
wisely
wryly

all righty
almighty
benignly
concisely
contritely
divinely
entirely
felinely
finitely
forthrightly
housewifely
politely
precisely
sublimely
supinely
unkindly
unsightly
untidy
untimely
unwifely

Aphrodite
asininely
eruditely
high and mighty
impolitely
imprecisely
poison ivy
saturninely
superfinely

once-over-lightly

IGHTNESS (see ITIS)
IGHTNING (see INDING)
IGHTON (see IGHTEN)
IGHTY (see IGHTLY)
IGI (see EASY)
IGID (see ITTED)
IGIL (see ITTLE)
IGILANT (see IVALENT)
IGINAL (see ITTABLE)
IGINALLY (see ISTICALLY)
IGINATE (see IMINATE)
IGING (see INDING)
IGION (see ITION)
IGIOUS 1 (see ESIS)
IGIOUS 2 (see ITIOUS)
IGIT (see ISTIC)
IGITAL (see ITTABLE)
IGITALLY (see ISTICALLY)
IGLET (see ISTIC)
IGLOO (see ISSUE)
IGM (see INE 1)
IGMA (see ILLA 1)
IGMENT (see INGENT)
IGN (see INE 1)
IGNAL (see ITTLE)
IGNANT (see INGENT)
IGNATURE (see ITIONER)
IGNEE (see IGHTLY)
IGNER (see IZER)

IGNIFY

dignify
ignify
lignify
signify
vilify

acidify
adsignify
consignify
foresignify
humidify
indignify
lapidify
malignify
nobilify

presignify
rigidify
solidify
dehumidify
disacidify

IGNING (see INDING)
IGNITY (see ILITY)
IGNLESS (see ITIS)
IGNLY (see IGHTLY)
IGNMENT (see ILEMENT)
IGNOR (see IZER)
IGNORANCE (see IVALENCE)
IGNORANT (see IVALENT)
IGO (see IO 1)
IGON (see YLON)
IGOR (see ITTER)
IGORLESS (see ITIONIST)
IGOROUS (see IVOROUS)
IGOT (see ISTIC)
IGOTRY (see ILITY)
IGRAPHIST (see IGAMIST)
IGRAPHY (see ILITY)
IGRATE (see YDRATE)
IGUE (see EED 1)
IGUING (see EATING 1)
IGUOUS (see IVOROUS)
IGURE (see ITTER)
IGURED (see ITTERED)
IGURELESS (see ITIONIST)
IGURING (see ITTERING)
IING (see EEDING)
IJI (see EASY)
IK 1 (see IP)
IK 2 (see EAT 1)
IKA (see IA)
IKABLE (see ITABLE 1)
IKE 1 (see IGHT)
IKE 2 (see IGHTLY)
IKELIER (see INIER)
IKELINESS (see IGHTLINESS)
IKELY (see IGHTLY)
IKEN (see IGHTEN)
IKENESS (see ITIS)
IKENING (see IGHTENING)
IKER (see IZER)
IKEY (see IGHTLY)
IKI (see EASY)
IKIE (see IGHTLY)
IKIER (see INIER)
IKINESS (see IGHTLINESS)
IKING (see INDING)

IKO (see IO 1)
IKY (see IGHTLY)
IL (see ILL)
ILA 1 (see IA)
ILA 2 (see ILLA 1)
ILABLY (see IETY)
ILAH (see IAH)
ILARY (see ILITY)
ILATE (see YDRATE)
ILBIN (see ILLION)
ILD 1 (see ILE 1)
ILD 2 (see ILL)
ILDE (see ILE 1)
ILDED (see ILTED)
ILDER 1 (see ILLER)
ILDER 2 (see IZER)
ILDEST (see ITIS)
ILDING (see ILLING)
ILDISH (see ITIS)
ILDLY (see IGHTLY)
ILDRED (see ILTED)
ILDREN (see ILLION)

ILE 1

aisle
child
file
guile
I'll
isle
mild
mile
Nile
pile
rile
smile
stile
style
tile
vile
while
wild
wile

argyle
awhile
beguile
brainchild
buck wild

card file
Carlisle
compile
cross-file
defile
erstwhile
exile
freestyle
gentile
godchild
grandchild
hairstyle
high style
hogwild
in style
last mile
lifestyle
lovechild
man-child
meanwhile
misfile
moonchild
nail file
old style
on file
profile
puerile
reptile
restyle
revile
Rothschild
run wild
sandpile
senile
servile
slush pile
stepchild
stockpile
textile
turnstile
with child
woodpile
worthwhile

after while
Anglophile
arctophile
Cajun style
country mile
crack a smile

cramp one's style
crocodile
domicile
down the aisle
flower child
for a while
Francophile
high-profile
in a while
in the wild
infantile
juvenile
latest style
letter file
mercantile
Oscar Wilde
out of style
peristyle
rank and file
reconcile
single file
unworthwhile
wedding aisle
western style
worth one's while
xenophile

bibliophile
call of the wild
circular file
Emerald Isle
family style
fingernail file
go out of style
mile after mile
nautical mile
once in a while

go the extra mile
Hillbilly Mobile
in a little while

every once in a while

ILE 2 (see EAL 1)
ILE 3 (see ITTY)

ILEMENT

guisement
pilement

acquirement
advisement
alignment
apprisement
aspirement
assignment
assizement
attirement
baptizement
beguilement
chastisement
compilement
confinement
consignment
contrivement
decidement
defilement
deprivement
derivement
designment
devisement
eloignment
enshrinement
enticement
excitement
exilement
franchisement
incitement
inditement
insignment
invitement
malignment
refinement
requirement
requitement
resignment
retirement
revilement
revisement
revivement

advertisement
aggrandizement
amortizement
emboitement
enfranchisement
misalignment
nonalignment
oxidizement
realignment

reassignment
recompilement
reconcilement
reconsignment

irreconcilement
overexcitement
oxygenizement
semiretirement
under advisement

disenfranchisement

solitary confinement

ILENCE (see ITIS)
ILER (see IZER)
ILEST (see ITIS)
ILEY (see IGHTLY)
ILFRED (see ILTED)
ILGRIM (see ILLION)
ILI 1 (see ITTY)
ILI 2 (see EASY)

ILIA

cilia
ilia
India
ixia
Libya
lindia
tibia
tilia
trivia

amphibia
Bolivia
brasilia
familia
Olivia
principia
reptilia
Valencia

aphrodisia
artemisia
pedophilia
residencia

memorabilia

ILIAN (see ILLION)
ILIAR (see ITTIER)
ILIARY (see ILITY)
ILIATE 1 (see IMINATE)
ILIATE 2 (see IVALENT)
ILIC (see ISTIC)
ILIENT (see ILLION)
ILIFY (see IGNIFY)
ILINESS (see IGHTLINESS)
ILING (see INDING)
ILION (see ILLION)
ILITANT (see IVALENT)
ILITANTS (see IVALENCE)
ILITATE (see IMINATE)

ILITY

bickery
bigamy
biggity
bigotry
bittery
blistery
chicory
chivalry
differently
dignity
dinnerly
distantly
fidgety
finicky
finity
fishery
fixity
flickery
flippancy
flittery
giddily
gimmickry
glittery
grittily
hickory
Hilary
history
imagery
industry
infamy

infancy
infantry
innerly
inquiry
instantly
Italy
jittery
liberty
lickety
liquidly
litany
livery
mimicry
ministry
misery
mistily
mystery
nittily
pittery
primity
quiddity
rickety
shivery
Sicily
silvery
simile
skittery
slickery
slithery
slivery
snippety
spinnery
stickily
symmetry
symphony
synergy
thickety
Tiffany
Timothy
tindery
trickery
trickily
trigamy
trilogy
trinity
twittery
viciously
victory
vility
villainy
visibly

wickedly
wittily
wizardry
ability
acclivity
acidity
activity
admissibly
affinity
agility
ambitiously
amenity
ancillary
anility
antiquity
applicably
artillery
assistantly
asymmetry
asynergy
auspiciously
auxiliary
calligraphy
capriciously
captivity
charivari
chemigraphy
civility
complicity
consistency
consistently
cupidity
debility
declivity
deficiency
deliciously
delivery
despicably
distillery
divinity
docility
ductility
duplicity
efficiency
epigraphy
epiphany
epitome
ethnicity
exility
explicitly

facility
facsimile
felicity
fertility
festivity
fictitiously
fissility
fluidity
fluxility
fragility
frigidity
futility
gentility
gracility
hability
hostility
humidity
humility
indignity
infinity
iniquity
initially
insistently
judiciously
lability
lascivity
lexigraphy
liquidity
lubricity
lucidity
maliciously
miserably
mobility
morbidity
motility
nativity
neurility
nihility
nobility
nubility
nutritiously
obliquity
obscenity
officiously
omnisciency
optimity
periphery
permissibly
persistently
persnickety

plasticity
polygamy
polyphony
proclivity
proficiency
prolixity
propitiously
proximity
publicity
rapidity
resistably
resistantly
rigidity
rotisserie
scurrility
sectility
senility
serenity
servility
simplicity
solidity
soliloquy
stability
sterility
stupidity
sublimity
submissively
subtility
sufficiency
suspiciously
tactility
tensility
timidity
tortility
toxicity
tractility
tranquility
ubiquity
ultimity
uniquity
utility
validity
vernility
vicinity
virginity
virility

addibility
affability
alibility

amability
asininity
audibility
authenticity
avariciously
capability
changeability
collectivity
conductivity
consimility
contractility
contradictory
countability
creativity
credibility
crocodility
crossability
cullibility
culpability
curability
damnability
disability
docibility
domesticity
durability
eccentricity
edibility
elasticity
electricity
equinimity
exclusivity
expeditiously
fallibility
feasibility
femininity
flammability
flexibility
floatability
fluxibility
friability
fusibility
gullibility
ignobility
imbecility
immobility
immotility
inability
inactivity
inadmissibly
inapplicably

inauspiciously
incivility
inconsistently
indocility
inductility
inefficiency
inexplicably
inextricably
infantility
infertility
inhability
instability
insufficiency
inutility
invirility
juvenility
laudability
legibility
liability
likability
livability
magnanimity
mailability
masculinity
miscibility
moral victory
movability
multiplicity
mutability
nonability
notability
objectivity
palpability
partibility
passibility
payability
peccability
placability
plausibility
pliability
ponibility
portability
possibility
potability
prehensility
probability
productivity
provability
puerility
ratability

readability
relativity
rentability
repetitiously
risibility
roadability
salability
salvability
sanability
self-sufficiency
sensibility
sensitivity
shareability
shiftability
solubility
solvability
specificity
sportability
stainability
suability
subjectivity
suitability
surreptitiously
tamability
tangability
tangibility
taxability
teachability
temptability
tenability
tensibility
testability
towability
traceability
tractability
treatability
trustability
tunability
unability
unanimity
uncivility
usability
vendibility
versability
versatility
viability
vibratility
vincibility
visibility
volatility
volubility

washability
workability
writability
absorbability
accendibility
acceptability
accessibility
accountability
acquirability
actionability
adaptability
addressibility
admirability
admissibility
adorability
advisability
affectibility
affordability
agreeability
alterability
amenability
amiability
amicability
amissibility
amovability
answerability
antifertility
appealability
appetibility
applicability
approachability
assignability
attainability
attractability
autostability
availability
combustibility
commutability
comparability
compatibility
compensibility
compressibility
computability
conceivability
conceptibility
condensibility
conducibility
conductibility
confluxibility
conformability

confusability
contemptability
contractibility
controllability
convertibility
corrigibility
corrodibility
corrosibility
corruptibility
creditability
deducibility
deductibility
defectibility
defensibility
deflagrability
demisability
demonstrability
dependability
deplorability
deportability
depressibility
descendibility
desirability
despicability
destructibility
detachibility
detestability
diffusibility
digestibility
disputability
dissolubility
dissolvability
distensibility
distractibility
divisibility
educability
effumability
egocentricity
eligibility
employability
enforceability
equitability
erectility
evolutility
exchangeability
excitibility
exhaustibility
expansibility
expendability
exportability

extendability
extensibility
fatigability
fermentability
figurability
filterability
fluctuability
foreseeability
formidability
frangibility
generability
governability
habitability
heritability
illegibility
imitability
immeability
immiscibility
immovability
immutability
impalpability
impartibility
impassability
impeccability
imperdibility
implacability
implausibility
impossibility
impregnability
impressibility
improbability
improvability
imputability
inaffability
inaudibility
incapability
inchangeability
incomparability
incredibility
inculpability
incurability
indellibility
indocibility
ineffability
inerrability
infallibility
infeasibility
inflammability
inflexibility
infrangibility

infusibility
insanability
insatiability
inscrutability
insensibility
insensitivity
inseparability
insociability
insolubility
insurability
intangibility
integrability
intermobility
intractability
invendibility
invincibility
invisibility
irascibility
irritability
knowledgeability
laminability
machinability
maintainability
malleability
manageability
marketability
marriageability
measureability
memorability
mensurability
merchantability
navigability
negotiability
obligability
operability
opposability
ordinability
ostensibility
oxidability
palatability
patentability
penetrability
perceptibility
perdurability
perfectability
perishability
permeability
permissibility
perspirability
persuasibility

perturbability
ponderability
practicability
predicability
predictability
preferability
prescriptibility
presentability
preventability
producibility
productibility
profitability
programmability
public utility
punishability
questionability
reasonability
receivability
receptibility
recyclability
redeemability
reducibility
reductibility
reflexibility
reformability
refrangibility
refutability
registrability
releasability
reliability
remissibility
renewability
reparability
repealability
replaceability
repressibility
reputability
resistibility
resolvability
respectability
respirability
responsibility
restorability
returnability
reusability
revealability
reversibility
reviewability
revocability
salvageability

separability
serviceability
settleability
severability
sociability
submergability
submersibility
suggestibility
survivability
susceptibility
suscitability
suspensibility
tenderability
terminability
transferability
transmissibility
transmutability
transportability
unflappability
unpossibility
unsalability
unsociability
unsuitability
untangibility
upward mobility
vaporability
variability
vegetability
venerability
verisimility
violability
vulnerability
weatherability
worshipability

alienability
assimilability
associability
commensurability
communicability
comprehensibility
decomposability
determinability
discoverability
disreputability
disrespectability
dissociability
falsifiability
hereditability
hypersensibility

imaginability
immeasurability
immensurability
impenetrability
imperceptibility
imperfectability
imperishability
impermeability
imprescriptibility
impressionability
impreventability
inaccessibility
inadmissability
inadvisability
inalterability
inappellability
inapplicability
incalculability
incombustibility
incommutability
incompatibility
incompressibility
inconceivability
incondensability
incontestability
inconvertibility
incorrigibility
incorruptibility
indefeasibility
indefectibility
indefensibility
indemonstrability
indescribability
indestructibility
indigestibility
indiscerpibility
indispensability
indisputability
indissolubility
indivisibility
ineducability
inelegibility
ineligibility
inevitability
inexcitability
inexcusability
inexhaustibility
inexorability
inexplicability
inexpressibility

inextricability
influenceability
inhabitability
inheritability
inimicability
inimitability
innumerability
insurmountability
insusceptibility
intelligibility
interchangeability
intolerability
intransmutability
invariability
inviolability
invulnerability
irredeemability
irreducibility
irrefragability
irrefrangibility
irrefutibility
irremobability
irreparability
irrepealability
irresistibility
irresolvability
irresponsibility
irretrievability
irreversibility
irrevocability
maneuverability
manipulability
modifiability
nonsusceptibility
objectionability
organizability
precipitability
radioactivity
realizability
recognizability
reconcilability
recoverability
substitutability
unacceptability
unaccountability
unamiability
unanswerability
unavailability
unavoidability
uncoformability
undesirability

unemployability
ungovernability
unimpeachability
unpredictability
unsatiability
verifiability

biodegradability
diversifiability
identifiability
inalieanability
incommensurability
incommunicability
incomprehensibility
incontrovertibility
ineffervescibility
irreconcilability
metabolizability
semirespectability

ILK (see ILT)
ILKEN (see ILLION)
ILKER (see ILLER)
ILKINESS (see IPPIEST)
ILKING (see ILLING)

ILKY

filmy
filthy
guilty
kilty
milky
quilty
realty
silky
silty
skilty
stilty
Sylvie
tilty
wilty

bloodguilty
inguilty
not guilty
subtilty

ILL

bill
build
chill
dill
drill
fill
film
frill
gild
gill
grill
guild
hill
ill
Jill
kill
mill
nil
Phil
pill
quill
rill
shrill
sill
skill
spill
still
swill
thrill
till
trill
twill
will

anthill
at will
be still
boat drill
boot hill
Brazil
Churchill
distill
downhill
fire drill
freewill
fulfill
gin mill
goodwill

handbill
ill will
instill
keep still
landfill
mixed grill
molehill
Nashville
Nob Hill
oil spill
playbill
quadrille
rebuild
refill
sawmill
Smallville
splitsville
standstill
top bill
treadmill
true bill
until
uphill
vaudeville
windmill

bar and grill
Benadryl
bitter pill
chlorophyll
coupe de ville
daffodil
degree mill
diet pill
dollar bill
Dr. Phil
dressed to kill
fill the bill
fit to kill
G.I. Bill
game of skill
Hooterville
Jack and Jill
Jacksonville
Lauryn Hill
Louisville
lumbermill
on the pill
overbuild
overkill

peppermill
rumor mill
shoot to kill
sleeping pill
take a pill
through the mill
water pill
windowsill

barbecue grill
Beverly Hills
Buffalo Bill
Capitol Hill
King of the Hill
license to kill
Mr. De Mille
Netflix and chill
over the hill
run-of-the-mill
Treasury bill
two-dollar bill
vitamin pill

Cruella De Vil

ILLA 1

HIPPA
Linda
ninja
sigma
Simba
squilla
stigma
Tricia
villa

ahimsa
barilla
cabrilla
chinchilla
enigma
Godzilla
gorilla
granilla
guerrilla
J Dilla
Leticia
Manila

manilla
mantilla
maxilla
militia
Morinda
papilla
Patricia
perilla
Priscilla
vanilla
vexilla
Virginia
zorilla

Abyssinia

Magilla Gorilla

The Thrilla in Manilla

ILLA 2 (see IA)
ILLABLE (see UILDABLE)
ILLAGE (see ITIOUS)
ILLAIN (see ITION)
ILLAINY (see ILITY)
ILLANT (see INGENT)
ILLAR (see ILLER)
ILLARY (see ILITY)
ILLE 1 (see ILL)
ILLE 2 (see EAL 1)

ILLER

builder
chiller
driller
filler
filter
gilder
griller
guilder
iller
killer
kilter
milker
miller
philter
pillar
Pilsner
quilter

silver
skilder
spiller
thriller
tilter
wilter

bewilder
distiller
fulfiller
housebuilder
instiller
man killer
painkiller
rebuilder
refiller
shipbuilder
stone pillar
Val Kilmer

bodybuilder
castlebuilder
caterpillar
killer-diller
lady-killer
Long John Silver
overkiller
underbuilder

cigarette filter

ILLERY (see ILITY)
ILLEST (see ITIOUS)
ILLET (see ISTIC)
ILLI (see ITTY)
ILLIAM (see ILLION)
ILLIAN (see IBBEAN)
ILLIANT (see ILLION)
ILLIE (see ITTY)
ILLIEST (see IPPIEST)
ILLIGAN (see IVALENT)
ILLIN (see ITION)
ILLINESS (see IPPIEST)

ILLING

billing
building
chilling
drilling

fielding
filling
filming
gilding
grilling
jilting
killing
milking
milling
quilting
schilling
shielding
shilling
spilling
swilling
thrilling
tilting
trilling
wielding
willing
wilting
yielding

distilling
fulfilling
God willing
instilling
oil drilling
refilling
top billing
unwilling
unyielding

mercy killing
self-fulfilling

ILLION

billion
billman
brilliant
children
Hilton
milken
million
Milton
pilgrim
silken
silvan

stilton
sylvan
tillman
trillion
William
Wilson
zillion

brainchildren
Brazilian
Castilian
civilian
cotillion
distillment
fulfillment
George Wilson
godchildren
grandchildren
instillment
pavilion
quadrillion
reptilian
resilient
schoolchildren
septillion
sextillion
Sicilian
stepchildren
vermilion

dissilient
Maximilian
nonfulfillment
Regis Philbin

Married with Children
one in a million

ILLIP (see ISTIC)
ILLMAN (see ILLION)
ILLMENT (see ILLION)
ILLO (see ILLOW)
ILLON (see ITION)

ILLOW

billow
bimbo
bingo
bisso

cisco
Crisco
dingo
disco
distro
ditto
Frisco
gizmo
gringo
hippo
indo
info
intro
ipso
kiddo
kimbo
limbo
limo
lingo
minnow
pillow
Pinto
Ringo
schizo
Shinto
sicko
widow
willow
window
winnow
Winslow
Zillow

akimbo
black widow
calypso
flamingo
golf widow
in limbo
Mandingo
Nabisco

Amarillo
armadillo
Monte Christo
peccadillo
pussy willow
S.S. Minnow
San Francisco
San Jacinto
weeping willow

Apocalypto

Hungry Hungry Hippo

ILLS (see ILL)
ILLUS (see ITIOUS)
ILLUSTRATE (see IMINATE)
ILLUSTRATION (see IMITATION)
ILLY (see ITTY)
ILM (see ILL)
ILMER (see ILLER)
ILMING (see ILLING)
ILMY (see ILKY)
ILO 1 (see IO 1)
ILOGY (see ILITY)
ILOQUY (see ILITY)
ILOT (see IET)
ILSNER (see ILLER)
ILSON (see ILLION)

ILT

bilk
built
filth
gilt
guilt
hilt
ilk
jilt
milk
quilt
silk
silt
spilt
stilt
tilt
tlilt
wilt

corn silk
full tilt
hand-quilt
rebuilt
skim milk
spilt milk
well built

buttermilk
crazy quilt
custom-built

do not tilt
out of guilt
patchwork quilt
soft as silk
to the hilt
Vanderbilt

cry over spilt milk

ILTED

gilded
hilted
jilted
kilted
lilted
Mildred
Milfred
quilted
silted
stilted
tilted
wilted

begilded
half-wilted
regilded

ILTER (see ILLER)
ILTH (see ILT)
ILTHY (see ILKY)
ILTING (see ILLING)
ILTON (see ILLION)
ILTRATION (see IMITATION)
ILTY (see ILKY)
ILVAN (see ILLION)
ILVER (see ILLER)
ILVERY (see ILITY)
ILY (see ITTY)
IM (see IN 1)
IMA 1 (see IA)
IMA 2 (see IAH)
IMACE (see ITIOUS)
IMACING (see IVELING)
IMAGE (see ITIOUS)
IMAGELESS (see IGAMIST)
IMAGERY (see ILITY)
IMAGING (see IVELING)
IMAL (see ITLE)
IMATE 1 (see YDRATE)

IMATE 2 (see IET)
IMB 1 (see IN 1)
IMB 2 (see INE 1)
IMBA (see ILLA 1)
IMBALE (see ITTLE)
IMBECILE (see ITTABLE)
IMBER 1 (see IZER)

IMBER 2

chinner
cincher
clincher
dimmer
dinner
flincher
glimmer
grimmer
grinner
incher
inner
limber
lyncher
pincher
pinner
rimmer
shimmer
simmer
sinner
skimmer
skinner
slimmer
spinner
swimmer
thinner
timber
timbre
trimmer
whimper
winner

beginner
born winner
light dimmer
mule skinner
paint thinner
prizewinner
tailspinner
tree trimmer

after dinner
penny-pincher
TV dinner

IMBERED (see ITTERED)
IMBERNESS (see ITIONIST)
IMBING (see INDING)
IMBLE (see ITTLE)
IMBO (see ILLOW)
IMBRE (see IMBER 2)
IMCHI (see INGY)
IME 1 (see INE 1)
IME 2 (see EEN 1)
IMEAN (see IBBEAN)
IMELESS (see ITIS)
IMELINESS (see IGHTLINESS)
IMELY (see IGHTLY)
IMENESS (see ITIS)
IMER (see IZER)
IMETER (see ITIONER)
IMEY (see IGHTLY)
IMI (see EASY)
IMIA (see ENIA)
IMIAN (see IBBEAN)
IMIC 1 (see ISTIC)
IMIC 2 (see ESIS)
IMICRY (see ILITY)
IMID (see ITTED)
IMIDATE (see IMINATE)
IMILAR (see ITIONER)
IMILE (see ILITY)
IMINAL (see ITTABLE)
IMINALLY (see ISTICALLY)

IMINATE

criminate
dissipate
fibrillate
filiate
illustrate
indicate
innovate
integrate
iterate
militate
simulate
stimulate
syndicate
titillate
vindicate

vitiate

accriminate
alliterate
anticipate
assimulate
conciliate
debilitate
defibrillate
deintegrate
discriminate
disintegrate
dissiumulate
eliminate
extimulate
facilitate
fertilitate
habilitate
humiliate
incriminate
initiate
insimulate
instimulate
intimidate
invitiate
militiate
nobilitate
novitiate
obliterate
officiate
originate
propitiate
recriminate
redintegrate
reintegrate
reiterate
revindicate
stabilitate
subindicate
subtiliate
transliterate

difficilitate
disaffiliate
dishabilitate
domiciliate
imbecilitate
overstimulate
reconciliate
rehabilitate

IMINESS (see IGHTLINESS)
IMING (see INDING)
IMIT (see ISTIC)

IMITATION

demigration
emigration
illustration
imitation
immigration
implication
impregnation
incubation
infiltration
innovation
instigation
insulation
integration
inundation
invitation
irrigation
limitation

delimitation
disintegration
illimitation
nonlimitation
prointegration
redintegration
reintegration
reinvitation

IMITED

fidgeted
limited
picketed
pivoted
ticketed

delimited
elicited
illimited
prelimited
solicited
unlimited

unsolicited

IMITER (see ITIONER)
IMITING (see IBITING)
IMITIVE (see IBUTIVE)
IMITY (see ILITY)
IMLESS (see ITIOUS)
IMMAGE (see ITIOUS)
IMME (see INGY)
IMMEL (see ITTLE)
IMMER (see IMBER 2)
IMMERED (see ITTERED)
IMMERING (see ITTERING)
IMMEST (see ITIOUS)
IMMICK (see ISTIC)
IMMICKING (see IBITING)
IMMIGRANT (see IVALENT)
IMMIGRATION (see IMITATION)
IMMING (see ITTING)
IMMY (see INGY)
IMNESS (see ITIOUS)
IMNEY (see INGY)
IMO 1 (see IO 1)
IMO 2 (see ILLOW)
IMOTHY (see ILITY)
IMP (see INK)
IMPAGE (see ITIOUS)
IMPER (see IMBER 2)
IMPERED (see ITTERED)
IMPERING (see ITTERING)
IMPEST (see ITIOUS)
IMPIE (see INGY)
IMPIER (see ITTIER)
IMPIEST (see IPPIEST)
IMPING (see ITTING)
IMPLE (see ITTLE)
IMPLICATION (see IMITATION)
IMPLY (see INGY)
IMPOTENCE (see IVALENCE)
IMPOTENT (see IVALENT)
IMPREGNATION (see IMITATION)
IMPSE (see INK)
IMPSON (see ITION)
IMPY (see INGY)
IMSA (see ILLA 1)
IMSEY (see INGY)
IMSICAL (see ITTABLE)
IMSIER (see ITTIER)
IMSIEST (see IPPIEST)
IMSON (see ITION)
IMSY (see ITTY)
IMULATE (see IMINATE)

IMULUS (see IVOROUS)
IMUS (see ITIS)
IMY (see IGHTLY)

IN 1

been
bin
bing
bling
brim
bring
chin
cling
dim
din
ding
fin
fling
Flynn
gin
grim
grin
gym
him
hymn
in
inn
Jim
Kim
kin
king
limb
pin
ping
prim
rim
ring
shin
sin
sing
skim
skin
slim
sling
spin
spring
sting
string

swim
swing
thin
thing
Tim
tin
trim
twin
vim
whim
win
wind
wing
wring
yin
zing

agrin
akin
all in
arm sling
bearskin
bee sting
begin
Beijing
Berlin
blend in
brass ring
break wind
break-in
buckskin
built-in
bullring
butt in
cash in
cave-in
cha-ching
chagrin
check-in
chin-chin
class ring
close-in
come in
coonskin
dig in
din-din
do in
downwind
drawstring

drive-in
drug ring
first-string
foreskin
G-string
give in
hairpin
hairspring
hamstring
hang in
hat pin
headwind
herein
horn in
key ring
kidskin
kingpin
kite string
left wing
linchpin
live-in
moleskin
mood ring
move in
no-win
offspring
pigskin
plaything
porch swing
prelim
rescind
run-in
sealskin
sharkskin
sheepskin
shoe-in
shoestring
shut-in
sidespin
Sin Sing
sit-in
snakeskin
something
stand-in
stickpin
straight pin
sure thing
swimfin
tailspin
tailwind

therein
thick skin
thin skin
topspin
trade-in
tradewind
trash bin
tune in
turn in
unpin
upswing
walk-in
wear thin
weigh in
wherein
whirlwind
wingding
within
woodwind
write-in

acronym
Adrienne
antonym
anything
apron string
B.B. King
bag of wind
bathtub gin
bathtub ring
bobbypin
bowling pin
boxing ring
Burger King
cherubim
chicken wing
deadly sin
diamond ring
ding-a-ling
discipline
do your thing
double chin
everything
homonym
in a spin
in full swing
julienne
kith and kin
lapel pin
Lion King

live in sin
loony bin
Mickey Finn
mortal sin
muffin tin
muscle in
napkin ring
next of kin
not a thing
on the chin
onion ring
paper-thin
paraffin
peregrine
pinkie ring
play to win
pseudonym
pull the pin
Rin Tin Tin
rolling pin
safety pin
second wind
second-string
seraphim
sheltering
shirttail kin
Silly String
sink or swim
skeltering
smeltering
static cling
Stephen King
swearing-in
synonym
teething ring
thick or thin
ultrathin
underpin
violin
wafer-thin
wearing thin
wedding ring

Bille Jean King
comedienne
engagement ring
equestrienne
fill to the rim
fraternal twin
gone with the wind
guilty as sin

Holiday Inn
out on a limb
ring-a-ding-ding
Rumpelstiltskin
self-discipline
Siamese twin
tear limb from limb
Teddy Ruxpin
through thick and thin
tragedienne
ugly as sin
under your skin
under your wing

Flintstones Vitamin
Huckleberry Finn
identical twin
original sin
puppet on a string
take it on the chin
three sheets to the wind

IN 2 (see AN 1)
INA 1 (see IA)
INA 2 (see IAH)
INABLE (see ITTABLE)
INACH (see ITIOUS)
INAL (see ITLE)
INALIST (see IVALIST)
INALLY (see IETY)
INC (see INK)
INCAN (see ITION)
INCE (see INK)
INCEABLE (see ITTABLE)
INCENT (see INGENT)
INCER (see INGER 1)
INCESS (see ITIOUS)
INCH (see INK)
INCHER (see IMBER 2)
INCHIER (see ITTIER)
INCHIEST (see IPPIEST)
INCHING (see ITTING)
INCHY (see INGY)
INCI (see INGY)
INCIBLE (see ITTABLE)
INCIDENCE (see IVALENCE)
INCIDENT (see IVALENT)
INCING (see ITTING)
INCIPAL (see ITTABLE)
INCIPALLY (see ISTICALLY)
INCIPLE (see ITTABLE)
INCOLN (see ITION)

INCOME

dinsome
income
kingdom
quindem
symptom
winsome
wisdom

Magic Kingdom
middle-income

INCT (see INK)
INCTION (see ITION)

INCTIVE

distinctive
instinctive

indistinctive
interstinctive
nondistinctive
undistinctive

contradistinctive

INCTLY (see INGY)
INCUBATION (see IMITATION)
INCY (see ITTY)
IND 1 (see INE 1)
IND 2 (see IN 1)
INDA (see ILLA 1)
INDAGE (see ITIOUS)
INDEM (see INCOME)
INDEN (see ITION)
INDER 1 (see IZER)
INDER 2 (see INGER 1)
INDERING (see ITTERING)
INDERY (see ILITY)
INDEST (see ITIS)
INDFUL (see ITLE)
INDIA (see ILIA)
INDICATE (see IMINATE)
INDIE (see INGY)
INDIER (see ITTIER)
INDIGENCE (see IVALENCE)
INDIGENT (see IVALENT)
INDIGNANCE (see IVALENCE)

INDING

biking
binding
biting
blinding
bribing
bridling
buying
chiming
citing
climbing
crying
cycling
dialing
dining
diving
driving
drying
dying
eyeing
fighting
filing
finding
fining
firing
flying
frying
gibing
gliding
grinding
griping
guiding
heisting
hiding
hiking
hiring
hying
hyping
icing
idling
jibing
jiving
knifing
knighting
lighting
lightning
liking
lying
miming

minding
mining
miring
piling
pining
piping
plying
pricing
priming
prizing
prying
psyching
rhyming
ricing
riding
rifling
righting
riling
rising
shining
siding
sidling
sighing
sighting
signing
siring
sizing
slicing
sliding
slighting
smiling
sniping
spiking
spiting
splicing
spying
squiring
stifling
striding
striking
striping
striving
styling
swiping
thriving
tiding
tiling
timing
tiring
tithing

titling
trifling
trying
twining
tying
typing
Viking
vining
vying
whining
wiling
winding
wining
wiping
wiring
writing

abiding
acquiring
admiring
advising
aligning
applying
apprising
arising
arriving
ascribing
aspiring
assigning
assizing
backbiting
backfiring
backsliding
baptizing
beguiling
bicycling
blow-drying
broadsiding
bullfighting
capsizing
chastising
co-signing
cockfighting
colliding
combining
compiling
complying
comprising
confiding
confining

conniving
conscribing
consigning
conspiring
contriving
crash-diving
deciding
declining
decrying
deep-frying
defiling
defining
defying
deicing
delighting
denying
depriving
deriving
describing
designing
desiring
despising
devising
discipling
disguising
disliking
dividing
drip-drying
drunk driving
enshrining
enticing
entitling
espying
excising
exciting
exiling
expiring
fistfighting
floodlighting
franchising
gang fighting
ghostwriting
greased lightning
gunfighting
handwriting
headlining
highlighting
hitchhiking
hogtying
hot wiring

igniting
implying
inciting
inclining
indicting
infighting
inquiring
inscribing
inspiring
intitling
inviting
jackknifing
joyriding
landsliding
maligning
midwifing
misfiring
misguiding
mistitling
moonlighting
nosediving
obliging
outlining
outpsyching
outriding
outshining
perspiring
pill fighting
prescribing
presiding
preslicing
prizefighting
profiling
proscribing
providing
reciting
reclining
redlining
refining
rehiring
relying
reminding
replying
reprising
requiring
residing
resigning
respiring
restyling
retyping

reviling
revising
reviving
rewiring
self-winding
sidelining
sideswiping
skin diving
skydiving
skywriting
smooth riding
speedwriting
spotlighting
stockpiling
streamlining
subscribing
subsiding
subtitling
sufficing
supplying
surmising
surprising
surviving
track lighting
transcribing
transpiring
two-timing
typewriting
umpiring
unbinding
uniting
untying
unwinding

advertising
aggrandizing
agonizing
amortizing
amplifying
analyzing
authorizing
awe-inspiring
beautifying
brutalizing
burglarizing
canonizing
centralizing
certifying
circumcising
circumscribing

civilizing
clarifying
classifying
codifying
coinciding
colonizing
compromising
copyrighting
countersigning
criticizing
crucifying
crystallizing
deifying
dignifying
disentitling
disentwining
disinclining
dramatizing
dynamiting
edifying
emphasizing
energizing
enfranchising
enterprising
equalizing
eulogizing
exercising
exorcising
expediting
extraditing
falsifying
fantasizing
feminizing
fertilizing
formalizing
fortifying
fossilizing
fraternizing
galvanizing
glorifying
gratifying
harmonizing
horrifying
horseback riding
humanizing
hypnotizing
idolizing
immunizing
improvising
intertwining

jeopardizing
justifying
law-abiding
legalizing
localizing
magnetizing
magnifying
masterminding
mechanizing
memorizing
merchandising
mesmerizing
minimizing
misapplying
mobilizing
modernizing
modifying
mollifying
moralizing
mortifying
motorbiking
motorizing
multiplying
mummifying
mystifying
neutralizing
notarizing
notifying
nullifying
occupying
organizing
ossifying
ostracizing
overbuying
overpricing
overriding
overtiring
pacifying
paralyzing
pasteurizing
patronizing
penalizing
petrifying
plagiarizing
pluralizing
polarizing
publicizing
purifying
qualifying
ramifying

ratifying
reacquiring
realigning
realizing
reapplying
recognizing
rectifying
redesigning
resubscribing
reuniting
sacrificing
sanctifying
satirizing
satisfying
scandalizing
scrutinizing
sensitizing
sermonizing
signifying
simplifying
socializing
specializing
specifying
stabilizing
standardizing
sterilizing
stigmatizing
stupefying
subdividing
subsidizing
summarizing
supervising
symbolizing
sympathizing
synchronizing
tantalizing
televising
temporizing
tenderizing
terrifying
terrorizing
testifying
theorizing
tranquilizing
traumatizing
typifying
tyrannizing
underbuying
underlining
underlying

undermining
underpricing
underwiring
underwriting
unifying
uninspiring
uninviting
urbanizing
utilizing
verbalizing
verifying
victimizing
vilifying
vitalizing
vocalizing
womanizing

acclimatizing
alphabetizing
antagonizing
apologizing
capitalizing
categorizing
characterizing
commercializing
decentralizing
declassifying
dehumanizing
demobilizing
democratizing
demoralizing
demystifying
deodorizing
devitalizing
disqualifying
dissatisfying
economizing
electrifying
epitomizing
exemplifying
extemporizing
familiarizing
hypothesizing
idealizing
identifying
immortalizing
indemnifying
intensifying
italicizing
legitimizing

militarizing
monopolizing
nationalizing
naturalizing
personifying
philosophizing
popularizing
preoccupying
rationalizing
refortifying
reorganizing
revitalizing
ritualizing
romanticizing
self-sacrificing
solidifying
systematizing
visualizing
wining and dining

materializing
memorializing
professionalizing
psychoanalyzing
revolutionizing

editorializing
institutionalizing
interior designing

INDLE (see ITTLE)
INDLESS (see ITIS)
INDLING (see IDDLING)
INDLY (see IGHTLY)
INDNESS (see ITIS)
INDO (see ILLOW)
INDOO (see ISSUE)
INDOW (see ILLOW)
INDRICAL (see ITTABLE)
INDSAY (see INGY)
INDU (see ISSUE)
INDUSTRY (see ILITY)
INDY (see INGY)

INE 1

bind
blind
chime
climb

crime
dime
dine
find
fine
grime
grind
hind
I'm
kind
Klein
lime
line
mime
mind
mine
nine
pine
prime
Rhine
rhyme
rime
rind
shine
shrine
sign
sine
slime
spine
stein
swine
thine
thyme
time
twine
vine
whine
wind
wine

A-line
align
all mine
all-time
alpine
arline
assign
baseline
bedtime
behind

benign
Bernstein
bigtime
bloodline
bovine
bustline
buy time
byline
canine
carbine
chow line
clothesline
cloud nine
co-sign
coal mine
coastline
combine
confine
consign
cruiseline
dateline
daytime
deadline
decline
define
design
divine
Einstein
enshrine
entwine
enzyme
fact-find
feline
fine line
fish line
food line
freightline
front line
frown line
full-time
goal line
gold mine
grapevine
great line
guideline
hairline
halftime
hard line
hard time
headline

hemline
high sign
high time
hot line
incline
keep time
kill time
land mine
laugh line
lead time
life time
lifeline
lunch line
lunch time
main line
make time
malign
mankind
May wine
mean time
moonshine
nap time
neckline
night time
noontime
old-line
old-time
online
opine
outline
outshine
part-time
pastime
peace sign
phone line
pipeline
playtime
post time
prime time
punchline
ragtime
real-time
recline
red wine
redline
refine
remind
resign
rewind
Rhine wine

salt mine
shoeshine
showtime
sideline
skyline
small-time
snow-blind
sometime
spring time
stag line
stateline
stop sign
straight line
streamline
sublime
sunshine
tell time
timeline
tow line
trunk line
turbine
two-time
unbind
unkind
unwind
war crime
wartime
white wine

aforetime
alkaline
anytime
aquiline
asinine
axe to grind
bacon rind
before time
blow your mind
borderline
bottom line
bump and grind
by design
call to mind
Calvin Klein
change of mind
checkout line
Christmas time
clinging vine
color line
color-blind

columbine
concubine
conga line
countersign
county line
credit line
cross your mind
curtain time
danger sign
dinner time
disincline
dollar sign
doorbell chime
dotted line
double-time
down the line
draw the line
drop a line
equal time
every time
fall behind
fall in line
Father Time
finish line
firing line
first in line
fishing line
five and dime
form a line
frame of mind
Frankenstein
free-throw line
hold the line
humankind
in a bind
in good time
in no time
intertwine
iodine
keep in mind
lemon rind
Liechtenstein
maritime
mastermind
Miller time
mountain climb
never mind
nick of time
on the line
on your mind

one more time
one thin dime
one-track mind
open mind
out of line
out of mind
overtime
overwind
Palestine
pantomime
paradigm
party line
pass the time
peace of mind
picket line
play for time
porcupine
private line
rain or shine
realign
redesign
rise and shine
royal line
same old line
saturnine
scrimmage line
shipping line
speak your mind
storyline
summer time
supper time
take your time
timberline
traffic fine
turpentine
underline
undermine
undersign
valentine
vintage wine
wait in line
warning sign
wine and dine
wintertime
womankind
yours and mine

above the line
Albert Einstein
all in good time

assembly line
boggle the mind
come from behind
electric line
end of the line
fifty-yard line
four of a kind
from time to time
Land Before Time
legally blind
make up your mind
marrying kind
nickel-and-dime
nursery rhyme
one at a time
one of a kind
out of your mind
partners in crime
piece of your mind
presence of mind
receiving line
stop on a dime
time after time
top-of-the-line
two of a kind
Venetian blind
victory sign

ahead of your time
better luck next time
daylight savings time
lay it on the line
Mason-Dixon line
once in a lifetime
once upon a time
One Day at a Time
where the sun don't shine

INE 2 (see EEN 1)
INE 3 (see IN 1)
INE 4 (see EASY)
INEA (see INGY)
INEAR (see ITTIER)
INELESS (see ITIS)
INELY (see IGHTLY)
INEM (see IGHTEN)
INEMENT (see ILEMENT)
INEN (see ITION)
INENESS (see ITIS)
INER (see IZER)
INERAL (see ITTABLE)

INERY 1 (see IETY)
INERY 2 (see EITY)
INEST (see ITIS)
INETY (see IGHTLY)
INEW (see ISSUE)
INFAMOUS (see IGAMIST)
INFAMY (see ILITY)
INFANCY (see ILITY)
INFANT (see INGENT)
INFANTRY (see ILITY)
INFINITE (see IVALENT)
INFO (see ILLOW)
INFREY (see INGY)
INFUL (see ITTLE)
ING (see IN 1)
INGDOM (see INCOME)
INGE (see INK)
INGEING (see ITTING)

INGENT

distant
figment
fitment
fringent
infant
instant
isn't
pigment
ringent
shipment
strigment
stringent
thrillant
tingent
trickment
Vincent

abridgement
acuitment
assistant
astringent
benignant
commitment
consistent
constringent
contingent
deficient
efficient
enlistment

equipment
existent
indignant
insistent
malignant
omniscient
persistent
proficient
refitment
remitment
reshipment
resistant
restringent
scintillant
subsistent
sufficient
transshipment
unshipment

co-existent
equidistant
inconsistent
inefficient
insufficient
nonmalignant
recommitment
self-sufficient

tamper-resistant

INGER 1

binger
blinker
cinder
clinger
cringer
dinger
drinker
finger
flinger
ginger
hinder
hinger
hinter
injure
inker
linger
linker

pincer
pinker
printer
ringer
shrinker
singer
sinker
slinger
splinter
springer
sprinter
squinter
stinger
stinker
stringer
swinger
thinker
tinder
tinker
tinter
twinger
winker
winter
wringer
zinger

and sinker
bellringer
blueprinter
convincer
dead-ringer
fast drinker
folk singer
free thinker
Goldfinger
gunslinger
headshrinker
hoodwinker
humdinger
impinger
imprinter
infringer
left-winger
lipsyncer
malinger
midwinter
misprinter
mud slinger
nondrinker
reprinter

rescinder
right-winger
ring finger
wingdinger
dead of winter
fingerprinter
ladyfinger
pull my finger
social drinker
trigger finger

hook, line, and sinker
not lift a finger

wrap around your little finger

INGER 2 (see INGER 1)
INGERED (see ITTERED)
INGERING (see ITTERING)
INGHY (see INGY)
INGIER (see ITTIER)
INGIEST (see IPPIEST)
INGINESS (see EAKINESS)
INGING 1 (see INKING)
INGING 2 (see ITTING)
INGLE (see ITTLE)
INGLER (see INKLER)
INGLING (see INKING)
INGLY (see INGY)
INGO (see ILLOW)
INGRAM (see ITION)
INGRID (see INTED)
INGUAL (see ITTLE)
INGUE (see AN 1)
INGUISH (see ITIOUS)
INGUIST (see ITIOUS)

INGY

bingy
Blimpie
blinky
chimney
chinchy
Cindy
clingy
crimpy
crinkly
dimmy
dimply

dinghy
dingy
dinky
findy
Finley
flimsey
fringy
gimme
gimpy
ginchy
Ginny
guinea
indie
Indy
inky
inly
Jimmy
jingly
kimchi
kingly
kinky
limply
Lindsay
lindy
linty
mingly
mingy
mini
Minnie
minty
ninny
pingy
pinkie
pinky
rindy
rinky
scrimpy
shimmy
shindy
shrimpy
simply
singly
skimpy
skinny
Slinky
springy
sprinkly
squinty
stingy
stinky

swimmy
swingy
thinly
tingly
tinny
Twinkie
twinkly
whimmy
whinny
Wimpy
windy
winky
wrinkly
zingy

Da Vinci
distinctly
Lewinsky
McKinley
New Guinea
succinctly

indistinctly
Mork and Mindy
Oprah Winfrey
Ren and Stimpy
rinky dinky
Tinky Winky

Monica Lewinski

INI 1 (see EASY)
INI 2 (see INGY)
INIA (see ILLA 1)
INIAN 1 (see IBBEAN)
INIAN 2 (see ITION)
INIC (see ISTIC)
INICAL (see ITTABLE)
INICALLY (see ISTICALLY)
INICAN (see IVALENT)
INICKY (see ILITY)
INICUS (see IVOROUS)
INIE (see IGHTLY)

INIER

brinier
dicier
feistier
icier

ivier
jivier
likelier
mightier
pinier
pricier
shinier
spicier
spikier
spinier
tidier
tinier
vinier
whinier
winier

INIMAL (see ITTABLE)
ININESS (see IGHTLINESS)
INING (see INDING)
INION (see ITION)
INISH (see ITIOUS)
INISHING (see IVELING)
INIST (see EANEST)
INISTER (see ITIONER)
INISTRESS (see IGAMIST)
INISTRY (see ILITY)
INITIVE (see IBUTIVE)
INITY (see ILITY)
INJA (see ILLA 1)
INJURE (see INGER 1)
INJURED (see ITTERED)
INJURING (see ITTERING)

INK

binge
blimp
blink
brink
chink
chintz
cinch
clinch
clink
crimp
cringe
dinge
dink
dint
drink

finch
flinch
flint
fringe
gimp
glimpse
glint
hinge
hint
inc.
inch
ink
jinx
kink
limp
link
lint
lymph
lynch
lynx
mince
mink
mint
minx
nymph
pimp
pinch
pink
plink
prince
print
quince
quint
rink
rinse
shrimp
shrink
since
singe
sink
skimp
sphinx
splint
sprint
squinch
squint
stink
stint
sync
think

tinge
tint
twinge
wimp
wince
winch
wink
zinc

blueprint
bullfinch
chain-link
cheese blintz
convince
crown prince
cuff link
distinct
extinct
fine print
footprint
goldfinch
hair rinse
handprint
hoodwink
hot pink
impinge
imprint
in sync
infringe
instinct
larynx
lipsync
misprint
mixed drink
newsprint
precinct
preshrink
reprint
rethink
small print
soft drink
succinct
syringe
unhinge

Derek Flint
Doublemint
ever since
fairy prince
fingerprint

Freddie Prinze
in a clinch
in a pinch
inch by inch
indistinct
interlink
kitchen sink
Little Prince
Merrill Lynch
missing link
on the brink
out of sync
out-of-print
pen and ink
penny-pinch
peppermint
rinky dink
roller rink
skating rink
take a drink
tickled pink
tiddlywink
U.S. Mint

back from the brink
lunatic fringe
no food or drink
Pretty in Pink

INKER (see INGER 1)
INKERING (see ITTERING)
INKIE (see INGY)
INKINESS (see EAKINESS)

INKING

blinking
bringing
clinging
clinking
crinkling
dinging
drinking
flinging
inking
inkling
jingling
kinging
linking
mingling
pinging
pinking

plinking
ringing
Ringling
shrinking
singing
singling
sinking
slinging
slinking
springing
sprinkling
stinging
stinking
stringing
swinging
thinking
tingling
tinkling
twinkling
winging
winking
winkling
wringing
wrinkling
zinging

besprinkling
commingling
hoodwinking
lipsyncing
mud-slinging
preshrinking
ratfinking
rethinking
unthinking
unwrinkling
upbringing

interlinking
intermingling
wishful thinking

INKISH (see ITIOUS)
INKLE (see ITTLE)

INKLER

crinkler
jingler
mingler
sprinkler
tingler
tinkler

twinkler
wrinkler

Henry Winkler

INKLING (see INKING)
INKLY (see INGY)
INKY (see INGY)
INLAND (see ITION)
INLET (see ISTIC)
INLEY (see INGY)
INLY (see INGY)
INN (see IN 1)
INNABLE (see ITTABLE)
INNACLE (see ITTABLE)
INNAGE (see ITIOUS)
INNAMON (see IVALENCE)
INNER (see IMBER 2)
INNERLESS (see ITIONIST)
INNERLY (see ILITY)
INNERNESS (see ITIONIST)
INNERY (see ILITY)
INNESS (see ITIOUS)
INNET (see ISTIC)
INNIE (see INGY)
INNIER (see ITTIER)
INNIEST (see IPPIEST)
INNINESS (see IPPIEST)
INNING (see ITTING)
INNISH (see ITIOUS)
INNOCENCE (see IVALENCE)
INNOCENT (see IVALENT)
INNOVATE (see IMINATE)
INNOVATION (see IMITATION)
INNOW (see ILLOW)
INNY (see INGY)
INO (see IO 1)
INO 1 (see INO 3)

INO 3

keno
niño
Reno
vino
Zeno

bambino
casino
El Niño
gambino
Latino

Al Pacino
Angeleno
cappuccino
El Camino
Filipino
Ford Torino
Valentino

San Bernardino
The Great Bambino

Vinnie Barbarino

INOR (see IZER)
INQUIRIST (see IGAMIST)
INQUIRY (see ILITY)
INQUISH (see ITIOUS)
INSE (see INK)
INSENG (see ITTING)
INSIC (see ISTIC)
INSICAL (see ITTABLE)
INSING (see ITTING)
INSKI (see INGY)
INSKY (see INGY)
INSLOW (see ILLOW)
INSOME (see INCOME)
INSTANCE (see ISTANCE)
INSTANT (see INGENT)
INSTANTLY (see ILITY)
INSTIGATION (see IMITATION)
INSULATION (see IMITATION)
INSY (see ITTY)
INT 1 (see INK)
INT 2 (see IGHT)
INTABLE (see ITTABLE)
INTAGE (see ITIOUS)

INTED

flinted
glinted
hinted
Ingrid
minted
printed
splinted
sprinted
squinted
stinted
tinted

blueprinted
fine printed
footprinted
handprinted
imprinted
misprinted
newsprinted
reprinted
spearminted

fingerprinted
pepperminted
U.S. Minted

INTEGER (see ITIONER)
INTEGRAL (see ITTABLE)
INTEGRATE (see IMINATE)
INTEGRATION (see IMITATION)
INTER (see INGER 1)
INTERED (see ITTERED)
INTEREST (see ITIOUS)
INTERING (see ITTERING)
INTERLESS (see ITIONIST)
INTH (see IGHT)
INTIMATE (see IVALENT)
INTIN (see ITION)
INTING (see ITTING)
INTO 1 (see ISSUE)
INTO 2 (see ILLOW)
INTON 1 (see ITION)
INTON 2 (see ITION)
INTRICATE (see IVALENT)
INTRO (see ILLOW)
INTSY (see ITTY)
INTY (see INGY)
INTZ (see INK)
INTZY (see ITTY)
INUE (see ISSUE)
INUM (see IGHTEN)
INUNDATION (see IMITATION)
INUOUS (see IVOROUS)
INUS (see ITIS)
INUTE (see ISTIC)
INVITATION (see IMITATION)
INX (see INK)
INY (see IGHTLY)
INYL (see ITLE)
INZE (see INK)

IO 1

cheapo
cheetoh
chemo
Chico
Cleo
credo
Debo
depot
ego
frio
Frito
Gino
Hilo
kilo
Leo
Nemo
Nino
primo
repo
rio
sego
Theo
Tito
Tivo
trio
veto

amigo
amino
bandito
Benito
burrito
Enrico
finito
gazebo
in vitro
libido
machismo
mosquito
placebo
Tampico
Toledo
torpedo
tuxedo
Yumiko

alter ego
Galileo

Ghostly Trio
Hirohito
incognito
Puerto Rico

IOLENCE (see ITIS)

ION 1

Brian
Bryant
client
giant
lion
pliant
riant
Ryan
Zion

compliant
defiant
Green Giant
Hawaiian
indictment
Lane Bryant
O'Brien
Orion
reliant
sea lion

dandelion
mountain lion
self-reliant

Cowardly Lion
Jolly Green Giant

ION 2 (see YLON)
IOR (see IER 1)
IORY (see IETY)
IOT (see IET)
IOTER (see IGHTENER)
IOUS (see ITIS)

IP

bit
blip
brick

chick
chip
chit
click
clip
dick
dip
drip
fit
flick
flip
flit
git
grip
grit
hick
hip
hit
it
kick
kit
knit
lick
lip
lit
mitt
nick
nip
nit
pick
pip
pit
prick
quick
quip
quit
Rick
rip
Schick
Schmidt
scrip
ship
shtick
sic
sick
sip
sit
skip
skit
slick

slip
slit
snip
snit
spit
split
stick
strict
strip
thick
tick
tip
tit
trick
trip
twit
whip
whit
wick
wit
writ
zip
zit

acquit
admit
afflict
airship
airsick
airstrip
alit
armpit
base hit
bean dip
beatnick
befit
big stick
Bisquick
blue chip
blue stick
bout it
Brad Pitt
broomstick
bullwhip
card trick
catnip
Chap Stick
chick flick
chopstick
close-knit

cockpit
commit
conflict
constrict
convict
Cool whip
courtship
cow chip
cowlick
CrossFit
cruise ship
deanship
depict
dimwit
dipstick
do stick
drag strip
drop kick
drumstick
emit
equip
evict
fat lip
field trip
film clip
flagship
friendship
goldbrick
guilt trip
hairclip
hairsplit
half-slip
half-wit
hand-knit
handgrip
handpick
hardship
hat trick
head trip
heartsick
homesick
horsewhip
hot tip
ice pick
inflict
joystick
judgeship
jump ship
kinship
lamplit

legit
let slip
lipstick
lordship
lovesick
mess kit
midship
misfit
moonlit
new stick
nitpick
nitwit
obit
oil slick
omit
outfit
outstrip
outwit
Peach Pit
permit
pinch-hit
pink slip
place-kick
predict
press kit
Q-Tip
rainslick
refit
remit
restrict
right-click
roach clip
rope trick
round trip
salt lick
sandpit
Sanskrit
seasick
side trip
sidekick
skin flick
slapstick
smash hit
snake pit
spaceship
St. Nick
starlit
steamship
submit
sunlit

switch-hit
tar pit
tight fit
tight-knit
Tip-it
to wit
tool kit
toothpick
top kick
township
transmit
troopship
true grit
two-bit
unfit
unsplit
unzip
warship
whip it
wingtip
witnit
yardstick

authorship
baby-sit
battleship
bit by bit
bite your lip
bone to pick
brinkmanship
business trip
caffeine fit
cancer stick
candlestick
candlewick
catcher's mitt
censorship
chips and dip
chocolate chip
clipper ship
comic strip
comradeship
contradict
counterfeit
Cousin Itt
crack the whip
craftsmanship
curl your lip
dirty trick
doctor kit

double-dip
double-knit
ego trip
every bit
fellowship
fiddlestick
filter tip
fingertip
first-aid kit
Gaza Strip
give the slip
have a fit
heretic
hit a lick
hockey stick
horsemanship
illegit
internship
ladyship
landing strip
leadership
lose your grip
manumit
membership
Messerschmitt
microchip
Moby Dick
nervous tic
Nestle Quik
overtip
ownership
paper clip
partnership
party whip
passion pit
penmanship
perfect fit
pillow slip
pirate ship
pistol-whip
pogo stick
poker chip
politic
power trip
readmit
recommit
repair kit
resubmit
rocket ship
salesmanship

scholarship
seamanship
sewing kit
shoe-shine kit
showmanship
skinny-dip
sponsorship
sportsmanship
statesmanship
stewardship
Sunset Strip
swizzle stick
take a dip
take a sip
throw a fit
trusteeship
undertip
walking stick
weatherstrip

acquaintanceship
apprenticeship
banana split
bargaining chip
bottomless pit
button your lip
championship
chancellorship
citizenship
companionship
computer chip
conniption fit
dictatorship
eggs Benedict
Freudian slip
good sportsmanship
guardianship
lay it on thick
lickety-split
licorice stick
Miracle Whip
one-upmanship
overcommit
partisanship
postnasal drip
potato chip
run a tight ship
shoot from the hip
stiff upper lip

emergency kit
short end of the stick

IPE (see IGHT)
IPELY (see IGHTLY)
IPEN (see IGHTEN)
IPENER (see IGHTENER)
IPENESS (see ITIS)
IPENING (see IGHTENING)
IPER (see IZER)
IPEST (see ITIS)
IPHANY (see ILITY)
IPHER (see IZER)
IPHERABLE (see IRABLE)
IPHERY (see ILITY)
IPHON (see IGHTEN)
IPHONED (see IGHTEN)
IPHONING (see IGHTENING)
IPIA (see ILIA)
IPID (see ITTED)
IPING (see INDING)
IPLE 1 (see ITLE)
IPLE 2 (see ITTLE)
IPLED (see ITTLED)
IPLESS (see ITIOUS)
IPLING 1 (see INDING)
IPLING 2 (see IDDLING)
IPMENT (see INGENT)
IPNESS (see ITIOUS)
IPOTENCE (see IVALENCE)
IPOTENT (see IVALENT)
IPPA (see ILLA 1)
IPPABLE (see ITTABLE)
IPPANCY (see ILITY)
IPPE (see ITTY)
IPPEE (see ITTY)
IPPER (see ITTER)
IPPERED (see ITTERED)
IPPERING (see ITTERING)
IPPERLESS (see ITIONIST)
IPPEST (see ITIOUS)
IPPET (see ISTIC)
IPPETY (see ILITY)
IPPI (see ITTY)
IPPIE (see ITTY)
IPPIER (see ITTIER)

IPPIEST

bingiest
bippiest
bitsiest
blippiest
busiest

chilliest
chilliness
chippiest
crispiest
dilliest
dingiest
dippiest
ditsiest
dizziest
dizziness
drippiest
fishiest
fishiness
fittiness
fizziest
flimsiest
flippiest
Frenchiest
frilliest
frilliness
fringiest
friskiest
frizziest
frizziness
giddiest
giddiness
giggliest
ginchiest
glitziest
grittiest
grittiness
grizzliest
gypsiest
hideous
hilliest
hilliness
hissiest
ickiest
idiot
iffiness
itchiness
jiggliest
kissiest
lippiest
lippiness
mingiest
missiest
mistiest
niftiest
nippiest

pickiest
pitchiness
Pixiest
prettiest
prettiness
prickliest
prissiest
prissiness
pygmiest
rippliest
riskiest
ritziest
shiftiest
shiftiness
sickliest
silkiness
silliest
silliness
sissiest
sissiness
sixtiest
sizzliest
skimpiest
skinniest
skinniness
skippiest
slippiness
snippiest
snippiness
spiffiest
squiggliest
squishiest
stickiest
stickiness
stingiest
swishiest
thriftiest
tibias
tinniest
tinniness
tippiest
tipsiest
tizziest
trickiest
twiggiest
twistiest
whimsiest
whizziest
wiggliest
williest

wishiest
wispiest
wittiest
wittiness
wriggliest
zippiest

fastidious
insidious
invidious
oblivious
Odysseus
perfidious

semioblivious

IPPINESS (see IPPIEST)
IPPING (see ITTING)
IPPLE (see ITTLE)
IPPLED (see ITTLED)
IPPLER (see IBBLER)
IPPLIER (see ITTIER)
IPPLIEST (see IPPIEST)
IPPLING (see IDDLING)
IPPO (see ILLOW)
IPPY (see ITTY)
IPROCAL (see ITTABLE)
IPSE (see IST 1)
IPSIER (see ITTIER)
IPSIEST (see IPPIEST)
IPSO (see ILLOW)
IPSTER (see ITTER)
IPSY (see ITTY)
IPT (see IST 1)
IPTIC (see ISTIC)
IPTICAL (see ITTABLE)
IPTING (see ITTING)
IPTION (see ITION)
IPTIONAL (see ITTABLE)
IPTIVE (see ITIOUS)
IPTURE (see ITTER)
IQUE (see EAT 1)
IQUEABLE (see IEVABLE)
IQUELY (see EASY)
IQUENESS (see ESIS)
IQUER (see EATER 1)
IQUEY (see ITTY)
IQUID (see ITTED)
IQUIDLY (see ILITY)
IQUING (see EATING 1)
IQUITIST (see IGAMIST)
IQUITOR (see ITIONER)

IQUITY (see ILITY)
IQUOR (see ITTER)
IR 1 (see ER 1)
IR 2 (see EAR 1)
IRA (see IAH)

IRABLE

firable
hirable
squirable
tirable
wirable

acquirable
aspirable
conspirable
desirable
expirable
inquirable
inspirable
perspirable
rehirable
requirable
retirable
rewirable
untirable

decipherable
reacquirable
undesirable
uninspirable

IRACLE (see ITTABLE)
IRACY (see IETY)
IRAL (see ITLE)
IRATE 1 (see IET)
IRATE 2 (see YDRATE)
IRBY (see IRTY)
IRCE (see IRTY)
IRCH (see IRST)
IRCHING (see ERTING)
IRCLE (see URTLE)
IRCUIT (see ERVICE)
IRCUITRY (see ERNITY)
IRCUS (see ERVICE)
IRD (see ORD 2)
IRDED (see URDED)
IRDER (see URNER)
IRDIE (see IRTY)

IRDING (see ERTING)
IRDLE (see URTLE)
IRDLING (see ERTING)

IRE

choir
dire
fire
hire
ire
lyre
mire
pyre
quire
sire
spire
squire
tire
wire

acquire
admire
afire
aspire
attire
backfire
barbed wire
bonfire
brush fire
campfire
catch fire
ceasefire
church choir
conspire
crossfire
desire
empire
entire
esquire
expire
flat tire
for hire
foxfire
gunfire
hang fire
haywire
hellfire
high wire
hotwire

inquire
inspire
live wire
McGuire
misfire
on fire
perspire
quagmire
rehire
require
respire
retire
rewire
sapphire
satire
shellfire
snow tire
spare tire
spitfire
surefire
transpire
tripwire
umpire
vampire
wildfire

ball of fire
line of fire
play with fire
rapid-fire
reacquire
set on fire
trial by fire
under fire
underwire
uninspire

down to the wire
Earth Wind and Fire
ready, aim, fire
under the wire

IRED

fired
hired
mired
sired
spired

squired
tired
wired

acquired
admired
aspired
attired
conspired
desired
dog-tired
expired
hotwired
inquired
inspired
misfired
perspired
rehired
required
retired
rewired
transpired
umpired

overtired
reacquired
sick and tired
undesired
uninspired

IRELY (see IGHTLY)
IREMENT (see ILEMENT)
IREN (see IGHTEN)

IRER

direr
firer
hirer
wirer

acquirer
admirer
aspirer
attirer
conspirer
desirer
expirer
inquirer
inspirer
perspirer

requirer

retirer

National Enquirer

IRES (see ITIS)
IRETY (see IETY)
IRGE (see ORD 2)
IRGIL (see URTLE)
IRGIN (see ERSION)
IRGO (see ERNO)
IRI (see EARY)
IRIAL (see ERIAL 1)
IRIC (see ISTIC)
IRICAL (see ITTABLE)
IRICALLY (see ISTICALLY)
IRING (see INDING)
IRIOUS (see ERIOUS)
IRIS (see ITIS)
IRISH (see ITIS)
IRIT (see ISTIC)
IRITUAL (see ITTABLE)
IRK (see ORK 1)
IRKER (see URNER)
IRKING (see ERTING)
IRKY (see IRTY)

IRL

burl

churl

curl

earl

furl

girl

hurl

pearl

purl

swirl

twirl

whirl

whorl

world

awhirl

call girl

dream girl

dream world

homegirl

pincurl

Playgirl

real world

recurl

Seaworld

show girl

Spice Girl

spitcurl

Third World

uncurl

unfurl

Wayne's World

attagirl

cover girl

Jheri Curl

Supergirl

Uptown Girl

Wally World

working girl

you go girl

Joy To The World

mother-of-pearl

out of this world

Powerpuff Girl

We Are The world

Little Red-Haired Girl

on top of the world

IRLER (see URNER)
IRLEY (see IRTY)
IRLING (see ERTING)
IRLY (see IRTY)
IRM (see URN)
IRMANCE (see ERSION)
IRMATIVE (see ERVATIVE)
IRMEST (see ERVICE)
IRMIER (see URLIER)
IRMING (see ERTING)
IRMISH (see ERVICE)
IRMITY (see ERNITY)
IRMLY (see IRTY)
IRMY (see IRTY)
IRO (see ERO 1)
IRON 1 (see IER 1)
IRON 2 (see IGHTEN)
IRONY (see IETY)
IROUS (see ITIS)
IRP (see ORK 1)
IRPIER (see URLIER)
IRPING (see ERTING)
IRPY (see IRTY)
IRREL (see URTLE)

IRRIGATION (see IMITATION)
IRRING (see ERTING)
IRRY (see IRTY)
IRS (see ARE 1)

IRST

berth

birch

birth

burst

church

curse

dearth

earth

erst

first

firth

girth

hearse

Hearst

lurch

mirth

Nerf

nurse

perch

Perth

purse

search

serf

smirch

smurf

surf

terse

thirst

turf

verse

worse

worst

worth

accurse

adverse

Amherst

asperse

at worst

averse

besmirch

blank verse

bratwurst

childbirth
cloudburst
coerce
commerce
converse
disburse
disperse
diverse
feetfirst
Fort Worth
headfirst
immerse
inverse
knackwurst
net worth
obverse
outburst
perverse
rebirth
rehearse
research
reverse
self-worth
soul-search
stillbirth
strip-search
submerse
sunburst
transverse
traverse
unearth
wet nurse
windsurf
Woolworth
Wordsworth

afterbirth
Astroturf
body surf
body-search
Cinn-a-burst
die of thirst
down-to-earth
intersperse
ladies first
Leavenworth
liverwurst
money's worth
Papa Smurf
Patty Hearst

reimburse
safety first
surf and turf
universe
what on earth?
chapter and verse
doggerel verse
for all it's worth
heaven on earth
salt of the earth

for better or worse
if worst comes to worst
move heaven and earth
Mrs. Butterworth

Masters of the Universe

IRSTING (see ERTING)
IRSTY (see IRTY)
IRT (see ORK 1)
IRTABLE (see URTABLE)
IRTED (see URDED)
IRTER (see URNER)
IRTH (see IRST)
IRTHING (see ERTING)
IRTIER (see URLIER)
IRTING (see ERTING)
IRTUAL (see URTABLE)

IRTY

Bernie
Bertie
birdie
blurry
blurty
burly
burpee
chirpy
churchy
churly
Circe
clergy
curly
curry
curtly
curvy
derby
dirty

Drury
early
earthly
ferny
firmly
flirty
flurry
Furby
furry
fury
germy
Gertie
girly
gurney
Herbie
Hershey
hurry
jerky
jersey
journey
jury
Kirby
lurchy
mercy
murky
Murphy
Murray
nerdy
nervy
nursey
pearly
Percy
perky
perty
purry
quirky
scurry
scurvy
Shirley
Slurpee
slurry
smirky
splurgy
spurty
squirmy
squirty
sternly
sturdy
surly
surrey

swervy
swirly
tersely
thirsty
thirty
tourney
turkey
twirly
whirly
whirry
wordy
wormy
worry
worthy

adversely
attorney
beef jerky
blameworthy
bloodthirsty
cold turkey
covertly
grand jury
inversely
invertly
Missouri
newsworthy
noteworthy
overtly
praiseworthy
Ralph Furley
Tandoori
unworthy

Albuquerque
Arthur Murray
at your mercy
Bert and Ernie
controversy
down and dirty
Eddie Murphy
herky-jerky
hurdy-gurdy
hurly-burly
hurry-scurry
metallurgy
not to worry
over thirty
overwordy

taciturnly
taxidermy
topsy-turvy
turkey-lurkey
watch the birdie
angel of mercy
district attorney
Laverne and Shirley

benefit of clergy
power of attorney

IRUS (see ITIS)
IRVING (see ERTING)
IRWIN (see ERSION)
IRY (see IGHTLY)
IS 1 (see IST 1)
IS 2 (see ID)
IS 3 (see EED 1)
IS 4 (see E 1)
IS 5 (see IZE 1)
ISA (see IA)
ISABLE (see ITABLE 1)
ISAL (see ITLE)
ISBEE (see ITTY)
ISBING (see ITTING)
ISC (see IST 1)
ISCAL (see ITTLE)
ISCER (see ITTER)
ISCHEIF (see ISTIC)
ISCIENCY (see ILITY)
ISCIENT (see INGENT)
ISCO (see ILLOW)
ISCUIT (see ISTIC)
ISCUS (see ITIOUS)
ISDOM (see INCOME)
ISE 1 (see IZE 1)
ISE 2 (see ICE 1)
ISE 3 (see EAT 1)
ISE 4 (see EED 1)
ISEL (see ITTLE)
ISELED (see ITTLED)
ISELY 1 (see IGHTLY)
ISELY 2 (see IGHTLY)
ISEMEN (see IGHTEN)
ISEMENT (see ILEMENT)
ISEN 1 (see ITION)
ISEN 2 (see IGHTEN)
ISENESS (see ITIS)
ISER (see IZER)
ISERABLY (see ILITY)
ISERY (see ILITY)

ISH 1 (see IST 1)
ISH 2 (see EAT 1)
ISHER (see ITTER)
ISHERY (see ILITY)
ISHES (see ITIOUS)
ISHFUL (see ITTLE)
ISHIER (see ITTER)
ISHIEST (see IPPIEST)
ISHINESS (see IPPIEST)
ISHING (see ITTING)
ISHIONER (see ITIONER)
ISHOLM (see ITION)
ISHOP (see ICCUP)
ISHY (see ITTY)
ISIA 1 (see ILIA)
ISIA 2 (see IA)
ISIAN (see ESIAN)
ISIBLE (see ITTABLE)
ISIBLY (see ILITY)
ISING (see INDING)
ISION (see ITION)
ISIS (see ITIS)
ISIT (see ISTIC)
ISITE (see ISTIC)
ISITER (see ITIONER)
ISITING (see IBITING)
ISITIVE (see IBUTIVE)
ISITOR (see ITIONER)
ISIVE (see ITIS)
ISK (see IST 1)
ISKER (see ITTER)
ISKERED (see ITTERED)
ISKERLESS (see ITIONIST)
ISKET (see ISTIC)
ISKEY (see ITTY)
ISKIER (see ITTER)
ISKIEST (see IPPIEST)
ISKING (see ITTING)
ISKY (see ITTY)
ISLAND (see IGHTEN)
ISLE (see ILE 1)
ISLL (see ITTLE)
ISLY (see ITTY)

ISM

ism
prism
rhythm
schism
baptism
deism

fascism
racism
seism
simplism
sophism
theism
truism

activism
altruism
anarchism
aneurysm
animism
aphorism
atheism
barbarism
botulism
cataclysm
catechism
centralism
chauvinism
communism
cretinism
criticism
cynicism
Darwinism
despotism
dogmatism
dualism
egotism
embolism
euphemism
exorcism
extremism
formalism
hedonism
heroism
humanism
hypnotism
idealism
journalism
Judaism
magnetism
mannerism
masochism
mechanism
mesmerism
modernism
monoism
moralism

mysticism
narcissism
nepotism
nihilism
optimism
organism
ostracism
pacifism
paganism
pantheism
pessimism
plagiarism
pragmatism
pugilism
realism
rheumatism
skepticism
socialism
solecism
solipsism
spoonerism
stigmatism
stoicism
syllogism
symbolism
synchronism
terrorism
tokenism
vandalism
voyeurism
vulgarism
witticism

alcoholism
amateurism
anachronism
animalism
antagonism
astigmatism
cannibalism
capitalism
Catholicism
commercialism
conservatism
consumerism
determinism
eroticism
evangelism
fanaticism
favoritism

federalism
hyperbolism
impressionism
liberalism
male chauvinism
metabolism
militarism
opportunism
parallelism
paternalism
patriotism
polytheism
provincialism
Puritanism
rationalism
recidivism
romanticism
separatism
ventriloquism
volunteerism

abolitionism
agrarianism
Americanism
anti-Semitism
colloquialism
colonialism
defense mechanism
exhibitionism
imperialism
indeterminism
industrialism
irrationalism
materialism
microorganism
professionalism
sadomasochism
sensationalism
spiritualism

animal magnetism
individualism
vegetarianism

humanitarianism

ISMAL (see ITTLE)
ISMO (see IO 1)
ISN'T (see INGENT)
ISNEY (see ITTY)
ISON 1 (see ITION)

ISON 2 (see IGHTEN)
ISONER (see ITIONER)
ISOR (see IZER)
ISORY (see IETY)
ISP (see IST 1)
ISPER (see ITTER)
ISPERED (see ITTERED)
ISPIER (see ITTIER)
ISPIEST (see IPPIEST)
ISPY (see ITTY)
ISQUE (see IST 1)
ISS (see IST 1)
ISSABLE (see ITTABLE)
ISSAL (see ITTLE)
ISSAN (see EON)
ISSAR (see ITTER)
ISSE (see EAT 1)
ISSER (see ITTER)
ISSERIE (see ILITY)
ISSES (see ITIOUS)
ISSFUL (see ITTLE)
ISSIBLE (see ITTABLE)
ISSIBLY (see ILITY)
ISSIER (see ITTER)
ISSIEST (see IPPIEST)
ISSILE (see ITTLE)
ISSINESS (see IPPIEST)
ISSING (see ITTING)
ISSION (see ITION)
ISSIONER (see ITIONER)
ISSIONING (see ITIONING)
ISSIPATE (see IMINATE)
ISSIVE (see ITIOUS)
ISSIVELY (see ILITY)
ISSO (see ILLOW)
ISSONANCE (see IVALENCE)
ISSONANT (see IVALENT)
ISSOR (see ITTER)
ISSORED (see ITTERED)

ISSUE

finew
hindoo
Hindu
igloo
into
issue
sinew
tissue
tribute

attribute
back issue
continue
contribute
dead issue
distribute
first issue
hereinto
insinew
scar tissue
thereinto
unsinew
whereinto

force the is issue
redistribute
toilet tissue

ISSURE (see ITTER)
ISSURED (see ITTERED)
ISSUS (see ITIOUS)
ISSY (see ITTY)

IST 1

bisque
bliss
blitz
brisk
Chris
cliff
crisp
crypt
cyst
dif
disc
dish
disk
diss
ditch
ditz
drift
fifth
fish
fist
fix
frisk
fritz
gift
gist

glitch
glitz
grist
hiss
hitch
if
itch
its
kiss
lift
lisp
list
Miff
miss
mist
mix
myth
niche
nix
pish
pitch
pix
priss
rich
riff
rift
risk
ritz
script
shift
shrift
sift
sis
six
sixth
smith
sniff
snitch
spitz
splish
spritz
squish
stiff
stitch
Styx
swift
swish
Swiss
switch
this

thrift
tiff
tryst
tsk
twist
twitch
which
whiff
whisk
whist
width
wish
wisp
witch
with
wrist

abyss
admix
adrift
affix
airlift
amiss
arm-twist
assist
bewitch
blacklist
blacksmith
bored stiff
cake mix
catfish
chairlift
checklist
cold fish
conscript
consist
day shift
dean's list
death wish
desist
dismiss
eclipse
encrypt
enlist
enrich
exist
eye twitch
face-lift
forklift
forthwith

French-kiss
gear shift
goldfish
goldsmith
guest list
gunsmith
hear this
Heathcliff
herewith
high pitch
high risk
hit list
insist
Ipswich
jock itch
kingfish
light switch
limp wrist
live with
locksmith
main dish
makeshift
midriff
near miss
night shift
persist
postscript
price list
quick fix
Radcliffe
remiss
resist
restitch
scared stiff
shoplift
side dish
ski lift
slipped disk
sneak diss
snowdrift
spendthrift
split shift
stick shift
subsist
Sunkist
swing shift
Swiss Miss
therewith
tongue twist
transcript

transfix
tsk tsk
unhitch
untwist
uplift
what if
Will Smith

Aerosmith
asterisk
bait-and-switch
birthday gift
birthday wish
Bolshevist
cable-stitch
candy kiss
Christmas list
coexist
compact disk
Cookie Crisp
coppersmith
dimmer switch
Exorcist
fever pitch
filthy rich
floppy disk
frozen stiff
get the drift
graveyard shift
hieroglyph
hit or miss
in a fix
intermix
jellyfish
mailing list
make a wish
manuscript
masterswitch
metalsmith
Mocha Mix
monolith
movie script
nondescript
obelisk
on the fritz
over with
perfect pitch
Pixy Stix
preexist
Richie Rich
secret tryst

shopping list
silversmith
slivovitz
solar disk
strike it rich
Sugar Crisp
sure and swift
theorist
waiting list
walk off with
Winsome Witch

apocalypse
burn to a crisp
cease and desist
drink like a fish
enemy list
glamour and glitz
grocery list
hand over fist
lunar eclipse
most-wanted list
on a par with
paleolith
River Phoenix
seven-year itch
slap on the wrist
solar eclipse
without a hitch

continental shift
over and done with
Werid Al Yankovic

Abercrombie & Fitch

Sabrina, the Teenage Witch

IST 2 (see ICE 1)
ISTABLE (see ITTABLE)
ISTABLY (see ILITY)

ISTANCE

distance
instance
pittance
admittance
assistance

consistence
enlistments
existence
insistence
long-distance
persistence
remittance
resistance
subsistence
transmittance

co-existence
go the distance
inconsistence
keep your distance
no admittance
preenlistments
readmittance
reenlistments
shouting distance

passive resistance

ISTANT (see INGENT)
ISTANTLY (see ILITY)
ISTATE (see YDRATE)
ISTE (see EAT 1)
ISTED (see ISTIC)
ISTEN (see ITION)
ISTENCE (see ISTANCE)
ISTENCY (see ILITY)
ISTENING (see ITIONING)
ISTENT (see INGENT)
ISTENTLY (see ILITY)
ISTER (see ITTER)
ISTERED (see ITTERED)
ISTERING (see ITTERING)
ISTERLESS (see ITIONIST)
ISTERY (see ILITY)
ISTFUL (see ITTLE)
ISTHMUS (see ITIOUS)
ISTIAN (see ITION)
ISTIBLE (see ITTABLE)
ISTIC (see ITIOUS)
ISTICAL (see ITTABLE)

ISTICALLY

biblically
clinically
criminally
critically
cyclically
cynically
digitally
fictionally
liberally
literally
lyrically
mystically
physically
pitifully
principally
trivially
typically
visually

artistically
ballistically
empirically
habitually
heuristically
holistically
linguistically
logistically
originally
politically
sadistically
simplistically
sophistically
statistically
stylistically
subliminally

agonistically
altruistically
atavistically
atheistically
casuistically
communistically
egotistically
fatalistically
futuristically
idealistically
optimistically
pantheistically

pluralistically
realistically
syllogistically

anachronistically
antagonistically
characteristically
opportunistically
ritualistically
stereotypically
surrealistically
unrealistically

ISTIER (see ITTER)
ISTIEST (see IPPIEST)
ISTILY (see ILITY)
ISTING (see ITTING)
ISTLE (see ITTLE)
ISTLED (see ITTLED)
ISTLER (see IBBLER)
ISTLING (see IDDLING)
ISTLY (see ITTY)
ISTMAS (see ITIOUS)
ISTMENT (see INGENT)
ISTMENTS (see ISTANCE)
ISTO (see ILLOW)
ISTOL (see ITTLE)
ISTOLED (see ITTLED)
ISTON (see ITION)
ISTONING (see ITIONING)
ISTOR (see ITTER)
ISTORY (see ILITY)
ISTRESS (see ITIOUS)
ISTRICT (see ITIOUS)
ISTRO (see ILLOW)
ISTY 1 (see ITTY)
ISTY 2 (see IGHTLY)
ISUAL (see ITTABLE)
ISUALLY (see ISTICALLY)
IT 1 (see IP)
IT 2 (see E 1)
ITA (see IA)

ITABLE 1

bicycle
bitable
bribable
citable
drivable
dryable

fightable
friable
guidable
hidable
hikable
icycle
jivable
liable
lightable
likable
pliable
prizeable
pryable
ridable
sighable
sightable
sizable
slidable
spikable
strikable
thrivable
tricycle
tryable
viable
writable

abidable
advisable
assizable
capsizable
compliable
contrivable
decidable
defiable
deniable
deprivable
despisable
devisable
disguisable
dislikable
dividable
excitable
franchisable
highlightable
ignitable
incitable
indictable
maniacal
recitable
reliable
revisable

revivable
surmisable
surprisable
survivable
unguidable
unitable
advertisable
analyzable
certifiable
civilizable
clarifiable
colonizable
compromisable
copyrightable
dignifiable
dramatizable
energizable
exorcisable
expeditable
falsifiable
fortifiable
hypnotizable
immunizable
justifiable
memorizable
minimizable
modernizable
modifiable
ostracizable
paralyzable
patronizable
polarizable
publicizable
realizable
recognizable
reunitable
satirizable
sensitizable
standardizable
sterilizable
subdividable
subsidizable
summarizable
televisable
terrorizable
undeniable
unreliable
verifiable

antagonizable
visualizable

ITABLE 2 (see ITTABLE)
ITAIN (see ITION)
ITAKER (see ITIONER)
ITAL (see ITLE)
ITALED (see ITTLED)
ITALY (see ILITY)
ITAN (see IGHTEN)
ITANY (see ILITY)
ITCH (see IST 1)
ITCHELL (see ITTLE)
ITCHEN (see ITION)
ITCHER (see ITTER)
ITCHES (see ITIOUS)
ITCHIER (see ITTER)
ITCHINESS (see IPPIEST)

ITCHING

ditching
hitching
itching
pitching
snitching
stitching
switching
twitching

bewitching
enriching
restitching
unhitching

cable-stitching

ITCHY (see ITTY)
ITE 1 (see IGHT)
ITE 2 (see EAT 1)
ITE 3 (see IGHTLY)

ITED 1

bided
chided
cited
glided
guided
kited
knighted
lighted

prided
righted
sided
sighted
sited
slighted
spited
whited

abided
alighted
broadsided
collided
confided
decided
delighted
derided
divided
elided
excited
far-sighted
floodlighted
forecited
foresighted
highlighted
ignited
incited
indicted
indited
invited
lopsided
misguided
moonlighted
near-sighted
one-sided
presided
provided
recited
requited
resided
respited
shortsighted
spotlighted
subsided
united
coincided
copyrighted
disunited

dynamited
expedited
extradited
forerecited
many-sided
nonunited
proselyted
reignited
reinvited
reunited
subdivided
undecided
undersided
unexcited
uninvited

overexcited

ITED 2 (see ITTED)
ITEFUL (see ITLE)
ITELY (see IGHTLY)
ITEM (see IGHTEN)
ITEMENT (see ILEMENT)
ITEN (see IGHTEN)
ITENER (see IGHTENER)
ITENESS 1 (see ITIS)
ITENESS 2 (see ESIS)
ITENING (see IGHTENING)
ITER 1 (see IZER)
ITER 2 (see EATER 1)
ITERAL (see ITTABLE)
ITERALLY (see ISTICALLY)
ITERANCE (see IVALENCE)
ITERANT (see IVALENT)
ITERATE 1 (see IMINATE)
ITERATE 2 (see IVALENT)
ITEY (see IGHTLY)
ITH (see IST 1)
ITHER (see ITTER)
ITHERED (see ITTERED)
ITHERING (see ITTERING)
ITHERY (see ILITY)
ITHIC (see ISTIC)
ITHING (see INDING)
ITHMIC (see ITIOUS)
ITI (see EASY)
ITIA (see ILLA 1)
ITIAL (see ITTLE)
ITIALED (see ITTLED)
ITIALLY (see ILITY)
ITIAN (see ITION)
ITIATE (see IMINATE)

ITIC (see ISTIC)
ITICAL (see ITTABLE)
ITICALLY (see ISTICALLY)
ITICUS (see IVOROUS)
ITIER (see ITTIER)
ITIFUL (see ITTABLE)
ITIFULLY (see ISTICALLY)
ITILLATE (see IMINATE)
ITIMATE (see IVALENT)
ITING (see INDING)

ITION

bidden
biffin
bitten
Britain
Briton
chicken
Chisholm
christen
Christian
Clinton
crimson
diction
dictum
Dillon
Dixon
driven
Dylan
England
fiction
Finland
fitten
friction
given
glisten
griffin
hidden
Incan
inland
kitchen
kitten
Lincoln
Linden
linen
listen
minion
mission
mitten

mizzen
Nixon
pidgin
pigeon
pinion
piston
prison
quicken
Quintin
richen
ridden
risen
scillain
sicken
Simpson
smidgen
smitten
stiffen
stricken
swidden
system
thicken
tiffin
Titian
victim
villain
vision
vixen
widgeon
women
written

addiction
addition
admission
affliction
ambition
arisen
ascription
attrition
audition
badminton
beautician
bedridden
Bill Clinton
Bob Dylan
clay pigeon
clinician
cognition
collision

commission
condition
conniption
conscription
constriction
contrition
conviction
decision
depiction
description
distinction
division
dominion
edition
Egyptian
elision
emission
enrichen
envision
eviction
extinction
flea bitten
forbidden
forgiven
frostbitten
fruition
George Clinton
God-given
Great Britain
grief-stricken
hagridden
handwritten
ignition
imprison
incision
infliction
inscription
instinction
intinction
logician
love-stricken
magician
Marge Simpson
Mark Ingram
Matt Dillon
Mel Gibson
munition
musician
New England
nonfiction

nutrition
omission
opinion
optician
outbidden
outvillain
partition
patrician
perdition
permission
petition
physician
position
precision
prediction
prescription
provision
rebidden
religion
remission
rendition
restinction
restriction
revision
rewritten
sedition
sex kitten
soup kitchen
spring chicken
stool pigeon
submission
subscription
suspicion
tactician
Tahitian
technician
tradition
transcription
transition
transmission
tuition
typewritten
unbidden
underwritten
unwritten
vanillin
Virginian
volition
abolition
acquisition
admonition

air-condition
ammunition
Ampicillin
apparition
apposition
benediction
buddy system
cascarillin
Church's Chicken
circumcision
circumscription
coalition
competition
composition
contradiction
cosmetician
crucifixion
definition
demolition
deposition
dereliction
dietician
disposition
double vision
drug addiction
electrician
erudition
exhibition
expedition
exposition
extradition
field of vision
first edition
free admission
Funky Chicken
good condition
imposition
in addition
indecision
indistinction
inhibition
inquisition
interdiction
intermission
intuition
jurisdiction
legal system
Lisa Simpson
long division
look and listen

Maggie Simpson
malnutrition
merit system
metric system
mint condition
New Edition
O.J. Simpson
obstetrician
Old Dominion
opposition
overridden
panic stricken
penicillin
pole position
politician
powerdriven
prediliction
premonition
preposition
prohibition
proper diction
proposition
rack and pinion
readmission
recognition
recondition
repetition
requisition
resubscription
rubber chicken
science fiction
split decision
statistician
subdistinction
subdivision
Super Chicken
superstition
supervision
supposition
television
terror-stricken
tunnel vision
valediction
West Virginian

A-1 condition
arithmetician
carrier pigeon
contradistinction
decomposition

fetal position
high-definition
juxtaposition
landmark decision
line of division
lotus position
mathematician
old-time religion
out of commission
out of condition
oversubscription
pediatrician
poverty-stricken
predisposition
public opinion
theoretician

chillin' like a villain
delicate condition
female intuition
fishing expedition
freedom of religion
Kentucky Fried Chicken
limited edition
unfair competition

ITIONAL (see ITTABLE)

ITIONER

fibular
integer
minister
prisoner
signature
similar
sinister
visitor

acquisitor
administer
antiquitor
attributer
auditioner
commissioner
conditioner
contributor
dissimilar
distributor

editioner
elicitor
exhibitor
exquisiter
funicular
inhibiter
iniquitor
inquisitor
navicular
parishioner
particular
perimeter
petitioner
positioner
practitioner
prime minister
prohibiter
proximiter
soliciter
solicitor
traditioner
ubiquitor
vehicular
ventricular
vestibular

admonitioner
air conditioner
coalitioner
exhibitioner
Forest Whitaker
hair conditioner
Johnny Whitaker
malpractitioner
perpendicular
repetitioner
requisitioner
verisimilar

extracurricular
vasoinhibitor

ITIONING

christening
divining
glistening
listening
pistoning

quickening
sickening
thickening

auditioning
commissioning
conditioning
enrichening
partitioning
petitioning
positioning
transitioning

air-conditioning
impositioning
reconditioning
requisitioning

juxtapositioning

ITIONIST

bitterness
figureless
fixtureless
gibberish
innerness
limberness
physicist
riverless
sisterless
stickerless
triggerless
vigorless
whiskerless
winnerless
winterless
zipperless

ambitionist
nutritionist
seditionist
traditionist

abolitionist
astrophysicist
biophysicist
coalitionist
demolitionist
exhibitionist

expeditionist
geophysicist
intuitionist
oppositionist
prohibitionist
requisitionist
superstitionist

ITIOUS

biggest
bigot
billet
biscuit
bitless
blisses
bridges
Bridget
brimless
brisket
britches
British
chillest
Christmas
citrus
civet
civic
clinic
cricket
crimpage
critic
cryptic
cynic
cystic
digit
dimmest
dimness
discus
dishes
district
ditches
divot
driblet
dripless
English
fidget
finish
finlet
Finnish
fishes

fitness
fittest
fixes
fridges
frigate
giblet
Gidget
gigot
gimmick
glibbest
glitches
grimace
grimmest
grimness
guinness
hipless
hipness
hippest
hisses
hitches
hitless
illest
image
impest
inlet
isthmus
itches
jibbest
kiddish
kisses
licit
limit
limpest
linguist
linnet
lipless
listed
litmus
lyric
mimic
mintage
minute
mischief
misses
missive
missus
misted
mistress
mixes
Mrs.

mystic
mythic
niches
nixes
pennage
Phillip
Phyllis
physic
picket
picnic
Piglet
pillage
pinkish
pinnage
pishes
pisses
pitches
pivot
primage
primmest
primness
princess
prisses
quickest
quickness
rhythmic
ribless
riblet
riches
ridges
rimless
rivet
scrimmage
shipless
shrillest
sickest
sickless
sickness
sinnet
sixes
skillet
skittish
slickest
slickness
slimmest
slimness
slitless
smidges
snippet
snitches

spigot
spillage
spinach
spinnet
spirit
stiffest
stiffness
stitches
strickless
stypic
swiftness
switches
thickest
thicket
thickness
thinness
ticket
tillage
tipless
triblet
trimmest
trimness
twisted
twitches
vicious
village
villus
vinquish
vintage
viscus
visit
whippet
whishes
wicket
widget
windage
wishes
witches
witless
witness
Yiddish

abridges
acidic
acrylic
addictive
admissive
admixes
affixes
afflictive

airsickness
ambitious
appendage
archimage
arillus
arthritic
artistic
ascriptive
assisted
auspicious
bacillus
ballistic
basilic
bewitches
bilinguist
blacklisted
cake mixes
carsickness
close-fisted
conflictive
consisted
constrictive
convicious
convictive
delicious
depictive
descriptive
desisted
dismisses
distinguish
drawbridges
elicit
elliptic
empiric
enlisted
enriches
evictive
exhibit
exilic
existed
explicit
exquisite
extinguish
extrinsic
eyewitness
factitious
fictitious
footbridges
free spirit
French-kisses

heartsickness
heuristic
hibiscus
high spirit
holistic
homesickness
horrific
idyllic
illicit
impennage
implicit
in stitches
inflictive
inhibit
inscriptive
insisted
interest
intrinsic
judicious
lambskinnet
last minute
lentiscus
linguistic
logistic
lovesickness
malicious
meal ticket
meniscus
narcissus
near misses
novitious
nutritious
officious
one minute
pacific
pactitious
paxillus
permissive
pernicious
persisted
phenicious
phoenicious
predictive
prescriptive
prodigious
prohibit
prolific
propitious
proscriptive
pulvillus

quick fixes
refinish
religious
relinquish
remissive
resisted
restiffness
restinguish
restitches
restrictive
revisit
sadistic
satiric
scamillus
seasickness
seditious
self-interest
Semitic
silicious
simplistic
solicit
sophistic
specific
speed limit
statistic
stylistic
submissive
subscriptive
subsisted
suspicious
team spirit
teen spirit
terrific
toll bridges
trainsickness
transcriptive
transfixes
transmissive
two-fisted
umbilic
unfitness
unhitches
unlisted
unwishes
vindictive
adventitious
afterimage
agonistic
altruistic
analytic

atavistic
atheistic
atmospheric
Bubblicious
casuistic
catalytic
co-existed
communistic
counterfeitness
crucifixes
diacritic
double digit
drama critic
evil spirit
exoteric
expeditious
fatalistic
football scrimmage
futuristic
go the limit
hieroglyphic
Holy Spirit
imbecilic
in a minute
inauspicious
inexplicit
injudicious
intermixes
irreligious
just a minute
litigious
masochistic
Mocha Mixes
movie critic
Mr. Fixit
Neolithic
nonmalicious
nonnutritious
nonreligious
obstitricious
optimistic
panegyric
pantheistic
paralytic
parasitic
parking ticket
photo finish
pluralistic
precipitious
preexisted

realistic
repetitious
sacrilegious
scientific
soporific
spitting image
splitting image
superstitious
syllogistic
unambitious
unauspicious
unpropitious
unreligious
unspecific
unsuspicious
veneficious
verticillus

anachronistic
animalistic
antagonistic
anti-Semitic
antireligious
apocalyptic
characteristic
Charlie Brown Christmas
from rags to riches
idealistic
interreligious
Jehovah's Witness
lactobacillus
lottery ticket
Ocean Pacific
opportunistic
overambitious
oversuspicious
Paleolithic
physical fitness
ritualistic
Smells Like Teen Spirit
streptobacillus
surrealistic
unrealistic
unscientific
up-to-the-minute
vital statistic
How the Grinch Stole Christmas
materialistic
Nightmare Before Christmas

ITIOUSLY (see ILITY)

ITIS

bias
blindest
blindness
bribeless
brightness
childish
crisis
cyclist
cypress
dryness
ficus
fineness
finest
guidance
guideless
hideless
highness
hiveless
hydrants
ibis
iceless
iris
Irish
Isis
kindness
knifeless
license
lifeless
lightness
likeness
Linus
miceless
Midas
mildest
mindless
minus
niceness
nighness
Picus
pious
priceless
prideless
primeness
Primus
psychic
rifeness
righteous
rightness

ripeness
ripest
science
shyness
signless
silence
sinus
slyness
snideness
spiceless
spineless
spryness
strifeless
stylish
stylist
stylus
tideless
tightness
timeless
triteness
typist
viceless
vilest
vineless
violence
virus
whiteness
wideness
wifeless
wildest
wineless
wiveless

abidance
affiance
alliance
appliance
arthritis
bronchitis
compliance
conciseness
decisive
defiance
derisive
desirous
divineness
divinest
divisive
Elias
hairstylist

incisive
Matthias
misguidance
night blindness
politeness
preciseness
red-eyeness
reliance
self-righteous
skylineless
sublimeness
subsidence
sunshineless
unpious
unrighteous
unripest
Weird Science
your highness

antivirus
Buenos Aires
Christian Science
coercitive
colorblindness
eruditeness
exact science
expeditive
gingivitis
hepatitis
impreciseness
in defiance
indecisive
laryngitis
medullitis
meningitis
mid-life crisis
misalliance
motorcyclist
nonalliance
noncompliance
on the bias
overrighteous
phonotypist
plus or minus
pseudoscience
racial bias
self-reliance
teletypist
underniceness
unicyclist

appendicitis
conjunctivitis
encephalitis
endocarditis
endometritis
myocarditis
pancreatitis
pericarditis
periostitis
Popular Science
sterotypist
thyroiditis

diverticulitis
gastroenteritis

ITISH (see ITIOUS)
ITIST (see ESIS)
ITIVE (see ITIS)
ITIZEN (see IVALENT)

ITLE

Bible
bridal
bridle
cycle
dial
Eiffel
eyeful
final
frightful
Highfill
idle
idol
idyll
libel
Michael
mindful
Nigel
NyQuill
prideful
primal
rhinal
rifle
rightful
rival
sighful

spinal
spiral
spiteful
spryful
stifle
tidal
title
trial
tribal
trifle
vial
vinyl
viral
vital

archival
archrival
arrival
Carmichael
contriteful
contrival
delightful
denial
deprival
disciple
entitle
exciteful
field trial
inciteful
insightful
life cycle
mistrial
on trial
pretrial
recital
recycle
reprisal
retrial
revival
subtitle
sundial
survival
unbridle
Billy Idol
homicidal
motorcycle
movie idol
royal title
self-denial
semifinal

suicidal
unicycle

old-time revival

ITLESS (see ITIOUS)
ITLING (see INDING)
ITMENT (see INGENT)
ITMUS (see ITIOUS)
ITNESS (see ITIOUS)
ITO (see IO 1)
ITOME (see ILITY)
ITOMIST (see IGAMIST)
ITON 1 (see ITION)
ITON 2 (see IGHTEN)
ITORAL (see ITTABLE)
ITORIS (see IVOROUS)
ITRIOL (see ITTABLE)
ITRO (see IO 1)
ITRUS (see ITIOUS)
ITS (see IST 1)
ITSIER (see ITTER)
ITSIEST (see IPPIEST)
ITSY (see ITTY)
ITT (see IP)

ITTABLE

biblical
binnacle
clinical
criminal
critical
cyclical
cynical
digital
fictional
fixable
fizzable
flickable
frizzable
givable
hittable
imbecile
integral
kickable
kissable
knittable
liberal

lickable
listable
literal
litoral
livable
lyrical
mineral
minimal
miracle
mystical
mythical
nickable
physical
pinnable
pinnacle
pitiful
pivotal
prickable
principal
principle
printable
quittable
quizzable
quizzical
risible
ritual
shippable
skinnable
spherical
spinnable
splittable
stickable
trickable
trivial
twistable
typical
visible
visual
vitriol
whimsical
winceable
winnable

acquittable
addictable
additional
admissible
admittable
alliteral

applicable
artistical
assidual
biliteral
blacklistable
committable
conditional
constrictable
convictable
convinceable
cylindrical
depictable
despicable
dismissible
divisible
elliptical
empirical
enlistable
equivocal
evictable
explicable
forbiddable
forgivable
habitual
hospitable
iliteral
inflictable
inscriptional
intrinsical
invincible
invisible
juridical
linguistical
logistical
nutritional
omissible
original
outfittable
permissible
permittable
political
predictable
reciprocal
relivable
remissible
remittable
residual
resistible
restrictable
satirical
spiritual

statistical
subliminal
submissible
submittable
traditional
transitional
transmittable
triliteral
unsplittable
volitional

aboriginal
analytical
apolitical
catalytical
compositional
contradictable
diacritical
disciplinable
duoliteral
egotistical
inadmissible
individual
indivisible
inexplicable
irresistible
jurisdictional
metaphysical
parasitical
pluriliteral
prepositional
quadriliteral
unconditional
unequivocal
unforgivable
uniliteral
unpredictable

antagonistical
characteristical
stereotypical

ITTAL (see ITTLE)
ITTANCE (see ISTANCE)

ITTED

fitted
flitted
frigid

gritted
ibid
kidded
knitted
lipid
liquid
livid
pitted
rigid
sipid
skidded
slitted
timid
twitted
vivid
wicked
witted

acquitted
admitted
befitted
committed
dimwitted
emitted
hand-knitted
insipid
nitwitted
nonrigid
omitted
outfitted
outwitted
permitted
remitted
submitted
subrigid
tightfitted
transmitted

benefited
manumitted
noncommitted
overrigid
readmitted
recommitted
resubmitted
semiliquid
semirigid
unpermitted

ITTEE (see ITTY)

ITTEN (see ITION)

ITTER

bicker
bidder
bigger
bitter
blister
brisker
chipper
clicker
clipper
cribber
crisper
critter
differ
digger
dipper
disher
ditcher
dither
drifter
dripper
fibber
figure
fisher
fissure
fixer
fixture
fizzer
flicker
Flipper
frisker
fritter
frizzer
gibber
giver
glibber
glitter
gripper
hipster
hisser
hither
hitter
itcher
jigger
jitter
kicker

kidder
kipper
kisser
knitter
libber
licker
lifter
liquor
lisper
litter
liver
misser
mister
mixer
mixture
nicker
nipper
nixer
picker
picture
pisser
pitcher
pitter
pricker
prisser
quicker
quipper
quitter
quiver
quizzer
ribber
richer
Richter
ridder
rigger
rigor
ripper
river
scissor
scripture
shifter
shipper
shiver
sicker
sifter
sipper
sister
sitter
skipper
skitter

slicker
slipper
slither
sliver
sniffer
snitcher
spitter
splitter
spritzer
squisher
sticker
stiffer
stricter
stricture
stripper
swifter
swigger
swisher
switcher
thicker
ticker
Tigger
tipper
tipster
titter
tricker
trickster
trigger
tripper
twister
twitcher
twitter
twizzler
vicar
victor
vigor
whiffer
whipper
whisker
whisper
whither
whizzer
wicker
wisher
wither
zipper
zither

acquitter
ad-libber

addictor
admitter
admixture
affixer
afflictor
aglitter
airlifter
aquiver
arm-twister
ass kicker
ass-kisser
assister
Big Dipper
big sister
blacklister
bootlicker
caregiver
chopped liver
come hither
committer
configure
conflictor
consider
constrictor
convictor
corn fritter
deliver
depictor
dismissar
ditchdigger
ditsier
downriver
drop kicker
East River
elixir
embitter
emitter
enlister
enricher
equipper
evictor
fence-sitter
fishier
forbidder
forgiver
forklifter
French-kisser
friskier
glass slipper
glitzier

golddigger
gravedigger
hair trigger
hairclipper
hairsplitter
hand mixer
hard liquor
high bidder
high liver
house slipper
inflictor
itchier
Jack Tripper
kingfisher
lawgiver
light fixture
lovesicker
low bidder
mistier
nitpicker
no-hitter
nose picker
omitter
outbidder
outfitter
outwitter
persister
pinch hitter
place kicker
potlicker
predictor
prefixer
prissier
pulitzer
rail-splitter
refitter
remitter
resister
restricter
ritzier
shoplifter
sidesplitter
sissier
squishier
stepsister
submitter
suffixer
swishier
tongue twister
transfixer

transistor
transmitter
twistier
twitchier
uplifter
upriver
weak sister
weightlifter
well-wisher
wishier
witchier

baby-sitter
bedroom slipper
bumper sticker
by a whisker
cement mixer
cherry picker
city slicker
contradictor
double-dipper
fever blister
garage clicker
get the picture
home-run hitter
in a dither
intermixer
Jack the Ripper
kitty litter
lily-liver
motion picture
overbidder
party mixer
reconfigure
reconsider
reminiscer
underbidder
up the river
whiskey jigger

boa constrictor
Claudia Schiffer
Eric Von Zipper
Indian giver
one hitter quitter
over deliver
pick of the litter
quick on the trigger
sell down the river
thingamajigger

designated hitter
Dr. Adam Bricker

ITTERED

bittered
blistered
blizzard
chippered
differed
dithered
figgered
figured
fissured
flickered
frittered
gibbered
gingered
gizzard
glimmered
glittered
injured
jittered
kippered
limbered
littered
livered
lizard
nickered
pictured
quivered
Richard
rivered
scissored
shimmered
shivered
simmered
skippered
skittered
slickered
slippered
slithered
slivered
snickered
splintered
stickered
strictured
swiggered
timbered

tittered
triggered
twittered
vizard
whimpered
whiskered
whispered
wickered
withered
wizard
zippered

considered
delivered
depictured
impicutred
lounge lizard

ITTEREST (see IGAMIST)

ITTERING

bickering
blinkering
blistering
blithering
clinkering
differing
figuring
fingering
flickering
flittering
frittering
glimmering
glittering
hindering
injuring
jiggering
kippering
lingering
littering
pittering
quivering
shimmering
shivering
simmering
sistering
skippering
skittering

slithering
slivering
splintering
tinkering
triggering
twittering
whimpering
wintering
withering
zippering

considering
delivering
embittering
malingering

administering
reconsidering

ITTERNESS (see ITIONIST)
ITTERY (see ILITY)
ITTEST (see ITIOUS)

ITTIER

bingier
bittier
busier
crispier
dingier
dittier
dizzier
drippier
drizzlier
fizzier
flimsier
flippier
fringier
frizzier
giddier
gigglier
ginchier
grittier
grizzlier
guiltier
ickier
jigglier
linear
mingier

niftier
nippier
nittier
pickier
pitier
pixier
prettier
pricklier
pygmier
ripplier
shiftier
sicklier
sixtier
sizzlier
skimpier
skinnier
skippier
snippier
spiffier
squigglier
stickier
stingier
swiftier
thriftier
tipsier
tizzier
trickier
twiggier
whispier
whizzier
wigglier
windier
wittier
wrigglier
zippier

familiar

unfamiliar

ITTIEST (see IPPIEST)
ITTILY (see ILITY)
ITTINESS (see IPPIEST)

ITTING

bidding
binging

Bisbing
blipping
blitzing
brimming
chinning
chipping
cinching
clicking
clinching
clipping
cribbing
crimping
cringing
digging
dimming
dipping
dishing
dribbling
drifting
dripping
fibbing
fishing
fitting
fixing
fizzing
flicking
flinching
flipping
flitting
fringing
frisking
frizzing
ginseng
giving
gridding
grinning
gripping
gritting
gypping
hinging
hinting
hissing
hitting
inching
inning
jigging
kicking
kidding
kissing
knitting

licking
lifting
limping
listing
living
lynching
miffing
mincing
minting
missing
misting
mixing
nibbling
nicking
nipping
nixing
picking
pimping
pinching
pinning
pissing
pitting
pricking
printing
quibbling
quipping
quitting
quizzing
ribbing
ridding
rifting
rigging
rimming
rinsing
ripping
risking
scribbling
scripting
shifting
shipping
sibling
sifting
singeing
sinning
sipping
sitting
skidding
skimming
skinning
skipping

slimming
slipping
slitting
sniffing
snipping
spitting
splinting
splitting
sprinting
spritzing
squinting
squishing
sticking
stiffing
stripping
swigging
swimming
swishing
thinning
ticking
tiffing
tinting
tipping
tricking
trimming
tripping
trysting
tsking
twinging
twisting
whiffing
whipping
whisking
whizzing
wincing
winning
wishing
zipping

acquitting
ad-libbing
addicting
admitting
admixing
affixing
afflicting
assisting
befitting
beginning
blacklisting

clean living
committing
conflicting
consisting
constricting
convicting
convincing
depicting
desisting
dismissing
drop-kicking
emitting
enlisting
equipping
evicting
evincing
existing
forbidding
forgiving
formfitting
gone fishing
hairsplitting
hand-knitting
handpicking
hard-hitting
horsewhipping
house-sitting
impinging
imprinting
inflicting
infringing
insisting
lawgiving
loose-fitting
misgiving
misprinting
ninth inning
no kidding
nonsticking
omitting
outbidding
outfitting
outliving
outstripping
outwitting
permitting
persisting
pinch-hitting
place-kicking
predicting

rebidding
refitting
reliving
remitting
reprinting
resisting
restricting
shoplifting
sidesplitting
spearfishing
submitting
subsisting
switch-hitting
Thanksgiving
tightfitting
transfixing
transmitting
unfitting
unflinching
unhinging
unpinning
untwisting
unwitting
unzipping
uplifting
weightlifting

benefitting
co-existing
contradicting
cost of living
counterfeiting
do your bidding
double dribbling
finger-licking
fingerprinting
intermixing
make a living
manumitting
overbidding
overtipping
penny-pinching
pistol-whipping
pre-existing
readmitting
recommitting
resubmitting
take a licking
underbidding
underpinning
undertipping

unforgiving
unremitting

alive and kicking
multiple listing
newspaper clipping
overcommitting

ITTISH (see ITIOUS)

ITTLE

bindle
binful
blissful
bristle
Bristol
brittle
chicle
chisel
civil
crimple
crinkle
cripple
crystal
cymbal
dibble
diddle
dimple
dismal
dribble
drivel
drizzle
dwindle
fickle
fiddle
fiscal
fistful
fizzle
fribble
frizzle
giggle
griddle
grinful
gristle
grizzle
hymnal
jiggle
jingle

kibble
kindle
little
middle
mingle
missal
missile
Mitchell
nibble
nickel
nimble
nipple
pickle
piddle
piffle
pimple
pistol
pixel
prickle
quibble
riddle
riffle
ripple
scribble
shingle
shrivel
Sibyl
sickle
signal
simple
sinful
single
sizzle
skiffle
skittle
sniffle
sniggle
snivel
spindle
spittle
sprinkle
squiggle
swindle
swivel
swizzle
symbol
thimble
this'll
thistle
tickle

timbale
tingle
tinkle
tipple
tittle
trickle
triple
twiddle
twinkle
victual
vigil
whiffle
whistle
whittle
wiggle
wishful
wriggle
wrinkle

abysmal
abyssal
acquittal
atingle
belittle
big nickel
bilingual
cap pistol
commingle
committal
cruise missile
dill pickle
dismissal
epistle
fo' shizzle
icicle
initial
judicial
Kriss Kringle
lead crystal
official
popsicle
rekindle
remissful
remittal
sex symbol
train whistle
transmittal
uncivil

artificial

beneficial
blow the whistle
Chicken Little
double dribble
guided missile
in a pickle
intermingle
Jimmy Kimmel
Mr. Whipple
noncommittal
pancake griddle
peanut brittle
periwinkle
phallic symbol
prejudicial
pumpernickel
Rip Van Winkle
sacrificial
status symbol
Stuart Little
superficial
unofficial
Vlasic Pickle
wet your whistle
Wienerschnitzel

around the middle
clean as a whistle
Dr. Dolittle
fit as a fiddle
hammer and sickle
hot as a pistol
little by little
play second fiddle
Professor Hinkle

fo' shizzle my nizzle

ITTLED

bristled
brittled
chiseled
crippled
crystaled
diddled
drizzled
fiddled
fizzled

frizzled
griddled
gristled
grizzled
middled
nippled
piddled
pistoled
riddled
rippled
sizzled
skittled
swizzled
tippled
tripled
twiddled
whistled
whittled

belittled
epistled
hospitaled
initialed

ITTLER (see IBBLER)
ITTLEST (see IGAMIST)
ITTLING (see IDDLING)
ITTNEY (see ITTY)
ITTO (see ILLOW)

ITTY

biggie
Billie
billy
bippy
bitsy
bitty
Bixby
blippy
bristly
Brittney
busy
chickee
Chile
chili
chilly
chintzy
chippy
Christy

ciggy
city
civvy
cliquey
crispy
dickey
dilly
dippy
Disney
ditsy
ditty
divvy
Dixie
dizzy
drippy
drizzly
fifty
filly
fishy
fitchy
fizzly
fizzy
flimsy
flippy
frilly
frisbee
frisky
Fritzi
frizzy
giddy
giggly
glitzy
grisly
gristly
gritty
grizzly
gypsy
hickey
hilly
hippie
hippy
hissy
icky
iffy
intsy
itchy
jiffy
jiggly
kiddie
kidney

kissy
kitty
lily
limsy
lippy
lispy
Mickey
MIDI
miffy
Millie
missy
misty
Mitzi
Nicky
nifty
nippy
nitty
picky
piggy
pitchy
pity
pixie
pretty
prickly
prissy
privy
pygmy
quickie
quickly
Quincy
quinsy
richly
risky
ritzy
shifty
sickie
sickly
sidney
silly
sissy
sixty
sizzly
skippy
skivvy
slickly
slimsy
sniffy
snippy
spiffy
squiggly

squishy
sticky
strictly
swiftly
swifty
swishy
switchy
Sydney
thickly
thistly
thrifty
tippy
tipsy
titty
tizzy
tricky
Trixie
twiggy
twisty
twitchy
Vicki
whiffy
whimsy
whiskey
whistly
whizzy
wiggly
willy
wishy
wispy
witchy
witty
wriggley
yippee
yippie
Ziggy
zippy

Bo Diddley
Chantilly
committee
doo hickey
Free Willy
hillbilly
lime rickey
Nowitzki
P-Diddy
Poughkeepsie
self-pity
unfrisky

unrisky
Xanthippe

Chilly Willy
Death of Richie
Easter lily
fifty-fifty
Gotham City
Hello Kitty
in a jiffy
inner city
Irish whiskey
itsy-bitsy
itty-bitty
Kansas City
kissy-kissy
Mississippi
nitty-gritty
Piccadilly
piccalilli
piggly wiggly
Salt Lake City
sitting pretty
water lily
whistling Dixie
willy nilly

Atlantic City
Lenny and Squiggy
Mexico City
Milli Vanilli
Pixie and Dixie

Oklahoma City

itty bitty titty committee

ITUAL (see ITTABLE)
ITUALLY (see ISTICALLY)
ITUM (see IGHTEN)
ITUP (see ICCUP)
ITY (see ITTY)
ITZ (see IST 1)
ITZEL (see ITTLE)
ITZER (see ITTER)
ITZI (see ITTY)
ITZIER (see ITTER)
ITZIEST (see IPPIEST)
ITZING (see ITTING)
ITZKI (see ITTY)
ITZY (see ITTY)

IUM (see EUM 1)
IV (see IGHTLY)
IVA 1 (see IA)
IVA 2 (see IAH)
IVABLE 1 (see ITABLE 1)
IVABLE 2 (see ITTABLE)
IVACY (see IETY)
IVAL (see ITLE)

IVALENCE

cinnamon
difference
dissonance
ignorance
impotence
incidence
indigence
indignance
innocence
iterance
malignance
militants
trivalence

ambivalence
beligerence
coincidence
considerance
equivalence
indifference
multivalence
nonmilitants
omnipotence
quadrivalence
quantivalence

IVALENT

bivalent
ciliate
citizen
different
digerent
dissonant
divalent
hypocrite
ignorant
immigrant

impotent
incident
indigent
infinite
innocent
intimate
intricate
iterant
ligament
literate
militant
trivalent
vigilant

affiliate
ambivalent
belligerent
certificate
cohibited
coincident
considerate
debilitant
Dominican
equivalent
exhibited
Gilligan
illegitimate
illiterate
indifferent
inhibited
legitimate
multivalent
nonmilitant
omnipotent
prohibited
quadrivalent
quantivalent
quinquivalent
reiterant

cobelligerent
equidifferent
incoincident
inconsiderate
nonbelligerent
noncoincident
reexhibited
rehabilitant
uninhibited
unprohibited

IVALIST

finalist
idolist
libelist

podiatrist
psychiatrist
revivalist
survivalist

quarterfinalist

IVALRY 1 (see IETY)
IVALRY 2 (see ILITY)
IVAN (see IGHTEN)
IVARI (see ILITY)
IVATE (see IET)
IVATIVE (see IBUTIVE)
IVE 1 (see IZE 1)
IVE 2 (see ID)
IVE 3 (see EED 1)
IVEL (see ITTLE)
IVELESS (see ITIS)
IVELINESS (see IGHTLINESS)

IVELING

driveling
finishing
fiveling
grimacing
imaging
riveling
shriveling
sniveling
swiveling

diminishing
refinishing

IVELY (see IGHTLY)
IVEMENT (see ILEMENT)
IVEN 1 (see ITION)
IVEN 2 (see IGHTEN)
IVENER (see IGHTENER)
IVENING (see IGHTENING)
IVER 1 (see IZER)
IVER 2 (see ITTER)
IVERED (see ITTERED)

IVERING (see ITTERING)
IVERLESS (see ITIONIST)
IVERY 1 (see ILITY)
IVERY 2 (see IETY)
IVET (see ISTIC)
IVIA (see ILIA)
IVIAL (see ITTABLE)
IVIALLY (see ISTICALLY)
IVIAN (see IBBEAN)
IVIC (see ISTIC)
IVID (see ITTED)
IVIER (see INIER)
IVIL (see ITTLE)
IVING 1 (see INDING)
IVING 2 (see ITTING)
IVINING (see ITIONING)
IVION (see IBBEAN)
IVIOUS (see IPPIEST)
IVITY (see ILITY)
IVO (see IO 1)
IVOCAL (see ITTABLE)
IVOR (see IZER)

IVOROUS

clitoris
limulus
rigorous
sinuous
stimulus
syllabus
syphilis
vigorous

ambiguous
carnivorous
continuous
dominicus
Leviticus
omnivorous
ridiculous
ventriculous

IVORY (see IETY)
IVOT (see ISTIC)
IVOTAL (see ITTABLE)
IVOTED (see IMITED)
IVOTING (see IBITING)
IVUM (see IGHTEN)
IVVY (see ITTY)
IVY 1 (see IGHTLY)

IVY 2 (see ITTY)
IWI (see EASY)
IX 1 (see IST 1)
IX 2 (see E 1)
IXABLE (see ITTABLE)
IXATIVE (see IBUTIVE)
IXBY (see ITTY)
IXEL (see ITTLE)
IXEN (see ITION)
IXER (see ITTER)
IXES (see ITIOUS)
IXIA (see ILIA)
IXIE (see ITTY)
IXIER (see ITTIER)
IXIEST (see IPPIEST)
IXING (see ITTING)
IXION (see ITION)
IXIR (see ITTER)
IXIT (see ISTIC)
IXITY (see ILITY)
IXON (see ITION)
IXTH (see IST 1)
IXTIER (see ITTIER)
IXTIEST (see IPPIEST)
IXTURE (see ITTER)
IXTURELESS (see ITIONIST)
IXTY (see ITTY)
IZ (see ID)
IZABLE (see ITABLE 1)
IZARD (see ITTERED)
IZARDRY (see ILITY)

IZE 1

buys
bys
chive
cries
dies
dive
dries
drive
dyes
eyes
five
flies
fries
guise
guys
highs
hive

I've
jive
lies
live
lyes
pies
plies
pries
prize
rise
rive
ryes
shies
sighs
size
skies
skive
spies
sties
strive
thighs
thrive
ties
tries
vies
vise
whys
wise

advise
alive
allies
applies
apprise
archive
arise
arrive
assize
baptize
beehive
belies
bite-size
blue skies
bye-byes
capsize
chastise
clockwise
complies
comprise
connive

contrive
crash-dive
crosswise
decries
deep-fries
defies
demise
denies
deprive
derive
despise
devise
disguise
door prize
drip-dries
edgewise
endive
espies
excise
fireflies
first prize
four-eyes
franchise
French fries
full-size
get wise
good-byes
hang five
hi-fis
high dive
high five
high-rise
implies
incise
king-size
leastwise
lengthwise
Levi's
life-size
likewise
line drive
magpies
make eyes
moonrise
mud pies
neckties
nosedive
outcries
outsize
pigsties

pile drive
pintsize
Popeye's
queen-size
red eyes
relies
replies
reprise
revise
revive
skin-dive
skydive
snake eyes
spin-dries
standbys
sunrise
supplies
surmise
surprise
survive
swan dive
take five
test drive
time flies
unties
unwise
widthwise
wiseguys

activize
advertise
aggrandize
agonize
alibis
amplifies
apple pies
atomize
authorize
bald-faced lies
bastardize
battle cries
beautifies
brutalize
burglarize
butterflies
calcifies
centralize
certifies
circumcise
civilize

clarifies
classifies
close your eyes
codifies
colonize
communize
compromise
criticize
crucifies
crystallize
deep-sea dive
deifies
dragonflies
dramatize
eagle eyes
edifies
emphasize
energize
enfranchise
enterprise
equalize
eulogize
evil eyes
exercise
exorcise
falsifies
feminize
fertilize
five-by-five
formalize
fortifies
fossilize
fraternize
galvanize
glorifies
goo-goo eyes
gratifies
harmonize
horrifies
humanize
hypnotize
idolize
immunize
improvise
Jackson Five
jeopardize
justifies
legal-size
legalize
liquefies

localize
lullabies
magnetize
magnifies
mechanize
memorize
mesmerize
minimize
misapplies
mobilize
modernize
modifies
mollifies
moralize
mortifies
motorize
multiplies
mummifies
mystifies
nasalize
neutralize
nine-to-five
Nobel Prize
notarize
notifies
nullifies
occupies
odorize
optimize
organize
ostracize
otherwise
overbuys
overdrive
oversize
oxidize
pacifies
pack of lies
pasteurize
patronize
penalize
petrifies
plagiarize
pluralize
polarize
private eyes
publicize
purifies
qualifies
quantifies

ramifies
ratifies
realize
rebaptize
recognize
rectifies
rhapsodize
sanctifies
satirize
satisfies
scrutinize
sensitize
sermonize
signifies
simplifies
skin alive
socialize
specialize
specifies
stabilize
standardize
sterilize
stigmatize
stupefies
subsidize
summarize
supervise
symbolize
sympathize
synchronize
take a dive
take the prize
tantalize
televise
temporize
tenderize
terrifies
terrorize
theorize
tiger eyes
tranquilize
traumatize
typifies
tyrannize
underlies
undersize
unifies
ups and dies
urbanize
utilize

vaporize
verbalize
verifies
victimize
vilifies
vitalize
vocalize
voter ayes
vulgarize
weather-wise
westernize
womanize

acclimatize
allegorize
anabaptize
antagonize
apologize
cannibalize
capitalize
characterize
chicken pot pies
commercialize
contrariwise
counterclockwise
cut down to size
decentralize
declassifies
dehumanize
demobilize
democratize
demoralize
demystifies
deodorize
devitalize
dichotomize
disenfranchise
disorganize
disqualifies
dissatisfies
economize
electric eyes
electrifies
epitomize
evade your eyes
exemplifies
familiarize
family ties
fanaticize
federalize
free enterprise

hip to the jive
hypothesize
idealize
identifies
immortalize
intensifies
italicize
legitimize
liberalize
little white lies
militarize
monopolize
natural highs
Olympic-size
open your eyes
personifies
philosophize
popularize
preoccupies
prioritize
Pulitzer Prize
refortifies
regularize
reorganize
revitalize
ritualize
romanticize
secularize
sensualize
sight for sore eyes
solidifies
soliloquize
spiritualize
systematize
theologize
try on for size
ventriloquize
visualize
word to the wise

Americanize
artificial highs
consolation prize
departmentalize
economy-size
legitimatize
materialize
memorialize
particularize
private enterprise

professionalize
revolutionize
Saturday Night Live
take by surprise
universalize

editorialize
institutionalize

IZE 2 (see EED 1)
IZEABLE (see ITABLE 1)
IZEMENT (see ILEMENT)

IZER

bider
biker
binder
biter
blinder
briber
brighter
chider
chimer
cider
cipher
climber
cyber
dialer
diaper
dicer
diner
diver
driver
fiber
fifer
fighter
filer
finder
finer
geyser
glider
grinder
griper
guider
hiker
hyper
icer
jiver

kaiser
kinder
kiper
knifer
lifer
liger
lighter
liner
milder
miler
minder
miner
minor
miser
nicer
Niger
Pfizer
piker
piler
piner
piper
pricer
primer
rhymer
rider
rifer
riler
riper
riser
Schneider
shiner
Shriner
signer
sizer
slicer
slider
slighter
smiler
snider
sniper
Snyder
spicer
spider
spiker
spiter
splicer
strider
striker
striver
styler

swiper
thriver
tiger
tighter
tiler
timer
triter
twiner
Tyler
typer
viler
viper
visor
whiner
whiter
wider
wilder
winder
wiper
wiser
writer

A-liner
abider
adviser
advisor
airliner
alighter
aligner
apprizer
ariser
arriver
ascriber
assigner
backslider
bagpiper
baptizer
baseliner
beguiler
benigner
bookbinder
Braunschweiger
byliner
cabdriver
chastiser
check signer
co-signer
coal miner
collider
combiner

compiler
confider
confiner
conniver
consignor
crime-fighter
cruiseliner
decider
decipher
decliner
defiler
definer
deicer
depriver
deriver
describer
designer
despiser
deviser
disguiser
divider
diviner
divisor
drunk driver
Dwayne Schneider
encipher
enticer
entwiner
exiler
eyeliner
firefighter
franchiser
freestyler
ghost rider
ghostwriter
gold miner
hair styler
hang glider
headliner
highlighter
hitchhiker
incisor
inciter
incliner
indicter
inscriber
insider
jackknifer
jetliner
Knight Rider

lamplighter
maligner
meat grinder
misguider
moonlighter
moonshiner
nail biter
nosediver
old-timer
one-liner
one-nighter
opiner
outliner
outshiner
outsider
pathfinder
pied piper
piledriver
prescriber
presider
pro lifer
profiler
provider
race driver
range finder
reciter
recliner
refiner
reminder
resider
resigner
restyler
reviler
reviser
reviver
rough rider
screwdiver
screwdriver
seasider
self-winder
shelf liner
shoeshiner
sideliner
sideswiper
sidewinder
sky writer
skydiver
slave driver
songwriter
speech writer

spellbinder
spotlighter
stockpiler
streamliner
sublimer
subscriber
subsider
sun visor
survivor
swandiver
transcriber
truckdriver
typewriter
unbinder
unkinder
unwinder
view finder

activizer
advertiser
aggrandizer
amortizer
analyzer
appetizer
apple cider
Asia Minor
atomizer
bareback rider
brutalizer
bump-and-grinder
centralizer
circumciser
circumscriber
civilizer
coffee grinder
coincider
colonizer
communizer
countersigner
dramatizer
emphasizer
energizer
enfranchiser
enterpriser
equalizer
exerciser
exorciser
fantasizer
feminizer
fertilizer

formalizer
forty-niner
fraternizer
freedom fighter
galvanizer
hair designer
harmonizer
horseback rider
humanizer
hypnotizer
immunizer
improviser
intertwiner
legalizer
letter filer
letter writer
magnetizer
masterminder
mechanizer
memorizer
mesmerizer
minimizer
mobilizer
modernizer
moralizer
motorizer
mountain climber
neutralizer
ocean liner
Oppenheimer
organ grinder
organizer
ostracizer
overrider
pantomimer
paralyzer
pasteurizer
patronizer
plagiarizer
publicizer
realigner
reconciler
redesigner
resuscriber
room divider
sacrificer
Sanforizer
sensitizer
social climber
socializer

specializer
sterilizer
stigmatizer
subsidizer
summarizer
supervisor
symbolizer
sympathizer
synthesizer
tantalizer
televisor
tenderizer
terrorizer
Toby Tyler
tranquilizer
traumatizer
underliner
underminer
underwriter
utilizer
vaporizer
vitalizer
windshield wiper
wine-and-diner
wisenheimer
womanizer

acclimatizer
antagonizer
apologizer
black widow spider
capitalizer
categorizer
center divider
decentralizer
demoralizer
deodorizer
disenfranchiser
economizer
epitomizer
fanaticizer
hit-and-run driver
hypothesizer
idealizer
immortalizer
legitimatizer
luxury liner
monopolizer
mystery writer
nationalizer

popularizer
rationalizer
reorganizer
revitalizer
romanticizer
self-sacrificer
Tony the Tiger
Winona Ryder

psychoanalyzer

IZING (see INDING)
IZMO (see ILLOW)
IZO (see ILLOW)
IZON (see IGHTEN)
IZZ (see ID)
IZZA (see IA)
IZZABLE (see ITTABLE)
IZZARD (see ITTERED)
IZZEN (see ITION)
IZZER (see ITTER)
IZZICAL (see ITTABLE)
IZZIER (see ITTIER)
IZZIEST (see IPPIEST)
IZZINESS (see IPPIEST)
IZZING (see ITTING)
IZZLE (see ITTLE)
IZZLED (see ITTLED)
IZZLER (see ITTER)
IZZLIER (see ITTIER)
IZZLIEST (see IPPIEST)
IZZLING (see IDDLING)
IZZLY (see ITTY)
IZZY (see ITTY)

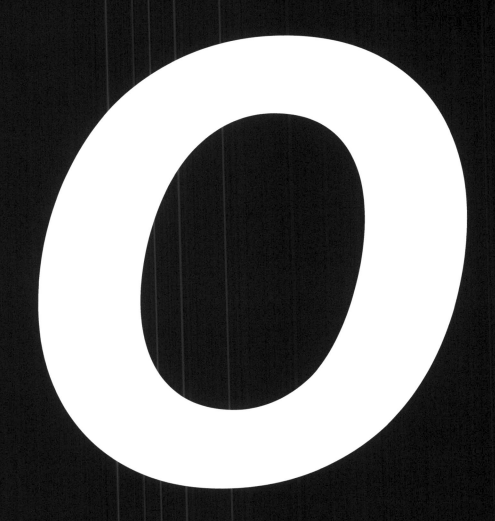

Rhyme Sounds

O 1 (see OW 1)
O 2 (see EW 1)
O'D (see OOM)
O'LL (see OOL 1)
O'RE (see EWER 1)
O'VE (see OOM)
OA 1 (see OLA)
OA 2 (see OW 1)
OABLE (see OOTABLE)
OACH (see OAT)
OACHABLE (see OTABLE)
OACHER (see OVER 1)
OACHES (see OSES)
OACHFUL (see OSAL)
OACHING (see OWING 1)
OAD 1 (see OSE 1)
OAD 2 (see OD)
OADABLE (see OTABLE)
OADED (see OASTED)
OADEN (see OTTEN)
OADER 1 (see OVER 1)
OADER 2 (see OLLAR)
OADIE (see ONY)
OADING (see OWING 1)
OADLY (see OCKEY)
OADNESS (see OLISH)
OADSTER (see OVER 1)
OADY (see ONY)
OAF (see OAT)
OAFER (see OVER 1)
OAFING (see OWING 1)
OAGIE (see ONY)
OAH (see OLA)
OAK (see OAT)
OAKEN (see OTION)
OAKER (see OVER 1)
OAKIER (see OKIER)
OAKILY (see OCALLY)
OAKING (see OWING 1)
OAKLEY (see ONY)
OAL (see OLE 1)
OALIE (see ONY)
OALY (see ONY)
OAM (see ONE 1)
OAMED (see OBED)
OAMING (see OWING 1)
OAMY (see ONY)
OAN (see ONE 1)
OANED (see OBED)
OANER (see OVER 1)
OANING (see OWING 1)
OANMENT (see ONEMENT)
OANY (see ONY)

OAP (see OAT)
OAPIER (see OKIER)
OAPING (see OWING 1)
OAPLESS (see OSES)
OAPY (see ONY)
OAR (see ORE 1)
OARABLE (see ORTABLE)

OARD

board
bored
chord
cord
cored
floored
ford
gored
gourd
hoard
Lord
sword
ward

abhorred
aboard
accord
adored
afford
award
backboard
billboard
blackboard
buckboard
cardboard
chalkboard
chess board
clipboard
Concorde
dart board
dashboard
deplored
discord
draft board
drainboard
floorboard
headboard
inboard
indoored
keyboard

landlord
lost chord
milord
on-board
outboard
reward
rip cord
scoreboard
seaboard
shipboard
sideboard
signboard
skateboard
slumlord
springboard
surfboard
switchboard
tackboard
tote board
warlord
washboard

above board
all aboard
bed and board
Betty Ford
boogieboard
by the board
checkerboard
clavichord
cutting board
diving board
drawing board
harpsichord
ill afford
in accord
ironing board
mortarboard
off-the-board
open-doored
Ouija Board
overboard
overlord
paddleboard
room and board
running board
shuffleboard
smorgasbord
sounding board
spinal chord
tape-record

across the board
bulletin board
electric cord
emery board
extension cord
governing board
Harrison Ford
model T Ford
stiff as a board

chairman of the board
executive board
Montgomery Ward
umbilical cord

Academy Award

OARDER (see ORDER)
OARDING (see ORMING 1)
OARING (see ORMING 1)
OARIOUS (see ORIOUS)
OARISH (see ORIST)
OARSE (see ORSE 1)
OARSELY (see ORY)
OARY (see ORY)
OAST (see OAT)
OASTAL (see OSAL)
OASTALLY (see OCALLY)

OASTED

bloated
boasted
boated
boded
coasted
coated
coded
doted
floated
ghosted
gloated
goaded
hosted
loaded
moded
noted
posted
quoted
roasted

toasted
toted
voted

connoted
corroded
decoded
denoted
devoted
emoted
eroded
exploded
misquoted
outmoded
outvoted
promoted
unloaded

overloaded
sugar-coated

OK, I'm Reloaded

OASTER (see OVER 1)
OASTFUL (see OSAL)
OASTIER (see OKIER)
OASTING (see OWING 1)
OASTY (see ONY)

OAT

bloat
bloke
boast
boat
bolt
both
broach
broke
brooch
choke
cloak
close
coach
coast
coat
coax
coke
colt
cope

croak
dolt
dope
dose
dote
float
folk
ghost
gloat
goat
grope
growth
hoax
hope
host
joke
jolt
loaf
loath
lope
molt
mope
most
nope
note
oaf
oak
oast
oat
oath
poach
poke
pope
post
quote
quoth
roach
roast
rope
rote
scope
shoat
slope
smoke
smote
soak
soap
spoke
stoke
stroke

taupe
throat
toast
tope
toque
tote
vote
woke
wrote
yoke
yolk

afloat
almost
approach
at most
awoke
backstroke
bad joke
basecoat
bedpost
Bob Hope
breaststroke
C-note
chain-smoke
cockroach
compost
connote
convoke
cutthroat
dead broke
deadbolt
deep throat
demote
denote
devote
down slope
downstroke
dreamboat
East Coast
egg yolk
elope
emote
encroach
evoke
fire boat
flat broke
footnote
foremost
French toast

glasnost
glucose
go broke
goalpost
Gold Coast
guest host
guidepost
gunboat
heatstroke
high note
houseboat
impost
in close
invoke
jocose
jump rope
keynote
kinfolk
lamppost
last hope
lifeboat
lose hope
Love Boat
love note
milepost
milktoast
misquote
misspoke
morose
no hope
no-host
of note
outgrowth
outpost
outvote
pot roast
pound note
promote
provoke
provost
raincoat
redcoat
regrowth
remote
reposte
reproach
revoke
revolt
rewrote
rowboat

sailboat
scapegoat
seacoast
showboat
sidestroke
signpost
slow boat
slowpoke
soft-soap
sore throat
sour note
Space Ghost
speedboat
stagecoach
steamboat
straw vote
strep throat
sunstroke
tightrope
too close
topcoat
topmost
townsfolk
towrope
trenchcoat
tugboat
turncoat
U-boat
unbolt
unquote
up close
utmost
voice vote
West Coast

aftergrowth
all she wrote
anecdote
antelope
antidote
antipope
artichoke
bar of soap
billy goat
cantaloupe
cloud of smoke
coast-to-coast
comatose
command post
countryfolk

diagnose
Diet Coke
dirty joke
envelope
ferryboat
furthermost
give up hope
go for broke
grandiose
gravy boat
Great White Hope
gyroscope
happi coat
hitching post
Holy Ghost
holy smoke
Holyoke
horoscope
innermost
interlope
isotope
Ivory Coast
lightning bolt
locomote
masterstroke
microscope
misanthrope
miss the boat
motorboat
nanny goat
nethermost
northernmost
okey-doke
otiose
outermost
overcoat
overdose
overgrowth
parcel post
periscope
petticoat
poison oak
powerboat
puff of smoke
quote/unquote
ray of hope
right to vote
riverboat
rock the boat
rootbeer float
rope a dope

running joke
seismoscope
self-reproach
southernmost
stethoscope
sugarcoat
take an oath
talk-show host
telescope
thunderbolt
trading post
under oath
undergrowth
underwrote
uppermost
uttermost
varicose
whipping post

absentee vote
Cape of Good Hope
cut your own throat
deciding vote
force down your throat
go up in smoke
hope against hope
in the same boat
Irish Spring Soap
jump down your throat
kaleidoscope
loyalty oath
lump in the throat
one man, one vote
popular vote
practical joke
Slippery slope
torpedo boat
Treasury note
white as a ghost

electoral vote
from pillar to post
Hippocratic oath
majority vote
population growth
promissory note
unanimous vote

at the end of your rope
Casper The Friendly Ghost

OATABLE (see OTABLE)
OATED (see OASTED)
OATEN (see OTION)
OATER (see OVER 1)
OATFUL (see OSAL)
OATH (see OAT)
OATHE (see OSE 1)
OATHER (see OVER 1)
OATHFUL (see OSAL)
OATHING (see OWING 1)
OATIER (see OKIER)
OATILY (see OCALLY)
OATING (see OWING 1)
OATY (see ONY)
OAX (see OAT)
OAXER (see OVER 1)
OAXING (see OWING 1)
OB (see OD)
OBABLE (see OGICAL)
OBABLY (see OMETRY)
OBAL (see OSAL)
OBALLY (see OCALLY)
OBBER (see OLLAR)
OBBERED (see OFFERED)
OBBERIES (see OLOGIES)
OBBERING (see OTTERING)
OBBERY (see OMETRY)
OBBIED (see OLLIED)
OBBIER (see OGGIER)
OBBIEST (see OGGIEST)
OBBILY (see OMETRY)
OBBIN (see OTTEN)
OBBINESS (see OCKINESS)
OBBING (see OCKING)
OBBISH (see OLISH)
OBBIT (see OCKET)
OBBITRY (see OMETRY)
OBBLE (see OTTLE)

OBBLED

bobbled
bottled
cobbled
coppled
Donald
dozzled
gobbled
grovled
hobbled
hoppled

jostled
mottled
nobbled
nozzled
pommeled
Ronald
stoppled
throttled
toggled
toppled
tottled
wobbled

bepommeled
McDonald

Old MacDonald

Joey Macdonald
Ronald McDonald

OBBLER

bobbler
bottler
cobbler
coddler
dawdler
Doppler
gobbler
hobbler
modeler
squabbler
toddler
toggler
twaddler
waddler
wobbler

cherry cobbler
turkey gobbler

OBBLERED (see OFFERED)
OBBLIER (see OGGIER)
OBBLIEST (see OGGIEST)
OBBLINESS (see OCKINESS)

OBBLING

bobbling
bottling

coddling
dawdling
fondling
gobbling
hobbling
squabbling
swaddling
throttling
toddling
waddling
wobbling

mollycoddling

OBBLY (see OCKEY)
OBBY (see OCKEY)
OBBYIST (see OGGIEST)
OBE 1 (see OSE 1)
OBE 2 (see ONY)

OBED

boned
chromed
cloned
closed
combed
coned
domed
don't
dozed
droned
foamed
globed
groaned
honed
hosed
loaned
lobed
moaned
nosed
owned
phoned
posed
probed
roamed
robed
stoned
strobed
toned

won't
zoned

atoned
bemoaned
big-boned
bulldozed
composed
condoned
deboned
deposed
dethroned
disclosed
disowned
disposed
disrobed
enclosed
enthroned
exposed
foreclosed
hardnosed
imposed
intoned
opposed
potponed
proposed
reposed
supposed
transposed

chaperoned
decomposed
honeycombed
ill-disposed
indisposed
juxtaposed
moaned and groaned
predisposed
presupposed
recomposed
self-imposed
telephoned

overexposed
superimposed

OBEL (see OSAL)
OBER (see OVER 1)
OBERLY (see OCALLY)
OBIA (see OLIA)
OBIAL (see OVIAL)

OBIAN (see ONIAN)
OBIC (see ONEMENT)
OBIL (see OSAL)
OBILE (see OSAL)
OBIN (see OTTEN)
OBING (see OWING 1)
OBIT (see ONEMENT)

OBJECT

complex
concept
context
convex
object
octet
offset
Paulette
project
prospect
spotcheck

top prospect

flying object
housing project

OBLE (see OSAL)
OBLEM (see OTTEN)
OBLESS (see OLISH)
OBLIN (see OTTEN)
OBLY (see ONY)
OBO (see OLO)
OBOE (see OLO)
OBRA (see OLA)
OBSTANCE (see OGICAL)
OBSTER (see OLLAR)
OBSTERING (see OTTERING)
OBULATE (see OMERATE)
OBVIOUS (see OGGIEST)
OBY (see ONY)
OBYL (see OSAL)
OC (see OT)
OCA (see OLA)
OCAL (see OSAL)

OCALLY

clonally
clovery

coastally
coterie
cozily
croakily
dopily
focally
globally
grocery
hopefully
hopelessly
hosiery
locally
modally
nodally
nosily
notably
notary
odory
openly
osiery
ovary
overly
poetry
pokily
postally
quotably
Rosalee
rosary
rosery
rosily
rotary
smokily
soberly
socially
soldierly
teetotally
throatily
tonally
totally
vocally
votary
woefully
zonally

anodally
antidotally
atonally
colloquially
diplomacy
hormonally

sacerdotally
upholstery

Madame Bovary

OCATIVE (see OSITIVE)
OCCAM (see OTTEN)

OCCASIN

Clonopin
moccasin
ottoman
oxygen
Solomon
Washington

George Washington

Denzel Washington
Freddie Washington
Isac Washington
metropolitan

OCCER (see OLLAR)
OCCHI (see OCKEY)
OCCHIO (see OLIO)
OCCO (see OTTO 1)
OCCOLI (see OMETRY)
OCCULATE (see OPULATE)
OCCULATION (see OPERATION)
OCCULENCE (see OMINENCE)
OCCUPATION (see OPERATION)
OCCUPY (see OLLIFY)
OCCUS (see AWLESS)
OCEAN (see OTION)
OCER (see OVER 1)
OCERY (see OCALLY)
OCHA (see OLA)
OCHLE (see UBBLE)
OCHO (see OLO)
OCIABLE (see OTABLE)
OCIAL (see OSAL)
OCIALLY (see OCALLY)
OCIATE (see ODIOUS)
OCILE (see OTTLE)
OCILELY (see OMETRY)
OCIOUS (see OSES)
OCITY (see OMETRY)
OCK (see OT)
OCKABLE (see OGICAL)

OCKAGE (see OTIC)
OCKER (see OLLAR)
OCKERED (see OFFERED)

OCKET

audit
bosset
brocket
closet
cocket
cosset
Crockett
docket
droplet
faucet
fosset
gossip
hobbit
hoppet
locket
moppet
plaudit
pocket
poppet
posit
posset
profit
prophet
rocket
scoppet
socket
sprocket
tophet

air pocket
apposite
back pocket
clothes closet
composite
deposit
disprofit
eye socket
hip pocket
light socket
non-profit
pickpocket
skyrocket
unprofit
unsocket

vest pocket
watch pocket

booster rocket
Farrah Fawcett
on the docket
out-of-pocket
Polly Pocket
redeposit
retrorocket
safe deposit
water faucet

hole in your pocket
out of the closet

skeleton in the closet

OCKETT (see OCKET)

OCKEY

Aldi
Aubrey
Audrey
Aussie
Autry
awfully
baldie
baldy
balky
ballsy
baubly
bawdry
bawdy
blotchy
blotty
bobbly
Bobby
body
boggy
bossy
botchy
boxy
broadly
chalky
choppy
cloddy
cloggy

clotty
cobbly
cocky
coffee
Coffy
copy
Cosby
costly
crotchy
doggie
dotty
falsely
faulty
floppy
flossy
foggy
foxy
froggy
frosty
gaudy
gauzy
gawky
glossy
gnocchi
gobbly
godly
halty
haughty
hobbly
hobby
hockey
hoppy
hotly
hottie
jockey
klatschy
knobby
knotty
lawfully
lobby
lofty
malty
mossy
moxie
naughty
Nazi
notchy
oddly
Ozzie
palsy

ploppy
poppy
poshly
posse
potty
proxy
quasi
rocky
Roxie
saki
salty
saucy
scoffy
Scottie
shoddy
slobby
sloppy
sloshy
smoggy
snobby
snotty
softly
softy
soggy
soppy
splotchy
spotty
squabbly
squatty
squawky
stalky
stocky
suavely
swabby
swazi
talkie
talky
tautly
tawdry
toddy
toffee
topsy
vaulty
waffly
walty
washy
wobbly
Yachtze

autopsy
Bill Cosby
Biloxi
biopsy
Bugatti
chapati
desk jockey
disc jockey
distraughtly
embody
epoxy
field hockey
flip-floppy
Gene Autry
god-awfully
hard body
hard copy
homebody
hot body
ice hockey
jalopy
karate
Milwaukee
nobody
Punjabi
recopy
ribaudry
rumaki
serape
somebody
souvlaki
swatchy
unfoxy
ungodly
unlawfully
unsloppy
Versace
Vivaldi
wide body

able body
antibody
anybody
busybody
carbon copy
everybody
Garibaldi
glitterati
Grand Ole Opry
Hammurabi

Jabberwocky
kamikaze
manicotti
mariachi
Nagasaki
orthodoxy
paparazzi
photocopy
sannyasi
student body
sukiyaki
Tamagotchi
teriyaki
training potty
vote by proxy
walkie-talkie
wishy-washy

Cerebral palsy
heavenly body
illiterati
illuminati
Joanie Loves Chachi
Maxwell House Coffee
Mr. Peabody
unorthodoxly

Gianni Versace

OCKEYED (see OLLIED)
OCKIER (see OGGIER)
OCKIEST (see OGGIEST)
OCKILY (see OMETRY)

OCKINESS

bawdiness
bossiness
boxiness
chalkiness
choppiness
clogginess
cockiness
costliness
floppiness
fogginess
foxiness
frostiness
gaudiness
gawkiness

glossiness
godliness
grogginess
jolliness
knobbiness
loftiness
mossiness
naughtiness
rockiness
sauciness
shoddiness
sloppiness
snottiness
sogginess
soppiness
spottiness
squashiness
squawkiness
stockiness
talkiness
washiness
wobbliness

OCKING

blocking
blotching
blotting
bobbing
bonging
bopping
bossing
botching
boxing
chopping
clocking
clotting
coifing
copping
costing
coughing
cropping
crossing
docking
dodging
doffing
donging
dotting
dropping

faulting
flocking
flopping
flossing
foxing
frosting
frothing
gawking
glossing
golfing
gonging
gosling
halting
hopping
joshing
jotting
knocking
knotting
lobbing
locking
lodging
longing
mobbing
mocking
mopping
notching
offing
opting
plotting
pocking
popping
potting
propping
quashing
robbing
rocking
rotting
salting
scoffing
shocking
shopping
slopping
sloshing
smocking
sobbing
socking
sopping
sploshing
splotching
spotting

squashing
squatting
squawking
stalking
stocking
stopping
swabbing
swapping
swashing
swatting
talking
throbbing
thronging
topping
tossing
vaulting
walking
washing
watching
whopping
wronging
yachting

accosting
adopting
allotting
assaulting
belonging
birdwatching
boycotting
brainwashing
cakewalking
carhopping
clip-clopping
concocting
crisscrossing
deadlocking
debauching
defaulting
defrocking
defrosting
detoxing
dishwashing
dislodging
ear-popping
eavesdropping
embossing
estopping
exalting
exhausting

fast-talking
flip-flopping
globe-trotting
gridlocking
handwashing
heartstopping
hip-hopping
hobnobbing
jaywalking
massaging
name-dropping
outcropping
outfoxing
outtalking
pole vaulting
prolonging
restocking
sharecropping
showstopping
silk stocking
sleepwalking
smooth-talking
spacewalking
speed-walking
sweet-talking
tick-tocking
unlocking
weight-watching
whitewashing
wife-swapping
Xeroxing

belly-flopping
bunnyhopping
camouflaging
dead man walking
double-talking
interlocking
overstocking
pillow-talking
railroad crossing
sabotaging
somersaulting
window-shopping

Pippi Longstocking

OCKISH (see OLISH)
OCKLE (see OTTLE)
OCKUS (see AWLESS)
OCKY (see OCKEY)

OCO (see OLO)
OCOA (see OLO)
OCOLATE (see OMERATE)
OCRACIES (see OLOGIES)
OCRACY (see OMETRY)
OCRATES (see OLOGIES)
OCRE (see OVER 1)
OCRISY (see OMETRY)
OCRITIES (see OLOGIES)
OCRITY (see OMETRY)
OCT (see OT)
OCTER (see OLLAR)
OCTET (see OBJECT)
OCTING (see OCKING)
OCTION (see OTTEN)
OCTOR (see OLLAR)
OCTORED (see OFFERED)
OCTORING (see OTTERING)
OCTRINE (see OTTEN)
OCUMENT (see OMERATE)
OCUMENTS (see OMINENCE)
OCUS (see OSES)

OD

blob
blog
Bob
bog
broad
Claude
clod
clog
cob
cod
daub
dodge
dog
flog
fob
fog
fraud
frog
glob
glogg
gob
God
grog
Hadj
hod

Hodge
hog
job
jog
knob
laud
lob
lodge
log
mob
mod
nod
nog
odd
plod
pod
Prague
prod
quad
rob
rod
scrod
shod
slob
smog
snob
sob
sod
squab
squad
suave
swab
throb
Todd
tog
trod
wad

abroad
agog
ah-hahed
applaud
athrob
backlog
bag job
befog
bipod
bird dog
bomb squad
boob job

bulldog
bullfrog
Cape Cod
collage
con job
corncob
corsage
death squad
defog
defraud
dense fog
dislodge
doorknob
downtrod
eggnog
facade
fat slob
flash mob
garage
goon squad
Greek god
groundhog
guard dog
heartthrob
hedgehog
hobnob
hodgepodge
hot dog
Hot Rod
hurrahed
kabob
leapfrog
maraud
massage
Mod Squad
montage
nabob
nose job
odd-job
pea pod
ramrod
red-dog
road hog
roughshod
roulade
ski lodge
slipshod
snowjob
spit-wad
thank God

tightwad
tin god
top dog
tripod
unclog
unshod
untrod
unwad
vice squad
warthog
watchdog
whole-hog
yule log

act of God
analog
Axelrod
bon voyage
bunco squad
camouflage
catalog
cattle prod
chili dog
cottonswab
decoupage
demagogue
demigod
dialogue
dog-eat-dog
entourage
epilogue
fishing rod
fuselage
give the nod
go whole hog
go with God
goldenrod
house of God
hunting lodge
inside job
la-de-dahed
Lamb of God
land of nod
lightning rod
monkeypod
monologue
navy grog
on-the-job
oohed and ahed
pea-soup fog

pedagogue
pettifog
promenade
pull a job
put-up job
reverse snob
riot squad
sabotage
salty dog
shish kebab
synagogue
Travelodge
travelogue
traverse rod
underdog
waterlog
wrath of God
wrist corsage

beware of dog
card catalog
corn on the cob
Deputy Dawg
divining rod
double garage
espionage
firing squad
Freddy the Frog
Kermit the Frog
Marquis de Sade
put on the dog
Scheherazade
Seeing-Eye dog
sleep like a log
Snoop Doggy Dogg
so help me God
thingamabob
yessireebob

lie down on the job
Sonic the Hedgehog

Clifford The Big Red Dog
Jefferson Davis Hogg

ODA (see OLA)
ODABLE (see OTABLE)
ODAL (see OSAL)
ODALLY (see OCALLY)
ODD (see OD)

ODDABLE (see OGICAL)
ODDED (see OLID)
ODDEN (see OTTEN)
ODDER (see OLLAR)
ODDESS (see OLISH)
ODDEST (see OLISH)
ODDIER (see OGGIER)
ODDIEST (see OGGIEST)
ODDILY (see OMETRY)
ODDINESS (see OCKINESS)
ODDING (see ALLING)
ODDITIES (see OLOGIES)
ODDITY (see OMETRY)
ODDLE (see OTTLE)
ODDLER (see OBBLER)
ODDLING (see OBBLING)
ODDLY (see OCKEY)
ODDY (see OCKEY)
ODE (see OSE 1)
ODED (see OASTED)
ODEFUL (see OSAL)
ODEL 1 (see OTTLE)
ODEL 2 (see OSAL)
ODELER (see OBBLER)
ODELING (see ANDERING 2)
ODEM (see OTION)
ODENT (see ONEMENT)
ODEO (see OLIO)
ODEON (see ONIAN)
ODER (see OVER 1)
ODERATE (see OMERATE)
ODERN (see OFFERED)
ODEST (see OLISH)
ODESY (see OMETRY)
ODGE (see OD)
ODGER (see OLLAR)
ODGING (see OCKING)
ODIA (see OLIA)
ODIAL (see OTABLE)
ODIAN (see ONIAN)
ODIC (see OTIC)
ODICAL (see OGICAL)
ODICE (see OLISH)
ODIE (see ONY)
ODIED (see OLLIED)
ODIFY (see OLLIFY)
ODIGAL (see OGICAL)
ODIGY (see OMETRY)
ODILY (see OMETRY)
ODIN (see OTION)
ODING (see OWING 1)

ODIOUS

associate
erroneous
felonious
harmonious
melodious

ceremonious

unceremonious

ODITY (see OMETRY)
ODIUM (see ONIAN)
ODKA (see ADA 1)
ODLIEST (see OGGIEST)
ODLINESS (see OCKINESS)
ODLY (see OCKEY)
ODO (see OLO)
ODOM (see OTTEN)
ODOMIES (see OLOGIES)
ODOMY (see OMETRY)
ODOR (see OVER 1)
ODORY (see OCALLY)
ODUS (see OSES)
ODY 1 (see OCKEY)
ODY 2 (see ONY)
ODYSSEY (see OMETRY)
ODYSSEYS (see OLOGIES)
OE 1 (see OW 1)
OE 2 (see EW 1)
OE 3 (see ONY)
OEBE (see EASY)
OEDER (see OVER 1)
OEFUL (see OSAL)
OEFULLY (see OCALLY)
OEING 1 (see OWING 1)
OEING 2 (see UING)
OEL (see OLE 1)
OELESS (see UENESS)
OEM (see ONE 1)
OENIX (see EANEST)
OER 1 (see EWER 1)
OER 2 (see OVER 1)
OES (see UG)
OESY (see ONY)
OET (see ONEMENT)
OETRY (see OCALLY)
OEUVRE (see ORD 2)
OEY (see ONY)
OF 1 (see UG)
OF 2 (see OFF)

OFA (see OLA)
OFAR (see OVER 1)
OFER (see OVER 1)

OFF

boff
boss
broth
cause
Claus
clause
cloth
cough
cross
doff
dross
floss
froth
gauze
gloss
golf
Goth
joss
loss
mauve
moss
moth
Nas
off
Oz
pause
prof
quaff
Rolf
Ross
Roth
Roz
sauce
schnozz
scoff
Slav
sloth
swath
toss
troth
trough

across
applause

bake-off
because
big boss
blast-off
Blue Cross
broadcloth
brush-off
castoff
cheesecloth
crisscross
cutoff
day off
dropoff
dummkopf
dust cloth
emboss
goof-off
hands off
hot sauce
improv
Khrushchev
kickoff
kiss-off
knockoff
lacrosse
lift-off
lip gloss
loincloth
lost cause
mirage
peat moss
Red Cross
ring toss
ripoff
runoff
send-off
show-off
slack off
soy sauce
spin-off
standoff
straw boss
take-off
tax loss
tee off
tip-off
trade-off
trail boss
turn-off
weight loss

well-off
write-off

albatross
applesauce
at a loss
better off
chicken broth
cocktail sauce
come across
common cause
dental floss
double-cross
escape clause
Gorbachev
gypsy moth
Haagen-Dazs
hearing loss
hit it off
hit the sauce
just because
knock it off
laugh it off
mazel tov
menopause
Molotov
on and off
run across
Santa Claus
smoker's cough
Southern Cross
stroganoff
tablecloth
tartar sauce
three-toed sloth
Toss Across
vichyssoise
Visigoth
water trough
whooping cough

A-1 Steak Sauce
Baryshnikov
beat the socks off
blow the lid off
Diana Ross
grandfather clause
male menopause
man of the cloth
memory loss

probable cause
profit and loss
round of applause
sign of the cross
Wizard of Oz

David Hasselhoff
miniature golf

Ferris Bueller's Day Off
Ragu Spaghetti Sauce

OFFA (see ADA 1)
OFFAL (see OTTLE)
OFFEE (see OCKEY)
OFFER (see OLLAR)

OFFERED

altered
Auburn
authored
awkward
boggard
bothered
clobbered
cobblered
cockered
coffered
collard
collared
coppered
coshered
doctored
faltered
fathered
fostered
goffered
haltered
hollered
Lollard
loppered
modern
offered
Oscared
Oxford
paltered
pollard
postured
pottered

proffered
prospered
rockered
slaughtered
soldered
stoppered
tottered
watered

bysmottered
coauthored
grandfathered
postmodern
unaltered
unoffered
unsoldered

Cindy Crawford
hot and bothered

OFFERING (see OTTERING)
OFFICE (see AWLESS)
OFFIN (see OTTEN)
OFFING (see OCKING)
OFFISH (see AWLESS)
OFFMAN (see OTTEN)
OFFSET (see OBJECT)
OFFY (see OCKEY)
OFIE (see ONY)
OFIT (see OCKET)
OFITOR (see OGRAPHER)
OFT (see ASH 2)
OFTED (see OLID)
OFTEN (see OTTEN)
OFTER (see OLLAR)
OFTIER (see OGGIER)
OFTIEST (see OGGIEST)
OFTINESS (see OCKINESS)
OFTING (see ALLING)
OFTLY (see OCKEY)
OFTNESS (see AWLESS)
OFTY (see OCKEY)
OG (see OD)
OGA (see OLA)
OGAMIST (see OLOGIST)
OGAMY (see OMETRY)
OGAN (see OTION)
OGANY (see OMETRY)
OGATIVE (see OSITIVE)
OGE (see OSE 1)
OGEE 1 (see ONY)
OGEE 2 (see ONY)

OGEL (see OSAL)
OGER (see OLLAR)
OGEY (see ONY)
OGG (see OD)
OGGAN (see OTTEN)
OGGARD (see OFFERED)
OGGER (see OLLAR)
OGGIE (see OCKEY)

OGGIER

blockier
blottier
boggier
bossier
boxier
choppier
cloddier
cloggier
cobbier
cockier
collier
copier
costlier
cottier
doggier
dossier
dottier
drossier
flockier
floppier
flossier
foggier
foxier
froggier
frostier
glossier
groggier
jollier
knobbier
knottier
loftier
loggier
loppier
mossier
nobbier
plottier
pockier
rockier
shoddier

sloppier
sloshier
smoggier
snobbier
snottier
soggier
soppier
spottier
squashier
stockier
washier
wobblier

peacockier
toploftier

photocopier

OGGIEST

balmiest
blockiest
blotchiest
blottiest
boggiest
bonniest
bossiest
botchiest
bottomless
boxiest
choppiest
cloddiest
cloggiest
cockiest
costliest
dottiest
drossiest
flauntiest
flockiest
floppiest
flossiest
foggiest
foxiest
froggiest
frostiest
glossiest
godliest
groggiest
hobbyist

jauntiest
jolliest
knobbiest
knottiest
lobbyist
loftiest
mossiest
motliest
obvious
ominous
omnibus
palmiest
paunchiest
plottiest
populace
qualmiest
raunchiest
rockiest
sauciest
scroggiest
shoddiest
slobbiest
sloppiest
smoggiest
snobbiest
snottiest
soggiest
soppiest
splotchiest
spottiest
stockiest
wobbliest
wonkiest

acropolis
anonymous
antonymous
autonomous
cosmopolis
Metropolis
monogamous
necropolis
preposterous
synonymous
ungodliest

heteronymous

Alcoholics Anonymous

OGGILY (see OMETRY)
OGGIN (see OTTEN)
OGGINESS (see OCKINESS)
OGGING (see ALLING)
OGGISH (see AWLESS)
OGGLE (see OTTLE)
OGGLED (see OBBLED)
OGGLER (see OBBLER)
OGGY (see OCKEY)
OGH (see OW 1)
OGI (see ONY)
OGIA (see OLIA)
OGIAN (see ONIAN)
OGIC (see OTIC)

OGICAL

audible
blockable
callable
causable
choppable
chronicle
clockable
comical
conical
coppable
crossable
dockable
droppable
follicle
hockable
knockable
laudable
launchable
lockable
logical
mockable
monocle
moppable
nautical
nominal
obstacle
optical
optimal
optional
pausable
pawnable
plausible
plottable

pockable
poppable
possible
probable
proddable
prodigal
rockable
shockable
sockable
solvable
spottable
squawkable
stalkable
stockable
stoppable
swappable
talkable
topical
toppable
tossable
tropical
walkable

abdominal
absolvable
applaudable
atomical
canonical
defraudable
demonical
diabolical
dissolvable
erotical
exhaustible
exotical
hypnotical
iconical
illogical
implausible
impossible
improbable
inaudible
ironical
melodical
methodical
mnemonical
outtalkable
outwalkable
padlockable
phenomenal

resolvable
restockable
seismotical
spasmodical
subtropical
sunblockable
symbolical
uncrossable
undauntable
unlockable
unsolvable
unstoppable

aeronautical
analogical
anatomical
astrological
astronomical
biological
chronological
cosmological
economical
gastronomical
geological
hyperbolical
idiotical
interlockable
mythological
neurological
overstockable
paradoxical
pathological
periodical
philanthropical
psychological
tautological
technological
theological
unresolvable
zoological

anthropological
archeological
climatological
etymological
genealogical
ideological
Mission Impossible
physiological
sociological

toxicological
uneconomical

meteorological

OGIE (see ONY)
OGIER (see OKIER)
OGING (see ALLING)
OGLE (see OSAL)
OGNA (see ONY)
OGNE (see ONE 1)
OGNITIVE (see OSITIVE)
OGO (see OLO)
OGOMOUS (see OGGIEST)

OGRAPHER

auditor
commoner
conifer
copular
follower
hollower
moniker
monitor
popular
positer
profitor
promiser
swallower
wallower

acknowledger
anthologer
astrologer
astronomer
barometer
biographer
chronologer
chronometer
geologer
hydrometer
kilometer
lithographer
odometer
philosopher
photographer
pornographer
speedometer
stenographer

sword-swallower
tachometer
thermometer
topographer
unpopular

bibliographer
choreographer
videographer

OGRAPHIES (see OLOGIES)
OGRAPHY (see OMETRY)
OGRE (see OVER 1)
OGRESS (see OLISH)
OGUE 1 (see OD)
OGUE 2 (see OSE 1)
OGUING (see OWING 1)
OGUL (see OSAL)
OGURT (see OVER 1)
OGUS (see OSES)
OGYNIST (see OLOGIST)
OGYNY (see OMETRY)
OH (see OW 1)
OHA (see OLA)
OHL (see OLE 1)
OHN (see ON 1)
OHNNY (see AWNY)
OHNSON (see OTTEN)
OI (see OID)
OIA (see OYA)
OIC (see ONEMENT)
OICE (see OID)
OICER (see ORDER)
OICING (see OILING)

OID

boy
choice
cloy
coif
coit
coy
droid
Floyd
Freud
hoist
joist
joy
Joyce

Lloyd
moist
noise
ploy
poi
poise
Roy
soy
toy
Troy
voice
void

ahoy
android
annoy
annoyed
anthoid
avoid
b-boy
blastoid
bok choy
boy toy
by choice
cowboy
deploy
deployed
destroy
destroyed
Detroit
devoice
devoid
employ
enjoy
enjoyed
envoy
exploit
fibroid
first choice
free choice
Gameboy
Hanoi
homeboy
invoice
keloid
killjoy
Kilroy
last choice
lymphoid
maioid

no choice
oh boy
one voice
outnoise
outvoice
Pink Floyd
Playboy
prochoice
rejoice
revoice
Rolls-Royce
Savoy
steroid
tabloid
tactoid
turquoise
uncoif
unmoist
viceroy

altar boy
antinoise
asteroid
attaboy
celluloid
Chips Ahoy
corduroy
counterpoise
embryoid
fair-haired boy
flavinoid
good ole boy
hoi polloi
Illinois
Iroquois
mama's boy
mongoloid
null and void
over joy
overjoyed
overmoist
paranoid
Polaroid
pride and joy
real McCoy
redeploy
rheumatoid
Sigmund Freud
still, small voice
Tinkertoy

traffic noise
unemploy
unemployed
water boy
whipping boy

Gidney and Cloyd
Helen of Troy
Josie McCoy
multiple choice
overexploit
Rinestone Cowboy
the real McCoy
Urban Cowboy

mama's little boy
Pillsbury Doughboy

OIDA (see OYA)
OIDABLY (see ORMITY)
OIDANCE (see OYANCE)
OIDANT (see OYMENT)
OIDER (see ORDER)
OIDERED (see ORDERED)
OIDERING (see ORDERING)
OIDERY (see ORMITY)
OIDING (see OILING)
OIF (see OID)
OIFING (see OCKING)
OIGNANT (see OYMENT)
OIKA (see OYA)

OIL

boil
broil
coil
Doyle
foil
loyal
oil
roil
royal
soil
spoil
toil

airfoil
coal oil
crude oil

despoil
disloyal
embroil
gargoyle
hard-boil
recoil
soft-boil
strike oil
tinfoil
topsoil
turmoil
uncoil
unspoil

baby oil
battle royal
boil in oil
castor oil
disembroil
olive oil
Olive Oyl
Standard Oil

cod-liver oil

aluminum foil
burn the midnight oil

OILER (see ORDER)
OILERY (see ORMITY)
OILET (see OYMENT)

OILING

boiling
broiling
coiling
foiling
hoisting
joining
oiling
oinking
pointing
roiling
soiling
spoiling
toiling
toying
voicing
voiding

annoying
anointing
appointing
avoiding
deploying
despoiling
destroying
embroiling
employing
enjoying
exploiting
invoicing
pinpointing
recoiling
rejoicing

disappointing
needlepointing
reappointing

OILY

boily
Boise
doily
noisy
oily
soily
spoily

hoity-toity

OIN (see OINT)
OINANT (see OYMENT)
OINE (see ON 1)
OINER (see ORDER)
OING 1 (see UING)
OING 2 (see OWING 1)
OINING (see OILING)
OINK (see OINT)
OINKING (see OILING)

OINT

boink
coin
doink
groin
join

joint
loin
oink
point

adjoin
anoint
appoint
ballpoint
beer joint
bluepoint
checkpoint
clip joint
conjoin
dew point
disjoin
disjoint
enjoin
high point
match point
midpoint
pinpoint
purloin
rejoin
sirloin
strip joint
viewpoint
West Point

at gunpoint
at sword's point
boiling point
breaking point
counterpoint
Dead Man's Point
disappoint
flip a coin
focal point
needlepoint
out of joint
reappoint
starting point
tenderloin
to the point
turning point
vantage point

break-even point
decimal point
get to the point

jumping-off point
nose out of joint

exclamation point

OINTING (see OILING)
OINTMENT (see OYMENT)
OINTMENTS (see OYANCE)
OIR 1 (see AR 1)
OIR 2 (see IRE)
OIRE (see AR 1)
OIS 1 (see A 1)
OIS 2 (see OID)
OISE 1 (see OID)
OISE 2 (see OILY)
OISE 3 (see OID)
OISE 4 (see OFF)
OISON (see OYMENT)
OIST (see OID)
OISTER (see ORDER)
OISTERED (see ORDERED)
OISTERING (see ORDERING)
OISTING (see OILING)
OISTURE (see ORDER)
OISY (see OILY)
OIT (see OID)
OITER (see ORDER)
OITERED (see ORDERED)
OITERING (see ORDERING)
OITING (see OILING)
OITY (see OILY)
OJECT (see OBJECT)
OJI (see ONY)
OJO (see OLO)
OK 1 (see OT)
OK 2 (see UP)
OKABLE (see OTABLE)
OKAH (see UNA)
OKE 1 (see OAT)
OKE 2 (see ONY)
OKEL (see OSAL)
OKEN (see OTION)
OKER (see OVER 1)
OKESTER (see OVER 1)
OKEY (see ONY)
OKIA (see OLIA)
OKIE (see ONY)

OKIER

blowier
bonier

chokier
cozier
croakier
crozier
dopier
dotier
dozier
floatier
ghostlier
Grolier
hokier
holier
logier
mopier
nosier
phonier
pokier
ropier
rosier
showier
smokier
snowier
soapier
stonier
throatier
toastier
tonier

billowier
unholier
willowier

OKILY (see OCALLY)
OKING (see OWING 1)
OKO (see OLO)
OKRA (see OLA)
OKUM (see OTION)
OKY (see ONY)
OKYO (see OLIO)
OL 1 (see OLE 1)
OL 2 (see ALL 1)

OLA

boa
chroma
cobra
coca
coda
cola

coma
Jonah
Kona
krona
Lola
mocha
Mona
Noah
Nola
nova
okra
Olga
Oprah
ova
polka
quota
Roma
Rona
rosa
Soca
soda
sofa
Sonia
stoa
toga
Yoda
yoga

Alcoa
aloha
ambrosia
ammonia
Angola
aroma
Balboa
begonia
Canova
club soda
corolla
corona
crapola
Crayola
cream soda
diploma
ebola
Estonia
glaucoma
iota
Jehovah
Loyola

mimosa
narcoma
nervosa
pagoda
Paloma
payola
pneumonia
Pomona
Samoa
Slavonia
Sonoma
sub rosa
Tacoma
Toyota
Verona
viola

Almond Roca
areola
Arizona
ayatollah
baking soda
Barcelona
bossa nova
carioca
Casanova
Coca-Cola
Espanola
Figueroa
gladiola
Gorgonzola
hematoma
ice cream soda
in a coma
John Travolta
Krakatoa
mariposa
Mauna Loa
Minnesota
My Sharona
North Dakota
Oklahoma
Pensacola
Pepsi-Cola
Ponderosa
root-beer soda
roseola
Saratoga
Scotch and soda
Shenandoah

South Dakota
supernova
tapioca
tokonoma
Villanova

Babylonia
Caledonia
Macedonia
Rocky Balboa

anorexia nervosa

OLABLE (see OTABLE)
OLACE (see AWLESS)
OLAN (see OTION)
OLAR 1 (see OVER 1)
OLAR 2 (see OLLAR)
OLD (see OSE 1)
OLDABLE (see OTABLE)
OLDAWAY (see OWAWAY)
OLDEN (see OTION)
OLDER 1 (see OVER 1)
OLDER 2 (see OLLAR)
OLDERED (see OFFERED)
OLDERING (see OTTERING)
OLDIE (see ONY)
OLDIER (see OVER 1)
OLDIERLY (see OCALLY)
OLDING (see OWING 1)
OLDY (see ONY)

OLE 1

boll
bowl
coal
cole
dole
droll
goal
hole
Joel
knoll
kohl
Lowell
mole
pole
poll
role

roll
scroll
Seoul
shoal
skoal
sol
sole
soul
stole
stroll
toll
troll
whole

armhole
bankroll
beanpole
bedroll
black hole
bridge toll
cajole
charcoal
condole
console
control
Creole
drum roll
egg roll
enroll
enscroll
extol
field goal
fishbowl
flagpole
foxhole
fur stole
half-sole
hellhole
insole
keyhole
knothole
light pole
logroll
loophole
manhole
Maypole
mudhole
North Pole
parole
patrol

payroll
peephole
pinhole
pothole
punch bowl
rathole
resole
Rose Bowl
sinkhole
South Pole
steamroll
straw poll
tadpole
unroll
washbowl

as a whole
aureole
barber pole
barrel roll
birth control
buttonhole
camisole
casserole
census poll
crowd control
cruise control
Dr. Scholl
Espanol
finger bowl
fishing hole
fishing pole
flood control
Gallup poll
goldfish bowl
ground control
heart and soul
Interpol
jelly roll
leading role
lose control
Manute Bol
metropole
money roll
Nat King Cole
nineteenth hole
Old King Cole
on a roll
on the whole
pest control

pigeonhole
rabbit hole
rigmarole
rock and roll
self-control
shore patrol
starring role
sugar bowl
Super Bowl
swimming hole
take control
take its toll
title role
toilet bowl
Tootsie Roll
totem pole
water hole

ace in the hole
bladder control
body and soul
Costa del Sol
disease control
Hollywood Bowl
magnetic pole
out of control
overcontrol
remote control
telephone pole
traffic control
under control
utility pole
watering hole

air-traffic control
quality control
shake, rattle and roll

OLE 2 (see ONY)
OLEE (see ONY)
OLEFUL (see OSAL)
OLELY (see ONY)
OLEM (see OTION)
OLEMAN (see OTION)
OLEMN (see OTTEN)
OLEN (see OTION)
OLEON (see ONIAN)
OLER (see OVER 1)
OLERANCE (see OMINENCE)
OLEY (see ONY)
OLF (see OFF)

OLFER (see ALTER)
OLFING (see OCKING)
OLGA (see OLA)
OLGER (see OVER 1)
OLI (see ONY)

OLIA

dolia
folia
Nokia
novia
olia
phobia
scholia
scolia
skolia

Arcoxia
colloquia
magnolia
melodia
myopia
utopia

acrophobia
analogia
claustrophobia
cornucopia
Ethiopia
homophobia
hydrophobia
xenophobia

agoraphobia

OLIAN (see ONIAN)
OLIC (see OTIC)
OLICAL (see OGICAL)
OLICY (see OMETRY)

OLID

bonded
clotted
dotted
frosted
knotted
lauded

lofted
nodded
olid
plodded
plotted
podded
potted
prodded
prompted
rotted
slotted
sodded
solid
spotted
squalid
squatted
stolid
swatted
trotted
wadded

absconded
accosted
allotted
applauded
carotid
defrosted
exhausted
marauded
responded
sursolid
unwadded

corresponded
polka-dotted
semsolid

OLIER (see OKIER)
OLING (see OWING 1)

OLIO

folio
olio
Oreo
polio
rodeo
Romeo
Scorpio
Tokyo

Antonio
Pinocchio
portfolio

OLISH

Amish
blobbish
bobbish
bodice
broadness
brockish
Chopness
cobless
cockish
congas
congress
conscious
goddess
honest
hospice
hotness
hottest
hottish
jobless
knobless
lobbish
mobbish
mobless
mockish
modest
monish
novice
oddest
polish
pompous
progress
promise
promptness
sawdust
schottish
Scottish
shamus
slobbish
slobless
snobbish
snobless
sobless
sottish
spotless

squabless
stockish
suaveness
swabless
tautest
Thomas
thoughtless
throbbish
throbless
Tongas
topless

abolish
accomplice
admonish
adonis
astonish
coronis
demolish
depolish
dishonest
doggonest
expolish
foreconscious
immodest
inconscious
maraudist
myopsis
parsonish
phoronis
preconscious
premonish
repolish
selfconscious
St. Thomas
subconscious
submonish
synopsis
unconscious
unpolish
withdrawnest

act of congress
babylonish
breach of promise
foreadmonish
overpolish
preadmonish
semiconscious
spit-and-polish

torticollis
under promise
unselfconscious
woebegonest

Speedy Gonzalez

OLISHING

polishing
promising
stonishing

abolishing
admonishing
astonishing
atomising
demolishing
depolishing
premonishing
repolishing
unpromising

OLITAN (see OCCASIN)
OLITY (see OMETRY)
OLIVE (see OTIC)
OLK (see OAT)
OLKA (see OLA)
OLKSY (see ONY)
OLL 1 (see ALL 1)
OLL 2 (see OLE 1)
OLLA (see OLA)
OLLABLE (see OTABLE)
OLLAH (see OLA)

OLLAR

augur
author
balker
baller
blocker
blogger
blotter
bobber
boffer
bogger
bomber
bopper

bosser
bother
boxer
brawler
broader
caller
calmer
chalker
Chaucer
chopper
clobber
clocker
clogger
clotter
cocker
codger
coffer
collar
copper
copter
cotter
cougher
crawler
crocker
cropper
crosser
daughter
docker
doctor
dodger
doffer
dogger
dollar
dotter
drawler
dropper
faller
father
flocker
flosser
fodder
fogger
foster
frocker
Frogger
froster
gawker
glosser
Gloucester
hauler
hawker

hogger
holler
hopper
hotter
jobber
jogger
jotter
knocker
knotter
lauder
lobber
lobster
locker
lodger
logger
loller
Mahler
mauler
mobber
mobster
mocker
modder
mopper
nodder
odder
offer
opter
Oscar
otter
palmer
pauper
plodder
plopper
plotter
popper
posture
pother
potter
proctor
proffer
proper
prosper
quaffer
quasher
robber
rocker
Roger
roster
rotter
saucer

scholar
scoffer
scrawler
shocker
shopper
slaughter
slobber
smaller
sobber
sobster
soccer
socker
softer
solder
spotter
sprawler
squalor
squasher
squatter
squawker
stalker
staller
stocker
stomper
stopper
swabber
swapper
swatter
talker
taller
tauter
throbber
tosser
totter
trawler
trodder
trotter
wadder
walker
waller
washer
watcher
water
whopper

accoster
allotter
appaller
applauder
backwater

bebopper
becalmer
bird caller
blackballer
Blackwater
bloodshotter
blue-collar
breakwater
bulldogger
catcaller
choke collar
Clearwater
coauthor
concocter
corn popper
crisscrosser
defogger
defrauder
defrocker
defroster
detoxer
dishwasher
dishwater
dislodger
distraughter
dive bomber
dog collar
dogtrotter
door knocker
doorstopper
eavesdropper
embalmer
embosser
enthraller
eye-popper
eyeballer
eyedropper
fast talker
firewater
flea collar
flip-flopper
floodwater
floor mopper
floorwalker
fly swatter
Foot Locker
forefather
forestaller
fox-trotter
free-faller

freshwater
globetrotter
godfather
grandfather
grasshopper
graverobber
half-dollar
heartstopper
heartthrobber
hobnobber
hot water
hot-rodder
ice water
impostor
improper
ink blotter
installer
jaywalker
leapfrogger
macabre
mad bomber
manslaughter
marauder
massager
men's locker
name-caller
name-dropper
napalmer
night stalker
no bother
Our Father
outtalker
padlocker
pill popper
pratfaller
rainwater
ramrodder
Rhodes scholar
rosewater
salt water
sea otter
sharecropper
shot caller
show-stopper
sleepwalker
smooth-talker
snowballer
speedballer
spitballer
spring water

stepdaughter
stepfather
still water
streetwalker
sunblocker
sweet-talker
tap water
top dollar
tread water
unclogger
white-collar
whitewasher
witch doctor
woodchopper
Xeroxer

above water
alma mater
baby-talker
belly-flopper
beta blocker
Betty Crocker
bobby soxer
bottled water
bread and water
caterwauler
cradle robber
creepy crawler
cup and saucer
Cyndi Lauper
double-crosser
double-talker
drink of water
flying saucer
founding father
Harry Potter
helicopter
holy water
hoot and holler
in hot water
interlocker
Knickerbocker
lindy-hopper
Luke Skywalker
make an offer
million-dollar
obscene caller
off your rocker

orthodoxer
overhauler
panty dropper
pettifogger
pillow talker
popcorn popper
snollygoster
teenybopper
teeter-totter
tightrope walker
toilet water
turkey-trotter
underwater
walk on water
window-shopper

almighty dollar
buttoned-down collar
compulsive shopper
dead in the water
fish out of water
flotation collar
Harlem Globetrotter
Live Long and Prosper
memory jogger

bet your bottom dollar
come hell or high water
hot under the collar
ring around the collar
you are not the father

OLLARD (see OFFERED)
OLLARED (see OFFERED)
OLLARING (see OTTERING)
OLLATIVE (see OSITIVE)
OLLEE (see ONY)
OLLEGE (see OTIC)
OLLEN 1 (see OTTEN)
OLLEN 2 (see OTION)
OLLER 1 (see OVER 1)
OLLER 2 (see OLLAR)
OLLERED (see OFFERED)
OLLERING (see OTTERING)
OLLEY (see OLLY 1)
OLLICK (see OTIC)
OLLICLE (see OGICAL)
OLLIE (see OLLY 1)

OLLIED

collied
dollied
jockeyed
jollied
lobbied
poppied
pottied
trollied

embodied
epoxied
full-bodied

OLLIER (see OGGIER)
OLLIEST (see OGGIEST)

OLLIFY

codify
jollify
modify
mollify
occupy
ossify
qualify

disqualify
preoccupy
remodify
reoccupy
unqualify

overmodify

OLLINESS (see OCKINESS)
OLLING 1 (see OWING 1)
OLLING 2 (see ALLING)
OLLIS (see OLISH)
OLLITY (see OMETRY)
OLLO (see OTTO 1)
OLLOW (see OTTO 1)
OLLOWER (see OGRAPHER)
OLLOWING (see ANDERING 2)
OLLSTER (see OVER 1)

OLLY 1

Ali
Bali
collie
crawly
Dali
dolly
drawly
folly
Golly
holly
jolly
Molly
Polly
Raleigh
scrawly
squally
trolley
volley
Wally

Bengali
by golly
finale
loblolly
Somali
Svengali
tamale

creepy-crawly
grand finale
hot tamale
melancholy

Muhammad Ali

OLLY 2 (see ONY)
OLM (see ONE 1)
OLMES (see ONE 1)

OLO

BOGO
bolo
Bozo
cocoa
Como
dodo
dojo

go-go
GoPro
hobo
lobo
loco
logo
mojo
no-go
oboe
ocho
photo
poco
Pogo
polo
popo
promo
Provo
so-so
solo
sotto
Togo
Toto
Volvo
yo-yo
Yoko
YOLO

DeSoto
Han Solo
kimono
Kyoto
risotto
rococo

Acapulco
barococo
grandioso
mafioso
Marco Polo
Matsumoto
quasimodo
Ruidoso
telephoto
virtuoso
water polo

affettuoso
capriccioso
poco a poco
Ralph Lauren Polo

OLOGER (see OGRAPHER)

OLOGIES

comedies
gaucheries
glossaries
homilies
hominies
lotteries
novelties
oddities
odysseys
ologies
potteries
robberies
snobberies
Socrates
sodomies
Wallabees

anthologies
apologies
apostasies
apostrophes
audiologies
autocracies
autonomies
biologies
chronologies
debaucheries
democracies
dichotomies
discographies
doxologies
ecologies
economies
filmographies
gemologies
geographies
geologies
graphologies
Hippocrates
holographies
isosceles
landocracies
lobotomies
mammographies
monopolies

monotonies
mythologies
necrologies
philosophies
phlebotomies
plutocracies
pornographies
spectrographies
taxonomies
theocracies
topographies
typographies

aristocracies
bibliographies
biographies
ideologies
immunologies
kakistocracies
mediocrities
meritocracies
methodologies
radiographies
sociologies
terminologies
thanatologies

autobiographies
cinematographies

OLOGIST

agronomist
anthologist
astrologist
biologist
chronologist
cosmologist
economist
geologist
misogynist
monogamist
mythologist
neurologist
oncologist
pathologist
philologist
phrenologist
psychologist

seismologist
synonymist
technologist
theologist
urologist
zoologist

anthropologist
archaeologist
archeologist
cardiologist
dermatologist
Egyptologist
etymologist
gynecologist
hematologist
ideologist
immunologist
lexicologist
phraseologist
physiologist
radiologist
sociologist
toxicologist

bacteriologist
meteorologist
paleontologist

anesthesiologist
epidemiologist

OLOGY (see OMETRY)
OLOMON (see OCCASIN)
OLON (see OTION)
OLONY (see OMETRY)
OLOR 1 (see USTER 1)
OLOR 2 (see OVER 1)
OLORING (see OVERING)
OLORLESS (see UDDERLESS)
OLPHIN (see OTTEN)
OLSEN (see OTION)
OLSTER (see OVER 1)
OLSTERY (see OCALLY)
OLT (see OAT)
OLTA (see OLA)
OLTAGE (see OSES)
OLTEN (see OTION)
OLTER (see OVER 1)
OLTING (see OWING 1)
OLTRON (see ORON)

OLUMN (see OTTEN)
OLVABLE (see OGICAL)
OLVE (see AULT)
OLVER (see ALTER)
OLVING (see ALLING)
OLVO (see OLO)
OLY 1 (see ONY)
OLY 2 (see OLLY 1)
OM 1 (see ON 1)
OM 2 (see UN)
OM 3 (see OOM)
OMA (see OLA)
OMACY (see OCALLY)
OMAGE (see OTIC)
OMAL (see OSAL)
OMALY (see OMETRY)

OMAN 1

cushion
tooken
woman
wooden
woolen

airwoman
Catwoman
chairwoman
newswoman
pincushion
saleswoman
spacewoman
spokeswoman
sportswoman
stateswoman

alderwoman
businesswoman
clergywoman
congresswoman
councilwoman
countrywoman
gentlewoman
I Am Woman
patrolwoman
police woman
Pretty Woman
whoopee cushion
Wonder Woman

OMAN 2 (see OTION)
OMAS (see OLISH)
OMB 1 (see ON 1)
OMB 2 (see ONE 1)
OMB 3 (see OOM)
OMBABLE (see OOTABLE)
OMBED (see OBED)
OMBER 1 (see OLLAR)
OMBER 2 (see OVER 1)
OMBER 3 (see ONOR 1)
OMBIE (see AWNY)
OMBING 1 (see ALLING)
OMBING 2 (see OWING 1)
OMBING 3 (see UTING 1)
OMBO (see ONDO)
OMBRE (see ANCE 3)
OME 1 (see ONE 1)
OME 2 (see UN)
OMED (see OBED)
OMEDIES (see OLOGIES)
OMEDY (see OMETRY)
OMELET (see ONIC)
OMELY (see ONY)
OMEN 1 (see OTION)
OMEN 2 (see ITION)
OMENAL (see OGICAL)
OMENT (see ONEMENT)
OMEO (see OLIO)
OMER 1 (see UMMER)
OMER 2 (see OVER 1)

OMERATE

chocolate
consulate
document
moderate
monument
obulate
opposite
osselet

conglobulate
conglomerate
immoderate
proconsulate

discombobulate

OMERY (see UTTERY)
OMET (see ONIC)

OMETER (see OGRAPHER)

OMETRY

awesomely
awkwardly
bawdily
blossomy
bobbery
bodily
bossily
botany
broccoli
cautiously
choppily
cloggily
cockily
colony
comedy
commonly
Conakry
constantly
cottony
daughterly
docilely
fatherly
floppily
foggily
foxily
gaudily
gawkily
glossary
glossily
gossipy
haughtily
hobbitry
homily
hominy
honesty
jobbery
jollity
lottery
naughtily
nobbily
novelty
novity
oddity
odyssey
paucity

pockily
policy
polity
possibly
pottery
poverty
probably
prodigy
pronity
quality
quantity
raucity
robbery
rockily
saucily
shoddily
slobbery
sloppily
snobbery
snobbily
snottily
sodomy
soggily
soppily
spottily
tossily
tottery
vomity
watery

agronomy
anomaly
anthology
apology
apostasy
apostrophe
astrology
astronomy
atrocity
autocracy
autonomy
biography
biology
bureaucracy
camaraderie
cartography
chronology
commodity
cosmography
cosmology

cryptography
debauchery
democracy
demography
dichotomy
ecology
economy
equality
ferocity
frivolity
gastrology
gastronomy
gemology
geodesy
geography
geology
geometry
graphology
high-quality
histology
hypocrisy
imbonity
lithography
lobotomy
mahogany
misogyny
monocracy
monogamy
monopoly
monotony
monstrosity
mythology
neurology
oncology
ontology
orthography
pathology
penology
philology
philosophy
phonology
photography
photology
phrenology
plutocracy
pomposity
pornography
precocity
proctology
psychology

scatology
seismology
stenography
synonymy
tautology
taxonomy
technocracy
technology
theocracy
theology
timocracy
topography
toxology
typography
urology
velocity
venosity
verbosity
vinosity
viscosity
zoology

animosity
anthropology
archeology
aristocracy
bibliography
cardiology
choreography
climatology
cosmetology
criminology
curiosity
dermatology
Deuteronomy
discommodity
Egyptology
entomology
eschatology
etymology
generosity
grandiosity
gynecology
hematology
hepatology
highway robbery
ichthyology
ideology
immunology
incommodity

inequality
lexicography
lexicology
luminosity
mediocracy
mediocrity
oceanography
ophthalmology
ornithology
pantheology
pharmacology
phraseology
physiography
physiology
piscatology
preciosity
radiology
reciprocity
scientology
sociology
terminology
toxicology
tracheotomy
virtuosity

autobiography
bacteriology
cinematography
endocrinology
impetuosity
kinesiology
meteorology
microbiology
paleontology
psychopathology
universology

anesthesiology
epidemiology

OMEY (see ONY)
OMFIEST (see UMPIEST)
OMFORT (see UMMER)
OMFY (see UNNY)
OMI (see ONY)
OMIAL (see OVIAL)
OMIC 1 (see ONIC)
OMIC 2 (see ONEMENT)
OMICA (see ONICA)
OMICAL (see OGICAL)
OMIE (see ONY)

OMILIES (see OLOGIES)
OMILY (see OMETRY)
OMINAL (see OGICAL)
OMINANCE (see OMINENCE)
OMINANT (see ONSONANT)
OMINATE (see OPULATE)
OMINATION (see OPERATION)
OMINDATE (see OPULATE)

OMINENCE

audience
competence
complements
compliments
confidence
documents
dominance
flocculence
opulence
oxidants
prominence
providence
tolerance

abominance
incompetence
predominance

antioxidants
omnicompetence
vote of confidence

OMINENT (see ONSONANT)

OMING 1

blunting
brunching
bumming
bumping
bunching
bunking
bunting
chumming
clumping
clunking
coming
crumpling

crunching
cunning
drumming
dumping
dumpling
dunking
dunning
flunking
fronting
funding
grumping
grunting
gumming
gunning
humming
humping
hunching
hunting
jumping
junking
lumping
lunching
lunging
munching
numbing
plumbing
plumping
plunging
plunking
pumping
punching
punning
punting
rumpling
running
scrunching
shunning
shunting
slumming
slumping
strumming
stumping
stunning
summing
sunning
thumbing
thumping
trumping
umping

affronting
becoming
benumbing
broad jumping
confronting
debunking
expunging
forthcoming
foxhunting
frontrunning
high jumping
homecoming
keypunching
manhunting
no dumping
nose-thumbing
oncoming
shortcoming
slam-dunking
succumbing
uncrumpling
witch hunting

apple dumpling
chicken dumpling
counterpunching
off and running
overcoming
second coming
treasure hunting
triple jumping
unbecoming
up and coming

OMING 2 (see OWING 1)
OMINIES (see OLOGIES)
OMINOUS (see OGGIEST)
OMINY (see OMETRY)
OMISE (see OLISH)
OMISER (see OGRAPHER)
OMISING (see OLISHING)
OMIT (see ONIC)
OMITY (see OMETRY)
OMMA (see ONNA)
OMMAGE (see OTIC)
OMMELED (see OBBLED)
OMMET (see ONIC)
OMMIE (see AWNY)
OMMING (see ALLING)
OMMON (see OTTEN)
OMMONER (see OGRAPHER)

OMMONLY (see OMETRY)
OMMY (see AWNY)
OMNIA (see AFIA)
OMNIBUS (see OGGIEST)
OMO (see OLO)
OMP (see ONT 2)

OMPANY

bumpily
company
dumpily
frumpily
grumpily
hungrily
jumpily
lumpily

accompany
curmudgeonly
discompany
repugnantly
Three's Company

intercompany
reaccompany

Electric Company

OMPASS (see UNLESS)
OMPER (see OLLAR)
OMPETENCE (see OMINENCE)
OMPETENT (see ONSONANT)
OMPING (see ONNING)
OMPLEMENTS (see OMINENCE)
OMPLEX (see OBJECT)
OMPLICE (see OLISH)
OMPLIMENTS (see OMINENCE)
OMPOUS (see OLISH)
OMPT (see ONT 2)
OMPTED (see OLID)
OMPTER (see ONOR 1)
OMPTING (see ONNING)
OMPTLY (see AWNY)
OMPTNESS (see OLISH)
OMSKY (see ONY)

ON 1

balm
blond
blonde
bomb
bond
bong
brawn
bronze
calm
con
dawn
don
dong
drawn
fawn
fond
Fong
Fonz
frond
g'wan
glom
gone
gong
Guam
John
Kahn
lawn
long
mom
on
palm
pawn
pond
prawn
prom
prong
psalm
qualm
Ron
song
spawn
strong
swan
thong
throng
Tom
tong
Vaughn

wan
wand
Wong
wrong
yawn
yon

A-bomb
abscond
add on
along
Antoine
bail bond
Bataan
baton
becalm
begone
belong
Bernbaum
beyond
bon-bon
bring on
catch on
chiffon
clip-on
come on
count on
coupon
daylong
Dear John
despond
ding-dong
diphthong
doggone
Don Juan
dot-com
dream on
embalm
ex-con
fire bomb
fishpond
folk song
furlong
go on
go wrong
gourmand
hands-on
hang on
headlong
headstrong

hereon
Hong Kong
hourlong
ice tong
Islam
James Bond
junk bond
keep calm
King Kong
LeBron
lifelong
long gone
love song
mahjongg
mesdames
Milan
millpond
move on
napalm
noncom
oblong
odds-on
pecan
ping-pong
pompom
predawn
prolong
proton
respond
right on
run-on
salon
San Juan
sarong
singsong
sitcom
so long
Sorbonne
Szechwan
Taiwan
Tehran
theme song
time bomb
tom-tom
torch song
triphthong
Tucson
turn on
two-prong
undrawn

upon
walk-on
wigwam
withdrawn
won ton
yearlong
Yukon
Yvonne

all along
all day long
all night long
Amazon
Audubon
autobahn
Avalon
Babylon
before long
billabong
bump along
cabochon
call upon
carillon
carry on
Cheech and Chong
Chipmunks Song
come along
come on strong
correspond
crack of dawn
decathlon
Donkey Kong
drinking song
early on
echelon
Elton John
fall back on
Genghis Khan
get along
get it on
go along
Goldie Hawn
grease your palm
Grey Poupon
hair salon
halcyon
Hans and Franz
hereupon
hexagon
hop-a-long

in the wrong
inchy palm
intercom
keep tabs on
Kublai Khan
Lebanon
leprechaun
lexicon
magic wand
mamasan
MazatlAn
move along
Neil Armstrong
octagon
off and on
on and on
overdrawn
overlong
papasan
parmesan
parthenon
peeping Tom
pentagon
Pokemon
polygon
Prairie Dawn
pro and con
right or wrong
run along
Sarah Vaughan
savings bond
senior prom
sing-along
Stretch Armstrong
string along
supermom
tagalong
take-along
talkathon
Tannenbaum
thereupon
tie one on
undergone
vagabond
Vietcong
Vietnam
walkathon
whereupon

atomic bomb
automaton
beauty salon
depend upon
grease someone's palm
keep an eye on
nuclear bomb
overly fond
phenomenon
Saskatchewan
strawberry blonde
Treasury bond
Twenty-third Psalm

Louis Farrakhan

Olivia Newton-John

ON 2 (see UN)
ON 3 (see ONE 1)
ON'T (see OBED)
ONA 1 (see OLA)
ONA 2 (see ONNA)
ONAGE 1 (see OD)
ONAGE 2 (see OTIC)
ONAH (see OLA)
ONAKRY (see OMETRY)
ONAL (see OSAL)
ONALD (see OBBLED)
ONALLY (see OCALLY)
ONAN (see OTION)
ONAS (see OSES)
ONCE 1 (see UMP)
ONCE 2 (see ANCE 3)
ONCENTRATION (see OPERATION)
ONCEPT (see OBJECT)
ONCHO (see ONDO)
ONCO (see ONDO)
OND (see ON 1)
ONDA (see ONNA)
ONDAGE (see OTIC)
ONDE (see ON 1)
ONDEAU (see ONDO)
ONDED (see OLID)
ONDER 1 (see ONOR 1)
ONDER 2 (see UMMER)

ONDERED

conjured
conquered

honored
onward
pondered
sponsored
squandered
wandered

cosponsored
dishonored
reconquered
unconquered
unhonored

ONDERING 1 (see ANDERING 2)
ONDERING 2 (see OVERING)
ONDEROUS (see UNLESS)
ONDIE (see AWNY)
ONDING (see ONNING)
ONDLE (see OTTLE)
ONDLER (see ONOR 1)
ONDLING (see OBBLING)
ONDLY (see AWNY)

ONDO

bongo
Bono
bronco
combo
condo
Congo
Gonzo
honcho
mambo
mondo
mono
poncho
rondeau
Rondo
Sanyo

cilantro
sforzando

Alejandro
Belgian Congo
chimichango

ONDOM (see OTTEN)
ONDON (see UNION 2)
ONDOR (see ONOR 1)

ONE 1

blown
bone
chrome
clone
comb
cone
dome
drone
flown
foam
gnome
groan
grown
home
hone
Joan
known
loam
loan
lone
moan
mown
own
phone
poem
pome
pone
prone
roam
roan
Rome
scone
sewn
shone
shown
Sloan
sown
stone
throne
thrown
tome
tone
zone

afoam
alone
at home
atone

backbone
bemoan
birthstone
bloodstone
blouson
breastbone
brimstone
brownstone
car loan
car phone
cellphone
cheekbone
cologne
condone
curbstone
cyclone
debone
dethrone
dial tone
disown
down home
earphone
end zone
enthrone
Firestone
fish bone
flagstone
flintstone
freestone
full-blown
full-grown
gallstone
gemstone
grindstone
hailstone
half-grown
headphone
headstone
high tone
hits home
home loan
homegrown
hormone
hot comb
ingrown
intone
iphone
jawbone
keystone
limestone

Malone
milestone
millstone
moonstone
outshone
ozone
pay phone
pine cone
postpone
Ramon
raw bone
rest home
rhinestone
sandstone
sea foam
shinbone
Simone
Sno-Kone
soupbone
Stockholm
strike zone
syndrome
T-bone
tailbone
time zone
tombstone
touch-tone
touchstone
trombone
unknown
unsewn
unshown
unsown
war zone
well known
whalebone
wishbone

Al Capone
all alone
anklebone
Astrodome
baritone
Blarney stone
broken home
buffer zone
carved in stone
catacomb
champignon
chaperone

cherrystone
chromosome
cobblestone
collarbone
combat zone
corazon
cornerstone
cortisone
crazy bone
Dictaphone
doggie bone
doubledome
fine-tooth comb
foster home
Fred Flintstone
frigid zone
funny bone
gastronome
grunt and groan
herringbone
hippodrome
hold your own
home sweet home
honeycomb
ice cream cone
kidney stone
knucklebone
Larry Holmes
lazybone
little known
loading zone
megaphone
methadone
metronome
microphone
moan and groan
mobile home
model home
monochrome
monotone
neutral zone
nursing home
on your own
overblown
overgrown
overthrown
overtone
palindrome
pleasure dome
rolling stone

saxophone
shaving foam
Sherlock Holmes
silicone
sousaphone
stand alone
stay-at-home
stepping-stone
Superdome
taxi zone
Teapot Dome
telephone
torrid zone
twilight zone
unbeknown
undertone
xylophone
Yellowstone

accident-prone
cast the first stone
cellular phone
Dom Perignon
extension phone
fire and brimstone
go it alone
hospital zone
mind of your own
no parking zone
no place like home
savings and loan
Temperate Zone
testosterone
to each his own
Wilma Flinstone
X chromosome
Y chromosome

come into your own
don't try this at home
dont try this at home
Moet & Chandon
Ponce de Leon
Sylvester Stallone

let well enough alone

ONE 2 (see UN)
ONE 3 (see ON 1)
ONE 4 (see ONY)
ONED (see OBED)

ONEL (see URTLE)
ONELY (see ONY)

ONEMENT

moment
phobic
poet
potent
quotient
rodent
stoic
Tobit

achromic
aerobic
atonement
bemoanment
component
condonement
dethronement
enthronement
exponent
heroic
opponent
postponement
proponent

homophobic

Day of Atonement

ONENESS (see UNLESS)
ONENT (see ONEMENT)
ONEOUS (see ODIOUS)
ONER 1 (see OVER 1)
ONER 2 (see ONOR 1)
ONEST (see OLISH)
ONESTY (see OMETRY)
ONEY 1 (see UNNY)
ONEY 2 (see ONY)
ONFIDENCE (see OMINENCE)
ONFIDENT (see ONSONANT)
ONG 1 (see ON 1)
ONG 2 (see UN)
ONGA (see ONNA)
ONGAS (see OLISH)
ONGE (see UN)
ONGER 1 (see UMMER)
ONGER 2 (see ONOR 1)

ONGERING (see OVERING)
ONGG (see ON 1)
ONGING (see OCKING)
ONGLY (see AWNY)
ONGO (see ONDO)
ONGOUS (see UNLESS)
ONGREGATE (see OPULATE)
ONGREGATION (see OPERATION)
ONGRESS (see OLISH)
ONGSTRESS (see AWLESS)
ONGUE (see UN)
ONGY (see UNNY)
ONHAM (see OTTEN)
ONI (see ONY)
ONIA (see OLA)
ONIAL (see OVIAL)

ONIAN

jovian
opium
podium
sodium

ammonium
Bostonian
Cambodian
colloquium
custodian
draconian
fallopian
jacksonian
jacobian
johnsonian
Mongolian
Napoleon
pavlovian
Smithsonian
utopian
zirconium

amazonian
apollonian
Arizonian
astrologian
Babylonian
Cameronian
Ethiopian
jeffersonian
Nickelodeon

pandemonium
patagonian
washingtonian

ONIC

bonnet
chronic
comet
comic
conic
gauntlet
grommet
omelet
onyx
phonic
sonic
sonnet
tonic
vomit

atomic
biggonnet
bionic
blaphomet
bluebonnet
bubonic
colonic
cordonnet
demonic
dubonnet
euphonic
harmonic
hedonic
iconic
ionic
ironic
islamic
laconic
mahomet
Masonic
mnemonic
moronic
Platonic
sardonic
sunbonnet
symphonic
Teutonic
unbonnet
anatomic

astronomic
catatonic
diatonic
economic
electronic
gin and tonic
Halley's comet
histrionic
isotonic
Panasonic
quadraphonic
stand-up comic
supersonic
telephonic
ultrasonic

Napoleonic
stereophonic

socioeconomic

ONICA

Hanukkah
Monica
optima
swastika
vomica

armonica
erotica
exotica
harmonica
hydromica
japonica
Veronica

amphibiotica
Santa Monica

Francis Ford Coppola

ONICAL (see OGICAL)
ONICLE (see OGICAL)
ONIER (see OKIER)
ONIFER (see OGRAPHER)
ONIKER (see OGRAPHER)
ONING (see OWING 1)
ONIO (see OLIO)
ONION (see UNION 2)

ONIOUS (see ODIOUS)
ONIS (see OLISH)
ONISH (see OLISH)
ONISHING (see OLISHING)
ONITOR (see OGRAPHER)
ONITY (see OMETRY)
ONIUM (see ONIAN)
ONJURE (see ONOR 1)
ONJURED (see ONDERED)
ONJURING (see ANDERING 2)
ONK 1 (see ONT 2)
ONK 2 (see UMP)
ONKA (see ONNA)
ONKER (see ONOR 1)
ONKEY 1 (see UNNY)
ONKEY 2 (see AWNY)
ONKIER (see AWNIER)
ONKIEST (see OGGIEST)
ONKING (see ONNING)
ONKY (see AWNY)
ONLY (see ONY)

ONNA

amah
Brahma
comma
conga
Donna
drama
Fonda
ganja
genre
Ghana
gonna
Hanta
Honda
lama
llama
mama
mantra
momma
Rama
Rhonda
ronda
sauna
Sonya
Tanya
Tonga
Tonka

trauma
Wanda
wanna

Bianka
big mama
Botswana
Chicana
iguana
Jane Fonda
lasagne
liana
Madonna
manana
nirvana
pajama
persona
piranha
Rwanda
Sri Lanka
Uganda

anaconda
baby momma
belladonna
Benihana
Casablanca
cinerama
Dalai Lama
diorama
docudrama
futurama
lingua franca
Maradona
marijuana
melodrama
prima donna
psychodrama
Rosh Hashanah
Tijuana
Willy Wonka
Yokohama

Barack Obama
double entendre

ONNE (see ON 1)
ONNER (see ONOR 1)
ONNET (see ONIC)
ONNIE (see AWNY)
ONNIEST (see OGGIEST)

ONNING

awning
bonding
bonking
bronzing
chomping
comping
conking
conning
daunting
dawning
donning
fawning
flaunting
haunching
haunting
honking
launching
paunching
pawning
pomping
prompting
romping
spawning
staunching
stomping
taunting
tromping
wanting
whomping
yawning
zonking

absconding
responding
unprompting

corresponding

ONNOR (see ONOR 1)
ONNOTATE (see OPULATE)
ONNOTATION (see OPERATION)
ONNY 1 (see AWNY)
ONNY 2 (see UNNY)
ONO 1 (see ONDO)
ONO 2 (see OLO)
ONOCLE (see OGICAL)
ONOMER (see OGRAPHER)
ONOMIES (see OLOGIES)
ONOMIST (see OLOGIST)

ONOMOUS (see OGGIEST)
ONOMY (see OMETRY)
ONOPIN (see OCCASIN)

ONOR 1

blonder
bonder
condor
conger
conjure
conker
conner
conquer
dawner
fawner
fonder
fondler
goner
honker
honor
launder
longer
monster
pawner
ponder
prompter
somber
spawner
sponsor
squander
stronger
wander
wanner
yawner
yonder

dishonor
O'Connor
responder

Boogiemonster
Cookie Monster
corresponder
debt of honor
field of honor
guest of honor
Loch Ness Monster
maid of honor
marathoner

on my honor
over yonder
place of honor
point of honor
roll of honor
wild blue yonder
word of honor

divide and conquer
matron of honor
Medal of Honor

ONOR 2 (see OVER 1)
ONORED (see ONDERED)
ONORING (see ANDERING 2)
ONQUER (see ONOR 1)
ONQUERED (see ONDERED)
ONQUERING (see ANDERING 2)
ONSCIOUS (see OLISH)
ONSE (see ONT 2)
ONSEN (see OTTEN)
ONSIN (see OTTEN)

ONSONANT

competent
confident
consonant
continent
dominant
nonsonant
opulent
prominent

inconsonant
inopulent
predominant
unconsonant

overprominent

ONSOR (see ONOR 1)
ONSORED (see ONDERED)
ONSORING (see ANDERING 2)
ONSTANT (see OTTEN)
ONSTANTLY (see OMETRY)
ONSTER (see ONOR 1)
ONSTIPATION (see OPERATION)
ONSULATE (see OMERATE)
ONSUMMATE (see OPULATE)

ONSUMMATION (see OPERATION)
ONT 1 (see UMP)

ONT 2

bonk
chomp
comp
conk
daunt
flaunt
font
gaunt
haunch
haunt
honk
jaunt
konk
launch
paunch
pomp
prompt
romp
staunch
stomp
swamp
taunt
tromp
want
whomp
wonk
wont
zonk

bouffant
detente
DuPont
piquant
response
savant
Vermont

ambiance
commandant
confidante
debutante
dilettante
no response
nonchalance
nonchalant

renaissance
restaurant

insouciance

conditioned response
piece de resistance

ONTABLE (see USTABLE)
ONTAL (see UMBLE)
ONTE (see AWNY)
ONTER (see UMMER)
ONTEXT (see OBJECT)
ONTH (see UMP)
ONTHLY (see UNNY)
ONTINENT (see ONSONANT)
ONTING (see OMING 1)
ONTO (see OTTO 1)
ONUMENT (see OMERATE)
ONUS (see OSES)
ONVEX (see OBJECT)
ONWARD (see ONDERED)

ONY

bloaty
bogey
bony
bowie
brodie
Chloe
closely
Cody
Coney
cony
cozy
crony
Dodie
dogie
Dopey
doty
doughy
drolly
floaty
foamy
fogey
Foley
folksy
ghostly
glowy

goalie
Goldie
groany
gropey
grossly
hoagie
hokey
holey
holy
homely
homey
homie
Hopi
Joey
Josie
Kobe
lonely
moany
moldy
mopey
mosey
mostly
nobly
nosy
oakley
OD
ogee
Okie
oldie
only
phony
poky
pony
posy
roadie
Rosie
rosy
shoaly
shogi
showy
slopey
slowly
smoky
snowy
soapy
Sofie
solely
Sony
Sophie
stogey

stony
throaty
toady
toasty
Toby
toesy
Tony
trophy
wholly
Yogi

Adobe
anchovy
baloney
bologna
cannoli
Capote
coyote
emoji
enrollee
jocosely
Marconi
morosely
Muskogee
Naomi
Noam Chomsky
not only
old fogey
Old Smokey
parolee
peyote
Quixote
remotely
Shoshone
spumoni
tea cozy
tortoni
unholy
verbosely

acrimony
alimony
cannelloni
ceremony
David Bowie
double bogey
golden oldie
guacamole
hokey-pokey
holy moly

in name only
Jeff Spicoli
Karaoke
macaroni
matrimony
minestrone
okey dokey
one and only
palimony
parsimony
patrimony
pepperoni
provolone
ravioli
Rice-A-Roni
rigatoni
roly-poly
sad and lonely
sanctimony
Shetland pony
testimony

My Little Pony
phony-baloney
zabaglione

holy matrimony
Leni Zavaroni
ring around the rosy
Vince Lombardi Trophy

Oscar Mayer Bologna

ONYA (see ONNA)
ONYMIST (see OLOGIST)
ONYMOUS (see OGGIEST)
ONYMY (see OMETRY)
ONYX (see ONIC)
ONZ (see ON 1)
ONZALEZ (see OLISH)
ONZE (see ON 1)
ONZING (see ONNING)
ONZO (see ONDO)
OO (see EW 1)
OOABLE (see OOTABLE)
OOB (see OOM)
OOBER (see UTER)
OOBIE (see UTY)
OOBOO (see ULU)
OOBY (see UTY)
OOCH 1 (see UTE)

OOCH 2 (see OAT)
OOCHEE (see UTY)
OOCHER (see UTER)
OOCHES (see OSES)
OOCHIE (see UTY)
OOCHING (see UTING 1)
OOCHY (see UTY)

OOD 1

could
good
hood
should
stood
wood
would

boyhood
childhood
deadwood
do-good
dogwood
driftwood
falsehood
firewood
for good
girlhood
hardwood
knighthood
make good
manhood
milkwood
no-good
plywood
priesthood
rainhood
redwood
sainthood
saw wood
Westwood
wildwood
withstood

adulthood
babyhood
bachelorhood
brotherhood
Clint Eastwood
cottonwood

Dollywood
fatherhood
Hollywood
knock on wood
likelihood
livelihood
maidenhood
motherhood
nationhood
neighborhood
not so good
parenthood
pretty good
Robin Hood
sisterhood
understood
widowhood
womanhood

misunderstood
Planned Parenthood
Red Riding Hood
second childhood
so far so good
unlikelihood

finger-licking good

Mister Rogers Neighborhood

OOD 2 (see OOM)
OOD 3 (see UG)
OODABLE (see USTABLE)
OODED (see USTED)
OODEN (see OMAN 1)
OODER (see USTER 1)
OODIE 1 (see OOGIE)
OODIE 2 (see UTY)
OODILY (see UITY 1)
OODINESS (see OOKINESS)
OODING (see USTING)

OODLE

boodle
brumal
brutal
bugle
croupal
crucial

doodle
drupal
dueful
dumal
duple
feudal
frugal
fruitful
fugal
futile
glumal
Google
googol
musal
neutral
noodle
poodle
pupal
pupil
ruble
rueful
ruthful
scruple
sleuthful
streusel
strudel
toothful
tootle
truthful
tubal
tupal
udal
useful
utile
youthful

abuseful
accusal
approval
bamboozle
caboodle
canoodle
communal
fiducial
French poodle
induceful
inutile
jejunal
lacunal
limp noodle

MacDougal
occlusal
octuple
paludal
perusal
quadruple
quintuple
rebukal
rebukeful
recruital
refusal
refutal
removal
reperusal
reproval
septuple
sextuple
subduple
tribunal
uncouthful
untruthful
whangdoodle

apple strudel
Daily Bugle
dipsy-doodle
disapproval
on approval
semitruthful
Snickerdoodle
Toaster Strudel
use one 's noodle
Yankee Doodle

kit and caboodle
limp as a noodle

OODLESS (see UTENESS)

OODLING

boodling
doodling
foozling
googling
noodling
scrupling
skrupling
tootling

bamboozling
canoodling
quadrupling

OODOO (see ULU)
OODY 1 (see UTY)
OODY 2 (see OOGIE)
OODY 3 (see UDDY)
OOER (see EWER 1)
OOEY (see EWY)
OOF 1 (see UTE)
OOF 2 (see OOK 1)
OOFA (see UNA)
OOFINESS (see OOKINESS)
OOFING (see UTING 1)
OOFLESS (see UTENESS)
OOFNESS (see UTENESS)
OOFY (see UTY)
OOGA (see UNA)
OOGE (see OOM)
OOGER (see OOKER)

OOGIE

boogie
bookie
bully
bushy
cookie
cushy
fully
goodie
hoodie
hooky
looky
noogie
nookie
nooky
pulley
pushy
pussy
rookie
Snooki
sooty
tushie
whoopee
woody
wookie
wussy

play hooky
Sam Goody
tough cookie

boogie-woogie
butter cookie
fortune cookie
shortbread cookie
sugar cookie

chocolate chip cookie
Electric Boogie
Oreo cookie

oatmeal raisin cookie
peanut butter cookie

OOGING (see UTING 1)
OOGLE (see OODLE)
OOGLING (see OODLING)
OOGOL (see OODLE)
OOH (see EW 1)
OOHING (see UING)
OOHOO (see ULU)
OOING (see UING)

OOK 1

book
brook
bush
butch
cook
crook
foot
hoof
hook
look
mush
nook
push
puss
put
rook
schnook
schuss
shook
shoosh
shush
snook
soot

took
tush
wuss

afoot
ambush
barefoot
betook
Bigfoot
Blackfoot
blue book
caput
casebook
checkbook
Chinook
closed book
clubfoot
cookbook
crow's foot
datebook
Facebook
fishhook
flatfoot
forsook
fry cook
George Bush
guidebook
handbook
hard-put
hotfoot
input
kaput
lead foot
light foot
logbook
matchbook
mistook
new look
notebook
outlook
output
partook
passbook
retook
rosebush
scrapbook
shotput
six foot
skyhook
slewfoot
songbook

sourpuss
square foot
stay put
textbook
unhook
webfoot

athlete's foot
backward look
by the book
Captain Cook
comic book
cozy nook
crack a book
dirty look
donnybrook
drizzlepuss
gingerroot
glamourpuss
gourmet cook
hand and foot
Jungle Book
knowing look
octopus
off the hook
open book
overcook
overlook
overtook
picklepuss
platypus
pocketbook
pussyfoot
rabbit's foot
small-time crook
Snagglepuss
tenderfoot
The Good Book
underfoot
undertook

coloring book
faraway look
gobble-de-gook
library book
little black book
short-order cook
telephone book

beat around the bush

OOK 2 (see UTE)
OOKA (see UNA)
OOKABLE (see OOTABLE)
OOKED 1 (see USHED)
OOKED 2 (see ULLET 1)
OOKEN (see OMAN 1)

OOKER

booger
booker
cooker
hooker
looker
musher
pusher
rooker
shoosher
shusher
snooker
sugar
Worcester

ambusher
dope pusher
good-looker
onlooker
unhooker

advance booker
backward looker
forward looker
overlooker
pressure cooker

OOKIE (see OOGIE)

OOKINESS

choosiness
droopiness
gloominess
goofiness
kookiness
looniness
moodiness
roominess
snootiness
spookiness

OOKING 1

booking
cooking
footing
hooking
looking
mushing
pudding
pushing
putting
rooking
shooshing
shushing
squooshing
swooshing
whooshing
wooshing

ambushing
fry-cooking
good-looking
unhooking
what's cooking?

advance booking
backward looking
forward looking
gourmet cooking
hasty pudding
overcooking
overlooking
pussyfooting
Yorkshire pudding

OOKING 2 (see UTING 1)
OOKLET (see ULLET 1)
OOKY 1 (see OOGIE)
OOKY 2 (see UTY)

OOL 1

cool
drool
fool
ghoul
mule
pool
pule
rule

school
spool
stool
tool
who'll
you'll
yule

air-cool
barstool
carpool
cesspool
damfool
gag rule
granule
high school
home rule
house rule
Kabul
law school
mob rule
module
night school
nodule
O'Toole
packmule
prep school
preschool
retool
sliderule
tidepool
toadstool
whirlpool

April fool
as a rule
blow your cool
boarding school
dirty pool
football pool
golden rule
Istanbul
Liverpool
lose your cool
minuscule
molecule
overrule
ridicule
Sunday school
supercool

swimming pool
traffic school
unit rule

finishing school
nobody's fool
nursery school
Princess Toadstool
too cool for school

I pitty the fool
majority rule

exception to the rule

OOL 2 (see ULL 1)
OOLABLE (see OOTABLE)
OOLANT (see UTION)
OOLANTS (see UDENCE)
OOLE (see OOL 1)
OOLEN (see OMAN 1)

OOLER

cooler
crueler
drooler
dueler
fooler
Mueller
pooler
ruler
schooler
stooler
tooler

bejeweler
preschooler
retooler
wine cooler

Ferris Bueller
overruler
water cooler

OOLERY (see UITY 1)
OOLEY (see UTY)
OOLIE (see UTY)

OOLING

cooling
drooling
fooling
fueling
pooling
puling
ruling
tooling

carpooling
retooling

overruling
ridiculing

OOLISH (see EWISH)
OOLLY (see UTY)
OOLY (see UTY)

OOM

bloom
boob
boom
boon
brood
broom
croon
crude
cube
doom
dude
dune
feud
flume
food
fume
gloom
goon
groom
groove
huge
June
lewd
loom
loon
lube

mood
moon
move
newb
noob
noon
nude
plume
prove
prude
prune
rheum
rood
room
rouge
rube
rude
rune
Scrooge
shrewd
smooth
snood
soon
soothe
spoon
spume
stooge
strewn
swoon
tomb
tube
tune
vroom
who'd
who've
whom
womb
wound
you'd
you've
zoom

abloom
allude
amove
approve
assume
attune
balloon
ballroom

barroom
bassoon
bedroom
behoove
bestrewn
boardroom
boob tube
boom-boom
bridegroom
buffoon
Calhoun
card room
cartoon
checkroom
cloakroom
cocoon
collude
commune
conclude
consume
costume
courtroom
dark room
delude
deluge
denude
disprove
dog food
dragoon
elude
entomb
etude
exclude
exhume
exude
false move
fast food
festoon
fine-tune
full moon
guest room
half-moon
harpoon
headroom
health food
heirloom
high noon
hit tune
homeroom
ice cube

immune	soup spoon	fortitude
improve	spare room	fuss and fume
impugn	spittoon	gloom and doom
include	stateroom	gratitude
intrude	storeroom	greasy spoon
jejune	subsume	harvest moon
junk food	tack room	honeymoon
Kaboom	taproom	importune
kamoom	tea room	in the groove
Khartoum	teaspoon	in the mood
lagoon	test tube	in the nude
lampoon	too soon	inner tube
leg room	tycoon	interlude
legume	typhoon	ladies' room
make room	Vroom Broom	lassitude
maroon	whiskbroom	latitude
men's room	YouTube	lead balloon
monsoon		locker room
mushroom	afternoon	longitude
Neptune	altitude	Looney Tune
new moon	amplitude	love in bloom
no room	anteroom	macaroon
obtrude	aptitude	magnitude
occlude	attitude	multitude
oppugn	baby boom	Name That Tune
perfume	baby food	nom de plume
plant food	beatitude	on the move
platoon	blue lagoon	opportune
pontoon	breathing room	out of tune
preclude	bride and groom	overstrewn
prelude	Brigadoon	picayune
presume	bust a move	picture tube
protrude	call the tune	platitude
pump room	Cameroon	plenitude
Quaalude	centrifuge	powder room
quadroon	certitude	pretty soon
racoon	change your tune	quietude
Rangoon	come unglued	reassume
rec room	consuetude	rectitude
refuge	crassitude	Rubik's Cube
remove	crescent moon	sanctitude
reprove	croon a tune	servitude
restroom	Daniel Boone	silver spoon
resume	desuetude	smoke-filled room
Saint Jude	disapprove	solitude
saloon	disquietude	sonic boom
seafood	down the tube	standing room
seclude	Dr. Doom	subterfuge
showroom	elbow room	tablespoon
soul food	finger food	trial balloon

turpitude
waiting room
women's room

carry a tune
decrepitude
exactitude
Family Feud
fruit of the loom
high altitude
hot-air balloon
inaptitude
ineptitude
inopportune
Legion of Doom
lower the boom
man in the moon
not in the mood
reception room
solicitude
twelve o'clock noon
vicissitude
Vidal Sassoon

crazy as a loon
Dark Side of the Moon
Meow Mix cat food
moral turpitude
National Lampoon
once in a blue moon
out of gratitude
wrinkled as a prune

Smokin' In the Boy's Room

OOMBA (see UNA)
OOMER (see UMER)
OOMIE (see UTY)
OOMINESS (see OOKINESS)
OOMING (see UTING 1)
OOMLESS (see UTENESS)
OOMPA (see UNA)
OOMY (see UTY)
OON (see OOM)
OONABLE (see OOTABLE)
OONBOW (see UNO)
OONE (see OOM)
OONER (see UMER)

OONEST

bluest
Buddhist
crudest
cruelest
cubist
cutest
flutist
hugest
lewdest
nudist
rudest
shrewdest
soonest

parachutist

OONEY (see UTY)
OONIE (see UTY)
OONINESS (see OOKINESS)
OONING (see UTING 1)
OONISH (see EWISH)
OONLESS (see UTENESS)
OONY (see UTY)
OOP (see UTE)
OOPA (see UNA)
OOPABLE (see OOTABLE)
OOPEE (see OOGIE)
OOPER (see UTER)
OOPERING (see UTORING)
OOPINESS (see OOKINESS)
OOPING (see UTING 1)
OOPLESS (see UTENESS)
OOPOO (see ULU)
OOPY (see UTY)
OOR 1 (see ORE 1)
OOR 2 (see URE 1)
OORAGE (see ORTAGE)
OORER (see URER)
OOREST (see URIST)
OORI (see IRTY)
OORLY (see URELY)
OOROO (see ULU)
OOSABLE (see OOTABLE)

OOSE 1

Bruce
deuce
goose

juice
loose
moose
mousse
noose
puce
sluice
spruce
truce
use
Zeus

abstruse
abuse
adduce
Bull Moose
burnoose
caboose
cayuse
chanteuse
chartreuse
cooked goose
deduce
educe
excuse
footloose
gone goose
hang loose
hangnoose
induce
masseuse
mongoose
no use
obtuse
papoose
produce
profuse
recluse
reduce
seduce
Spruce Goose
traduce
turn loose
unloose
vamoose
wild goose

Ballet Russe
calaboose
call a truce

charlotte russe
child abuse
Christmas goose
cook your goose
Dr. Seuss
Duck Duck Goose
fast and loose
hangman's noose
introduce
lemon juice
mass-produce
Mother Goose
no excuse
on the loose
orange juice
out of use
overuse
reproduce
silly goose
what's the use?

chocolate mousse
have a screw loose
hypotenuse
no earthly use
overproduce
put to good use
vegetable juice

OOSE 2 (see USE 1)
OOSELY (see UTY)
OOSEN (see UTION)
OOSENECK (see OULETTE)
OOSENESS (see UTENESS)
OOSER (see UTER)
OOSEY (see UTY)
OOSH 1 (see OOK 1)
OOSH 2 (see UTE)
OOSHED (see USHED)
OOSHER (see OOKER)
OOSHING (see OOKING)
OOSHY (see UTY)
OOSIER (see UTER)
OOSINESS (see OOKINESS)
OOSING 1 (see UTING 1)
OOSING 2 (see UTING 1)
OOST (see UTE)
OOSTER (see UTER)
OOSTING (see UTING 1)
OOSY 1 (see UTY)
OOSY 2 (see UTY)

OOT 1 (see UTE)
OOT 2 (see OOK 1)

OOTABLE

beautiful
brewable
bruisable
chewable
choosable
coolable
coopable
croonable
croupable
crucible
cruisable
cubicle
cuticle
doable
droolable
droopable
dukable
dutiful
feudable
foolable
fuelable
funeral
fusable
goopable
groovable
groupable
hoopable
hootable
loopable
lootable
losable
movable
musical
mutable
nukable
poolable
poopable
provable
prunable
pukable
rulable
schoolable
scoopable
screwable
shootable

sloopable
snoopable
soupable
spookable
spoolable
spoonable
stoopable
suable
suitable
swoonable
swoopable
toolable
tootable
troopable
tunable
usable
usual
viewable

abusable
accruable
accusable
air-coolable
alludable
amusable
approvable
assumable
attunable
balloonable
carpoolable
cartoonable
communable
commutable
computable
concludable
confusable
construable
consumable
deducible
defusable
deludable
delusional
denudable
diffusable
dilutable
disprovable
disputable
effusable
ensuable
entombable

eschewable
excludable
exclusional
excusable
exhumable
exudable
fine-tunable
granulable
harpoonable
immovable
immunable
immutable
improvable
impugnable
imputable
includable
inducible
infusible
inscrutable
intrudable
lampoonable
maroonable
modulable
perfumable
permutable
perusable
pollutable
precludable
presumable
producible
protrudable
pursuable
pursuitable
rebukable
recoupable
recruitable
redoable
reducible
refusable
refutable
regroupable
removable
renewable
reprovable
resumable
retoolable
reusable
salutable
secludable
seducible

shampooable
subduable
subsumable
teaspoonable
tidepoolable
transfusible
transmutable
undoable
unscrewable
unsuitable
unusable
unusual
uprootable
whirlpoolable

April foolable
Broadway musical
constitutional
convolutable
distributional
evolutional
executable
High School Musical
hula hoopable
importunable
indisputable
inexcusable
institutional
introducible
irreducible
mass-producible
opportunable
overrulable
pharmaceutical
prosecutable
reassumable
reproducible
ridiculable
substitutable
therapeutical
unassumable
unconsumable
undilutable

electrocutable
reconstitutable

OOTCHY (see UTY)
OOTED (see UTED)
OOTER (see UTER)

OOTH 1

booth
couth
Ruth
sleuth
sooth
tooth
truth
youth

Babe Ruth
bucktooth
eyetooth
false tooth
forsooth
half-truth
phone booth
sawtooth
shark's tooth
sweet tooth
toll booth
uncouth
untruth
vermouth
whole truth

baby tooth
Dr. Ruth
gospel truth
kissing booth
naked truth
polling booth
sabertooth
snaggletooth
supersleuth
voting booth
wisdom tooth

fountain of youth
moment of truth
projection booth
telephone booth

nothing but the truth

OOTH 2 (see OOM)
OOTHE (see OOM)
OOTHER (see UTER)
OOTHFUL (see OODLE)
OOTHIE (see UTY)

OOTHING (see UTING 1)
OOTHLY (see UTY)
OOTHNESS (see UTENESS)
OOTIE (see UTY)
OOTILY (see UITY 1)
OOTINESS (see OOKINESS)
OOTING 1 (see UTING 1)
OOTING 2 (see OOKING)
OOTLE (see OODLE)
OOTLING (see OODLING)
OOTY 1 (see UTY)
OOTY 2 (see OOGIE)
OOVABLE (see OOTABLE)
OOVE (see OOM)
OOVER (see UTER)
OOVING (see UTING 1)
OOVY (see UTY)
OOZA (see UNA)
OOZE (see USE 1)
OOZER (see UTER)
OOZING (see UTING 1)
OOZLE (see OODLE)
OOZLING (see OODLING)
OOZY (see UTY)
OP (see OT)
OPAL (see OSAL)
OPANT (see ONEMENT)
OPE (see OAT)
OPEFUL (see OSAL)
OPEFULLY (see OCALLY)
OPELESS (see OSES)
OPELESSLY (see OCALLY)
OPEN (see OTION)
OPENLY (see OCALLY)
OPER 1 (see OVER 1)
OPER 2 (see OLLAR)
OPERA (see ADA 1)
OPERATE (see OPULATE)

OPERATION

automation
concentration
congregation
connotation
constipation
consummation
copulation
domination
flocculation
nomination

occupation
omination
operation
oscillation
ovulation
oxidation
population
properation

abomination
agnomination
annomination
cooperation
deconcentration
denomination
deoxidation
depopulation
disoccupation
disoxidation
improperation
inoccupation
inoperation
peroxidation
predomination
prenomination
preoccupation
renomination
reoccupation
repopulation

noncooperation
overpopulation
retrocopulation

creative constipation

OPERATIVE (see OSITIVE)
OPEY (see ONY)
OPF (see OFF)
OPHER (see OVER 1)
OPHET (see OCKET)
OPHIC (see OTIC)
OPHIE (see ONY)
OPHY (see ONY)
OPI (see ONY)
OPIA (see OLIA)
OPIAL (see OVIAL)
OPIAN (see ONIAN)
OPIC (see OTIC)
OPICAL (see OGICAL)
OPIER 1 (see OKIER)

OPIER 2 (see OGGIER)
OPILY (see OCALLY)
OPING (see OWING 1)
OPIUM (see ONIAN)
OPLESS (see OLISH)
OPLET (see OCKET)
OPNESS (see OLISH)
OPO (see OLO)
OPOLIES (see OLOGIES)
OPOLIS (see OGGIEST)
OPOLY (see OMETRY)
OPPA (see ADA 1)
OPPABLE (see OGICAL)
OPPAGE (see OTIC)
OPPER (see OLLAR)
OPPERED (see OFFERED)
OPPET (see OCKET)
OPPIED (see OLLIED)
OPPIER (see OGGIER)
OPPIEST (see OGGIEST)
OPPILY (see OMETRY)
OPPINESS (see OCKINESS)
OPPING (see OCKING)
OPPLE (see OTTLE)
OPPLED (see OBBLED)
OPPLER (see OBBLER)
OPPOLA (see ONICA)
OPPOSITE (see OMERATE)
OPPY (see OCKEY)
OPRAH (see OLA)
OPRY (see OCKEY)
OPSIS (see OLISH)
OPSY (see OCKEY)
OPT (see OT)
OPTER (see OLLAR)
OPTIC (see OTIC)
OPTICAL (see OGICAL)
OPTIMA (see ONICA)
OPTIMAL (see OGICAL)
OPTING (see OCKING)
OPTION (see OTTEN)
OPTIONAL (see OGICAL)
OPULACE (see OGGIEST)
OPULAR (see OGRAPHER)

OPULATE

automate
brominate
congregate
connotate

consummate
copulate
dominate
flocculate
nominate
ominate
operate
oscillate
ovulate
oxidate
populate
properate

abominate
agnominate
annominate
cooperate
denominate
deoxidate
depopulate
disoxidate
inconsummate
innominate
inovulate
predominate
preomindate
renominate
repopulate
suroxidate
unconsummate

overpopulate

OPULATION (see OPERATION)
OPULENCE (see OMINENCE)
OPULENT (see ONSONANT)
OPY (see OCKEY)
OQUE (see OAT)
OQUIA (see OLIA)
OQUIAL (see OVIAL)
OQUIALLY (see OCALLY)
OQUIUM (see ONIAN)
OR (see ORE 1)

ORA

aura
Cora
Dora
flora

hora
Laura
Nora
Torah

angora
Aurora
begorra
fedora
menorah
Pandora
senora
Sonora

Bora Bora
Isadora

Sodom and Gomorrah

ORABLE (see ORTABLE)
ORACE (see ORIST)
ORACLE (see ORTABLE)
ORAGE (see ORTAGE)
ORAH (see ORA)
ORAL (see ORMAL)
ORALLY (see ORMITY)
ORANGE (see ORTANCE)
ORANT (see ORIST)
ORATIVE (see OSITIVE)
ORBABLE (see ORTABLE)
ORBETT (see ORIST)
ORBID (see ORIST)
ORBIDLY (see ORMITY)
ORBIN (see ORTION)
ORBING (see ORMING 1)
ORBIT (see ORIST)
ORBITAL (see ORTABLE)
ORCE (see ORSE 1)
ORCEABLE (see ORTABLE)
ORCEFUL (see ORMAL)
ORCEFULLY (see ORMITY)
ORCELAIN (see ORIAN)
ORCEMENT (see ORTION)
ORCER (see ORDER)
ORCERESS (see ORIOUS)
ORCERING (see ORDERING)
ORCERY (see ORMITY)
ORCESTER (see OOKER)
ORCH (see ORSE 1)
ORCHARD (see ORDERED)
ORCHER (see ORDER)
ORCHING (see ORMING 1)

ORCIBLE (see ORTABLE)
ORCIBLY (see ORMITY)
ORCING (see ORMING 1)
ORCIVE (see ORSIVE)
ORD 1 (see OARD)

ORD 2

berg
bird
blurb
burg
curb
curd
curve
dirge
gird
heard
herb
herd
merge
nerd
nerve
purge
scourge
Serb
serge
serve
splurge
surge
swerve
third
turd
urge
verb
verge
verve
word

absurd
acerb
adverb
bean curd
Big Bird
blackbird
bluebird
buzzword
byword
code word
conserve

converge

crossword

deserve

deterge

disturb

diverge

emerge

F word

God's Word

hors d'oeuvre

iceberg

jailbird

jaybird

keyword

last word

lovebird

news blurb

observe

one-third

password

perturb

preserve

proverb

railbird

reserve

resurge

reword

Salzburg

self-serve

send word

snowbird

songbird

submerge

subserve

suburb

superb

swearword

unheard

unnerve

upsurge

watchword

yardbird

dirty word

early bird

Gettysburg

gold reserve

have a word

Hindenburg

household word

in reserve

just a word

keep your word

ladybird

Larry Bird

Luxembourg

mark my word

mockingbird

on the curve

on the verge

overheard

reemerge

resubmerge

say the word

seen not heard

solemn word

take my word

throw a curve

word for word

bundle of nerves

do not disturb

eat like a bird

first-come first-serve

four-letter word

free as a bird

funeral dirge

Johannesburg

Whoopi Goldberg

as good as your word

tip of the iceberg

Florida Orange Bird

Thurston Howell III

ORDABLE (see ORTABLE)

ORDABLY (see ORMITY)

ORDAL (see ORMAL)

ORDAN (see ORTION)

ORDANCE (see ORTANCE)

ORDANT (see ORTION)

ORDE (see OARD)

ORDED (see URDED)

ORDEN (see ORTION)

ORDER

boarder

boiler

border

broiler

chorder

cloister

coiler

corker

corner

courter

foiler

forcer

forder

forger

forker

former

foyer

gorger

hoarder

hoister

horner

horror

joiner

lawyer

loiter

moister

moisture

mortar

mourner

oiler

order

oyster

porker

porter

quarter

roiler

roister

Sawyer

scorcher

scorner

shorter

soiler

sorter

spoiler

stormer

swarmer

thwarter

toiler

torture

voider

voyeur

warmer
warner

aborter
accorder
adjoiner
adorner
airfoiler
annoyer
assorter
awarder
back-order
barnstormer
benchwarmer
cavorter
chairwarmer
conformer
conjoiner
consorter
contorter
court order
deployer
deporter
destroyer
disjoiner
disorder
distorter
divorcer
embroider
embroiler
employer
enforcer
enjoiner
escorter
exhorter
exploiter
exporter
forewarner
French Quarter
gag order
heart-warmer
importer
in order
informer
invoicer
leg warmer
mail order
New Yorker
performer

purloiner
recoiler
recorder
reforger
reformer
rejoicer
rejoiner
reporter
rewarder
ripsnorter
rush order
short order
stop order
supporter
tall order
Transformer
transporter
uncorker

amen-corner
breakfast order
brick and mortar
call to order
come to order
court reporter
custom-order
flight recorder
in short order
Latin Quarter
law and order
made-to-order
misinformer
money order
out of order
outperformer
pecking order
point of order
reinforcer
rules of order
star reporter
tape recorder

Little Jack Horner
Mexican border
pay to the order

athletic supporter
Canadian border
video recorder

ORDERED

bordered
broidered
cloistered
cornered
forward
goitered
loitered
orchard
ordered
roistered
tortured
toward

disordered
embordered
embroidered
fast-forward
imbordered
reordered
straightforward
untoward

pay it forward
reconnoitered

ORDERING

bordering
broidering
cloistering
cornering
loitering
moidering
ordering
oystering
portering
quartering
roistering
sorcering
torturing

disordering
embroidering
headquartering
imbordering
no loitering
reordering

reconnoitering

ORDERLY (see ORMITY)
ORDIALLY (see ORMITY)
ORDIAN (see ORIAN)
ORDIER (see URLIER)
ORDIG (see ORMING 1)
ORDINANCE (see ORTUNATE)
ORDINATE (see ORTUNATE)
ORDING 1 (see ORMING 1)
ORDING 2 (see ERTING)
ORDION (see ORIAN)
ORDIST (see ORIST)
ORDMENT (see ORTION)
ORDON (see ORTION)
ORDSTROM (see ORUM)
ORDY 1 (see IRTY)
ORDY 2 (see ORY)

ORE 1

boar
bore
chore
core
corps
door
drawer
floor
for
fore
four
gore
hoar
lore
more
nor
oar
or
ore
pore
roar
score
shore
snore
soar
sore
spore
store
swore
Thor
tore

war
whore
wore
yore
your

abhor
adore
afore
ashore
at war
backdoor
bedsore
before
cash drawer
chain store
cold sore
cold war
dance floor
decor
deplore
detour
downpour
drugstore
Dutch door
encore
explore
eyesore
fall for
folklore
footsore
forswore
fourscore
front door
galore
hard-core
heartsore
hoped-for
ignore
implore
in for
indoor
keep score
liqueur
masseur
mentor
next-door
no more
offshore
onshore

outdoor
outscore
Peace Corps
postwar
pray for
press corps
price war
rapport
restore
seashore
señor
soft-core
sophomore
stage door
ten-four
therefore
threescore
tie score
top drawer
top floor
trapdoor
uproar
wait for
wherefore
wild boar
work for
world war

act of war
albacore
all ashore
antiwar
anymore
apple core
army corps
at death's door
Baltimore
bar the door
Barrymore
blood and gore
bottom floor
canker sore
carnivore
civil war
commodore
Connect Four
connoisseur
corridor
cuspidor
declare war

dinosaur
discount store
doggie door
door-to-door
dresser drawer
Ecuador
either or
evermore
furthermore
guarantor
hardware store
have the floor
heretofore
household chore
humidor
know the score
lion's roar
man-of-war
Marine Corps
matador
metaphor
mind the store
mirador
neither/nor
nevermore
open door
orator
paramour
perfect score
petit four
picador
pinafore
piscator
pompadour
por favor
raconteur
rich or poor
saboteur
saddle sore
ship-to-shore
signal corps
Singapore
sliding door
spoils of war
state of war
swinging door
sycamore
take the floor
ten-cent store
Theodore

to die for
to the core
Trojan War
troubadour
tug-of-war
two-by-four
unasked-for
uncalled-for
uncared-for
underscore
unpaid-for

Army Air Corps
conservator
conspirator
convenience store
cutting-room floor
department store
Drew Barrymore
El Salvador
Fantastic Four
forevermore
grocery store
Korean War
mixed metaphor
revolving door
settle the score
titanosaur
toreador
Vietnam War

prisoner of war

declaration of war
Studio 54

ORE 2 (see ORY)
OREAL (see ORIAL)
ORED (see OARD)
OREDOM (see ORUM)
OREGON (see ORIAN)
OREGONE (see ORON)
OREIGN (see ORTANCE)
OREMAN (see ORTION)
ORENCE (see ORTANCE)
ORENESS (see ORIST)
OREO (see OLIO)
OREST (see ORIST)
ORESTRY (see ORMITY)
ORF (see ORSE 1)
ORFEIT (see ORIST)

ORGAN (see ORTION)
ORGANIST (see ORTUNATE)
ORGE (see ORSE 1)
ORGEOUS (see ORIST)
ORGER (see ORDER)
ORGERY (see ORMITY)
ORGHUM (see ORUM)
ORGIAN (see ORIAN)
ORGIE (see ORY)
ORGING (see ORMING 1)
ORGON (see ORTION)
ORGY (see ORY)
ORI (see ORY)

ORIA

cornea
Gloria

consortia
euphoria
Pretoria
Victoria

California

ORIAL

boreal
oriole

corporeal
memorial
pictorial
raptorial
sartorial
temporeal
tonsorial
tutorial

categorial
dictatorial
editorial
equatorial
professorial
promissorial
senatorial
territorial

accusatorial
supervisorial
time immemorial

ORIAM (see ORIAN)

ORIAN

formian
Georgian
gordian
Morphean
Oregon
orient
porcelain
scorpion

accordion
censorian
Delorian
emporium
Gregorian
historian
luxuriant
New Orlean
stentorian
Victorian

auditorium
Californian
crematorium
in memoriam
Kenny Florian
moratorium
sanitorium

Dr. Kevorkian
valedictorian

ORIC (see ORIST)
ORICAL (see ORTABLE)
ORICALLY (see ORMITY)
ORID (see ORIST)
ORIENT (see ORIAN)

ORIFY

fortify
glorify

horrify
Lorilei
mortify
scorify
storify

corporify
disglorify
unglorify

ORILEI (see ORIFY)
ORING 1 (see ORMING 1)
ORING 2 (see ERTING)
ORIOLE (see ORIAL)

ORIOUS

glorious
Morpheus
Scorpius
sorceress

censorious
euphorious
inglorious
laborious
notorious
stentorious
uproarious
victorious

meritorious
unvictorious

ORIS (see ORIST)
ORISH (see ORIST)

ORIST

boarish
Boris
chorist
chorus
corant
Corbett
cornice
cornist
Corpus
corset

courant
Doric
Doris
dorkus
florid
florist
flourish
forest
forfeit
gorgeous
Horace
hornet
horrid
moorish
morbid
Morris
orbit
poorish
porous
porpoise
portrait
shortest
soreness
sorest
Taurus
torrid
tortoise
warmest
whorish

arborist
caloric
Centaurus
conformist
deforest
disforest
enforest
enormous
euphoric
folklorist
forlornest
Green Hornet
herborist
historic
phosphoric
recordist
reforest
reformist
rhetoric
sonorant

temporist
thesaurus

allegoric
allegorist
amateurish
brontosaurus
categoric
categorist
harpischordist
hydrochloric
megasaurus
metaphoric
metaphorist
meteoric
nonconformist
oratoric
paregoric
prehistoric
sophomoric
stegosaurus
unconformist
uniformest

brachiosaurus
Enchanted Forest
nonuniformist
tyrannosaurus

Natasha and Boris
probabilitorist

ORITY (see ORMITY)
ORIUM (see ORIAN)

ORK 1

Berk
Bert
blurt
burnt
burp
chirp
clerk
curt
dirk
dirt
flirt
hurt

irk
jerk
kirk
learnt
lurk
murk
perk
pert
quirk
shirk
shirt
skirt
slurp
smirk
spurt
squirt
Turk
twerk
twerp
work

alert
Antwerp
artwork
assert
avert
berserk
bookwork
brainwork
bridgework
bulwark
clockwork
convert
covert
daywork
desert
dessert
divert
eat dirt
excerpt
exert
fast work
fieldwork
file clerk
flatwork
footwork
framework
Frankfurt
groundwork
guesswork

homework
housework
inburnt
inert
insert
invert
knee jerk
legwork
network
nightshirt
overt
patchwork
pay dirt
pervert
piecework
Q-Bert
redshirt
revert
rework
schoolwork
stuffed shirt
subvert
sunburnt
t-shirt
teamwork
town clerk
unburnt
usurp
windburnt
woodwork

busy work
Captain Kirk
controvert
dirty work
disconcert
dish the dirt
extrovert
flannel shirt
handiwork
hula skirt
introvert
latticework
line of work
little twerp
lose your shirt
men at work
miniskirt
needlework
out of work

overwork
red alert
right-to-work
smog alert
undershirt
underskirt
underwork
women's work
Wyatt Earp

animadvert
DJ Kool Herc
Hawaiian shirt
overexert
spoiler alert
yellow alert

ORK 2 (see ORP)
ORKER 1 (see ORDER)
ORKER 2 (see URNER)
ORKI (see ORY)
ORKIAN (see ORIAN)
ORKIE (see ORY)
ORKIN (see ORTION)
ORKING 1 (see ERTING)
ORKING 2 (see ORMING 1)
ORKUS (see ORIST)
ORKY (see ORY)
ORL (see IRL)
ORLD (see IRL)
ORLEAN (see ORIAN)
ORLON (see ORON)
ORM 1 (see ORN)
ORM 2 (see URN)

ORMAL

aural
choral
chordal
chortle
coral
dorsal
floral
forceful
formal
laurel
moral
morsel
mortal

normal
oral
portal
quarrel
sorrel
sourceful

abnormal
amoral
clitoral
immoral
immortal
informal
mayoral
pastoral
remorseful
resourceful
subnormal
unmoral

above normal
lovers' quarrel
semiformal
unremorseful

ORMALIST (see ORTUNATE)
ORMALLY (see ORMITY)
ORMAN (see ORTION)
ORMANCE (see ORTANCE)
ORMANT (see ORTION)
ORMENT (see ORTION)
ORMER (see ORDER)
ORMERLY (see ORMITY)
ORMEST (see ORIST)
ORMIAN (see ORIAN)

ORMING 1

boarding
boring
chordig
cording
coring
corking
Corning
coursing
courting
dwarfing
flooring
forcing

fording
forging
forking
forming
gorging
goring
hoarding
horning
horsing
lording
morning
mourning
oaring
orbing
pouring
roaring
scorching
scoring
scorning
shorting
snoring
snorting
sorting
sporting
storing
storming
swarming
swording
thorning
thwarting
torching
warding
warming
warning
warping
warring
whoring

abhorring
aborning
aborting
absorbing
according
adoring
adorning
affording
assorting
awarding
barnstorming
benchwarming

brainstorming
cavorting
comporting
conforming
consorting
contorting
deforcing
deforming
dehorning
deploring
deporting
discording
disgorging
distorting
divorcing
downpouring
efforcing
encoring
endorsing
enforcing
engorging
escorting
exhorting
exploring
exporting
extorting
flood warning
forewarning
gale warning
good morning
heartwarming
ignoring
imploring
importing
indorsing
informing
midmorning
misforming
outpouring
outscoring
performing
preforming
prewarning
purporting
reboarding
recording
reflooring
reforging
reforming
reporting

resorting
restoring
retorting
rewarding
rewarming
riproaring
skateboarding
suborning
supporting
surfboarding
transforming
transporting
uncorking
unhorsing
uproaring

air-raid warning
chloroforming
global warming
habit-forming
misinforming
nonconforming
outperforming
prerecording
reabsorbing
reinforcing
reinforming
rerecording
subendorsing
thunderstorming
unconforming
uniforming
weatherboarding

top of the morning

ORMING 2 (see ERTING)
ORMIST (see ORIST)

ORMITY

broidery
broilery
chorally
cordially
Dorothy
florally
forcefully
forcibly

forestry
forgery
formally
formerly
horribly
joyfully
loyalty
morally
morbidly
mortally
normally
oilery
orally
orderly
portably
porterly
quarterly
royalty
sorcery
warranty

abnormally
abnormity
affordably
amorally
authority
avoidably
biformity
conformity
corporally
deformity
difformity
disloyalty
doctorally
embroidery
enormity
historically
informally
informity
majority
minority
misformity
pastorally
pectorally
priority
rhetorically
seniority
sonority
sorority
subnormally

temporally
viceroyalty

allegorically
categorically
deiformity
disconformity
electorally
inconformity
incorporally
metaphorically
multiformity
nonconformity
nontemporally
omniformity
oratorically
paranormally
port authority
preconformity
unavoidably
unconformity
uniformity

inferiority
moral majority
police authority
silent majority
simple majority
superiority

ORMLY (see ORY)
ORMON (see ORTION)
ORMOUS (see ORIST)
ORMY 1 (see ORY)
ORMY 2 (see IRTY)

ORN

born
borne
corn
dorm
form
horn
morn
mourn
norm
porn
scorn
shorn

storm
swarm
sworn
thorn
torn
warm
warn
worn

acorn
adorn
air horn
airborne
bad form
barnstorm
bighorn
brainstorm
bullhorn
careworn
conform
deform
duststorm
firestorm
firstborn
foghorn
forewarn
forlorn
forsworn
free-form
freeborn
French horn
greenhorn
highborn
inborn
inform
longhorn
lovelorn
lukewarm
newborn
outworn
perform
platform
popcorn
prewarn
rainstorm
reborn
reform
rewarm
sandstorm
shoehorn

shopworn
snowstorm
tax form
timeworn
tinhorn
transform
unborn
unshorn
unsworn
untorn
well-worn
windstorm

barleycorn
Capricorn
chloroform
co-ed dorm
ear of corn
early morn
flugelhorn
foreign-born
Maidenform
Matterhorn
misinform
native born
order form
outperform
peppercorn
proper form
take by storm
thunderstorm
unadorn
unicorn
uniform

around the horn
dance up a storm
Foghorn Leghorn
ride out the storm
toot your own horn

Children of the Corn
Jiffy Pop Popcorn
out of uniform

tropic of Capricorn

ORNE (see ORN)
ORNEA (see ORIA)
ORNER (see ORDER)
ORNERED (see ORDERED)

ORNERING (see ORDERING)
ORNEST (see ORIST)
ORNET (see ORIST)
ORNEY (see IRTY)
ORNIA (see ORIA)
ORNIAN (see ORIAN)
ORNICAL (see ORTABLE)
ORNICE (see ORIST)
ORNING (see ORMING 1)
ORNIST (see ORIST)
ORNY (see ORY)

ORON

boron
foregone
moron
Orlon
Voltron

oxymoron

OROTHY (see ORMITY)
OROUGH (see ERNO)
OROUS (see ORIST)

ORP

cork
corp
court
dork
fork
fort
forte
gorp
ort
pork
port
quart
short
snort
sort
sport
stork
thwart
tort
torte
warp

wart
York

abort
airport
assort
backcourt
bad sport
carport
cavort
cohort
comport
consort
contort
cut short
deport
distort
escort
exhort
export
extort
fall short
good sport
high court
hold court
home port
import
in short
moot court
New York
Newport
night court
passport
pitchfork
purport
report
resort
retort
salt pork
seaport
sell short
Shreveport
Southfork
spoilsport
support
time warp
transport
uncork

center court
child support

circuit court
contact sport
davenport
day in court
divorce court
Duke of York
heliport
last resort
nonsupport
on report
out-of-court
pop the cork
Rapoport
Sacher torte
small claims court
Supreme Court
tennis court
traffic court
tuning fork
worrywart

contempt of court
kangaroo court
laugh out of court
moral support
police escort
spectator sport
spousal support
weather report

make a long story short

ORPHAN (see ORTION)
ORPHEAN (see ORIAN)
ORPHEUS (see ORIOUS)
ORPHIN (see ORTION)
ORPIO (see OLIO)
ORPION (see ORIAN)
ORPIUS (see ORIOUS)
ORPOISE (see ORIST)
ORPORAL (see ORTABLE)
ORPORATE (see ORTUNATE)
ORPS (see ORE 1)
ORPSE (see ORSE 1)
ORPSMAN (see ORTION)
ORPTION (see ORTION)
ORPUS (see ORIST)
ORRA (see ORA)
ORRAH (see ORA)
ORRE (see ORY)
ORRED (see OARD)
ORREL (see ORMAL)

ORRENCE (see ORTANCE)
ORRENT (see ORTION)
ORRIBLE (see ORTABLE)
ORRIBLY (see ORMITY)
ORRID (see ORIST)
ORRIDGE (see ORTAGE)
ORRIER (see URLIER)
ORRIFY (see ORIFY)
ORRING (see ORMING 1)
ORRIS (see ORIST)
ORROR (see ORDER)
ORROW (see ARGO)
ORRUGATE (see ORTUNATE)
ORRY 1 (see ARTY 1)
ORRY 2 (see IRTY)
ORSABLE (see ORTABLE)
ORSAL (see ORMAL)
ORSCHE (see ORSE 1)
ORSCHT (see ORSE 1)

ORSE 1

borscht
coarse
corpse
course
dwarf
force
forge
forth
fourth
George
gorge
hoarse
horse
Morse
Norse
north
porch
porsche
quartz
Schwartz
scorch
source
swarth
torch
wharf

air force
back porch

blowtorch
bring forth
brute force
by force
clothes horse
come forth
concourse
crash course
dark horse
discourse
disgorge
divorce
due course
endorse
enforce
engorge
front porch
gift horse
go forth
golf course
henceforth
high horse
in force
main course
midcourse
of course
one-fourth
packhorse
racecourse
racehorse
recourse
remorse
resource
rose quartz
sawhorse
seahorse
set forth
strike force
sun porch
task force
thenceforth
up north
warhorse
workforce
workhorse

and so forth
back and forth
but of course
charley horse

Crazy Horse
driving force
Dusseldorf
hobbyhorse
Human Torch
in due course
intercourse
iron horse
July Fourth
labor force
magnum force
police force
quarter horse
reinforce
rocking horse
show of force
stay the course
tour de force
Valley Forge
watercourse
wooden horse

beat a dead horse
carry a torch
collision course
Curious George
grounds for divorce
have intercourse
Jennifer North
matter of course
obstacle course
Olympic torch
refresher course

cart before the horse
centrifugal force
correspondence course
so on and so forth

ORSE 2 (see IRST)
ORSEFUL (see ORMAL)
ORSEL (see ORMAL)
ORSEMENT (see ORTION)
ORSEN (see ERSION)
ORSER (see URNER)
ORSET (see ORIST)
ORSEY (see ORY)
ORSHIP (see ERVICE)
ORSING (see ORMING 1)
ORSION (see ORTION)

ORSIVE

sportive
tortive

abortive
contortive
distortive
divorcive
enforcive
extorsive
extortive
purportive
retortive
supportive

ORST (see IRST)
ORT 1 (see ORP)
ORT 2 (see ORE 1)

ORTABLE

boardable
chordable
corporal
courtable
forcible
fordable
fornical
horrible
oracle
orbital
portable
portional
pourable
soarable
sortable
storable

abhorable
abortable
absorbable
adorable
affordable
antorbital
assortable
contortable
deplorable
deportable

distortable
distortional
endorsable
enforceable
enforcible
escortable
exhortable
explorable
exportable
extortable
historical
ignorable
importable
outscorable
postorbital
preorbital
proportional
purportable
recordable
reportable
restorable
retortable
rewardable
rhetorical
suborbital
supportable
transorbital
transportable
unpourable
unscorable

allegorical
anteorbital
categorical
disproportional
infraorbital
insupportable
interorbital
metaphorical
nonproportional
oratorical
prehistorical
supraorbital

ORTABLY (see ORMITY)

ORTAGE

borage
corage

floorage
forage
moorage
mortgage
porridge
portage
shorage
shortage
storage

cold storage
colportage
reportage

ORTAL (see ORMAL)
ORTALLY (see ORMITY)

ORTANCE

Florence
foreign
Lawrence
orange
Warren

abhorrence
accordance
concordance
conformance
discordance
importance
performance
recordance
supportance
transformance
transportance

nonperformance
unimportance

ORTAR (see ORDER)
ORTE (see ORP)
ORTEM (see ORUM)
ORTEN (see ORTION)
ORTER (see ORDER)
ORTERING (see ORDERING)
ORTERLY (see ORMITY)
ORTEST (see ORIST)
ORTGAGE (see ORTAGE)
ORTH 1 (see ORSE 1)

ORTH 2 (see IRST)
ORTHLESS (see ERVICE)
ORTHY (see IRTY)
ORTIA (see ORIA)
ORTIE (see ORY)
ORTIFY (see ORIFY)
ORTING (see ORMING 1)

ORTION

Borden
corbin
cordon
corpsman
Corwin
doorman
dormant
floorman
forcement
foreman
formant
fortune
Gordon
Gorgon
horrent
Horton
Jordan
mordant
Morgan
morkin
Mormon
Norman
Norton
organ
orphan
portion
shorten
sorbin
sortment
torment
torrent
torsion
warden
warrant
Wharton

abhorrent
aborsement
abortion
abortment

absorption
accordant
accordment
afforcement
affordment
apportion
assortment
bench warrant
biorgan
churchwarden
comportment
concordant
contortion
deforcement
deportment
discordant
distortion
distortment
divorcement
endorphin
endorsement
enforcement
extortion
firewarden
foreshorten
game warden
idorgan
indorsement
informant
longshoreman
misfortune
proportion
rain torrent
search warrant
supportment
transportment

decachordon
disaccordant
in proportion
inaccordant
jury foreman
law enforcement
manichordon
Michael Jordan
misinformant
nonenforcement
proenforcement
reapportion
reassortment

reenforcement
reinforcement
Wheel of Fortune

ORTIONAL (see ORTABLE)
ORTIONIST (see ORTUNATE)
ORTIVE (see ORSIVE)
ORTLE (see ORMAL)
ORTLY (see ORY)
ORTMENT (see ORTION)
ORTOISE (see ORIST)
ORTON (see ORTION)
ORTRAIT (see ORIST)

ORTUNATE

corporate
corrugate
disordinance
formalist
fortunate
ordinance
organist
portionist

abortionist
contortionist
coordinate
extortionist
importunate
infortunate
inordinate
misfortunate
unfortunate
unportunate

insubordinate

ORTUNE (see ORTION)
ORTURE (see ORDER)
ORTURED (see ORDERED)
ORTURING (see ORDERING)
ORTY (see ORY)

ORUM

boredom
forum
jorum

Nordstrom
quorum
sorghum
whoredom

decorum
postmortem

indecorum
open forum
variorum

ORUS (see ORIST)
ORWARD (see ORDERED)
ORWIN (see ORTION)

ORY

corky
corny
courtly
Courtney
dorky
dory
forty
Georgie
glory
Gorki
gory
hoarsely
hoary
horny
horsey
Laurie
Lordy
orgy
porgy
porky
portly
quarry
shortly
shorty
Snorky
sortie
sporty
stormy
story
thorny

Tory
warbly
warmly
warty
yorkie

Daugherty
fish story
John Dory
love story
Maori
Old Glory
one-story
rock quarry
sob story
tall story
Top 40
Toy Story
true story
two-story
vainglory

a priori
allegory
amatory
auditory
bedtime story
cacciatore
category
Christmas Story
con amore
cover story
crematory
De La Torre
dictatory
dilatory
dormitory
flammatory
Georgie Porgie
horror story
hunky-dory
inventory
laboratory
laudatory
lavatory
mandatory
migratory
morning glory

oratory
promissory
promontory
purgatory
second-story
territory
transitory
uniformly

accusatory
admonitory
ambulatory
circulatory
cock-and-bull story
commendatory
compensatory
conservatory
declaratory
depilatory
derogatory
detective story
explanatory
exploratory
inflammatory
no guts, no glory
obligatory
observatory
preparatory
reformatory
regulatory
repository
respiratory

conciliatory
congratulatory
discriminatory
hallucinatory
interlocutory
interrogatory
never ending story
noninflammatory
self-explanatory

antiinflammatory

OS 1 (see OSE 1)
OS 2 (see OW 1)
OSA (see OLA)
OSABLE 1 (see OTABLE)
OSABLE 2 (see OOTABLE)
OSAGE (see OSES)

OSAL

boastful
boatful
bodeful
bromal
coastal
doleful
domal
focal
global
hopeful
loathful
local
Mobil
mobile
modal
mogul
mopeful
noble
nodal
noteful
ogle
opal
oval
postal
prosal
Sobel
social
somal
soulful
tonal
total
vocal
Vogel
woeful
yodel
yokel

anomal
bicoastal
bifocal
Chernobyl
deposal
disposal
ennoble
exposal
go postal
ignoble
immobile

opposal
petrosal
prodromal
proposal
reposal
reproachful
subtotal
supposal
teetotal
transposal
trifocal

anecdotal
chromosomal
interposal
local yokel
presupposal
ribosomal
sacerdotal

at your disposal
garbage disposal
marriage proposal

OSALEE (see OCALLY)
OSARY (see OCALLY)
OSBY (see OCKEY)
OSCAR (see OLLAR)
OSCARED (see OFFERED)
OSCELES (see OLOGIES)
OSCILLATE (see OPULATE)
OSCILLATION (see OPERATION)

OSE 1

beaus
bode
bold
brogue
chose
close
clothe
clove
code
cold
cove
dove
doze
drove
fold

froze
globe
goad
gold
gross
grove
hold
hose
hove
load
loathe
lobe
lode
loge
mode
mold
node
nose
ode
old
pose
probe
prose
road
robe
rode
rogue
rose
rove
scold
sold
Spode
stove
strobe
strode
strove
those
toad
told
trove
Vogue
wove

abode
age-old
airhose
alcove
arm hold
arose
back road

bandeaux	lactose	a la mode
bath robe	lap robe	adios
behold	leasehold	Axel Rose
billfold	lymph node	bellicose
blindfold	microbe	big and bold
bluenose	Morse Code	by a nose
brown-nose	oppose	catch a cold
bulldoze	out cold	centerfold
carload	pathos	claustrophobe
caseload	payload	common cold
catch cold	planeload	Comstock Lode
choir robe	prefold	damask rose
choke hold	primrose	days of old
commode	propose	decompose
compose	pug nose	electrode
corrode	railroad	episode
cosmos	red rose	fluff and fold
crossroad	reload	garden hose
decode	repose	good as gold
depose	resold	grab a hold
dextrose	rewove	heart of gold
disclose	shipload	hit the road
dispose	ski nose	hot and cold
disrobe	space probe	hundredfold
download	spun gold	interpose
dress code	stronghold	interwove
earlobe	suppose	Irish rose
enclose	tea rose	Jell-O mold
enfold	tenfold	juxtapose
engross	threshold	liquid gold
erode	toehold	manifold
ethos	toll road	marigold
explode	transpose	mother lode
expose	truckload	nose-to-nose
fanfold	twice-told	on the nose
fire hose	twofold	open road
fool's gold	unclothe	overload
foothold	unfold	overrode
forebode	unfroze	oversold
foreclose	unload	panty hose
foretold	unsold	penal code
freehold	untold	pirate cove
freeload	uphold	pot of gold
hardnose	upload	predispose
head cold	verbose	presuppose
high road	wardrobe	pure as gold
household	white gold	purple prose
ice-cold	withhold	recompose
implode	workload	Roman nose
impose	zip code	runny nose

solid gold
stranglehold
thousandfold
treasure trove
undersold
water hose

area code
bibliophobe
carry the load
lead by the nose
lo and behold
one for the road
open and close
out in the cold
overexpose
pay through the nose
superimpose
underexpose

accordion-fold
middle of the road
my wild Irish rose
to have and to hold
Underground Railroad
worth your weight in gold

OSE 2 (see OAT)
OSE 3 (see USE 1)
OSED (see OBED)
OSELY (see ONY)
OSEN (see OTION)
OSENESS (see OSES)
OSER 1 (see OVER 1)
OSER 2 (see UTER)
OSERY (see OCALLY)

OSES

bogus
bonus
broaches
brooches
closeness
closes
coaches
crocus
dosage
dozes
focus

gnosis
grossness
hocus
hopeless
hoses
Jonas
locus
lotus
modus
Moses
motive
noses
notice
notive
onus
poaches
poses
postage
proses
roaches
ropeless
roses
soapless
voltage
votive

airhoses
approaches
atrocious
bluenoses
brown-noses
bulldozes
cockroaches
composes
connotive
corrosive
demotive
deposes
discloses
disposes
emotive
encloses
encroaches
erosive
explosive
exposes
ferocious
fire hoses
forecloses
hardnoses

hypnosis
imposes
in focus
moroseness
neurosis
opposes
osmosis
precocious
primroses
prognosis
proposes
psychosis
pug noses
red roses
refocus
reposes
reproaches
ski noses
stagecoaches
supposes
tea roses
thrombosis
transposes
verboseness

acidosis
automotive
damask roses
decomposes
diagnosis
garden hoses
halitosis
hocus-pocus
interposes
Irish roses
juxtaposes
locomotive
out of focus
predisposes
presupposes
purple proses
recomposes
Roman noses
runny noses
scoliosis
self-hypnosis
unferocious
unprecocious
water hoses

cystic fibrosis
overexposes
superimposes
tuberculosis
underexposes

mononucleosis
osteosclerosis
ulterior motive

OSET (see OCKET)
OSEY (see ONY)
OSH (see ASH 2)
OSHER (see OVER 1)
OSHERED (see OFFERED)
OSHIER (see OGGIER)
OSHING (see OCKING)
OSHLY (see OCKEY)
OSHY (see OCKEY)
OSIA (see OLA)
OSIE 1 (see ONY)
OSIE 2 (see ONY)
OSIER (see OKIER)
OSIERY (see OCALLY)
OSILY (see OCALLY)
OSING 1 (see OWING 1)
OSING 2 (see OWING 1)
OSING 3 (see UTING 1)
OSION (see OTION)
OSIS (see OSES)
OSIT (see OCKET)
OSITE (see OCKET)
OSITER (see OGRAPHER)

OSITIVE

auditive
causative
cognitive
collative
operative
positive
talkative
vocative

abrogative
appositive
arrogative
avocative
compositive
cooperative

corroborative
derogative
dispositive
evocative
expositive
inoperative
nonoperative
oppositive
postoperative
postpositive
precognitive
preoperative
prepositive
prerogative
provocative
recognitive
revocative
suppositive
transpositive
unoperative

interrogative
noncooperative
noncorroborative
reciprocative
uncooperative

electropositive
supererogative

OSITY (see OMETRY)
OSIVE (see OSES)
OSK (see ASH 2)
OSLING (see OCKING)
OSMIC (see OTIC)
OSMOND (see OTTEN)
OSNIA (see AFIA)
OSO (see OLO)
OSOPHER (see OGRAPHER)
OSOPHIES (see OLOGIES)
OSOPHY (see OMETRY)
OSP (see OX)
OSPECT (see OBJECT)
OSPEL (see OTTLE)
OSPER (see OLLAR)
OSPERED (see OFFERED)
OSPERING (see OTTERING)
OSPICE (see OLISH)
OSQUE (see ASH 2)
OSS 1 (see OFF)
OSS 2 (see OSE 1)

OSSABLE (see OGICAL)
OSSAGE (see OTIC)
OSSAL (see OTTLE)
OSSARIES (see OLOGIES)
OSSARY (see OMETRY)
OSSE 1 (see OCKEY)
OSSE 2 (see OFF)
OSSELET (see OMERATE)
OSSER 1 (see OLLAR)
OSSER 2 (see OVER 1)
OSSET (see OCKET)
OSSIBLE (see OGICAL)
OSSIBLY (see OMETRY)
OSSIER (see OGGIER)
OSSIEST (see OGGIEST)
OSSIFY (see OLLIFY)
OSSIL (see OTTLE)
OSSILY (see OMETRY)
OSSINESS (see OCKINESS)
OSSING 1 (see OCKING)
OSSING 2 (see OWING 1)
OSSIP (see OCKET)
OSSIPY (see OMETRY)
OSSLE (see OTTLE)
OSSLY (see ONY)
OSSNESS (see OSES)
OSSOM (see OTTEN)
OSSOMY (see OMETRY)
OSSUM (see OTTEN)
OSSY (see OCKEY)
OST 1 (see OAT)
OST 2 (see ASH 2)
OSTA (see ADA 1)
OSTAGE 1 (see OTIC)
OSTAGE 2 (see OSES)
OSTAL 1 (see OSAL)
OSTAL 2 (see OTTLE)
OSTALLY (see OCALLY)
OSTASIES (see OLOGIES)
OSTASY (see OMETRY)
OSTE (see OAT)
OSTED 1 (see OLID)
OSTED 2 (see OASTED)
OSTEL (see OTTLE)
OSTER 1 (see OLLAR)
OSTER 2 (see OVER 1)
OSTERED (see OFFERED)
OSTERING (see OTTERING)
OSTEROUS (see OGGIEST)
OSTIC (see OTIC)
OSTIER (see OGGIER)
OSTIEST (see OGGIEST)
OSTILE (see OTTLE)

OSTINESS (see OCKINESS)
OSTING 1 (see OCKING)
OSTING 2 (see OWING 1)
OSTLE (see OTTLE)
OSTLED (see OBBLED)
OSTLIER 1 (see OGGIER)
OSTLIER 2 (see OKIER)
OSTLIEST (see OGGIEST)
OSTLINESS (see OCKINESS)
OSTLY 1 (see ONY)
OSTLY 2 (see OCKEY)
OSTON (see OTTEN)
OSTOR (see OLLAR)
OSTRIL (see OTTLE)
OSTROPHE (see OMETRY)
OSTROPHES (see OLOGIES)
OSTURE (see OLLAR)
OSTURED (see OFFERED)
OSTURING (see OTTERING)
OSTY (see OCKEY)
OSURE (see OVER 1)
OSY (see ONY)

OT

auk
Bach
baht
balk
block
blot
bop
bot
bought
brought
caught
caulk
chalk
chock
chop
clock
clop
clot
cock
cop
cot
crock
crop
doc
dock

dot
drop
flock
flop
fop
fought
fraught
frock
gawk
Glock
glop
got
hawk
hock
hop
hot
Jacques
jock
jot
knock
knot
lock
lop
lot
Mach
mock
mop
naught
not
opt
ought
plop
plot
pock
pop
pot
prop
roc
rock
rot
Scott
shock
shop
shot
slop
slot
smock
snot
sock
sop

sought
spot
squat
squawk
stalk
stock
stop
strop
swap
swat
talk
taught
taut
thought
top
tot
trot
walk
watt
whop
wok
wrought
yacht

ad hoc
adopt
Aesop
air drop
allot
armlock
atop
backdrop
backstop
backtalk
bakeshop
Bangkok
bank shot
bar hop
beanstalk
bebop
bedrock
begot
bellhop
best shot
big shot
big top
blackrot
blacktop
blind spot
blood clot

bloodshot
boardwalk
box top
boycott
buckshot
bus stop
cakewalk
cannot
car lock
carhop
catwalk
cellblock
chalk talk
cheap shot
chip shot
chop-chop
Chris Rock
clip-clop
closed shop
co-op
concoct
cooktop
cornstalk
cough drop
crack shot
crackpot
crosswalk
damp-mop
deadlock
desktop
dewdrop
distraught
dogtrot
doo-wop
doorstop
dreadlock
dry rot
duckwalk
dust mop
earshot
eavesdrop
fast-talk
fat lot
five-spot
flattop
fleshpot
flip-flop
forethought
forgot
foxtrot

French knot
full stop
girltalk
gluepot
grapeshot
gridlock
gumdrop
gunshot
hamhock
handwrought
hard rock
hardtop
headlock
headshop
hedgehop
hemlock
hilltop
Hip-Hop
Hitchcock
hockshop
hot pot
hot shot
hot spot
in stock
inkblot
jackpot
jayhawk
jaywalk
jive talk
job lot
knock-knock
kumquat
laptop
livestock
long shot
loquat
mail drop
mail slot
malt shop
mascot
milksop
Mohawk
mug shot
name-drop
night spot
nonstop
o'clock
odd lot
on top
onslaught

outcrop
outtalk
outwalk
padlock
pawnshop
peacock
pep talk
Pet Rock
pit stop
pork chop
post doc
post-op
pro shop
punk rock
ragmop
raindrop
red-hot
rest stop
restock
roadblock
robot
rooftop
Rorshach
sales talk
sandlot
self-taught
shamrock
sharecrop
shellshock
Sherlock
shoptalk
shortstop
shylock
sidewalk
sleepwalk
slingshot
slipknot
small talk
smooth-talk
smudge pot
snapshot
snowdrop
sock hop
soft spot
spacewalk
speed walk
square knot
stinkpot
store-bought
stovetop

sunblock
sunspot
sweatshop
sweet-talk
take stock
talk shop
tank top
teapot
teardrop
Ted Talk
ten-spot
The Rock
thrift shop
tick-tock
tight spot
time clock
tiptop
topknot
treetop
truck stop
tube sock
tube top
Tupac
uncaught
unlock
untaught
upshot
vox pop
warlock
warm spot
wedlock
wet-mop
whatnot
wife-swap
windsock
woodblock
woodcock
Woodstock
workshop

acid rock
aeronaut
aftershock
afterthought
alarm clock
all for naught
antilock
apricot
aquanaut
Argonaut

astronaut
auction block
baby talk
barbershop
beauty spot
belly flop
blue-chip stock
body shop
boiling hot
booster shot
born to shop
bumper crop
bunny hop
butcher block
Camelot
candid shot
carrot-top
caveat
chamber pot
chicken hawk
chopping block
coffee pot
coffee shop
come to naught
cosmonaut
counterplot
cuckoo clock
culture shock
curly top
diddly-squat
double-talk
eagle hawk
empty lot
flower pot
food for thought
future shock
glottal stop
go to pot
granny knot
hammerlock
hatch a plot
hit the spot
hollyhock
hot to trot
Hottentot
interlock
Jiffy Pop
John Hancock
juggernaut
keystone cop

kilowatt
knockout drop
Lancelot
laughingstock
lemon drop
lindy hop
Little Rock
liver spot
lobster pot
lollipop
loves me not
malaprop
megawatt
melting pot
mental block
microdot
mom and pop
mountaintop
Mr. Spock
nature walk
not so hot
ocelot
on the block
on the dot
on the spot
open stock
out of stock
overshot
overstock
overwrought
parking lot
parting shot
pepper pot
pillow talk
piping hot
polka dot
polyglot
poppycock
put the shot
reach the top
riding crop
round-the-clock
saddle block
Schoolhouse Rock
second thought
set up shop
shorty wop
shuttlecock
soda pop
starting block

stumbling block
summer stock
Super Jock
table talk
table top
table-hop
take a shot
take a walk
thanks a lot
tie the knot
tomahawk
tommyrot
traffic stop
trouble spot
turboprop
turkey trot
undershot
union shop
weathercock
What's Up Doc?
whistle-stop
window-shop
Windsor knot
writer's block

Alfred Hitchcock
around-the-clock
burial plot
by a long shot
capital stock
cream of the crop
digital clock
electric shock
forget-me-not
grandfather's clock
grocery shop
hard as a rock
Hoppity Hop
karate chop
like it or not
on second thought
out of wedlock
over the top
overhead shot
some like it hot
sweeten the pot
tie in a knot
whether or not
Winter Warlock
x marks the spot

believe it or not
chip off the old block
comparison shop
malice aforethought
new kid on the block
not by a long shot
Rosie The Robot
security lock
Snap! Crackle! and Pop!

biological clock
hit me with your best shot
strike while the iron's hot

she loves me she loves me not

OTA (see OLA)

OTABLE

broachable
closable
coachable
floatable
foldable
goadable
holdable
loadable
motional
mouldable
mowable
notable
notional
osable
poachable
pokable
posable
potable
quotable
rollable
rowable
smokable
sociable
strollable
tokable
totable
towable
votable

allodial
approachable
bestowable
bulldozable
commotional
composable
consolable
controllable
corrodable
custodial
decodable
demotable
demotional
denotable
devotional
disposable
emotional
enclosable
enrollable
erodable
evokable
explodable
exposable
extollable
misquotable
parolable
patrollable
promotable
promotional
reproachable
resolable
supposable
transposable
unloadable
unquotable

episodial
indisposable
interposable
juxtaposable
monopodial
unapproachable
uncontrollable
unemotional

OTABLY (see OCALLY)
OTAL (see OSAL)
OTALLY (see OCALLY)
OTANY (see OMETRY)
OTARY (see OCALLY)
OTCH (see ASH 2)

OTCHA (see ADA 1)
OTCHECK (see OBJECT)
OTCHI (see OCKEY)
OTCHIEST (see OGGIEST)
OTCHING (see OCKING)
OTCHY (see OCKEY)
OTE 1 (see OAT)
OTE 2 (see ONY)
OTED (see OASTED)
OTEFUL (see OSAL)
OTEGE (see OWAWAY)
OTELY (see ONY)
OTEM (see OTION)
OTEN (see OTION)
OTENT (see ONEMENT)
OTER (see OVER 1)
OTERIE (see OCALLY)
OTFUL (see OTTLE)
OTH 1 (see OFF)
OTH 2 (see OAT)
OTHE (see OSE 1)
OTHEL (see OTTLE)
OTHER 1 (see USTER 1)
OTHER 2 (see OLLAR)
OTHERED (see OFFERED)
OTHERING 1 (see OVERING)
OTHERING 2 (see OTTERING)
OTHERLESS (see UDDERLESS)
OTHIC (see OTIC)
OTHING 1 (see OWING 1)
OTHING 2 (see USTING)
OTHING 3 (see OCKING)
OTHLESS (see UTENESS)
OTIAN (see OTION)

OTIC

baltic
blockage
bondage
caustic
colic
college
Coptic
cosmic
costage
cottage
crossage
dockage
folic
frolic

fromage
Gnostic
gothic
haulage
homage
hostage
knowledge
lockage
logic
mockage
olive
optic
otic
pommage
rollick
sausage
Slavic
stoppage
topic
toxic
tropic
Vonage
wattage

acknowledge
acrostic
agnostic
anthropic
aquatic
biotic
bucolic
carbolic
chaotic
despotic
erotic
estoppage
exotic
foreknowledge
hydraulic
hypnotic
melodic
methodic
myopic
narcotic
neurotic
nostalgic
prognostic
psychotic
quixotic
robotic

semmotic
spasmodic
subtopic
subtropic
symbolic

aeronautic
alcoholic
apostolic
apostrophic
carnal knowledge
catastrophic
chocoholic
diabolic
diagnostic
Ethiopic
foodaholic
fun and frolic
idiotic
junior college
melancholic
metabolic
microscopic
misanthropic
paradoxic
pathologic
patriotic
periodic
philanthropic
philosophic
semiotic
sleepaholic
symbiotic
telescopic
unerotic
unexotic
vagabondage
vitriolic
workaholic

antibiotic
antispasmotic
heliotropic
kaleidoscopic
macrobiotic

OTICA (see ONICA)
OTICAL (see OGICAL)
OTICE (see OSES)
OTID (see OLID)
OTIENT (see ONEMENT)

OTIER (see OKIER)
OTING (see OWING 1)

OTION

bolden
bowman
broken
chosen
cloven
Coleman
colon
Conan
frozen
golden
golem
hogan
hokum
holden
Logan
lotion
modem
molten
motion
Nolan
nomen
notion
notum
novum
oaken
oaten
ocean
Odin
olden
omen
open
ovum
Owen
potion
quotum
Roman
Rosen
scrotum
showman
slogan
sloven
spoken
stolen
swollen
token

totem
woken
woven
yeoman
yolden

arrosion
awoken
Beethoven
beholden
bespoken
bus token
cognomen
commotion
corrosion
demotion
devotion
displosion
embolden
emotion
encolden
erosion
explosion
factotum
fresh frozen
golf open
hand lotion
heartbroken
Hoboken
Hulk Hogan
imbolden
implosion
love potion
love token
misspoken
outspoken
plainspoken
promotion
pronotum
reopen
rewoven
slow motion
soft-spoken
symplosion
teetotum
unchosen
unfrozen
unspoken
unyolden
verboten

well-spoken
wide-open
withholden

do not open
forward motion
interwoven
Jimmy Olsen
lederhosen
locomotion
magic potion
make a motion
man in motion
mesonotum
metanotum
monkey motion
Nova Scotian
semicolon
sleeping potion
spastic colon
unbeholden

Atlantic Ocean
by the same token
Pacific Ocean

perpetual motion
poetry in motion

OTIONAL (see OTABLE)
OTIVE (see OSES)
OTLE (see OTTLE)
OTLESS (see OLISH)
OTLIEST (see OGGIEST)
OTLY (see OCKEY)
OTNESS (see OLISH)
OTO (see OLO)
OTOMIES (see OLOGIES)
OTOMY (see OMETRY)
OTONIES (see OLOGIES)
OTONY (see OMETRY)
OTOPLAY (see OWAWAY)
OTOR (see OVER 1)
OTSA (see ADA 1)
OTSMAN (see OTTEN)
OTT (see OT)
OTTA (see ADA 1)
OTTABLE (see OGICAL)
OTTAGE (see OTIC)
OTTAL (see OTTLE)
OTTED (see OLID)

OTTEN

almond
auction
Austin
autumn
awesome
blossom
bobbin
Boston
bottom
Brahman
broaden
caution
coffin
column
common
condom
constant
cotton
coxswain
Datsun
dobbin
doctrine
dolphin
fallen
goblin
gotten
Hoffman
Johnson
noggin
often
option
Osmond
oxen
pollen
possum
problem
robin
rotten
Scotsman
shaman
slalom
sobbin
sodden
Sodom
soften
solemn
sponsen
Stalin
Swanson

tauten
toxin
trodden
watchman

adoption
au gratin
befallen
begotten
concoction
crestfallen
downfallen
downtrodden
forgotten
hobgoblin
ill-gotten
McLaughlin
misgotten
opossum
play possum
precaution
rock bottom
round robin
spoiled rotten
squash blossom
Steve Austin
toboggan
Top Ramen
uncommon
untrodden
Wisconsin

apple blossom
Donny Osmond
have in common
Magic Johnson
Marie Osmond
misbegotten
orange blossom
sauerbraten
semicolumn
spinal column
Tutankhamen
unforgotten

Christopher Walken
every so often
proceed with caution
William H. Bonham
William of Occam

OTTER (see OLLAR)
OTTERED (see OFFERED)
OTTERIES (see OLOGIES)

OTTERING

authoring
bothering
clobbering
collaring
daughtering
doctoring
fostering
hollering
mobstering
offering
posturing
pottering
proffering
prospering
slaughtering
slobbering
soldering
watering

mouth-watering

OTTERY (see OMETRY)
OTTEST (see OLISH)
OTTI (see OCKEY)
OTTIE (see OCKEY)
OTTIED (see OLLIED)
OTTIER (see OGGIER)
OTTIEST (see OGGIEST)
OTTILY (see OMETRY)
OTTINESS (see OCKINESS)
OTTING (see OCKING)
OTTISH (see OLISH)

OTTLE

awful
bauble
bobble
boggle
bottle
brothel
caudle
causal

cobble
cockle
coddle
dawdle
docile
fondle
fossil
glossal
glottal
gobble
goggle
gospel
grovel
hobble
hostel
hostile
joggle
jostle
lawful
model
mottle
nostril
novel
nozzle
offal
popple
potful
squabble
swaddle
thoughtful
throttle
toddle
toggle
topple
tossle
twaddle
waddle
waffle
wassail
watchful
wobble

apostle
boondoggle
Coke bottle
colossal
debacle
distraughtful
duck waddle
falafel

floor model
full throttle
god-awful
hornswoggle
old fossil
remodel
role model
undocile
unlawful
unthoughtful
youth hostel

airplane model
Aristotle
baby bottle
Eggo waffle
fashion model
hit the bottle
mollycoddle
Pentecostal
spin the bottle
supermodel
water bottle
working model

OTTLED (see OBBLED)
OTTLER (see OBBLER)
OTTLING (see OBBLING)

OTTO 1

Aldo
also
auto
bravo
Cabo
follow
grotto
hollow
lotto
macho
mano
motto
Otto
Pablo
Prado
pronto
swallow
taco
Tahoe

Tonto
wallow

Apollo
bravado
Chicago
Chicano
cuidado
Del Taco
Delgado
Diablo
fidalgo
gazpacho
Gustapo
hidalgo
Iago
Lake Tahoe
lumbago
Mikado
Morocco
mulatto
paisano
palazzo
Picasso
Romano
São Paulo
sirocco
staccato
Toronto
vibrato
Where's Waldo?
Zhivago

Alvarado
avocado
Capistrano
catafalco
Coronado
desperado
Eldorado
Esperanto
hard to swallow
Johnny Bravo
obligato
parmigiano
pizzicato
Robert Wadlow
Santiago

Americano
inamorato
mano y mano

aficionado
incommunicado

OTTO 2 (see OLO)
OTTOM (see OTTEN)
OTTOMAN (see OCCASIN)
OTTOMLESS (see OGGIEST)
OTTON (see OTTEN)
OTTONY (see OMETRY)
OTTY (see OCKEY)
OTUM (see OTION)
OTUS (see OSES)
OTY (see ONY)
OU 1 (see EW 1)
OU 2 (see OW 2)
OU'D (see OOM)
OU'LL (see OOL 1)
OU'RE (see URE 1)
OU'VE (see OOM)
OUBLE (see UBBLE)
OUBLER (see USTER 1)
OUBLING (see UFFLING)
OUBLY (see UDDY)
OUBT (see OUT)
OUBTER (see OWSER)
OUBTFUL (see OUSAL)
OUBTFULLY (see OWERY)
OUBTING (see OUNTING)
OUBTLESS (see OUTNESS)
OUCESTER (see OLLAR)
OUCH 1 (see OUT)
OUCH 2 (see UFF)
OUCHABLE (see USTABLE)
OUCHE (see UTE)
OUCHER 1 (see OWSER)
OUCHER 2 (see USTER 1)
OUCHING 1 (see OUNTING)
OUCHING 2 (see UTING 1)
OUCHY 1 (see OWDY)
OUCHY 2 (see UDDY)
OUD (see OUT)
OUDER (see OWSER)
OUDEST (see OUTEST)
OUDING (see OUNTING)
OUDLESS (see OUTNESS)
OUDLY (see OWDY)
OUDNESS (see OUTNESS)
OUDY (see OWDY)

OUGAR (see UTER)
OUGE (see OUT)
OUGER (see OWSER)
OUGH 1 (see EW 1)
OUGH 2 (see UFF)
OUGH 3 (see OW 1)
OUGH 4 (see OFF)
OUGH 5 (see OW 2)
OUGHEN (see UTTON)
OUGHER 1 (see USTER 1)
OUGHER 2 (see OLLAR)
OUGHIE (see UDDY)
OUGHING 1 (see OCKING)
OUGHING 2 (see USTING)
OUGHLY (see UDDY)
OUGHNESS (see UCKET)
OUGHT 1 (see OT)
OUGHT 2 (see OUT)
OUGHTA (see ADA 1)
OUGHTFUL (see OTTLE)
OUGHTLESS (see OLISH)
OUGHY (see ONY)
OUGING (see OUNTING)
OUGLAS (see UCKET)
OUI (see E 1)
OUIJA (see EASY)
OUILLE (see EWY)
OUIS (see UENESS)
OUK (see UTE)
OUKA (see UNA)
OUL 1 (see OLE 1)
OUL 2 (see OWL 1)
OUL 3 (see OOL 1)
OULD (see OOD 1)
OULDABLE (see OTABLE)
OULDER (see OVER 1)
OULER (see OWSER)
OULEST (see OUTEST)

OULETTE

duet
duplex
gooseneck
roulette
Suzette

crepe suzette

Russian roulette

OULFUL (see OSAL)
OULING (see OUNTING)
OULISH (see EWISH)
OULNESS (see OUTNESS)
OUM (see OOM)
OUN 1 (see OUND 1)
OUN 2 (see OOM)
OUNAL (see OUSAL)
OUNCE (see OUT)

OUNCED

bounced
browsed
doused
drowsed
flounced
groused
housed
pounced
roused
soused
trounced

announced
aroused
caroused
denounced
espoused
pronounced
renounced

mispronounced
rabble-roused

OUNCEMENT

fountain
mountain
thousand

accountant
announcement
denouncement
endowment
enouncement
inbowment
indowment
pronouncement
renouncement

disavowment
disendowment
drinking fountain
Magic Mountain
preannouncement
soda fountain

Escape to Witch Mountain

OUNCER (see OUNDER)
OUNCING (see OUNTING)
OUNCY (see OWDY)

OUND 1

bound
brown
browse
clown
crown
down
drown
drowse
found
frown
gown
ground
hound
lounge
mound
noun
pound
round
rouse
scrounge
sound
town

abound
aground
all-round
around
arouse
astound
back down
background
ballgown
Bean Town
bloodhound
boomtown

break ground
breakdown
burn down
campground
carouse
chow down
chowhound
clampdown
close down
comedown
compound
confound
countdown
cow town
crackdown
crosstown
dogpound
downtown
dumbfound
earthbound
expound
face-down
fairground
foreground
Georgetown
ghosttown
goose down
greyhound
hands-down
hardbound
hick town
hidebound
high ground
hoedown
hometown
icebound
impound
inbound
James Brown
Jamestown
knockdown
lay down
letdown
lowdown
markdown
meltdown
Motown
newfound
nightgown
outbound
playground

profound
pronoun
propound
putdown
rebound
redound
renown
rubdown
scale-down
shakedown
showdown
shutdown
sit down
slowdown
small-town
snowbound
spellbound
sundown
surround
takedown
thumbs-down
Toon Town
touchdown
unbound
unfound
unsound
unwound
uptown
wash down
wind down
wolfhound
year-round

above ground
all around
battleground
breeding ground
broken-down
buttoned-down
cap and gown
Charlie Brown
Chinatown
circus clown
Cooperstown
dressing gown
dressing-down
duty-bound
eiderdown
evening gown
fool around
fox and hound

Foxy Brown
go to town
hallowed ground
hand-me-down
homeward bound
honorbound
kiss the ground
knuckle down
leather-bound
lightning round
lost and found
musclebound
neutral ground
off the ground
on the town
out-of-town
outward-bound
paint the town
pitcher's mound
proving ground
rabble-rouse
round and round
run aground
runaround
shantytown
solid ground
stamping ground
stand your ground
trickle-down
triple crown
tumbledown
ultrasound
underground
up and down
upside down
watered-down
wedding gown
westward bound
wraparound

Bozo The Clown
burial ground
chocolate brown
ear to the ground
Fox and the Hound
get off the ground
Homie The Clown
in and around
Koreatown
man about town
merry go round

out on the town
run rings around
take lying down
up and around

Huckleberry Hound
only game in town
pussyfoot around
run into the ground

Santa Caus is Comin' to Town

OUND 2 (see OOM)
OUNDABLE (see OUNTIFUL)
OUNDARY (see OWDY)
OUNDED (see OUNTED)

OUNDER

bouncer
bounder
counter
downer
flouncer
flounder
founder
frowner
grounder
hounder
lounger
mounter
pouncer
pounder
rounder
scrounger
sounder
trouncer

accounter
announcer
astounder
cofounder
confounder
denouncer
discounter
dismounter
encounter
expounder
impounder
inbounder

lunch counter
miscounter
profounder
pronouncer
rebounder
recounter
renouncer
surmounter
surrounder

bargain counter
chance encounter
checkout counter
Geiger counter
mispronouncer
quarter pounder

over the counter
under the counter

OUNDING

bounding
founding
grounding
hounding
pounding
rounding
sounding

abounding
astounding
compounding
confounding
dumbfounding
expounding
impounding
inbounding
propounding
rebounding
strange sounding
surrounding

OUNDLESS (see OUTNESS)
OUNDLY (see OWDY)
OUNDREL (see OUSAL)
OUNDRESS (see OUTNESS)
OUNDRY (see OWDY)
OUNG (see UN)
OUNGE (see OUND 1)

OUNGER 1 (see OUNDER)
OUNGER 2 (see UMMER)
OUNGING (see OUNTING)
OUNGY (see OWDY)
OUNSEL (see OUSAL)
OUNSELING (see OUNTING)
OUNT (see OUT)
OUNTABLE (see OUNTIFUL)
OUNTABLY (see OWERY)
OUNTAIN (see OUNCEMENT)
OUNTANT (see OUNCEMENT)

OUNTED

bounded
counted
founded
hounded
pounded
rounded
sounded

abounded
astounded
compounded
confounded
dumbfounded
expounded
impounded
inbounded
propounded
rebounded
redounded
surrounded
unfounded
well founded
well-rounded

OUNTER (see OUNDER)
OUNTESS (see OUTNESS)
OUNTIE (see OWDY)

OUNTIFUL

boundable
bountiful
countable
foundable
groundable

houndable
mountable
poundable
roundable
soundable

accountable
astoundable
compoundable
confoundable
discountable
dismountable
dumbfoundable
expoundable
impoundable
propoundable
reboundable
recountable
remountable
spellboundable
surmountable
surroundable
unboundable
unfoundable
unsoundable

insurmountable
unaccountable

OUNTING

blousing
bouncing
bowing
browning
browsing
chowing
clouding
clowning
couching
counting
cowling
crouching
crowding
crowning
doubting
dousing
downing
drowning

drowsing
flouncing
flouting
fouling
frowning
gouging
grouching
grousing
grouting
growling
housing
howling
jousting
lounging
mounting
mouthing
ousting
outing
plowing
pouncing
pouting
prowling
rousing
rousting
routing
scouting
scowling
scrounging
shouting
slouching
spouting
sprouting
touting
trouncing
vouching
vowing
wowing

accounting
allowing
amounting
announcing
arousing
avowing
befouling
blood counting
bow-wowing
carousing
counseling
delousing

denouncing
discounting
dismounting
endowing
enshrouding
espousing
head counting
kowtowing
meowing
miscounting
pronouncing
recounting
remounting
renouncing
roughhousing
snowplowing
surmounting
warehousing

body counting
catamounting
cost accounting
disallowing
disavowing
mispronouncing
overclouding
overcrowding
rabble-rousing

OUNTLESS (see OUTNESS)
OUNTRY (see UNNY)
OUNTY (see OWDY)
OUP 1 (see UTE)
OUP 2 (see EW 1)
OUPABLE (see OOTABLE)
OUPAL (see OODLE)
OUPE 1 (see UTE)
OUPE 2 (see OAT)
OUPER (see UTER)
OUPIE (see UTY)
OUPING (see UTING 1)
OUPLE (see UBBLE)
OUPLET (see UCKET)
OUPY (see UTY)
OUR 1 (see ORE 1)

OUR 2

dour
flour
hour

our
scour
sour

devour
half hour
lunch hour
manhour
noonhour
rush hour
sweet-sour

cocktail hour
dinner hour
happy hour
miles per hour
sweet and sour
whiskey sour
witching hour
zero hour

OUR 3 (see URE 1)
OURABLE (see ORTABLE)
OURAGE (see ERVICE)

OURAGEMENT

furnishment
nourishment
permanent
turbulent

discouragement
disfurnishment
encouragement
impermanent
malnourishment
nonpermanent
refurbishment
refurnishment

disencouragement
semipermanent
semopermanent
undernourishment

OURANT (see ORIST)
OURBON (see ERSION)
OURCE (see ORSE 1)
OURCEFUL (see ORMAL)

OURD (see OARD)
OUREST 1 (see OUTEST)
OUREST 2 (see URIST)
OURI (see IRTY)
OURIER (see URLIER)
OURING 1 (see OWERING)
OURING 2 (see ORMING 1)
OURISH 1 (see ERVICE)
OURISH 2 (see ORIST)
OURISHMENT (see OURAGEMENT)
OURLY 1 (see OWERY)
OURLY 2 (see URELY)
OURN (see ORN)
OURNER (see ORDER)
OURNEY (see IRTY)
OURNING (see ORMING 1)
OURSE (see ORSE 1)
OURSING (see ORMING 1)
OURT (see ORP)
OURTABLE (see ORTABLE)
OURTER (see ORDER)
OURTH (see ORSE 1)
OURTING (see ORMING 1)
OURTLY (see ORY)
OURTNEY (see ORY)
OURY (see OWERY)
OUS (see USE 1)

OUSAL

counsel
doubtful
nounal
scalpel
scoundrel
spousal
tousle

arousal
carousal
devoutful
espousal
respousal

OUSAND (see OUNCEMENT)
OUSE 1 (see OUT)
OUSE 2 (see OUND 1)
OUSED 1 (see OUNCED)
OUSED 2 (see OUNCED)
OUSELESS (see OUTNESS)
OUSER (see OWSER)

OUSESS (see OUTNESS)
OUSIN (see UTTON)
OUSING 1 (see OUNTING)
OUSING 2 (see OUNTING)
OUSINLY (see UTTERY)
OUSLE (see OUSAL)
OUST (see OUT)
OUSTER (see OWSER)
OUSTIC (see EWISH)
OUSTING (see OUNTING)
OUSY 1 (see OWDY)
OUSY 2 (see OWDY)

OUT

blouse
bounce
bout
cloud
clout
couch
count
crouch
crowd
doubt
douse
drought
Faust
flounce
flout
fount
gouge
gout
grouch
grouse
grout
house
joust
kraut
Laos
loud
louse
lout
mount
mouse
mouth
ouch
ounce
oust
out

pouch
pounce
pout
proud
roust
rout
scout
shout
shroud
slouch
snout
souse
south
spouse
spout
sprout
stout
Strauss
tout
trounce
trout
vouch

about
account
all out
aloud
amount
announce
bad-mouth
bail out
bathhouse
beachhouse
bean sprout
belt out
big mouth
birdhouse
blackout
blood count
blowout
boathouse
boy scout
breakout
bughouse
bugout
burnout
campout
cathouse
church mouse
close-out

clubhouse
cookout
courthouse
cross out
cub scout
cutout
deep South
delouse
denounce
devout
dine out
discount
dismount
doghouse
dollhouse
downspout
drag out
dropout
dugout
enshroud
espouse
ex-spouse
fade-out
fallout
far out
field house
field mouse
firehouse
flame-out
flophouse
full house
girl scout
greenhouse
guardhouse
guest house
handout
hangout
head count
holdout
in-crowd
jailhouse
knockout
layout
lighthouse
lights out
lockout
lookout
loudmouth
madhouse
mail pouch

make out
miscount
no doubt
no-count
outhouse
outloud
pass out
penthouse
playhouse
poorhouse
pronounce
psych-out
rain spout
raincloud
rained out
recount
remount
renounce
reroute
roadhouse
roughhouse
roundhouse
row house
self-doubt
sellout
shoot-out
shutout
smoke out
smokehouse
sold-out
stakeout
standout
steak house
storehouse
stressed-out
strung out
surmount
take-out
teahouse
throughout
townhouse
tryout
turnout
uncloud
walkout
war cloud
warehouse
washed out
washout
way out

White House
whorehouse
wipeout
without
workout

all about
bank account
beyond doubt
blabbermouth
boarding house
body count
bring about
Brussels sprout
casting couch
cat and mouse
catamount
chicken out
coffeehouse
coming-out
Count Von Count
dish it out
do without
down and out
falling-out
figure out
gadabout
go without
halfway house
hand-to-mouth
haunted house
hoof and mouth
house-to-house
in and out
inside out
knockabout
Levi Strauss
live without
long-drawn-out
Mickey Mouse
Mighty Mouse
Minnie Mouse
mispronounce
mouth-to-mouth
mushroom cloud
no-account
odd man out
on account
on the house
open house

ounce for ounce
out-and-out
overblouse
overcrowd
overshout
paramount
porterhouse
powerhouse
psyched you out
rainbow trout
roundabout
roustabout
runabout
sauerkraut
scenic route
set up house
shut your mouth
slaughterhouse
talent scout
tantamount
the big house
three's a crowd
thundercloud
truth will out
turnabout
walkabout
waterspout
Westinghouse
without doubt
word of mouth

atomic cloud
big as a house
bring down the house
day in, day out
down for the count
easy way out
eat your heart out
expense account
knock-down-drag-out
on no account
on or about
Oscar The Grouch
over and out
Pee-Wee's Playhouse
stick your neck out
up and about
with or without
without a doubt
year in, year out
for crying out loud

quiet as a mouse
reasonable doubt
Rosemary Woodhouse
shadow of a doubt
Speaker of the House
take into account

benefit of the doubt

OUTE (see OUT)
OUTER (see OWSER)

OUTEST

brownest
brownist
Daoist
flautist
foulest
loudest
Maoist
proudest
sourest
stoutest

devoutest

OUTFUL (see OUSAL)
OUTH (see OUT)
OUTHER (see UTER)
OUTHERN (see USTER 1)
OUTHESS (see OUTNESS)
OUTHFUL (see OODLE)
OUTHING (see OUNTING)
OUTHLESS (see OUTNESS)
OUTING (see OUNTING)
OUTLESS (see OUTNESS)
OUTLY (see OWDY)

OUTNESS

boundless
browless
cloudless
countess
countless
doubtless
foulness
foundress

groundless
houseless
loudness
mouthless
nowness
outhess
outness
proudness
prowess
shroudless
soundless
spouseless
spousess
spoutless
stoutness
vowless

devoutless
devoutness
viscountess

roundaboutness

OUTRE (see UTER)
OUTWARDLY (see OWERY)
OUTY (see OWDY)
OUVEAU (see UNO)
OUVER (see UTER)
OUX (see EW 1)
OV 1 (see OFF)
OV 2 (see OFF)
OV 3 (see UG)
OVA (see OLA)
OVABLE 1 (see OOTABLE)
OVABLE 2 (see USTABLE)
OVAH (see OLA)
OVAL 1 (see OODLE)
OVAL 2 (see OSAL)
OVARY (see OCALLY)
OVE 1 (see UG)
OVE 2 (see OSE 1)
OVE 3 (see OOM)
OVEL 1 (see UBBLE)
OVEL 2 (see OTTLE)
OVELESS (see UCKET)
OVELIEST (see UBBIEST)
OVELING 1 (see OVERING)
OVELING 2 (see ANDERING 2)
OVELTIES (see OLOGIES)
OVELTY (see OMETRY)
OVELY (see UDDY)
OVEMENT (see UTION)

OVEN 1 (see OTION)
OVEN 2 (see UTION)
OVEN 3 (see UTTON)
OVENANT (see UCCULENT)
OVENLY (see UTTERY)

OVER 1

bloater
blower
boaster
boater
bolder
Bolger
bolster
boner
boulder
bowler
broker
chauffeur
choker
choler
cloner
closer
closure
clover
coaster
coaxer
coder
colder
comber
coper
croaker
crower
dolor
donor
doper
doser
doter
Dover
dozer
droner
floater
foamer
folder
gaucher
gloater
goader
goer
gofer

gopher
groaner
grocer
grosser
grower
hoer
holder
holster
homer
honer
joker
jokester
jolter
kosher
loader
loafer
loaner
loather
loner
lower
moaner
molar
molder
moper
motor
mower
noter
odor
ogre
older
over
owner
phoner
poacher
poker
polar
poller
pollster
poser
poster
prober
proner
quoter
roadster
roamer
roaster
rober
roller
roper
rotor

rover
rower
Schroeder
scolder
scroller
sewer
shofar
shoulder
slower
smoker
smolder
soaker
sober
solar
soldier
sower
stoker
stoner
stroker
stroller
thrower
toaster
toner
toter
troller
volar
voter
wholer
yogurt
zoner

all over
aloner
atoner
beachcomber
beholder
bemoaner
bipolar
blindfolder
blow over
boil over
bowl over
brown-noser
bulldozer
cajoler
cardholder
chain-smoker
changeover
churchgoer
co-owner

cold shoulder
cold sober
composer
composure
condoler
condoner
connoter
consoler
controller
convoker
corroder
deboner
decoder
demoter
denoter
deposer
dethroner
disclosure
disowner
disrober
do over
eloper
emoter
enclosure
enfolder
enroller
eroder
evoker
exploder
exposer
exposure
extoller
fire stoker
flamethrower
flip over
foreclosure
fork over
four-poster
freeloader
greengrocer
gun holster
hair roller
hand over
hangover
high roller
holdover
homeowner
householder
imposer
intoner

invoker
knock over
Land Rover
landholder
lawnmower
layover
leaseholder
leftover
log roller
makeover
mindblower
misnomer
misquoter
moreover
nonsmoker
October
once-over
opposer
paroler
part owner
Passover
patroller
pawn broker
pearl choker
pick over
popover
postponer
potholder
promoter
proposer
provoker
pullover
pushover
Red Rover
reloader
revoker
roll over
run over
shalomer
shareholder
sleep over
soft shoulder
spillover
steamroller
stockbroker
stockholder
strikeover
strip poker
supposer
switchover
takeover
talk over

think over
throw over
transposer
turnover
unfolder
unloader
upholder
upholster
verboser
warmed-over
withholder
work over

air controller
carryover
Dannon Yogurt
death warmed over
diagnoser
four-leaf clover
going-over
grandslam homer
holy roller
mediocre
overloader
partygoer
penny loafer
powerbroker
pull a boner
red-hot poker
reupholster
Ricky Schroder
rock-and-roller
roller coaster
Super Soaker
telephoner
turkey roaster

absentee voter
bigger and bolder
chip on your shoulder
cry on my shoulder
keep your composure
Love Roller Coaster
manila folder
over and over
overexposure
policy holder
shoulder-to-shoulder

indecent exposure

OVER 2 (see USTER 1)
OVER 3 (see UTER)

OVERING

blundering
blustering
buffering
buggering
bunkering
buttering
clustering
cluttering
coloring
covering
duffeling
flustering
fluttering
governing
hoveling
hovering
hungering
hunkering
lumbering
mothering
mustering
muttering
numbering
plundering
puckering
pummeling
puttering
shoveling
shuddering
slumbering
smothering
sputtering
structuring
stuttering
succoring
suckering
suffering
thundering
tuckering
ushering
uttering
wondering
wuthering

book covering

cloud covering
discoloring
dust covering
encumbering
godmothering
ground covering
outnumbering
rebuffering
recovering
renumbering
slipcovering
uncovering
unpuckering
warmongering

disencumbering
movie ushering
scandalmongering

OVERLAY (see OWAWAY)
OVERLY (see OCALLY)
OVERN (see USTER 1)
OVERNING (see OVERING)
OVERNMENT (see UCCULENT)
OVERPAY (see OWAWAY)
OVERPLAY (see OWAWAY)
OVERSTAY (see OWAWAY)
OVERTY (see OMETRY)
OVERY 1 (see UTTERY)
OVERY 2 (see OCALLY)
OVET (see UCKET)
OVETT (see UCKET)
OVEY (see UDDY)
OVIA (see OLIA)

OVIAL

jovial

acromial
binomial
colloquial
colonial
microbial
monomial
trinomial

ceremonial
circumjovial
diagonial

matrimonial
microscopial
oxygonial
patrimonial
polynomial
quadrinomial
sanctimonial
testimonial

antimicrobial
intercolonial
neocolonial

OVIAN (see ONIAN)
OVICE (see OLISH)
OVIDENCE (see OMINENCE)
OVIE (see UTY)
OVING 1 (see UTING 1)
OVING 2 (see USTING)
OVING 3 (see OWING 1)
OVITY (see OMETRY)
OVLED (see OBBLED)
OVO (see OLO)
OVULATE (see OPULATE)
OVULATION (see OPERATION)
OVUM (see OTION)
OVY (see ONY)

OW 1

beau
blow
bow
bro
crow
doe
dough
faux
floe
flow
foe
fro
glow
go
grow
hoe
Joe
know
lo
low

Moe
mow
no
O
oh
owe
Poe
pro
Rho
roe
row
schmo
sew
show
sloe
slow
snow
so
sow
stow
though
throw
toe
tow
whoa
woe
yo

aglow
ago
all pro
all show
although
bateau
below
bestow
Bordeaux
cash-flow
chapeau
chateau
CO
Cousteau
crossbow
death blow
death row
flambeau
floorshow
forego
freak show
free flow

game show
golf pro
heave-ho
heigh-ho
hum ho
ice floe
in tow
Jane Doe
Jim Crow
Joe Blo
John Doe
Kwang-Chow
lie low
light show
longbow
low blow
Monroe
moon glow
no show
old crow
outflow
outgo
outgrow
oxbow
peep show
plateau
Play-Doh
quiz show
Rain-Blo
road show
Rousseau
say-so
scarecrow
sideshow
ski tow
skid row
sourdough
stone's throw
talk show
tent show
tiptoe
Van Gogh
Wham-o
workflow
you know

afterglow
Alamo
all for show
apropos

best in show
blow by blow
body blow
BTO
camel toe
CEO
CIO
cookie dough
Cosby Show
crowning blow
cup of Joe
cupid's bow
daddy-o
do-si-do
ebb and flow
embryo
even so
even though
fall below
fashion show
fatal blow
friend or foe
G.I. Joe
go below
hammerthrow
hammertoe
heel-and-toe
high and low
IMO
in the know
Ivanhoe
Jackie O
Jill Monroe
Kokomo
long ago
minstrel show
mistletoe
on the go
on tiptoe
one-man show
overflow
overgrow
overthrow
piccolo
picture show
pompano
puppet show
quid pro quo
right-to-know
run the show

Russell Crowe
semipro
send below
Sloppy Joe
so-and-so
SRO
status quo
steal the show
stop and go
stop the show
strike a blow
tale of woe
talent show
tally ho
tic-tac-toe
tippytoe
TKO
to and fro
toe-to-toe
touch and go
TV show
undergo
underthrow
undertow
white as snow
Wild West show
years ago
yes and no

Flip Wilson Show
from the word go
get-up-and-go
go with the flow
medicine show
pay as you go
ready to go
ready, set, go
star of the show

dog-and-pony show
Hawaii five-O
Marilyn Monroe
Michelangelo
pianissimo
That 70s Show

easy come easy go
Mary Tyler Moore Show
Pilsbury Cookie Dough
pure as the driven snow

eeny meeny miny mo
one monkey don't stop no show
Rocky Horror Picture Show

OW 2

bough
bow
brow
chow
ciao
cow
how
now
ow
plough
plow
pow
prow
scow
tau
thou
vow
wow

allow
and how
avow
bow wow
endow
eyebrow
highbrow
know-how
kowtow
landau
lowbrow
luau
Mau Mau
meow
Moscow
nohow
powwow
snowplow
somehow

anyhow
cat's meow
disallow
disavow

even now
here and now
holy cow
marriage vow
sacred cow
solemn vow
take a bow

holier than thou

OWABLE (see OTABLE)
OWABLY (see OWERY)
OWAL (see OWEL)
OWARD 1 (see OWER 1)
OWARD 2 (see ORDERED)
OWARDLY (see OWERY)

OWAWAY

foldaway
overlay
overpay
overplay
overstay
photoplay
protégé
stowaway
throwaway
towaway

OWD (see OUT)
OWDER (see OWSER)
OWDERING (see OWERING)
OWDING (see OUNTING)

OWDY

Audi
blousy
blowsy
bouncy
boundary
bounty
brownie
cloudy
county
dowdy
downy
drowsy

foundry
frowsy
gouty
grouchy
howdy
Howie
loudly
lousy
Maui
mountie
mousy
ouchy
pouchy
pouty
powie
roundly
rowdy
Saudi
scroungy
slouchy
snouty
soundly
stoutly
tousy
townie
wowie
yowie
zowie

cum laude
pandowdy
profoundly
uncloudy

Ronda Rousey
rowdydowdy

apple pandowdy
magna cum laude
summa cum laude

OWE (see OW 1)

OWEL

bowel
dowel
Powell
towel

trowel
vowel

avowal

Colin Powell
crying towel
disembowel

throw in the towel

OWELER (see OWSER)
OWELL (see OWEL)
OWEN (see OTION)

OWER 1

Bauer
bower
coward
cower
flower
Howard
plower
power
shower
tower
vower
wower

allower
avower
bell tower
brain power
clock tower
cold shower
cornflower
deflower
empower
endower
firepower
gray power
horsepower
lung power
manpower
Mayflower
rain shower
Ron Howard
safflower
sea power

snowplower
sunflower
wallflower
watchtower
wildflower
willpower
world power

baby shower
bridal shower
candlepower
cauliflower
control tower
Devil's Tower
disallower
disavower
Eiffel Tower
Eisenhower
ivory tower
overpower
passion flower
superpower
veto power
woman power

atomic power
balance of power
electric power
nuclear power

OWER 2 (see OVER 1)

OWERING

cowering
flouring
flowering
powdering
powering
scouring
showering
souring
towering

deflowering
devouring
empowering

overpowering

OWERY

bowery
cowardly
doubtfully
dowry
floury
flowery
hourly
outwardly
showery
sourly

accountably
allowably

OWESS (see OUTNESS)
OWIE 1 (see OWDY)
OWIE 2 (see ONY)
OWIER (see OKIER)

OWING 1

bloating
blowing
boasting
boating
boding
Boeing
bolting
boning
bowling
broaching
choking
chroming
cloning
closing
clothing
coaching
coasting
coating
coaxing
coding
combing
coning
coping
croaking
crowing
doling
doping

dosing
doting
dozing
droning
floating
flowing
foaming
folding
ghosting
gloaming
gloating
glowing
goading
going
groaning
groping
grossing
growing
hoeing
holding
homing
honing
hoping
hosing
hosting
joking
jolting
knowing
loading
loafing
loaning
loathing
loping
lowing
moaning
molding
molting
moping
mowing
nosing
noting
owing
owning
phoning
poaching
poking
polling
posing
posting
probing

quoting
roaming
roasting
robing
roguing
rolling
roping
roving
rowing
scolding
scoping
sewing
showing
sloping
smoking
snowing
soaking
soaping
sowing
stoking
stoning
stowing
stroking
strolling
throwing
toasting
toeing
toning
toting
towing
trolling
voting
zoning

all-knowing
approaching
atoning
bankrolling
beholding
bemoaning
bestowing
blindfolding
bulldozing
cajoling
chain-smoking
churchgoing
composing
condoling
condoning
connoting

consoling
controlling
convoking
corroding
deboning
decoding
demoting
denoting
deposing
dethroning
devoting
disclosing
disowning
disposing
disrobing
eloping
emoting
enclosing
encroaching
enfolding
engrossing
enrolling
enscrolling
enthroning
eroding
evoking
exploding
exposing
extolling
fast growing
flamethrowing
foreboding
foreclosing
foregoing
free-flowing
handholding
imposing
intoning
invoking
logrolling
mind-blowing
misquoting
no smoking
ongoing
opposing
outflowing
outgoing
outvoting
paroling
postponing

OWING 2 (continued)

prefolding
promoting
proposing
provoking
remolding
reposing
reproaching
resoling
revoking
revolting
steamrolling
stonethrowing
supposing
tiptoeing
transposing
unfolding
unloading
unrolling
upholding
withholding

chaperoning
color coding
decomposing
diagnosing
easygoing
honeycombing
interloping
interposing
overdosing
overflowing
overloading
overthrowing
partygoing
pigeonholing
predisposing
presupposing
recomposing
rock-and-rolling
telephoning
tippytoeing
undergoing
unimposing

overcontrolling
overexposing
superimposing
wolf in sheep's clothing

OWING 2 (see OUNTING)

OWL 1

cowl
foul
fowl
growl
howl
jowl
owl
prowl
scowl
yowl

afoul
befoul
hoot owl
night owl

fish or fowl
on the prowl
waterfowl
wise old owl

technical foul
wise as an owl

OWL 2 (see OLE 1)
OWLEDGE (see OTIC)
OWLEDGER (see OGRAPHER)
OWLER 1 (see OWSER)
OWLER 2 (see OVER 1)
OWLESS (see OUTNESS)
OWLING 1 (see OUNTING)
OWLING 2 (see OWING 1)
OWLY (see ONY)
OWMAN (see OTION)
OWMENT (see OUNCEMENT)
OWN 1 (see OUND 1)
OWN 2 (see ONE 1)
OWNED (see OBED)
OWNER 1 (see OVER 1)
OWNER 2 (see OUNDER)
OWNESS (see OUTNESS)
OWNEST (see OUTEST)
OWNIE (see OWDY)
OWNING 1 (see OUNTING)
OWNING 2 (see OWING 1)
OWNIST (see OUTEST)
OWNY (see OWDY)
OWRY (see OWERY)
OWSE (see OUND 1)
OWSED (see OUNCED)

OWSER

bowser
browser
chowder
coucher
croucher
doubter
drowser
flouter
fouler
gouger
groucher
grouter
growler
houser
howler
jouster
louder
oucher
ouster
outer
pouter
powder
prouder
prowler
rouser
router
schnauzer
scouter
scowler
shouter
sloucher
souser
sprouter
stouter
touter
trouser
voucher
yowler

arouser
bath powder
carouser
clam chowder
enshrouder
espouser
gun powder
mail router

disemboweler
Doogie Howser
overcrowder
rabble-rouser

OWSING (see OUNTING)
OWSY (see OWDY)
OWTH (see OAT)
OWY (see ONY)

OX

box
cox
fox
knosp
Knox
lox
ox
pox
sox
wasp

bandbox
beat box
black box
breadbox
call box
cashbox
detox
dumb ox
Fort Knox
fuse box
gift box
hatbox
icebox
inbox
jukebox
lockbox
lunchbox
mailbox
matchbox
outfox
pillbox
poor box
press box
Red Sox
sandbox
shoebox
smallpox

snot box
snuff box
soap box
squawk box
squeezebox
strongbox
sweatbox
toy box
voice box
White Sox
Xerox

ballot box
bobby sox
cardboard box
chatterbox
chickenpox
cigar box
crackerbox
equinox
flowerbox
jury box
letter box
music box
orthodox
paradox
shadowbox
silver fox
tinderbox
windowbox
witness box

collection box
Jack In The Box
jewelry box
Michael J. Fox
Pandora's box
Patty Simcox
penalty box
post office box
sly as a fox
suggestion box
unorthodox

vernal equinox

first crack out of the box

OXEN (see OTTEN)
OXER (see OLLAR)
OXFORD (see OFFERED)

OXI (see OCKEY)
OXIA (see OLIA)
OXIC (see OTIC)
OXICAL (see OGICAL)
OXIDANTS (see OMINENCE)
OXIDATE (see OPULATE)
OXIDATION (see OPERATION)
OXIE (see OCKEY)
OXIED (see OLLIED)
OXIER (see OGGIER)
OXIEST (see OGGIEST)
OXILY (see OMETRY)
OXIN (see OTTEN)
OXINESS (see OCKINESS)
OXING (see OCKING)
OXIOUS (see AWLESS)
OXLY (see OCKEY)
OXSWAIN (see OTTEN)
OXY (see OCKEY)
OXYGEN (see OCCASIN)
OY (see OID)

OYA

Goya
moya
soya
troika

Sequoia

annuloida
paranoia

OYAL (see OIL)
OYALTY (see ORMITY)

OYANCE

buoyance
joyance
noyance
ointments
voidance

annoyance
anointments
appointments
avoidance
clairvoyance

flamboyance
upbuoyance

disappointments
reappointments

OYANT (see OYMENT)
OYCE (see OID)
OYD (see OID)
OYED (see OID)
OYER (see ORDER)
OYEUR (see ORDER)
OYFULLY (see ORMITY)
OYING (see OILING)
OYL (see OIL)
OYLE (see OIL)

OYMENT

buoyant
joinant
ointment
poignant
poison
toilet
toison

adjoinant
anointment
appointment
avoidant
chatoyant
clairvoyant
deployment
disjointment
employment
empoison
enjoyment
flamboyant
impoison
unpoison

disappointment
disemployment
foreappointment
misemployment
nonappointment
preappointment
reappointment
redeployment

reemployment
reenjoyment
unemployment

underemployment

OYO (see OLO)
OYSTER (see ORDER)
OYSTERING (see ORDERING)
OZ (see OFF)
OZABLE (see OTABLE)
OZE (see OSE 1)
OZED (see OBED)
OZEN 1 (see UTTON)
OZEN 2 (see OTION)
OZER (see OVER 1)
OZES (see OSES)
OZIE (see UTY)
OZIER (see OKIER)
OZILY (see OCALLY)
OZING (see OWING 1)
OZO (see OLO)
OZY (see ONY)
OZZ (see OFF)
OZZIE (see OCKEY)
OZZLE (see OTTLE)
OZZLED (see OBBLED)

U

Rhyme Sounds

U (see EW 1)
UABLE (see OOTABLE)
UAD (see OD)
UAL (see EWAL)
UALITY (see OMETRY)
UALLY (see UITY 1)
UANCE (see UDENCE)
UANCY (see UITY 1)
UANT (see UTION)
UANTITY (see OMETRY)
UAVE (see OD)
UB (see UG)
UBA (see UNA)
UBAL (see OODLE)
UBAN (see UTION)
UBBA (see USSIA)
UBBABLE (see USTABLE)
UBBER (see USTER 1)
UBBERY (see UTTERY)

UBBIEST

bubbliest
buggiest
bustiest
chubbiest
clubbiest
crustiest
duckiest
dustiest
fluffiest
fussiest
fustiest
fuzziest
grubbiest
gushiest
gustiest
gutsiest
guttiest
huffiest
loveliest
luckiest
lustiest
muckiest
muddiest
muggiest
mussiest
mustiest
muttiest
muzziest
nubbiest

nuttiest
pluckiest
plushiest
puffiest
pussiest
rubbliest
ruddiest
rustiest
scrubbiest
scruffiest
shrubbiest
slushiest
sluttiest
smuttiest
snubbiest
snuffiest
stubbiest
stubbliest
studliest
stuffiest
touchiest
trustiest
tubbiest
ugliest
illustrious
industrious
unluckiest

UBBING (see USTING)
UBBISH (see UFFISH)

UBBLE

bubble
buckle
bustle
buttle
chuckle
couple
cuddle
double
duffel
fuddle
guzzle
hovel
hubble
huddle
hustle
juggle
knuckle

muddle
muffle
muscle
mussel
muzzle
nubble
nuzzle
puddle
puzzle
rubble
ruffle
Russell
rustle
scuffle
scuttle
shovel
shuffle
shuttle
smuggle
snuffle
snuggle
struggle
stubble
subtle
suckle
supple
trouble
truckle
truffle
tuggle
tussle
Tuttle

air bubble
befuddle
belt buckle
car trouble
corpuscle
dust ruffle
fast shuffle
in trouble
Kurt Russell
mud puddle
pinochle
rebuttle
redouble
reshuffle
see double
soap bubble
space shuttle

steam shovel
swashbuckle
unbuckle
unruffle
unsubtle
white-knuckle

borrow trouble
daily double
Double Bubble
double trouble
facial stubble
flex your muscle
honeysuckle
hustle bustle
married couple
Mr. Bubble
on the double
smooth and supple
Super Bubble
takeout double
too much trouble
water puddle

UBBLER (see USTER 1)
UBBLIEST (see UBBIEST)
UBBLING (see UFFLING)
UBBLY (see UDDY)
UBBORN (see USTER 1)
UBBORNLY (see UTTERY)
UBBY (see UDDY)
UBE (see OOM)
UBELESS (see UTENESS)
UBEN (see UTION)
UBER (see UTER)
UBERANT (see UMINANT)
UBEROUS (see UBIOUS)
UBERTY (see UITY 1)
UBIC (see EWISH)
UBICLE (see OOTABLE)
UBIK (see EWISH)
UBILANT (see UMINANT)
UBILATE (see UMINATE)
UBILOUS (see UBIOUS)
UBINARY (see UITARY)
UBING (see UTING 1)

UBIOUS

crucifix
dubious

Eucharist
fugitive
humorous
lucrative
ludicrous
luminous
lunatic
neutralist
nubilous
nucleus
numerous
pugilist
punitive
rubious
studious
tuberous
tumorous
uterus

delusionist
exclusionist
gratuitous
illuminist
illuminous
illusionist
intrusionist
intuitive
obstrusionist
protuberous
seclusionist
voluminous

constitutionist
distributionist
elocutionist
evolutionist
Orange Julius
overnumerous
resolutionist
revolutionist

UBIST (see OONEST)
UBLE (see OODLE)
UBLIC (see UCKET)
UBLISH (see UFFISH)
UBRICANT (see UMINANT)
UBRIS (see UENESS)
UBSEQUENT (see UCCULENT)
UBSIDY (see UTTERY)
UBSY (see UDDY)

UBTLE (see UBBLE)
UBTLER (see USTER 1)
UBTLETY (see UTTERY)
UBU (see ULU)
UBY (see UTY)
UCA (see UNA)
UCAS (see UENESS)
UCCI (see UTY)
UCCOR (see USTER 1)
UCCORING (see OVERING)

UCCULENT

covenant
government
punishment
subsequent
succulent
supplement
truculent

self-government
UCE (see OOSE 1)
UCEFUL (see OODLE)
UCELESS (see UTENESS)
UCENCE (see UDENCE)
UCENT (see UTION)
UCER (see UTER)
UCH (see UFF)
UCHARIST (see UBIOUS)
UCHESS (see UCKET)
UCHIEST (see UBBIEST)
UCHING (see USTING)
UCIAL (see OODLE)
UCIALLY (see UITY 1)
UCIAN (see UTION)
UCIANT (see UMINANT)
UCIBLE (see OOTABLE)
UCID (see UTED)
UCIFER (see UTIONER)
UCIFIX (see UBIOUS)
UCING (see UTING 1)
UCIOUS (see UENESS)
UCIUS (see UENESS)
UCIVE (see USIVE)
UCK (see UP)
UCKA (see USSIA)
UCKABLE (see USTABLE)
UCKER (see USTER 1)
UCKERING (see OVERING)
UCKERY (see UTTERY)

UCKET

bucket
budget
buffet
couplet
covet
crumpet
cupless
cutlet
Douglas
duchess
fustic
gullet
gusset
junket
justice
loveless
luckless
mullet
Muppet
Muscrat
musket
nugget
plummet
public
pundit
puppet
ruckus
rustic
rustless
smugness
strumpet
stuffless
summit
toughness
trumpet

abruptness
Augustus
chief justice
Chip Douglas
ear trumpet
gold nugget
injustice
lardbucket
low-budget
Lyle Lovett
Nantucket
paint bucket

republic
robustness
slopbucket

chicken cutlet
Hall of justice
Jimmy Buffet
kick the bucket
sink a bucket
tea and crumpet

poetic justice

Banana Republic
miscarriage of justice

UCKIE (see UDDY)
UCKIEST (see UBBIEST)
UCKILY (see UTTERY)
UCKING (see USTING)
UCKISH (see UFFISH)
UCKLE (see UBBLE)
UCKLESS (see UCKET)
UCKLING (see UFFLING)
UCKSTABLE (see USTABLE)
UCKUS (see UCKET)
UCKY (see UDDY)
UCLEAR (see UTIONER)
UCLEUS (see UBIOUS)
UCOUS (see UENESS)
UCRATIVE (see UBIOUS)
UCRE (see UTER)
UCT (see UP)
UCTANTLY (see UTTERY)
UCTED (see USTED)
UCTIBLE (see USTABLE)
UCTING (see USTING)
UCTINOAL (see USTABLE)

UCTION

suction
Upton

abduction
conduction
construction
corruption
deduction
destruction

disruption
eruption
induction
instruction
obstruction
production
reduction
seduction

child abduction
dance instruction
interruption
introduction
liposuction
mass production
reconstruction
reproduction
self-destruction

army induction
movie production
overproduction
UCTIONAL (see USTABLE)

UCTIVE

adjunctive
compulsive
conductive
conjunctive
constructive
consultive
convulsive
deductive
destructive
disjunctive
disruptive
impulsive
inductive
injunctive
instructive
obstructive
productive
repulsive
resultive
revulsive
seductive
subjunctive
subsultive

introductive
reconstructive
reproductive
self-destructive
unproductive

counterproductive

UCTOR (see USTER 1)
UCTURAL (see USTABLE)
UCTURE (see USTER 1)
UCTURELESS (see UDDERLESS)
UCTURING (see OVERING)
UCULENT (see UCCULENT)
UCUS (see UENESS)
UCY (see UTY)
UD (see UG)
UDA (see UNA)
UDABLE (see OOTABLE)
UDAH (see UNA)
UDAL (see OODLE)
UDAS (see UENESS)
UDD (see UG)
UDDED (see USTED)
UDDEN (see UTTON)
UDDENLY (see UTTERY)
UDDER (see USTER 1)
UDDERING (see OVERING)

UDDERLESS

colorless
hungerless
lusterless
motherless
numberless
rudderless
slumberless
structureless
supperless
thunderless
udderless
usherless

UDDHA (see UNA)
UDDHIST (see OONEST)
UDDIEST (see UBBIEST)
UDDING 1 (see OOKING)
UDDING 2 (see USTING)
UDDLE (see UBBLE)
UDDLER (see USTER 1)

UDDLING (see UFFLING)

UDDY

bloody
bubbly
buddy
buggy
bulgy
bulky
busty
chubby
Chuckie
chuggy
clubby
clucky
clutchy
covey
cruddy
crusty
cubby
doubly
ducky
Dudley
Duffy
dully
dusky
dusty
fluffy
fuddy
fudgy
fussy
fuzzy
grubby
gucky
gully
guppie
gushy
gussy
gusty
gutsy
gutty
hubby
huffy
huggy
husky
hussy
juggly
lovely

lucky
lushly
lusty
mucky
muddy
muggy
multi
mushy
musky
mussy
musty
mutty
nubby
nutty
plucky
plushy
pudgy
puffy
puppy
putty
roughie
roughly
rubbly
ruddy
rusty
rutty
scrubby
scuzzy
slushy
slutty
smudgy
smugly
smutty
snuffy
snuggy
snugly
stubbly
stubby
study
stuffy
sully
sultry
touchy
trustee
trusty
tubby
Tubsy
ugly
yucky
Yuppie

abruptly
adultery
corruptly
dune buggy
golf buddy
good buddy
hush puppy
Kentucky
peanutty
unlucky
unmuddy
unstuffy
walnutty

buddy-buddy
coconutty
drinking buddy
fuddy-duddy
horse and buggy
lovey-dovey
nature study
rubber ducky
Silly Putty
understudy

character study
happy-go-lucky

Siberian husky

UDE (see OOM)
UDED (see UTED)
UDEL (see OODLE)
UDELY (see UTY)

UDENCE

coolants
lucence
mutants
nuisance
prudence
students
usance

affluence
confluence
congruence
connusance
imprudence

impudence
influence
nonusance
pollutants
protrudence
pursuance
translucence
unprudence

incongruence
jurisprudence

UDENESS (see UTENESS)
UDENT (see UTION)
UDENTLY (see UITY 1)
UDENTS (see UDENCE)
UDER (see UTER)
UDEST (see OONEST)
UDGABLE (see USTABLE)
UDGE (see UG)
UDGEL (see UMBLE)
UDGEON (see UTTON)
UDGEONLY (see OMPANY)
UDGER (see USTER 1)
UDGERY (see UTTERY)
UDGET (see UCKET)
UDGING (see USTING)
UDGY (see UDDY)
UDIC (see EWISH)
UDICANT (see UMINANT)
UDICATE (see UMINATE)
UDICROUS (see UBIOUS)
UDIE (see UTY)
UDING 1 (see UTING 1)
UDING 2 (see USTING)
UDIOUS (see UBIOUS)
UDIST (see OONEST)
UDITY (see UITY 1)
UDLE (see OTTLE)
UDLEY (see UDDY)
UDLIEST (see UBBIEST)
UDO (see UNO)
UDOR (see UTER)
UDSABLE (see USTABLE)
UDU (see ULU)
UDY 1 (see UDDY)
UDY 2 (see UTY)
UE (see EW 1)
UEFUL (see OODLE)
UEGER (see UTER)
UEL 1 (see EWAL)
UEL 2 (see EWAL)

UELA (see ASIA)
UELABLE (see OOTABLE)
UELER (see OOLER)
UELESS (see UENESS)
UELEST (see OONEST)
UELING (see OOLING)
UELLER (see OOLER)
UELLY (see UTY)
UENCE (see UDENCE)
UENCY (see UITY 1)

UENESS

blueness
Brutus
clueless
crewless
dewless
dueness
fewness
fucus
hubris
hueless
Judas
Lewis
Louis
Lucas
Lucius
lupus
mucous
mucus
newness
Plutus
Rufus
shoeless
skewness
trueness
upas
viewless

arbutus
astucious
Confucius
scorbutus
St. Louis
undueness

barracudas
Jerry Lewis

Emmanuel Lewis

UENO (see ADO 2)
UENT (see UTION)
UER (see EWER 1)
UERY (see EARY)
UES (see USE 1)
UEST (see OONEST)
UET (see OULETTE)
UEY (see EWY)
UF (see UFF)

UFF

bluff
blush
brush
brusque
buff
bus
buss
bust
clutch
crush
crust
crutch
crux
cuff
cuss
duff
dusk
dust
dutch
fluff
flush
flux
fuss
gruff
guff
gush
gust
huff
hush
husk
hutch
just
luff
lush
lust
lux
much

muff
musk
muss
must
plus
plush
puff
pus
rough
ruff
rush
rust
scruff
scuff
slough
slush
smutch
snuff
stuff
such
thrush
thrust
thus
touch
tough
truss
trust
tuft
tusk
tux
us

a must
ablush
adjust
agush
airbrush
as such
beer bust
brain-trust
bulrush
bum rush
cheek blush
clothes brush
coal dust
combust
cornhusk
cost-plus
cream puff
crop-dust

dehusk
deluxe
discuss
disgust
distrust
drug bust
ear muff
encrust
enough
entrust
foodstuff
French cuff
go Dutch
gold dust
gold rush
hairbrush
handcuff
hang tough
hard stuff
hot stuff
hush-hush
influx
kid stuff
light touch
McGruff
mistrust
nonplus
not much
onrush
paintbrush
pie crust
rebuff
restuff
retouch
right stuff
robust
rough stuff
sagebrush
school bus
soft touch
some such
stardust
straight flush
tongue-thrust
too much
toothbrush
unjust

angel dust
antitrust

at first blush
between us
bite the dust
blindman's bluff
blunderbus
boom-or-bust
bottlebrush
breach of trust
call one's bluff
Cocoa Puff
common touch
double dutch
dry as dust
fair enough
final touch
fisticuff
gloomy Gus
huff and puff
in the buff
in the rough
inasmuch
insomuch
make a fuss
Midas touch
minibus
off the cuff
on the cuff
overmuch
overstuff
powder puff
pretty much
public trust
rabbit hutch
readjust
rough and tough
royal flush
semitough
shuttle bus
strut your stuff
such-and-such
sure enough
thank you much
two hand touch
underbrush
up to snuff
uppercrust
wanderlust

ever so much

Marshmallow Fluff
more than enough
Starsky and Hutch
Ziggy Stardust

diamond in the rough
H.R. Pufnstuf

UFFABLE (see USTABLE)
UFFEL (see UBBLE)
UFFELING (see OVERING)
UFFER (see USTER 1)
UFFERING (see OVERING)
UFFERY (see UTTERY)
UFFET (see UCKET)
UFFIEST (see UBBIEST)
UFFIN (see UTTON)
UFFING (see USTING)

UFFISH

buckish
clubbish
cubbish
dullish
dunnish
gruffish
gullish
huffish
hummus
hunnish
muffish
muggish
nunnish
publish
puckish
puggish
pumice
punish
punnish
rubbish
ruttish
sluggish
sluttish
snubbish
suffix
thuggish
tuffish
uppish

UFFIX (see UFFISH)
UFFLE (see UBBLE)

UFFLER (see USTER 1)
UFFLESS (see UCKET)

UFFLING

bubbling
buckling
bumbling
chuckling
cuddling
doubling
duckling
fumbling
grumbling
guzzling
huddling
humbling
juggling
jumbling
knuckling
muddling
muffling
mumbling
muzzling
nuzzling
puzzling
ruffling
rumbling
scuffling
scuttling
shuffling
shuttling
smuggling
snuffling
snuggling
struggling
stumbling
suckling
troubling
truckling
truffling
tuggling
tumbling

befuddling
belt buckling
bemuddling
dust ruffling
fast shuffling
rebuttling

redoubling
reshuffling
swashbuckling
unbuckling
unruffling
untroubling

UFFY (see UDDY)
UFIC (see EWISH)
UFT (see UFF)
UFUS (see UENESS)

UG

blood
blub
bub
bud
budge
bug
buzz
chub
chug
club
crud
cub
cud
cuz
does
dove
drub
drudge
drug
dub
dud
dug
flood
flub
fudge
fuzz
glove
glug
Gov
grub
grudge
hub
HUD
hug
judge
jug

love
lug
mud
mug
nub
nudge
of
plug
pub
pug
rub
rug
scrub
scud
scuzz
shove
shrub
shrug
sludge
slug
smudge
smug
snub
snug
spud
stub
stud
sub
thud
thug
trudge
tub
tug
ugh
was

above
abuzz
adjudge
backrub
bad blood
bathtub
bear cub
bear hug
bear rug
bedbug
beer mug
begrudge
blue blood
bridge club
check stub

debug
earplug
fan club
firebug
fireplug
flash flood
flubdub
forejudge
glee club
golf club
handrub
health club
hereof
hot blood
hot fudge
hot tub
hubbub
humbug
June bug
kid glove
lifeblood
light plug
Love Bug
Milk Dud
misjudge
new blood
nightclub
nose plug
peach fuzz
prejudge
rosebud
self-love
sort of
spark plug
sweat blood
taste blood
taste bud
thereof
tired blood
true love
unplug
washtub
whereof
white-glove
young blood

auto club
Beelzebub
billy club
boxing glove

chug-a-lug
clear as mud
creeping crud
cut a rug
doodlebug
draw first blood
Elmer Fudd
Endless Love
fall in love
flesh and blood
flub the dub
get rid of
grow tired of
hand and glove
in cold blood
jitterbug
ladybug
ladylove
lightning bug
lion cub
litterbug
mile-high club
pull the plug
puppy love
rise above
rubber glove
secret love
shutterbug
ticket stub
turtledove
unheard of
up above
well-thought-of
whiskey jug
wonder drug
Wonderbug

a cut above
alcohol rub
brotherly love
curdle your blood
designer drug
fit like a glove
good ol' boys club
here come da judge
illicit love
in favor of
labor of love
make a mess of
Mickey Mouse Club

miracle drug
motherly love
nip in the bud
platonic love
potato bug
prescription drug
push comes to shove
Rotary Club
rub a dub dub
stick in the mud
To Sir, With Love
tunnel of love

fertility drug
none of the above
Oriental rug
over and above
sober as a judge

crazy as a bedbug

snug as a bug in a rug

UGA (see UNA)
UGAL (see OODLE)
UGALLY (see UITY 1)
UGAR (see OOKER)
UGE (see OOM)
UGELY (see UTY)
UGENESS (see UTENESS)
UGENT (see UTION)
UGER (see UTER)
UGEST (see OONEST)
UGGABLE (see USTABLE)
UGGER (see USTER 1)
UGGERING (see OVERING)
UGGERY (see UTTERY)
UGGET (see UCKET)
UGGIEST (see UBBIEST)
UGGING (see USTING)
UGGISH (see UFFISH)
UGGLE (see UBBLE)
UGGLER (see USTER 1)
UGGLING (see UFFLING)
UGGLY (see UDDY)
UGGY (see UDDY)
UGH (see UG)
UGHES (see USE 1)
UGILIST (see UBIOUS)
UGING (see UTING 1)
UGITIVE (see UBIOUS)
UGLE (see OODLE)
UGLIEST (see UBBIEST)

UGLY (see UDDY)
UGN (see OOM)
UGNABLE (see OOTABLE)
UGNANTLY (see OMPANY)
UGNER (see UMER)
UGNESS (see UCKET)
UGNING (see UTING 1)
UGO (see UNO)

UH

bruh
duh
huh
the
no duh
uh-huh
UI (see AY)
UICE (see OOSE 1)
UICER (see UTER)
UICING (see UTING 1)
UICY (see UTY)
UID (see UTED)
UIDANCE (see ITIS)
UIDE (see IDE)
UIDELESS (see ITIS)
UIDER (see IZER)
UIDING (see INDING)
UIE (see EWY)
UILD (see ILL)

UILDABLE

billable
buildable
chillable
drillable
fillable
grillable
killable
spillable
syllable
thrillable
tillable
willable

distillable
fulfillable
instillable
refillable

UILDER (see ILLER)
UILE (see ILE 1)
UILEMENT (see ILEMENT)
UILING (see INDING)
UILT (see ILT)
UILTIER (see ITTIER)
UIN 1 (see UTION)
UIN 2 (see EEN 1)
UINER (see UTIONER)

UING

bluing
booing
brewing
chewing
crewing
cuing
doing
gluing
mooing
poohing
queueing
ruing
screwing
shoeing
spewing
stewing
suing
viewing
wooing

accruing
boo-booing
canoeing
construing
cuckooing
debuting
ensuing
eschewing
imbuing
Jock Ewing
miscuing
outdoing
pooh-poohing
pursuing
redoing
renewing
reviewing
shampooing
subduing
tattooing

undoing
unscrewing
wrongdoing
yoo-hooing

barbecuing
countersuing
interviewing
misconstruing
nothing doing
overdoing
Patrick Ewing
peek-a-booing
toodle-ooing
up-and-doing

UIRKY (see IRTY)
UISABLE (see OOTABLE)
UISANCE (see UDENCE)
UISE (see USE 1)
UISER (see UTER)
UISH (see EWISH)
UISING (see UTING 1)
UIT (see UTE)
UITABLE (see OOTABLE)
UITABLY (see UITY 1)
UITAL (see OODLE)

UITARY

luminary
routinary

ablutionary
concubinary
illuminary
matutinary
pituitary

devolutionary
evolutionary
institutionary
revolutionary
substitutionary

hyperpituitary
proevolutionary

antirevolutionary
counterrevolutionary

UITED (see UTED)

UITER (see UTER)
UITFUL (see OODLE)
UITFULLY (see UITY 1)
UITING (see UTING 1)
UITIVE (see UBIOUS)
UITOR (see UTER)
UITOUS (see UBIOUS)

UITY 1

brewery
brutally
crucially
crudity
dually
dutifully
eulogy
feudally
fluency
foolery
frugally
fruitfully
futilely
humanly
jewelry
lewdity
moodily
mutiny
neutrally
nudity
prudently
prudity
puberty
punity
rudity
scrutiny
snootily
suitably
truancy
truthfully
unity

affluency
annuity
circuity
community
congruency
congruity
diffluency

disunity
effluency
fortuity
gratuity
immunity
imprudently
impudently
impunity
inhumanly
refluency
tomfoolery
vacuity

ambiguity
contiguity
continuity
exiguity
importunity
incongruency
incongruity
ingenuity
interluency
opportunity
perpetuity
promiscuity
superfluity

equal opportunity
photo opportunity

diplomatic immunity

UITY 2 (see UTY)
UJI (see UTY)
UJO (see UNO)
UJU (see ULU)
UK (see UP)
UKABLE (see OOTABLE)
UKAL (see OODLE)
UKE (see UTE)
UKEFUL (see OODLE)
UKER (see URNER)
UKEY (see UTY)
UKI (see UTY)
UKING (see UTING 1)
UKKER (see USTER 1)
UKY (see UTY)
UL 1 (see OOL 1)
UL 2 (see ULT)
ULA (see UNA)

ULABLE (see OOTABLE)
ULAN (see UTION)
ULB (see ULT)
ULCAN (see ULTAN)
ULCER (see ULGAR)
ULCH (see ULT)
ULCO (see OLO)
ULE 1 (see OOL 1)
ULE 2 (see UTY)
ULER (see OOLER)
ULF (see ULT)
ULFING (see ULLING)
ULFUR (see ULGAR)

ULGAR

Bulgar
bulger
bulgur
bulker
culture
culver
duller
gulper
huller
hulver
luller
muller
pulser
sculker
sculpter
skulker
sulfur
sulker
sulphur
ulcer
vulgar
vulture

annuller
consulter
convulser
divulger
indulger
insulter
invulgar
subculture

agriculture
catapulter
counterculture

culture vulture
floriculture
horticulture
multiculture
supravulgar

overindulger

ULGE (see ULT)
ULGER (see ULGAR)
ULGING (see ULLING)
ULGUR (see ULGAR)
ULGY (see UDDY)
ULING (see OOLING)
ULISH (see EWISH)
ULIUS (see UBIOUS)
ULK (see ULT)
ULKER (see ULGAR)
ULKING (see ULLING)
ULKY (see UDDY)

ULL 1

bull
full
pull
wool

bell pull
chock-full
cram full
half-full
lamb's wool
pit bull
push-pull
steel wool

cock and bull
shoot the bull
Sitting Bull
taffy pull
virgin wool

dyed in the wool

ULL 2 (see ULT)
ULLA (see UNA)
ULLAH (see UNA)
ULLER (see ULGAR)
ULLERY (see UTTERY)
ULLEST (see ULLET 1)

ULLET 1

booklet
bullet
bullock
crooked
fullest
pullet
pulpit

bite the bullet
Sandra Bullock

ULLET 2 (see UCKET)
ULLEY (see OOGIE)
ULLIBLE (see USTABLE)

ULLING

bulging
bulking
culling
dulling
gulfing
gulping
hulking
hulling
lulling
mulling
nulling
pulping
pulsing
sculling
skulking
sulking

annulling
consulting
convulsing
divulging
effulging
engulfing
expulsing
exulting
impulsing
indulging
insulting
occulting
promulging
repulsing

resulting
catapulting
disannulling

overindulging

ULLISH (see UFFISH)
ULLOCK (see ULLET 1)
ULLY 1 (see UDDY)
ULLY 2 (see OOGIE)
ULOGY (see UITY 1)
ULP (see ULT)
ULPER (see ULGAR)
ULPHUR (see ULGAR)
ULPING (see ULLING)
ULPIT (see ULLET 1)
ULPT (see ULT)
ULPTER (see ULGAR)
ULSE (see ULT)
ULSER (see ULGAR)
ULSING (see ULLING)
ULSION (see ULTAN)
ULSIVE (see UCTIVE)

ULT

bulb
bulge
bulk
cull
cult
dull
gulf
gull
gulp
hulk
hull
lull
mulch
mull
null
pulp
pulse
scull
sculpt
skulk
skull
sulk

adult
annul

consult
convulse
divulge
expulse
exult
impulse
indulge
insult
lightbulb
numskull
occult
penult
repulse
result
tumult

catapult
difficult
end result
young adult

antepenult
Castle Grayskull
Incredible Hulk
out of your skull
overindulge

Battle of the Bulge
consenting adult

personality cult

ULTAN

sultan
Vulcan

compulsion
convulsion
divulsion
emulsion
expulsion
impulsion
propulsion
repulsion
revulsion

ULTER (see ULGAR)
ULTERY (see UDDY)
ULTI (see UDDY)
ULTING (see ULLING)

ULTIPLE (see USTABLE)   UMBERING (see OVERING)   UMBLER (see UMMER)
ULTIVE (see UCTIVE)   UMBERLESS (see UDDERLESS)   UMBLIEST (see UMPIEST)
ULTRY (see UDDY)   UMBIEST (see UMPIEST)   UMBLING (see UFFLING)
ULTURAL (see USTABLE)   UMBING (see OMING 1)   UMBLY (see UNNY)
ULTURE (see ULGAR)

UMBLE

ULU

bumble

booboo   bundle
boohoo   bungle
FUBU   crumble
gooroo   crumple
guru   cudgel
hoodoo   frontal
hoopoo   fumble
juju   fungal
kudu   funnel
lulu   grumble
pudu   humble
pulu   jumble
sulu   jungle
trubu   mumble
tutu   pummel
voodoo   punful
woohoo   rumble
yoohoo   scumble
Zulu   stumble
                    trundle
Isuzu   tumble
mahoohoo   tunnel
urubu   uncle

                    carbuncle
Honolulu   confrontal
                    disgruntle
ULVER (see ULGAR)   Dutch uncle
ULY (see UTY)   Repunzel
UM (see UN)   say uncle
UMA (see UNA)   unbundle
UMABLE (see OOTABLE) wind tunnel
UMAL (see OODLE)
UMAN (see UTION)   antifungal
UMANLY (see UITY 1) concrete jungle
UMANN (see UTION)   drop a bundle
UMB (see UN)   rough-and-tumble
UMBA (see UNA)   take a tumble
UMBAA (see UNA)
UMBABLE (see USTABLE) George of the Jungle
UMBENT (see UNION 2) law of the jungle
UMBER 1 (see UMMER)
UMBER 2 (see UMMER) Simon and Garfunkel

UMBO

bunco
bungo
Dumbo
gumbo
GungHo
jumbo
junco
junto
mumbo
mungo
punto
umbo
unco

Columbo
Motumbo
rotundo

mumbo jumbo

UMBUS (see UNLESS)
UMBY (see UNNY)
UME (see OOM)
UMELESS (see UTENESS)
UMEN (see UTION)
UMENT (see UTION)

UMER

bloomer
boomer
crooner
fumer
groomer
humor
junior
lunar
mooner
pruner
rumor
schooner
sooner

spooner
swooner
tumor
tuner

assumer
ballooner
black humor
brain tumor
Carl's Jr.
communer
consumer
costumer
exhumer
fine-tuner
good humor
harpooner
ill humor
impugner
lampooner
late bloomer
marooner
perfumer
pet groomer
presumer
resumer

baby boomer
early bloomer
honeymooner

Frankenstein Jr.
piano tuner

John Kennedy Jr.

Martin Luther King Jr.

UMERANT (see UMINANT)
UMERATE (see UMINATE)
UMEROUS (see UBIOUS)
UMIC (see EWISH)
UMICE (see UFFISH)
UMID (see UTED)
UMIN (see UTION)

UMINANT

jubilant
lubricant

luminant
ruminant

conjubilant
dijudicant
extuberant
exuberant
illuminant
insouciant
nonruminant
prejudicant
protuberant

equinumerant

UMINARY (see UITARY)

UMINATE

jubilate
luminate
nubilate
numerate
ruminate

abjudicate
accuminate
adjudicate
annumerate
dijudicate
enubilate
enumerate
exuperate
illuminate
obnubilate
prejudicate
recuperate
rejuvenate
renumerate
volubilate

imprejudicate
reilluminate

UMING (see UTING 1)
UMINIST (see UBIOUS)
UMINOUS (see UBIOUS)
UMLESS (see UNLESS)
UMLY (see UNNY)
UMMABLE (see USTABLE)

UMMARY (see UTTERY)
UMMEL (see UMBLE)
UMMELING (see OVERING)

UMMER

blunder
blunter
bummer
bumper
bunker
bunter
clunker
comer
crumber
cruncher
drummer
drunker
dumber
dumper
dumpster
dunker
fronter
funder
glummer
grunter
gummer
gunner
hummer
hunger
hunker
hunter
jumper
juncture
junker
lumber
mummer
muncher
number
plumber
plumper
plunder
plunger
plunker
pumper
puncher
puncture
punker
punter

runner
shunner
shunter
slumber
slummer
strummer
stumper
stunner
stunter
summer
sunder
sunner
thumber
thumper
thunder
trumper
tumbler
umber
under
wonder
younger

affronter
asunder
becomer
benumber
boy wonder
broad jumper
call number
claim-jumper
confronter
cowpuncher
cucumber
discomfort
down under
encumber
fishmonger
front-runner
go under
grand juncture
hatemonger
headhunter
high jumper
hot number
humdrummer
keypuncher
latecomer
long jumper
manhunter
midsummer

newcomer
newsmonger
no wonder
old clunker
outnumber
refunder
renumber
roadrunner
rotunder
slam-dunker
spelunker
tailgunner
tire puncture
warmonger
wrong number

acupuncture
Archie Bunker
Bible-thumper
blood and thunder
die of hunger
disencumber
Donna Summer
Eddie Munster
Endless Summer
fife and drummer
Herman Munster
ironmonger
knuckle under
loot and plunder
lucky number
number cruncher
out from under
overcomer
paint by number
puddle jumper
rumormonger
scandalmonger
Stevie Wonder
The Road Runner
triple jumper
unencumber
up-and-comer
without number

bumper to bumper
cardinal number
Crocodile Hunter
Indian summer
ninety-day wonder

parachute jumper
steal someone's thunder

cool as a cucumber
Josephine The Plumber

UMMERY (see UTTERY)
UMMET (see UCKET)
UMMING (see OMING 1)
UMMINS (see UTTON)
UMMIT (see UCKET)
UMMON (see UNION 2)
UMMUS (see UFFISH)
UMMY (see UNNY)
UMNUS (see UNLESS)
UMO (see UNO)
UMOR (see UMER)
UMORING (see UTORING)
UMOROUS (see UBIOUS)

UMP

blunt
brunch
brunt
bump
bunch
bunk
bunt
chump
chunk
clump
clunk
crunch
drunk
dump
dunce
dunk
flunk
front
frump
funk
grump
grunch
grunt
hump
hunch
hunk
hunt
jump

junk
lump
lunch
monk
month
munch
once
plump
plunk
pump
punch
punk
punt
rump
runt
schlump
scrunch
shrunk
shunt
skunk
slump
slunk
spunk
stump
stunk
stunt
sump
sunk
thump
thunk
trump
trunk
ump
unk

adjunct
affront
at once
beachfront
blue funk
box lunch
breast pump
broad jump
chipmunk
cold front
confront
conjunct
debunk
defunct
disjunct

do lunch
forefront
fox hunt
free lunch
fruit punch
gas pump
goose bump
high jump
homefront
injunct
kerplunk
keypunch
long jump
manhunt
no trump
out front
Podunk
preshrunk
punch-drunk
school lunch
ski jump
slam dunk
speed bump
storefront
trash dump
tree stump
undrunk
up front
whole bunch
witch hunt

all at once
business lunch
Cap'N Crunch
city dump
counterpunch
Donald Trump
Forest Gump
honeybunch
Humpty Hump
in a slump
oceanfront
on a hunch
one-two punch
out to lunch
overtrump
Phillies Blunt
pile of junk
quantum jump
rabbit punch

shooting slump
steamer trunk
stomach pump
sucker-punch
suction pump
sugar lump
Sunday brunch
treasure hunt
triple jump
umpty-ump
up a stump
water pump
waterfront

dowager's hump
drunk as a skunk
energy crunch
Hawaiian Punch
hop, skip, and jump
over the hump
parachute jump
The Brady Bunch

Cinnamon Toast Crunch
Nut & Honey Crunch
Peanut Butter Crunch

UMPABLE (see USTABLE)
UMPER (see UMMER)
UMPET (see UCKET)
UMPHREY (see UNNY)

UMPIEST

bumpiest
bunchiest
chunkiest
clumpiest
clumsiest
comfiest
crumbiest
crumbliest
crunchiest
dumpiest
duskiest
frumpiest
funkiest
funniest
grumpiest
grungiest

hungriest
huskiest
jumpiest
junkiest
lumpiest
muskiest
punchiest
runniest
runtiest
spunkiest
stumpiest
sunniest

UMPILY (see OMPANY)
UMPING (see OMING 1)
UMPKIN (see UNION 2)
UMPLE (see UMBLE)
UMPLING (see OMING 1)
UMPSTER (see UMMER)
UMPTION (see UNION 2)
UMPTIOUS (see UNLESS)
UMPUSS (see UNLESS)
UMPY (see UNNY)
UMSIEST (see UMPIEST)
UMSY (see UNNY)
UMULATE (see IMINATE)
UMVEE (see UNNY)
UMY (see UTY)

UN

sun
brung
bum
bun
chum
Chung
clung
come
crumb
done
drum
dumb
dun
dung
flung
from
fun
fund
glum

grunge
gum
gun
hum
hun
hung
lung
lunge
mum
none
numb
nun
one
plum
plumb
plunge
pun
rum
run
rung
scum
shun
slum
slung
some
son
sponge
sprung
spun
strum
strung
stun
stung
sum
sung
swum
swung
thumb
ton
tongue
tun
um
won
wrung
young
yum

all done
alum
among

bass drum
bay rum
beach bum
become
begun
benumb
blowgun
bread crumb
burp gun
cap gun
come from
cow dung
day one
dog run
dry run
dumdum
eardrum
earned run
end run
expunge
far-flung
finespun
first-come
forked tongue
grandson
green thumb
hail from
hamstrung
handgun
hear from
high-strung
hired gun
ho-hum
home run
homespun
how come?
humdrum
lump sum
make fun
Neil Young
no one
oil drum
outcome
outdone
outrun
Pier One
poke fun
popgun
redone
refund

rerun
rotund
rum-dum
shantung
shogun
short run
shotgun
six gun
ski run
slush fund
someone
square one
squirt gun
succumb
Tom Thumb
Top Gun
trial run
trust fund
undone
unhung
unrun
unstrung
unsung
unwon
well done
well hung
year one
yum-yum

411
911
Air Force One
all or none
anyone
BB gun
bite your tongue
bubblegum
cattlerun
chewing gum
cookie crumb
cut and run
deaf and dumb
egg foo yung
everyone
fife and drum
Flying Nun
Gatling-gun
hit-and-run
hold your tongue
hole in one

honeybun
hot dog bun
hurry some
iron lung
jump the gun
just begun
kettle drum
kingdom come
midnight sun
mother tongue
murder one
native son
noonday sun
number one
on the run
one by one
one-on-one
overcome
overdone
overrun
pack a gun
pension fund
rule of thumb
setting sun
smoking gun
take the plunge
to and from
Tweedledum
underdone
unearned run
VH-1
World War I
worrisome

back to square one
chrysanthemum
cost overrun
favorite son
fe fi fo fum
forever young
fun in the sun
hamburger bun
hot buttered rum
in the long run
KRS-One
over and done
place in the sun
prodigal son
slip of the tongue

son of a gun
under the gun
under the sun

Attila the Hun
committee of one
each and every one
every other one

girls just want to have fun
on the tip of your tongue

UNA

Beulah
Buddha
chouka
Cuba
Fuga
Gouda
hookah
hula
Judah
loofa
luna
pluma
pooka
puca
puma
pupa
Roomba
ruga
scuba
stupa
tuba
tuna
Tuza
Yuga
Yuma
Zuma
Zumba

Abdullah
Aruba
bazooka
beluga
Bermuda
lacuna
laguna
mazuma

medulla
medusa
mezuzah
Missoula
palooka
vicuna

barracuda
Chattanooga
Montezuma
Oompa Loompa
Petaluma
Starkist Tuna

King Bowser Koopa
Lollapalooza
Madame Medusa
Timon and Pumbaa

Bumble Bee canned tuna

Chicken of the Sea tuna

UNABLE (see OOTABLE)
UNAL (see OODLE)
UNAR (see UMER)
UNATIC (see UBIOUS)
UNCAN (see UNION 2)
UNCE (see UMP)
UNCH (see UMP)
UNCHABLE (see USTABLE)
UNCHEON (see UNION 2)
UNCHER (see UMMER)
UNCHIEST (see UMPIEST)
UNCHING (see OMING 1)
UNCHY (see UNNY)
UNCIE (see UNNY)
UNCLE (see UMBLE)
UNCO (see UMBO)
UNCT (see UMP)
UNCTION (see UNION 2)
UNCTIOUS (see UNLESS)
UNCTIVE (see UCTIVE)
UNCTURE (see UMMER)
UND (see UN)
UNDABLE (see USTABLE)
UNDANT (see UNION 2)
UNDER (see UMMER)
UNDERING (see OVERING)
UNDERLESS (see UDDERLESS)
UNDI (see UNNY)
UNDING (see OMING 1)

UNDIT (see UCKET)
UNDLE (see UMBLE)
UNDO (see UMBO)
UNDRED (see UNLESS)
UNDY (see UNNY)
UNE (see OOM)
UNEAU (see UNO)
UNELESS (see UTENESS)
UNEMENT (see UTION)
UNER (see UMER)
UNERAL (see OOTABLE)
UNFUL (see UMBLE)
UNG (see UN)
UNGAL (see UMBLE)
UNGE (see UN)
UNGEE (see UNNY)
UNGENT (see UNION 2)
UNGER 1 (see UMMER)
UNGER 2 (see UMMER)
UNGERING (see OVERING)
UNGERLESS (see UDDERLESS)
UNGHO (see UMBO)
UNGIEST (see UMPIEST)
UNGING (see OMING 1)
UNGLE (see UMBLE)
UNGO (see UMBO)
UNGRIEST (see UMPIEST)
UNGRILY (see OMPANY)
UNGRY (see UNNY)
UNGSTEN (see UTTON)
UNGUS (see UNLESS)
UNGY (see UNNY)
UNI (see UTY)
UNIC (see EWISH)
UNICH (see EWISH)
UNING (see UTING 1)
UNION 1 (see UTION)

UNION 2

bumpkin
bunion
Bunyan
cumbent
drunken
Duncan
function
junction
London
luncheon
onion

pumpkin
pungent
shrunken
summon
sunken
unction

abundant
adjunction
assumption
conjunction
consumption
disjunction
dysfunction
incumbent
injunction
malfunction
preshrunken
presumption
rambunction
redundant

railroad junction

Conjunction Junction
overabundant
superincumbent

UNIOR (see UMER)
UNISH (see UFFISH)
UNISHMENT (see UCCULENT)
UNIT (see EWISH)
UNITIVE (see UBIOUS)
UNITY (see UITY 1)
UNK (see UMP)
UNKABLE (see USTABLE)
UNKEL (see UMBLE)
UNKEN (see UNION 2)
UNKER (see UMMER)
UNKERING (see OVERING)
UNKET (see UCKET)
UNKIE (see UNNY)
UNKIEST (see UMPIEST)
UNKING (see OMING 1)
UNKY (see UNNY)

UNLESS

compass
doneness

fungus
gumless
gunless
hundred
oneness
rumpuss
runless
scrumptious
shunless
sunless
unless
wonderous
alumnus
Columbus
compunctious
encompass
humongous
rambunctious

UNNABLE (see USTABLE)
UNNEL (see UMBLE)
UNNER (see UMMER)
UNNERY (see UTTERY)
UNNIEST (see UMPIEST)
UNNING (see OMING 1)
UNNISH (see UFFISH)

UNNY

bluntly
bumpy
Bundy
bungee
bunny
chummy
chunky
clumpy
clumsy
clunky
comfy
country
crumbly
crummy
crunchy
dummy
dumpy
flunky
frumpy
funky
funny

glumly
glummy
grumpy
grungy
gumby
gummy
honey
humbly
Humphrey
humpy
humvee
hungry
hunky
jumpy
junkie
junky
lumpy
money
monkey
monthly
mummy
mumsy
munchy
Muncie
punchy
punky
punny
rummy
runny
runty
scummy
slummy
slumpy
sonny
spongy
spunky
stumpy
sunny
thumpy
tummy
yummy

Al Bundy
beach bunny
bi-monthly
blood money
Bugs Bunny
Burundi
dumb bunny
gin rummy

grease monkey
hush money
mad money
Sea Monkey

Easter bunny
easy money
even money
junk-food junky
Kelly Bundy
Peggy Bundy
Playboy Bunny
for love or money
one for the money
right on the money

a run for your money
Energizer Bunny
land of milk and honey

UNO

Bruno
bureau
Cujo
duo
Euro
Hugo
judo
Juneau
Juno
kudo
moonbow
neuro
nouveau
Ouzo
Pluto
pseudo
sumo
uno
utro

art nouveau
Inugo
Jacques Clouseau
Menudo
prosciutto

Census Bureau
Politburo

numero uno

UNSTER (see UMMER)
UNT (see UMP)
UNTABLE (see USTABLE)
UNTER (see UMMER)
UNTIEST (see UMPIEST)
UNTING (see OMING 1)
UNTLE (see UMBLE)
UNTLY (see UNNY)
UNTO (see UMBO)
UNTY (see UNNY)
UNY (see UTY)
UNYAN (see UNION 2)
UNZEL (see UMBLE)
UO (see UNO)
UOY (see EWY)

UP

buck
but
butt
chuck
cluck
cup
cut
duck
duct
glut
guck
gut
hut
jut
luck
muck
mutt
nut
pluck
puck
pup
putt
ruck
rut
schmuck
shuck
shut
slut
smut
struck
strut
stuck

suck
sup
truck
tuck
tut
up
what
whup
yuck
yuk
yup

abduct
abrupt
abut
act up
air duct
all but
amok
awestruck
B-cup
backup
bad luck
bankrupt
blowup
bone up
breakup
bring up
buck up
buildup
burn up
bust-up
catch up
catgut
checkup
chestnut
clean-cut
cleanup
clear-cut
closeup
cold duck
conduct
construct
corrupt
crackup
crewcut
cut-up
dead duck
deduct
destruct

disrupt
dress-up
dumbstruck
dump truck
egg cup
erupt
fast buck
fess up
fire truck
fix up
flare-up
food truck
foul-up
gear up
get up
give up
good luck
grown-up
haircut
hang-up
hard up
heads up
holdup
hookup
induct
instruct
King Tut
knock up
lame duck
lay up
let up
lineup
lockup
lovestruck
low-cut
makeup
matchup
mess up
mixup
moonstruck
mop up
obstruct
own up
pent up
pinup
pop-up
potluck
precut
pushup
putt-putt

rebut
recut
roll up
rotgut
rough cut
rough up
roundup
sawbuck
say what?
setup
shakeup
shortcut
show up
shut up
size up
slip up
so what?
somewhat
sound truck
speak up
spit up
spruce up
stagestruck
stand up
starstruck
stickup
straight up
stuck up
sunup
tank up
teacup
tear duct
throw up
thumbs-up
tossup
touchup
tough luck
tow truck
trip up
tuneup
turn up
turnt up
uncut
unstuck
upchuck
wake up
walkup
washed-up
what's up?

wind up
woodchuck
woodcut
World Cup
worse luck
wrap-up
write-up
wrought-up

7UP
all shook up
all washed up
ante up
aqueduct
belly up
bottoms up
bring it up
buckle up
bundle up
bust a gut
butter up
buttercup
butternut
coconut
coffee cup
come unstuck
coverup
cuddle up
Daffy Duck
divvy up
Dixie cup
Donald Duck
double up
Dynomutt
fill 'er up
giddy-up
halibut
hazelnut
higher-up
hockey puck
horror-struck
in a rut
interrupt
Lady Luck
Lilliput
listen up
loving cup
nip and tuck
nothing but

out of luck
panel truck
paper cup
paper cut
pass the buck
Peking duck
pick-me-up
pitch-and-putt
Pizza Hut
press your luck
reconstruct
reinstruct
rotten luck
run amok
runner up
Scroog McDuck
scuttlebutt
self-destruct
shoot 'em-up
sitting duck
Solo cup
split a gut
Stanley Cup
straighten up
suction cup
terror-struck
thunderstruck
training cup
tummy tuck
uncorrupt
undercut
up and up
uppercut
viaduct
whoop it up
wickiup

anything but
auto-destruct
beginner's luck
cigarette butt
down on your luck
emerald cut
high muck-a-muck
Jabba the Hutt
open-and-shut
poverty-struck
Rachel Haircut
sunnyside up

America's Cup
high muckety-muck
Million Dollar Duck
on the up-and-up
put up or shut up

tempest in a teacup

UPA (see UNA)
UPAL (see OODLE)
UPAS (see UENESS)
UPE (see UTE)
UPEE (see UTY)
UPER (see UTER)
UPERATE (see UMINATE)
UPERING (see UTORING)
UPID (see UTED)
UPIL (see OODLE)
UPING (see UTING 1)
UPITER (see UTIONER)
UPLE (see OODLE)
UPLESS (see UCKET)
UPLEX (see OULETTE)
UPLING 1 (see OODLING)
UPLING 2 (see USTING)
UPOR (see UTER)
UPPER (see USTER 1)
UPPERLESS (see UDDERLESS)
UPPET (see UCKET)
UPPIE (see UDDY)
UPPING (see USTING)
UPPISH (see UFFISH)
UPPLE (see UBBLE)
UPPLEMENT (see UCCULENT)
UPPLER (see USTER 1)
UPPY (see UDDY)
UPT (see UP)
UPTABLE (see USTABLE)
UPTER (see USTER 1)
UPTIBLE (see USTABLE)
UPTING (see USTING)
UPTION (see UCTION)
UPTIVE (see UCTIVE)
UPTLY (see UDDY)
UPTNESS (see UCKET)
UPTON (see UCTION)
UPUS (see UENESS)
UQUE (see UTE)
UR (see ER 1)
URA (see ORA)

URABLE

curable
durable
urinal

assurable
endurable
incurable
insurable
procurable
securable
unendurable
unsecurable

URABLY

Curity
durably
purity
surety

impurity
maturity
obscurity
security
unsurety

immaturity
insecurity
prematurity

lack of security
social security

URAL

crural
dural
jural
mural
neural
pleural
plural
rural
sural
ural

procural

extramural
intermural
intramural
semirural

URANCE

assurance
endurance
insurance
procurance

life insurance
reassurance
self-assurance

URB (see ORD 2)
URBABLE (see URTABLE)
URBAN (see ERSION)
URBANCE (see ERSION)
URBID (see URDED)
URBING (see ERTING)
URBISH (see ERVICE)
URBISHMENT (see OURAGEMENT)
URBO (see ERNO)
URBULENT (see OURAGEMENT)
URBY (see IRTY)
URCH (see IRST)
URCHASE (see ERVICE)
URCHER (see URNER)
URCHILL (see URTLE)
URCHIN (see ERSION)
URCHING (see ERTING)
URCHY (see IRTY)
URD (see ORD 2)

URDED

blurted
curded
flirted
furkid
girded
herded
skirted
spurted
squirted

turbid
turgid
worded

alerted
asserted
averted
converted
deserted
diverted
exerted
inserted
inverted
perverted
reverted
reworded
subverted

disconcerted
extroverted
introverted

overexerted

URDEN (see ERSION)
URDER (see URNER)
URDING (see ERTING)
URDITY (see ERNITY)
URDLE (see URTLE)
URDLER (see URNER)
URDLING (see ERTING)
URDY (see IRTY)

URE 1

boor
cure
lure
moor
poor
pour
pure
spoor
sure
tour
you're

abjure
allure
amour
assure
azure
bon jour
brochure
cocksure
contour
cook's tour
couture
demure
dirt poor
endure
ensure
grand tour
impure
insure
inure
l'amour
make sure
mature
obscure
parkour
piss-poor
procure
secure
unsure
velour

curvature
epicure
haute couture
immature
insecure
manicure
overture
pedicure
premature
reassure
reinsure
simon-pure
sinecure
soupe du jour
take the cure

URE 2 (see EWER 1)
UREAU (see UNO)

URED

cured
lured
toured

assured
contoured
detoured
endured
ensured
insured
inured
matured
obscured
procured
secured
manicured
reassured
unsecured

URELY

dourly
poorly
purely
surely

demurely
impurely
maturely
obscurely
securely
unsurely

amateurly
immaturely
insecurely
prematurely

URER

curer
furor
juror
lurer
poorer

purer
surer
tourer

allurer
assurer
contourer
demurer
endurer
ensurer
grand juror
insurer
maturer
obscurer
procurer
securer
unsurer

immaturer
insecurer
manicurer
reassurer

UREST (see URIST)
URETY (see URABLY)
URF (see IRST)
URFABLE (see URTABLE)
URFACE (see ERVICE)
URFER (see URNER)
URFING (see ERTING)
URG (see ORD 2)
URGE (see ORD 2)
URGENCE (see ERSION)
URGENCY (see ERNITY)
URGENT (see ERSION)
URGENTLY (see ERNITY)
URGEON (see ERSION)
URGER 1 (see URNER)
URGER 2 (see URNER)
URGERY (see ERNITY)
URGICAL (see URTABLE)
URGID (see URDED)
URGING (see ERTING)
URGLAR (see URNER)
URGLARY (see ERNITY)
URGLE (see URTLE)
URGLER (see URNER)
URGUNDY (see ERNITY)
URGY (see IRTY)
URIAL (see ARABLE)
URIANT (see ORIAN)
URINAL (see URABLE)

URING (see ERTING)

URIOUS

curious
furious
spurious

incurious
injurious
luxurious
perjurious
uncurious
usurious

illuxurious
noninjurious
overcurious

URIST

dourest
jurist
poorest
purest
purist
surest
tourist

maturest
obscurest
securest

immaturest
insecurest
manicurist

caricaturist

Madge The Manicurist

URITY (see URABLY)
URK (see ORK 1)
URKEL (see URTLE)
URKER (see URNER)
URKEY (see IRTY)
URKID (see URDED)
URKIER (see URLIER)
URKING (see ERTING)

URKISH (see ERVICE)
URKY (see IRTY)
URL (see IRL)
URLABLE (see URTABLE)
URLER (see URNER)
URLEY (see IRTY)

URLIER

blurrier
burlier
chirpier
churlier
courier
curlier
curvier
dirtier
earlier
furrier
hurrier
murkier
pearlier
scurrier
slurrier
squirmier
wordier
worrier

mail courier

URLING (see ERTING)
URLY (see IRTY)
URMITY (see ERNITY)

URN

burn
churn
derm
earn
ern
fern
firm
germ
learn
perm
sperm
spurn
squirm

stern
term
tern
turn
urn
worm
yearn

adjourn
affirm
Ahern
astern
bookworm
concern
confirm
deworm
discern
downturn
earthworm
full-term
Glo Worm
glowworm
heartburn
infirm
intern
Jules Verne
lectern
long-term
midterm
nocturne
return
ringworm
sauterne
short-term
silkworm
slow burn
sojourn
sunburn
tapeworm
U-turn
unlearn
upturn
windburn

angleworm
disaffirm
epiderm
Howard Stern
live and learn
out of turn
overturn
pachyderm

reaffirm
reconfirm
taciturn
tax return
toss and turn
unconcern
wiggleworm

at every turn
done to a turn
money to burn
third-degree burn

point of no return

URNABLE (see URTABLE)
URNACE (see ERVICE)
URNAL (see URTLE)
URNALIZE (see ERSIFY)
URNALLY (see ERNITY)
URNE (see URN)

URNER

blurter
burger
burglar
burner
burper
churner
curler
cursor
curter
curver
earner
fervor
flirter
furler
girder
gurgler
herder
hurdler
hurler
hurter
irker
jerker
learner
Lerner
lurcher
lurker

Mercer
merger
murder
nurser
nurture
percher
perjure
purger
purler
purser
searcher
server
shirker
slurper
smirker
splurger
spurner
spurter
squirter
sterner
surfer
surger
swerver
swirler
turner
twirler
urger
verdure
verger
verser
whirler
worker
worser
yearner

absurder
adjourner
alerter
asserter
averter
back burner
barn-burner
berserker
bra-burner
caseworker
coercer
conserver
converger
converser
converter

coverter
dayworker
deserter
deserver
discerner
diverter
emerger
exerter
frankfurter
front burner
hair curler
hamburger
Hamburglar
inerter
inserter
inverter
observer
overter
perverter
precursor
preserver
recurler
researcher
reserver
resurger
returner
reverter
slow learner
sojourner
submerger
subverter
tearjerker
uncurler
unfurler
unnerver
wage earner

back yard burger
baton twirler
bloody murder
Bunsen burner
butter churner
eyelash curler
life preserver
migrant worker
money earner
overturner
pancake turner
process server
Tina Turner
Whataburger

URNEY (see IRTY)
URNING (see ERTING)
URNISH (see ERVICE)
URNISHMENT (see OURAGEMENT)
URNLY (see IRTY)
URNT (see ORK 1)
URO (see UNO)
UROR (see URER)
URP (see ORK 1)
URPEE (see IRTY)
URPER (see URNER)
URPHY (see IRTY)
URPING (see ERTING)
URPLE (see URTLE)
URPOSE (see ERVICE)
URR (see ER 1)
URRANT (see ERSION)
URRAY (see IRTY)
URRENCY (see ERNITY)
URRENT (see ERSION)
URRENTLY (see ERNITY)
URREY (see IRTY)
URRIER (see URLIER)
URRING (see ERTING)
URRO (see ERNO)
URROW (see ERNO)
URRY (see IRTY)
URSABLE (see URTABLE)
URSAL (see URTLE)
URSE (see IRST)
URSER (see URNER)
URSERY (see ERNITY)
URSEY (see IRTY)
URSIBLE (see URTABLE)
URSING (see ERTING)
URSION (see ERSION)
URSIVE (see ERVICE)
URSIVELY (see ERNITY)
URSOR (see URNER)
URSORY (see ERNITY)
URST (see IRST)
URSTABLE (see URTABLE)
URSTING (see ERTING)
URT (see ORK 1)

URTABLE

blurtable
burnable
burstable
cervical

curlable
cursable
flirtable
germinal
hurtable
liturgical
merciful
mergable
nursable
personal
skirtable
spurtable
surfable
surgical
terminal
vertical
vertigo
virtual

assertable
avertable
coercible
conversible
convertible
desertable
disbursible
dispersible
disturbable
divertible
exertable
immersible
insertable
invertible
nonsurgical
presurgical
preterminal
proverbial
referrable
rehearsable
reversible
revertible
submersible
subvertible
traversable

disconcertable
interspersible
microsurgical
neurosurgical
nonliturgical
reimbursible
unassertable

incontrovertible

URTAIN (see ERSION)
URTED (see URDED)
URTER (see URNER)
URTESY (see ERNITY)
URTFULLY (see ERNITY)
URTING (see ERTING)
URTIS (see ERVICE)
URTIVE (see ERVICE)
URTIVELY (see ERNITY)

URTLE

burgle
circle
colonel
curdle
dermal
fertile
gerbil
girdle
gurgle
herbal
Herschel
hurdle
hurtle
journal
kernel
myrtle
purple
squirrel
thermal
turtle
Urkel
verbal
vernal
Virgil

commercial
conferral
crape myrtle
deferral
disbursal
dispersal
engirdle
eternal
external
fraternal
inertial
infernal
infertile

internal
maternal
mock turtle
nocturnal
paternal
referral
rehearsal
reversal
Steve Urkel

chicken colonel
controversial
daily journal
dress rehearsal
epidermal
hypothermal
noncommercial
pachydermal
role reversal
uncommercial
universal
Winston Churchill

family circle

Teenage Mutant Ninja Turtle

URTLY (see IRTY)
URTON (see ERSION)
URTURE (see URNER)
URTY (see IRTY)
URU (see ULU)
URVE (see ORD 2)
URVER (see URNER)
URVIER (see URLIER)
URVING (see ERTING)
URVY (see IRTY)
URY 1 (see IRTY)
URY 2 (see ARY)
US 1 (see UFF)
US 2 (see EW 1)
US 3 (see OOK 1)
USA (see UNA)
USABLE (see OOTABLE)
USAL (see OODLE)
USAN (see UTION)
USANCE (see UDENCE)
USANT (see UTION)
USBAND (see UTTON)
USCAN (see UTTON)
USCANT (see USTMENT)
USCANY (see UTTERY)

USCLE (see UBBLE)
USCLER (see USTER 1)
USCRAT (see UCKET)

USE 1

blues
booze
bruise
choose
cruise
Cruz
fuse
Hughes
lose
muse
news
ooze
ruse
snooze
use
whose
yous

abuse
accuse
adieus
amuse
bad news
bayous
bemuse
charmeuse
confuse
defuse
diffuse
disuse
effuse
enthuse
excuse
froufrous
good news
infuse
make news
peruse
refuse
short fuse
suffuse
Tom Cruise
transfuse

blow a fuse
born to lose
breaking news
caribous
disabuse
in the news
pick and choose
Santa Cruz
Syracuse
win or lose

Caribbean cruise

Parker Lewis Can't Lose

an offer you can't refuse

USE 2 (see OOSE 1)
USEAU (see UNO)
USEFUL (see OODLE)
USELESS (see UTENESS)
USEMENT (see UTION)
USER 1 (see UTER)
USER 2 (see UTER)
USH 1 (see UFF)
USH 2 (see OOK 1)
USHABLE (see USTABLE)

USHED

booked
bushed
cooked
hooked
looked
mushed
pushed
rooked
schussed
shooshed
smushed
whooshed

unhooked

overcooked
overlooked

USHER 1 (see USTER 1)
USHER 2 (see OOKER)

USHERING (see OVERING)
USHERLESS (see UDDERLESS)
USHI (see UTY)
USHIE (see OOGIE)
USHIEST (see UBBIEST)
USHING 1 (see USTING)
USHING 2 (see OOKING)
USHION (see OMAN 1)
USHLY (see UDDY)
USHY 1 (see UDDY)
USHY 2 (see OOGIE)
USIBLE (see OOTABLE)
USIC (see EWISH)
USICAL (see OOTABLE)
USIER (see ITTIER)
USIEST (see IPPIEST)
USING 1 (see UTING 1)
USING 2 (see USTING)
USION (see UTION)
USIONAL (see OOTABLE)
USIONIST (see UBIOUS)

USIVE

abusive
allusive
collusive
conclusive
conducive
delusive
diffusive
effusive
elusive
exclusive
illusive
in fusive
inclusive
intrusive
obtrusive
occlusive
preclusive
profusive
protrusive
reclusive
seclusive

inconclusive
unobtrusive

USK (see UFF)
USKER (see USTER 1)
USKET (see UCKET)
USKIEST (see UMPIEST)
USKING (see USTING)
USKY (see UDDY)
USQUE (see UFF)
USS 1 (see OOK 1)
USS 2 (see UFF)
USSABLE (see USTABLE)
USSE (see OOSE 1)
USSED (see USHED)
USSEL (see UBBLE)
USSELL (see UBBLE)
USSEN (see UTION)
USSER (see USTER 1)
USSET (see UCKET)

USSIA

Bubba
busta
crusta
frusta
gutta
Prussia
pucka
Russia
sucka
sutta

Augusta
Calcutta
locusta

USSIAN (see UTTON)
USSIEST (see UBBIEST)
USSIN (see UTTON)
USSING (see USTING)
USSION (see UTTON)
USSLE (see UBBLE)
USSLER (see USTER 1)
USSY 1 (see UDDY)
USSY 2 (see OOGIE)
UST (see UFF)
USTA (see USSIA)

USTABLE

brushable
buggable
bumpable
bunchable
bustable
chuggable
chunkable
clubbable
clumpable
clutchable
crummable
crunchable
crushable
cuffable
cullible
cultural
cuttable
druggable
drummable
dubbable
dumpable
dunkable
dustable
floodable
fluffable
flunkable
flushable
fundable
gullible
huffable
huggable
huntable
judgable
jumpable
lovable
luggable
lustable
multiple
pluckable
pluggable
plumbable
puffable
pumpable
punchable
puntable
puttable
runnable

rustable
scrubbable
shovable
shuttable
sluggable
smudgable
structural
strummable
stuffable
stumpable
stunnable
suckable
suctional
sudsable
summable
thumpable
touchable
trumpable
trustable
tubbable
tuggable
abductible
adjustable
airbrushable
bankruptable
combustible
conductible
conductinoal
confrontable
constructible
constructional
corruptible
cross-cultural
debunkable
deductible
destructible
destructional
discussable
disruptable
eruptable
inductible
inductional
industrial
instructible
instructional
obstructible
obstructional
outrunnable
productional
rebuffable

recuttable
reductional
refundable
rerunnable
retouchable
self-lovable
slamdunkable
uncuttable
unpluggable
unrunnable
upchuckable

Dr. Huckstable
indestructible
interruptable
multicultural
noncombustible
readjustable
reconstructional
self-destructional
uncorruptable

USTANT (see USTMENT)
USTARD (see USTER 1)

USTED

budded
busted
butted
crusted
dusted
flooded
glutted
gusted
gutted
jutted
lusted
putted
rusted
strutted
studded
thudded
trusted
tutted

abducted
abutted
adjusted
blue-blooded

cold-blooded
combusted
disgusted
distrusted
encrusted
entrusted
full-blooded
mistrusted
rebutted
red-blooded
star-studded

flat-out busted
readjusted

USTEE (see UDDY)

USTER 1

blubber
bluffer
blusher
bluster
brother
brusher
bubbler
bucker
budder
budger
buffer
bugger
busser
buster
bustler
butler
butter
buzzer
chucker
clubber
clucker
cluster
clutter
color
cover
crusher
cuddler
cuffer
cusser
custard
Custer

cutter
drubber
drudger
dubber
ducker
duffer
duster
flooder
flubber
fluffer
flusher
fluster
flutter
fuddler
fudger
fusser
fuzzer
glutter
govern
grubber
grudger
gruffer
gusher
gutter
guzzler
hover
huddler
huffer
hugger
husher
husker
hustler
judger
juggler
juster
jutter
lover
lusher
luster
mother
mucker
mudder
muddler
muffler
mugger
muscler
musser
mustard
muster
mutter

muzzler
nother
nudger
nuzzler
other
plucker
plusher
pucker
puffer
putter
puzzler
rougher
rubber
rudder
ruffler
rusher
ruster
rustler
scrubber
shover
shudder
shuffler
shutter
shuttler
slougher
sludger
slugger
smother
smudger
smuggler
snubber
snuffer
snuffler
snuggler
southern
sputter
structure
struggler
strutter
stubborn
stuffer
stutter
subtler
succor
sucker
suffer
supper
suppler
thruster
thudder

toucher
tougher
troubler
trucker
trudger
truster
tucker
tussler
upper
usher
utter
yukker

abductor
abrupter
abutter
adjuster
aflutter
another
backbuster
ball-buster
bankrupter
befuddler
begrudger
big brother
blockbuster
blood brother
bloodsucker
bone crusher
book cover
book lover
burn rubber
clear cutter
cloud cover
conductor
constructor
corn shucker
cornhusker
corrupter
crimebuster
crop duster
deductor
dehusker
discolor
discover
discusser
disrupter
distruster
Dustbuster
dustcover

each other
Earth Mother
egg custard
entruster
erupter
foam rubber
forejudger
french mustard
fuzzbuster
gangbuster
gas guzzler
Ghostbuster
godmother
golf putter
grandmother
ground cover
haircutter
handcuffer
hardcover
housemother
inductor
instructor
lackluster
landlubber
Last Supper
misjudger
mistruster
none other
obstructor
off color
oh, brother
oil gusher
pass muster
pot scrubber
prejudger
queen mother
rain gutter
rebuffer
recover
restuffer
retoucher
robuster
seersucker
slipcover
sodbuster
some other
sponge rubber
stepmother
take cover

thumb-sucker
trustbuster
unclutter
uncover
unjuster
unpucker
upchucker
whale blubber
woodcutter

any other
blow your cover
bread and butter
bronco buster
candlesnuffer
chicken plucker
coast guard cutter
cookie cutter
cut the mustard
feather duster
filibuster
fixer-upper
Fluffernutter
Holy Mother
interrupter
money grubber
movie usher
Nutter Butter
one another
paper cutter
peanut butter
picker-upper
reconstructor
red-hot lover
run for cover
self-destructor
silent butler
stocking stuffer
Technicolor
toilet flusher
train conductor
tummy-tucker
uncorrupter
undercover
undercutter
uppercutter
watercolor

huffer and puffer
Land O Lakes Butter
one or another
rougher and tougher
somehow or other
one thing or another
one way or the other
significant other

Peter Pan Peanut Butter

horse of a different color

USTER 2 (see UTER)
USTERING (see OVERING)
USTERLESS (see UDDERLESS)
USTIBLE (see USTABLE)
USTIC (see UCKET)
USTICE (see UCKET)
USTIEST (see UBBIEST)
USTIN (see UTTON)

USTING

bluffing
blushing
brushing
bucking
budding
budging
buffing
bugging
busing
bussing
busting
butting
buzzing
chucking
chugging
clubbing
clucking
clutching
coupling
crushing
crusting
cuffing
cupping
cussing
cutting

drubbing
drugging
dubbing
ducking
ducting
dusting
flooding
flubbing
fluffing
flushing
fussing
fuzzing
gushing
gusting
gutting
huffing
hugging
hushing
husking
hussing
hustling
judging
jutting
loving
lugging
lusting
muffing
mugging
mussing
nothing
nudging
plucking
plugging
puffing
roughing
rubbing
ruffing
rushing
rusting
scrubbing
scuffing
shoving
shrugging
shucking
shutting
slugging
slushing
smudging
snubbing
snuffing

strutting
stubbing
stuffing
subbing
sucking
supping
thrusting
thudding
touching
trucking
trudging
trussing
trusting
tucking
tugging
upping
whupping
yupping

abducting
abrupting
abutting
adjudging
adjusting
airbrushing
backrubbing
bankrupting
begruding
bone-crushing
combusting
conducting
constructing
corrupting
crop-dusting
deducting
defuzzing
discussing
disgusting
disrupting
distrusting
encrusting
entrusting
erupting
forejudging
handcuffing
humbugging
inducting
instructing
misjudging
mistrusting

nightclubbing
obstructing
precutting
prejudging
rebuffing
rebutting
recutting
retouching
toothbrushing
unplugging
upchucking

everloving
interrupting
jitterbugging
overstuffing
readjusting
reconstructing
reinstructing
self-destructing
Stove Top Stuffing
tummy-tucking
uncorrupting
undercutting

USTION (see UTTON)
USTLE (see UBBLE)
USTLER (see USTER 1)
USTLESS (see UCKET)
USTLING (see USTING)

USTMENT

adjustment
betrustment
coruscant
encrustment
entrustment
incrustment
pregustant

coadjustment
maladjustment
misadjustment
preadjustment
readjustment

USTNESS (see UCKET)

USTODY (see UTTERY)
USTOM (see UTTON)
USTON (see UTION)
USTRIAL (see USTABLE)
USTRIOUS (see UBBIEST)
USTUS (see UCKET)
USTY (see UDDY)
USUAL (see OOTABLE)
USURING (see UTORING)
USY (see ITTY)
UT 1 (see UP)
UT 2 (see OOK 1)
UT 3 (see EW 1)
UT 4 (see UTE)
UTABLE (see OOTABLE)
UTAL (see OODLE)
UTALLY (see UITY 1)
UTAN (see UTION)
UTANT (see UTION)
UTANTS (see UDENCE)
UTCH 1 (see UFF)
UTCH 2 (see OOK 1)
UTCHABLE (see USTABLE)
UTCHING (see USTING)
UTCHY (see UDDY)

UTE

beaut
bloop
boost
boot
brute
butte
chute
coop
coot
coup
coupe
croup
cuke
cute
douche
droop
duke
dupe
fluke
flute

fruit
goof
goop
group
hooch
hoop
hoot
jute
kook
loop
loot
Luke
lute
mooch
moot
mute
newt
nuke
pooch
poof
poop
proof
puke
roof
roost
root
route
scoop
scoot
shoot
sloop
smooch
snoop
snoot
soup
spoof
spook
stoop
stoup
stupe
suit
swoop
swoosh
toot
troop
uke
whoop
whoosh
zoot

acute
age group
aloof
archduke
astute
Beirut
breadfruit
cheroot
childproof
commute
compute
confute
crapshoot
deaf mute
dilute
disproof
dispute
door stoop
Dubuque
duck soup
en route
Farouk
file suit
fireproof
flameproof
foolproof
Froot Loop
Fruit Brute
galoot
grapefruit
hirsute
impute
in-group
jumpsuit
lawsuit
long suit
mail route
minute
offshoot
outshoot
pea soup
peer group
permute
peruke
pollute
pursuit
rap group
reboot
rebuke
recoup
recruit

refute
regroup
repute
salute
scout troop
soundproof
spacesuit
square root
strong suit
trade route
transmute
trapshoot
trump suit
uproot
wet suit
youth group
zoot suit

absolute
alley-oop
arrowroot
bathing suit
Betty Boop
birthday suit
bulletproof
chicken coop
chicken soup
chute-the-chute
constitute
convolute
cowboy boot
destitute
disrepute
dissolute
diving suit
ethnic group
execute
fly the coop
follow suit
galley proof
Guadeloupe
hot pursuit
hula hoop
ice-cream suit
ill repute
in the soup
inside scoop
institute
interest group
involute

Juicy Fruit
laundry chute
leisure suit
loop-the-loop
malemute
monkey suit
Nike swoosh
nincompoop
one fell swoop
overshoot
parachute
party poop
passionfruit
persecute
pooper-scoop
pressure group
prosecute
prostitute
resolute
restitute
retribute
splinter group
substitute
three-piece suit
troubleshoot
turkey shoot
tutti-fruit
undershoot
waterproof
Whiffenpoof

alternate route
burden of proof
class action suit
come home to roost
Debbie the Bloop
electrocute
encounter group
forbidden fruit
Freddy the Flute
irresolute
newspaper scoop
not give a hoot
not worth a hoot
reconstitute

house of ill repute
Trivial Pursuit

twenty-one gun salute

UTED

booted
cupid
druid
feuded
fluid
fluted
fruited
hooted
humid
looted
lucid
mooted
mucid
muted
rooted
routed
scooted
stupid
suited
tooted
tumid

alluded
colluded
commuted
computed
concluded
confuted
Dan Cupid
deluded
denuded
dilucid
diluted
disputed
eluded
excluded
exuded
imputed
included
intruded
obtruded
occluded
pellucid
polluted
precluded
protruded

recruited
refuted
reputed
saluted
secluded
translucid
transmuted
uprooted
constituted
convoluted
executed
instituted
parachuted
persecuted
prosecuted
prostituted
semifluid
substituted

electrocuted
reconstituted

UTELY (see UTY)

UTENESS

bloomless
boothless
bruteness
couthless
crudeness
cuteness
foodless
fumeless
hoopless
hugeness
lewdness
looseness
moonless
muteness
nudeness
plumeless
proofless
prudeness
roofless
roomless
rudeness

ruthless
shrewdness
smoothness
soothness
toothless
truceless
truthless
tubeless
tuneless
useless
acuteness
aloofness
arguteness
astuteness
diluteness
minuteness

absoluteness
destituteness
dissoluteness
resoluteness

nonabsoluteness

UTER

blooper
booster
boozer
Brewster
bruiser
chooser
cooper
cooter
cougar
couther
cruder
cruiser
cuter
drooper
duper
feuder
fuser
future
goober
gooser
groover
grouper

hooper
Hoosier
hooter
Hoover
juicer
lewder
looper
looser
looter
loser
louver
lucre
luger
Luther
moocher
mover
muser
muter
neuter
oozer
pewter
pooper
prover
rooster
rooter
ruder
Schuster
scooper
scooter
shooter
shrewder
sleuther
smoocher
smoother
snooper
snoozer
soother
sprucer
stooper
stupor
suitor
super
suture
swooper
trooper
trouper
Tudor
tutor
uber
user
whooper

abuser
accoutre
accuser
acuter
alluder
amuser
approver
astuter
bad loser
bemuser
born loser
commuter
computer
concluder
confuser
crapshooter
defuser
deluder
denuder
diffuser
diluter
disprover
disputer
drug user
earthmover
eluder
excluder
excuser
exuder
good loser
improver
includer
inducer
infuser
intruder
Lex Luthor
maneuver
minuter
misuser
nonuser
obtuser
occluder
peashooter
polluter
prime mover
producer
profuser
protruder
recouper
recruiter

reducer
refuser
refuter
regrouper
remover
Rod Stewart
saluter
seducer
sharpshooter
state trooper
uncouther
uprooter
vamooser
Vancouver

Alice Cooper
cabin cruiser
child abuser
disabuser
disapprover
Freddy Krueger
Herbert Hoover
hula hooper
ice cream scooper
instituter
Martha Stewart
Martin Luther
mass-producer
motor scooter
outmaneuver
overshooter
parachuter
paratrooper
party pooper
people mover
persecutor
pooper scooper
prosecutor
stain remover
substituter
super-duper
troubleshooter
two-time loser

electrocuter
Heimlich maneuver
polish remover
wave of the future

public prosecutor

UTERING (see UTORING)
UTERUS (see UBIOUS)
UTEST (see OONEST)
UTH (see OOTH 1)
UTHER (see UTER)
UTHERING (see OVERING)
UTHFUL (see OODLE)
UTHFULLY (see UITY 1)
UTHLESS (see UTENESS)
UTHOR (see UTER)
UTIAN (see UTION)
UTIC (see EWISH)
UTICAL (see OOTABLE)
UTICLE (see OOTABLE)
UTIE (see UTY)
UTIFUL (see OOTABLE)
UTIFULLY (see UITY 1)
UTILE (see OODLE)
UTILELY (see UITY 1)
UTIN (see UTION)
UTINARY (see UITARY)

UTING 1

blooming
blooping
booming
boosting
booting
boozing
brooming
bruising
choosing
cooping
couping
crooning
cruising
cubing
deucing
dooming
douching
drooping
duping
feuding
fuming
fusing
glooming
goofing
goosing

grooming
grooving
grouping
hooping
hooting
juicing
looming
looping
loosing
looting
losing
louping
lubing
mooching
mooning
moving
muting
nooning
noosing
oozing
pooching
pooping
proofing
proving
pruning
puking
roofing
rooming
roosting
scooping
scooting
shooting
sleuthing
sluicing
smooching
smoothing
snooping
snoozing
soothing
souping
spoofing
spooking
spooning
sprucing
stooging
stooking
stooping
suiting
swooning
swooping

toothing
tooting
trooping
trouping
trucing
tubing
tuning
using
vrooming
whooping
zooming

abducing
abusing
accusing
adducing
aggrouping
alluding
amusing
approving
assuming
attuning
ballooning
behooving
bemusing
cartooning
childproofing
chirruping
cocooning
colluding
commoving
communing
commuting
computing
concluding
conducing
confusing
consuming
costuming
crapshooting
debouching
deducing
defusing
deluding
deluging
denuding
detruding
diffusing
diluting
disproving

disputing
dragooning
earthmoving
educing
eluding
entombing
excluding
excusing
exhuming
extruding
exuding
festooning
fine-tuning
fireproofing
foolproofing
foredooming
foretuning
good grooming
harpooning
illuding
improving
impugning
imputing
including
inducing
infusing
intruding
lampooning
landluping
larruping
marooning
mistuning
misusing
mushrooming
obtruding
occluding
oppugning
permuting
perusing
petuning
platooning
polluting
pontooning
precluding
preluding
presuming
producing
protruding
rattooning
reblooming

rebuking
recouping
recruiting
reducing
refuging
refusing
refuting
regrouping
removing
reproving
resuming
retruding
retuning
saluting
secluding
seducing
shockproofing
soudnproofing
subtruding
suffusing
traducing
transducing
transfusing
transmuting
transuding
unloosing
unmoving
unroofing
uprooting
vamoosing

bulletproofing
constituting
convoluting
counterproving
disabusing
disapproving
everblooming
executing
honeymooning
importuning
inconcluding
instituting
intercluding
introducing
mass-producing
nonconcluding
outproducing
overshooting
parachuting

persecuting
prosecuting
prostituting
reassuming
reinducing
reproducing
self-abusing
substituting
time-consuming
troubleshooting
unapproving
unassuming
unconcluding
undershooting
unobtruding
waterproofing
weatherproofing

electrocuting
intercommuning
overproducing
reconstituting
reintroducing
superinducing
underproducing

cruising for a bruising
up to and including

UTING 2 (see UING)
UTINY (see UITY 1)

UTION

Bhutan
bruin
chulan
coolant
Cuban
cumin
cutin
Ewan
fluent
fusion
glutin
Houston
hulan
human
jument
koulan

kulan
loosen
lucent
moutan
movement
mutant
Newman
proven
prudent
Putin
Reuben
ruin
rutin
Schumann
Steuben
student
Susan
truant
Truman
trusion
ulan
union
yulan
ablution
abstrusion
abusion
accusant
accusement
acumen
affluent
affusion
albumen
Aleutian
allusion
amusement
approvement
attunement
collusion
communion
conclusion
confluent
Confucian
confusion
conglutin
congruent
contusion
delusion
darn tootin
detrusion
diffusion

dilution
disclusion
disproven
disunion
effusion
elusion
exclusion
excusement
extrusion
Fig Newton
hortulan
illusion
improvement
inclusion
infusion
inhuman
intrusion
Laputan
misusement
nonproven
nonunion
obtrusion
obtusion
occlusion
Paul Newman
perfusion
pertusion
pollutant
pollution
preclusion
preunion
profusion
prolusion
protrusion
prounion
pursuant
rambutan
Rasputin
Rasmussen
reclusion
refusion
retrusion
reunion
seclusion
solution
subhuman
suffusion
Ted Nugent
transfusion
unloosen

unproven
volution

absolution
advolution
air pollution
antiunion
attribution
blood transfusion
bowel movement
circumclusion
circumfusion
comminution
consecution
constitution
contribution
convolution
countermovement
destitution
devolution
diminution
disillusion
disimprovement
dissolution
distribution
elocution
evolution
excommunion
execution
exolution
exsolution
hifalutin
highfalutin
imminution
in conclusion
inconfusion
incongruent
insecution
institution
interclusion
interfusion
intrafusion
involution
Isaac Newton
labor union
Lilliputian
malocclusion
misconclusion
misimprovement
noncommunion

nonsolution
persecution
prosecution
prostitution
rack and ruin
redargution
reinfusion
resolution
restitution
retribution
revolution
self-improvement
semiglutin
smog pollution
substitution
super human
Whitney Houston

antecommunion
antipollution
electrocution
foregone conclusion
high school reunion
high-resolution
inexecution
intercommunion
interlocution
intervolution
irresolution
malexecution
nondistribution
nonexecution
reconstitution
redistribution
reinstitution
subinvolution
ventrilocution
water pollution

counterrevolution
marriage dissolution
New Year's resolution
optical illusion
stay of execution
superinstitution
U.S. Constitution

Evolution Revolution

UTIONAL (see OOTABLE)
UTIONARY (see UITARY)

UTIONER

crucifer
Jupiter
Lucifer
nuclear
ruiner

executioner
resolutioner
revolutioner

UTIONIST (see UBIOUS)
UTIST (see OONEST)
UTLER (see USTER 1)
UTLET (see UCKET)
UTO (see UNO)
UTOR (see UTER)

UTORING

coopering
humoring
neutering
rumoring
supering
tutoring
usuring

accoutering
maneuvering

outmaneuvering

UTRALIST (see UBIOUS)
UTRALLY (see UITY 1)
UTRO (see UNO)
UTSIEST (see UBBIEST)
UTSY (see UDDY)
UTT (see UP)
UTTA (see USSIA)
UTTABLE (see USTABLE)
UTTE (see UTE)
UTTED (see USTED)
UTTER (see USTER 1)

UTTERING (see OVERING)
UTTERLY (see UTTERY)

UTTERY

blubbery
buggery
bummery
buttery
buttony
cluttery
cousinly
custody
drudgery
flummery
fluttery
fubbery
gluttony
gullery
gunnery
guttery
lovery
luckily
luxury
mummery
muttony
nummary
nunnery
nuttery
puckery
puffery
rubbery
shrubbery
skullery
slovenly
sluttery
snuggery
sputtery
stubbornly
stuttery
subsidy
subtlety
suddenly
summary
summery
thuggery
Tuscany
utterly

discovery
humbuggery

Montgomery
recovery
reluctantly
skullduggery

indiscovery
nondiscovery
oversubtlety
prediscovery
rediscovery

UTTI (see UTY)
UTTIEST (see UBBIEST)
UTTING 1 (see USTING)
UTTING 2 (see OOKING)
UTTISH (see UFFISH)
UTTLE (see UBBLE)
UTTLER (see USTER 1)
UTTLING (see UFFLING)
UTTO (see UNO)

UTTON

bludgeon
button
buxom
cousin
coven
cozen
Cummins
custom
dozen
dudgeon
Dustin
glutton
husband
Justin
muffin
mutton
oven
Prussian
puffin
roughen
Russian
sudden
Sutton
toughen
tungsten
Tuscan

accustom
Antrustion
combustion
concussion
discussion
excussion
percussion
precustom
push button
unbutton
unbuxom
baker's dozen
bellybutton
country cousin
dime a dozen
disaccustom
E. F. Hutton
English muffin
kissing cousin
leg-of-mutton
on the button
panic button
ragamuffin
reaccustom
repercussion
Robitussin
unaccustom

all of a sudden
Byelorussion
Easy-Bake Oven

UTTONY (see UTTERY)
UTTY (see UDDY)
UTU (see ULU)
UTURE (see UTER)
UTUS (see UENESS)

UTY

beauty
boobie
booby
bootie
booty
boozy
broody
brutely
choosy

coolie
coolly
cootie
croupy
crudely
cruelly
cutely
cutie
doobie
doozie
drooly
droopy
duly
duty
floozy
fluky
foodie
fruity
Fuji
gloomy
goofy
Goonie
goony
goopy
goosy
groovy
groupie
Gucci
hoochie
Hootie
hooty
hugely
Judy
juicy
kewpie
kooky
lewdly
looby
loony
loopy
loosely
Lucy
moochy
moody
moony
moosey
movie
mutely
newbie
newly

newsy
nudely
nudie
nudy
oozy
plumy
poochy
poofy
pukey
puny
rheumy
roomie
roomy
Rooney
ruby
rudely
Rudy
rupee
shrewdly
smoochy
smoothie
smoothly
snoopy
snooty
soothly
soupy
spoofy
spooky
stooly
SUNY
sushi
Suzie
swoopy
swooshy
tootie
Trudy
truly
tule
uzi
woozy
Zuni

acutely
argutely
astutely
George Clooney
gilhooley
guard duty
Jacuzzi
Judge Judy

kabuki
minutely
night duty
off duty
on duty
perfumy
spring beauty
Suzuki
uncruelly
unduly
ungloomy
unroomy
unruly
yours truly

absolutely
acey-deucy
active duty
bathing beauty
call of duty
Chattahoochee
convolutely
destitutely
do your duty
double-duty
heavy-duty
hootchy-kootchy
Howdy Doody
I Love Lucy
jury duty
line of duty
Sleeping Beauty
sweet patooty
tour of duty
tutti-frutti
Yamaguchi

cutie patootie
nonabsolutely

military duty

Amerigo Vespucci
Father Guido Sarducci

UU (see EW 1)
UVENATE (see UMINATE)
UVERING (see UTORING)
UX (see UFF)
UXE (see UFF)
UXOM (see UTTON)

UXURY (see UTTERY)
UYS (see IZE 1)
UZ 1 (see USE 1)
UZ 2 (see UG)
UZA (see UNA)
UZAH (see UNA)
UZETTE (see OULETTE)
UZI (see UTY)
UZIE (see UTY)
UZO (see UNO)
UZU (see ULU)
UZZ (see UG)
UZZER (see USTER 1)
UZZI (see UTY)
UZZIEST (see UBBIEST)
UZZING (see USTING)
UZZLE (see UBBLE)
UZZLER (see USTER 1)
UZZLING (see UFFLING)
UZZY (see UDDY)

Y

Rhyme Sounds

Y

aye
buy
by
bye
cry
die
dry
dye
eye
fly
fry
guy
hi
high
I
lie
lye
my
nigh
phi
pi
pie
ply
pry
rye
shy
sigh
sky
sly
spy
sty
Thai
thigh
thy
tie
try
vie
why
wry
Y

ace high
ally
apply
awry
aye aye
bird's-eye
black eye
black tie
blow-dry
blue sky

bone-dry
bonzai
bow tie
buckeye
bull's-eye
bye-bye
comply
curvey
deadeye
decry
deep-fry
defy
deny
drip dry
fall guy
far cry
firefly
fish fry
fisheye
fly high
French fry
get by
GI
glass eye
goodbye
gun-shy
hereby
hi-fi
hogtie
horsefly
I Spy
imply
July
knee-high
magpie
mai tai
McFly
medfly
mind's eye
mud pie
nearby
necktie
outcry
pigsty
pinkeye
Popeye
porkpie
rabbi
red-eye
refi
rely
reply
run by

sci-fi
Shanghai
shuteye
sky-high
slip by
small fry
sneak by
spin dry
standby
stir-fry
supply
thereby
thigh-high
tie-dye
tongue-tie
two-ply
untie
Versailles
war cry
whereby
wise guy

alibi
alkali
all-time high
Alpha Chi
Alpha Phi
amplify
apple pie
battle cry
beady eye
beautify
bold-faced lie
butterfly
by and by
camera-shy
catch your eye
cherry pie
clarify
counterspy
crucify
cutie pie
deify
DIY
do or die
eagle eye
evil eye
eye-to-eye
falsify
FBI
flying high
FYI
Gemini

high and dry
humble pie
justify
liquefy
live a lie
Lorelei
lullaby
metrify
misapply
multiply
mummify
mystify
naked eye
notify
nullify
on the sly
overbuy
Paraguay
petrify
pizza pie
private eye
purify
quantify
ramify
reapply
right-to-die
rockaby
samurai
sanctify
seeing eye
Sigma Chi
simplify
stupefy
Superfly
typify
underbuy
underlie
unify
up and die
Uruguay
what a guy
When Doves Cry
you and I

chicken pot pie
demystify
easy as pie
eat humble pie
Eskimo Pie
exemplify
Fourth of July
identify
in short supply

indemnify
intensify
Jefferson High
little white lie
Marty McFly
Mother, May I?
Mr. Nice Guy
mud in your eye
natural high
never say die
personify
pie in the sky
power supply
refortify
see eye-to-eye
Spy vs. Spy
Sweet Valley High
vox populi
wink of an eye

Alpha Delta Pi
an eye for an eye
apple of my eye
artificial high
bigger fish to fry
catcher in the rye
easy on the eye
Treaty of Versailles

Fast Times at Ridgemont High

Levi's 501 Button Fly

YABLE (see ITABLE 1)
YAN (see ION 1)
YANT (see ION 1)
YATT (see IET)
YBER (see IZER)
YBRID (see IET)
YCH (see IGHT)
YCHE (see IGHTLY)
YCHIC (see ITIS)
YCHING (see INDING)
YCLE (see ITLE)
YCLICAL (see ITTABLE)
YCLICALLY (see ISTICALLY)
YCLING (see INDING)
YCLIST (see ITIS)
YDE (see IDE)
YDEN (see IGHTEN)
YDER (see IZER)
YDNEY (see ITTY)
YDRANTS (see ITIS)

YDRATE

bistate
dilate
gyrate
hydrate
irate
migrate
primate
thymate
tristate
vibrate

archprimate
dehydrate
rehydrate
remigrate
transmigrate

carbohydrate

YDRON (see IGHTEN)
YE (see Y)
YED (see IDE)
YEING (see INDING)
YER (see IER 1)
YES (see IZE 1)
YFUL (see ITLE)
YGAMIST (see IGAMIST)
YGAMY (see ILITY)
YGMIER (see ITTIER)
YGMIEST (see IPPIEST)
YGMY (see ITTY)
YGONE (see YLON)
YING (see INDING)
YKE (see IGHT)
YL (see ILL)
YLAN (see ITION)
YLE (see ILE 1)
YLER (see IZER)
YLIC (see ISTIC)
YLING (see INDING)
YLISH (see ITIS)
YLIST (see ITIS)
YLL (see ILL)
YLLABLE (see UILDABLE)
YLLABUS (see IVOROUS)
YLLIC (see ISTIC)
YLLIS (see ITIOUS)

YLON

bygone
icon
ion
micron
nylon
phylon
pylon
python
Saigon
scion
trigon

millimicron

YLUM (see IGHTEN)
YLUS (see ITIS)
YLVAN (see ILLION)
YLVIE (see ILKY)
YLY (see IGHTLY)
YM (see IN 1)
YMATE (see YDRATE)
YMBAL (see ITTLE)
YMBOL (see ITTLE)
YME (see INE 1)
YMEN (see IGHTEN)
YMER (see IZER)
YMIE (see IGHTLY)
YMING (see INDING)
YMMETRY (see ILITY)
YMN (see IN 1)
YMNAL (see ITTLE)
YMPH (see INK)
YMPHONIST (see IGAMIST)
YMPHONY (see ILITY)
YMPTOM (see INCOME)
YMY (see IGHTLY)
YNASTY (see IETY)
YNC (see INK)
YNCER (see INGER 1)
YNCH (see INK)
YNCHER (see IMBER 2)
YNCHING (see ITTING)
YNCING (see INKING)
YNDICATE (see IMINATE)
YNE (see EEN 1)
YNERGY (see ILITY)
YNESS (see ITIS)

YNIC (see ISTIC)
YNICAL (see ITTABLE)
YNICALLY (see ISTICALLY)
YNN (see IN 1)
YNX (see INK)
YOR (see IER 1)
YPE (see IGHT)
YPER (see IZER)
YPH (see IST 1)
YPHEN (see IGHTEN)
YPHENED (see IGHTEN)
YPHENING (see IGHTENING)
YPHIC (see ISTIC)
YPHILIS (see IVOROUS)
YPHONY (see ILITY)
YPIC (see ISTIC)
YPICAL (see ITTABLE)
YPICALLY (see ISTICALLY)
YPING (see INDING)
YPIST (see ITIS)
YPOCRITE (see IVALENT)
YPPING (see ITTING)
YPRESS (see ITIS)
YPSE (see IST 1)
YPSIEST (see IPPIEST)
YPSO (see ILLOW)
YPSY (see ITTY)
YPT (see IST 1)
YPTIAN (see ITION)
YPTIC (see ISTIC)
YPTO (see ILLOW)
YQUILL (see ITLE)
YRATE (see YDRATE)
YRE (see IRE)
YRIA (see ERIA 1)
YRIAD (see ERIOUS)
YRIAN (see ERIAN)
YRIC (see ISTIC)
YRICAL (see ITTABLE)
YRICALLY (see ISTICALLY)

YRO

bio
Cairo
Fido
gyro
hydro

hypo
maestro
micro
psycho
pyro
rhino
silo
typo
tyro
wino

albino
Ohio
Tamayo

YRON (see IGHTEN)
YRRH (see ER 1)
YRTLE (see URTLE)
YRUM (see IGHTEN)
YS (see IZE 1)
YSIC (see ISTIC)
YSICAL (see ITTABLE)
YSICALLY (see ISTICALLY)
YSICIST (see ITIONIST)
YSIUM (see ELIUM)
YSM (see ISM)
YSMAL (see ITTLE)
YSON (see IGHTEN)
YSS (see IST 1)
YSSAL (see ITTLE)
YSSEUS (see IPPIEST)
YSSOP (see ICCUP)
YST (see IST 1)
YSTAL (see ITTLE)
YSTALED (see ITTLED)
YSTEM (see ITION)
YSTERY (see ILITY)
YSTIC (see ITIOUS)
YSTICAL (see ITTABLE)
YSTICALLY (see ISTICALLY)
YSTING (see ITTING)
YTE (see IGHT)
YTED (see ITED 1)
YTH (see IST 1)
YTHIC (see ISTIC)
YTHICAL (see ITTABLE)
YTHM (see ISM)
YTIC (see ISTIC)
YTICAL (see ITTABLE)
YX (see IST 1)
YZABLE (see ITABLE 1)
YZER (see IZER)
YZING (see INDING)